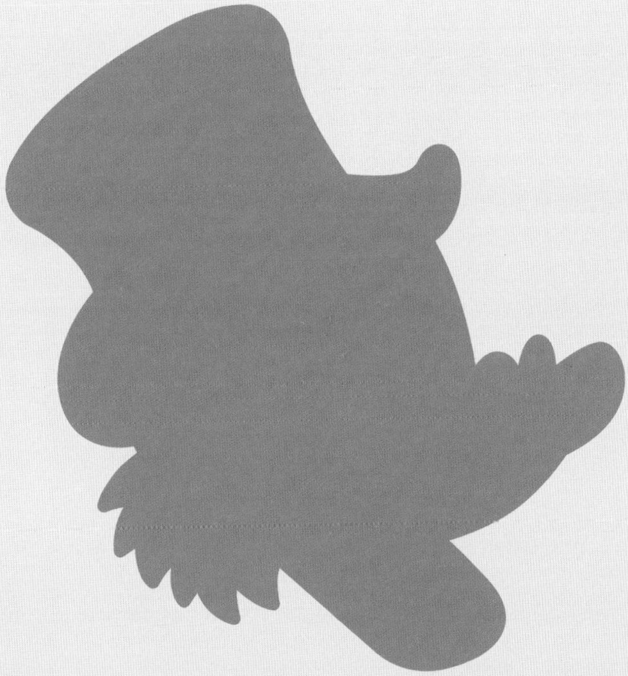

DISNEY MASTERS

UNCLE SCROOGE: PIE IN THE SKY

by William Van Horn

FANTAGRAPHICS | SEATTLE

Publisher: GARY GROTH • Editor: DAVID GERSTEIN • Production: PAUL BARESH
Designers: KEELI McCARTHY, DAVID GERSTEIN, and CHELSEA WIRTZ
Associate Publisher: ERIC REYNOLDS

Disney Masters showcases the work of internationally acclaimed Disney artists. Many of the stories presented in the *Disney Masters* series appear in English for the first time. This is *Disney Masters* Volume 18. Permission to quote or reproduce material for reviews must be obtained from the publisher.

Fantagraphics Books, Inc. • 7563 Lake City Way NE • Seattle WA 98115 • (800) 657-1100

Visit us at fantagraphics.com. Follow us on Twitter at @fantagraphics and on Facebook at facebook.com/fantagraphics.

Cover art by William Van Horn; color by David Gerstein and Chelsea Wirtz.
Title page art by William Van Horn; color by William Van Horn and David Gerstein.
Special thanks to John Clark, Thomas Jensen, Christos Kentrotis, John Lustig, Fernando Ventura, and William Van Horn.

Second printing: September 2023 • ISBN 978-1-68396-441-4
Printed in China • Library of Congress Control Number: 2017956971

The stories in this volume were originally created in English in the United States,
and were first published in the following magazines:

"Pie in the Sky" in *Uncle Scrooge* #243, June 1990 (KU 0190). "A Prickly Relation" in *Uncle Scrooge* #226, May 1988 (AR 111). "Tightrope Gag" in *Donald Duck* #264, July 1988 (AR 115). "A Sound Deal" in *Mickey and Donald* #2, May 1988 (AR 112). "Fly Now, Pay Later" in *Donald Duck* #263, June 1988 (AR 114). "Dime Collector" in *Uncle Scrooge* #227, July 1988 (AR 117). "Backyard Bet" in *Donald Duck* #265, August 1988 (AR 120). "Floating Alone" in *Uncle Scrooge Adventures* #6, August 1988 (AR 121). "Large Deduction" in *Uncle Scrooge* #229, September 1988 (AR 123). "Tents, Anyone?" in *Donald Duck Adventures* [series I] #7, September 1988 (AR 122). "Lost On a Dog" in *Uncle Scrooge Adventures* #8, October 1988 (AR 124). "His Money's Worth" in *Uncle Scrooge* #230, October 1988 (AR 126). "Poisoned Palate" in *Donald Duck* #268, November 1988 (AR 127). "The Bright Side" in *Donald Duck* #269, January 1989 (AR 131). "Shaping Up" in *Uncle Scrooge* #231, November 1988 (AR 129). "Heavy Duty" in *Walt Disney's Comics and Stories* #537, March 1989 (AR 133). "Duel Personalities" in *Mickey and Donald* #9, March 1989 (AR 134). "The Three Bs" in *Uncle Scrooge Adventures* #12, April 1989 (AR 135). "Seafood Blues" in *Donald Duck Adventures* [series I] #12, May 1989 (AR 137). "Quick Trim" in *Uncle Scrooge* #234, May 1989 (AR 138). "Tree's a Crowd" in *Donald Duck* #271, June 1989 (AR 140). "Be My Gust" in *Donald Duck* #272, July 1989 (AR 141). "Shooting to the Top" in *Uncle Scrooge* #235, July 1989 (AR 144). "False Economy" in *Uncle Scrooge* #237, September 1989 (AR 147). "Another Vine Mess" in *Walt Disney's Comics and Stories* #545, December 1989 (AR 149). "Call Off the Wild" in *Mickey and Donald* #17, March 1990 (AR 150). "The Amazon Queen" in *Donald Duck Adventures* [series I] #20, April 1990 (AR 154). "Rootin', Tootin' Duck" in *Donald Duck Adventures* [series II] #2, July 1990 (KD 0290). "Beachhead Bathos" in *Donald Duck Adventures* [series II] #3, August 1990 (KD 0690). "The Bees Have It!" in *Donald Duck Adventures* [series II] #4, September 1990 (KD 0790). "Snore Losers" in *Donald Duck Adventures* [series II] #5, October 1990 (KD 0890). "It's Bats, Man!" in *Donald Duck Adventures* [series II] #6, November 1990 (KD 0990).

Walt Disney

Uncle $crooge

Pie in the Sky

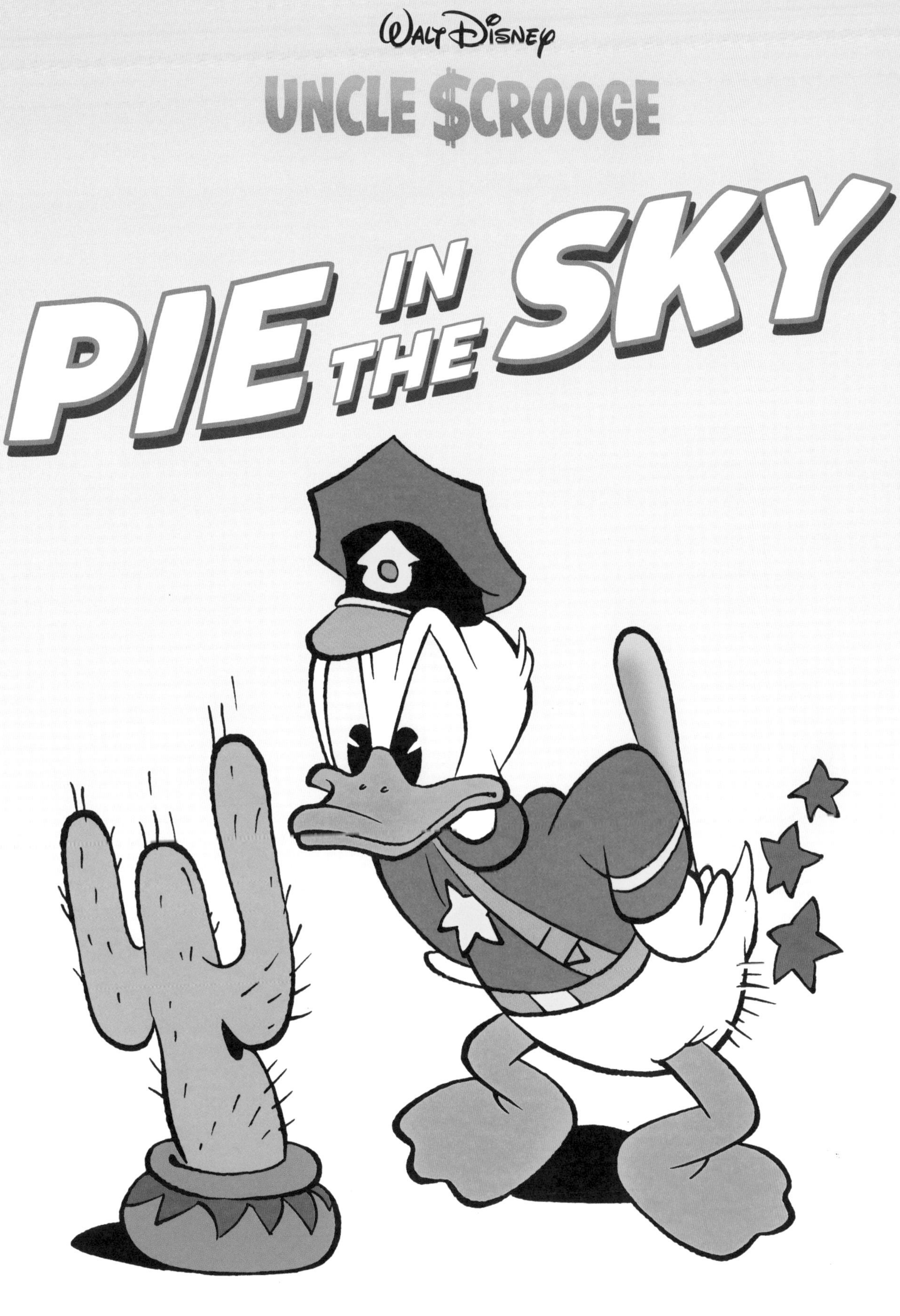

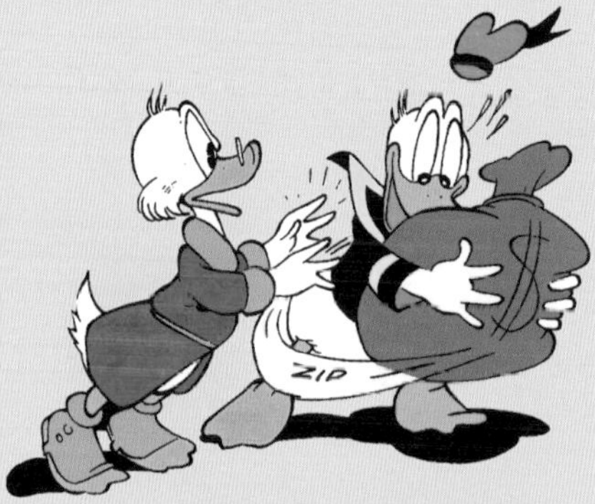
ZIP

CONTENTS

All stories and covers drawn and lettered by William Van Horn.
All stories written by William Van Horn unless noted.

The stories in this volume are presented here in their entirety as first created in 1988-1990.

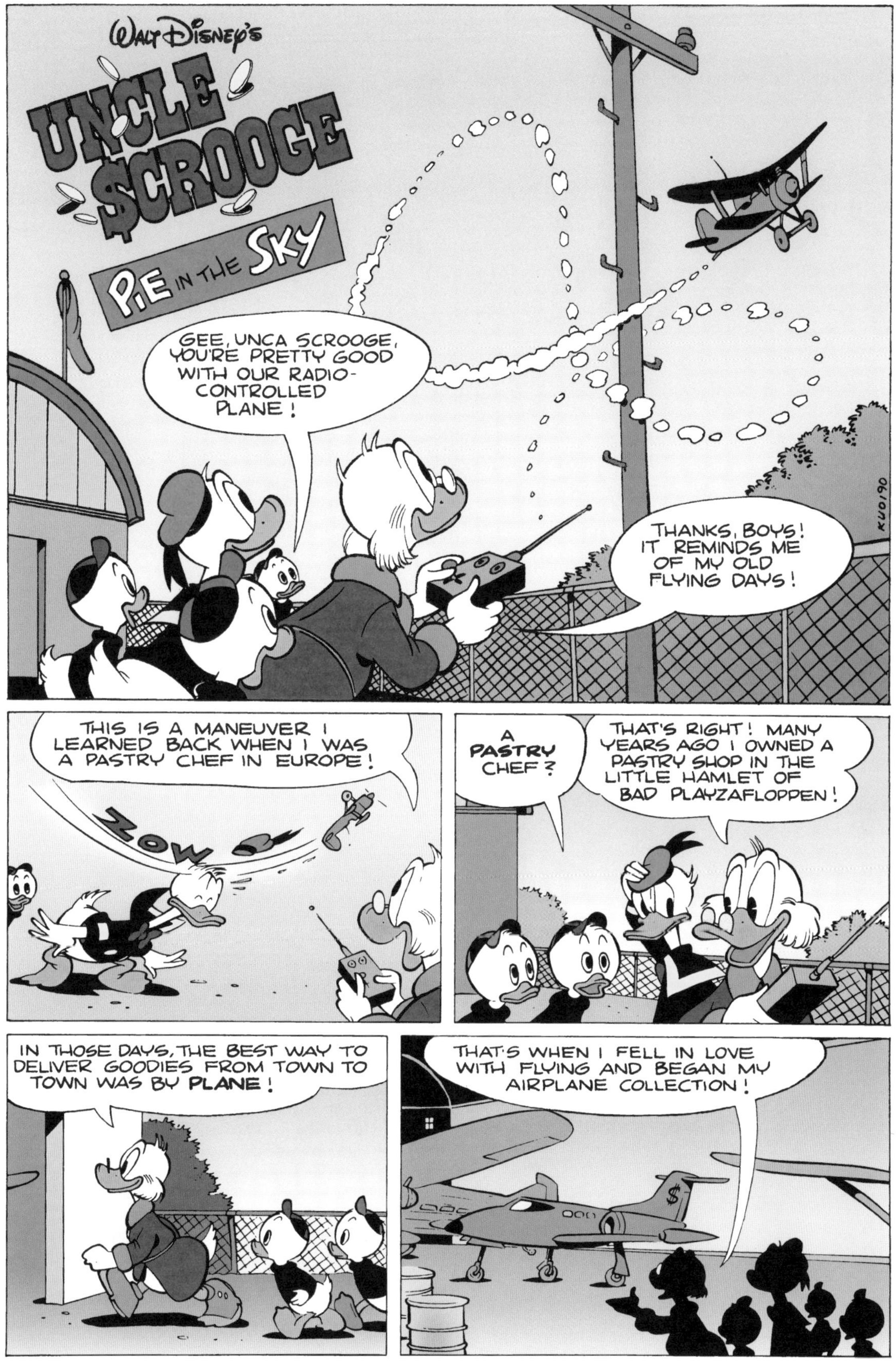
Walt Disney's
Uncle $crooge
Pie in the Sky
GEE, UNCA SCROOGE, YOU'RE PRETTY GOOD WITH OUR RADIO-CONTROLLED PLANE!
THANKS, BOYS! IT REMINDS ME OF MY OLD FLYING DAYS!
KUO/90
THIS IS A MANEUVER I LEARNED BACK WHEN I WAS A PASTRY CHEF IN EUROPE!
ZOW
A PASTRY CHEF?
THAT'S RIGHT! MANY YEARS AGO I OWNED A PASTRY SHOP IN THE LITTLE HAMLET OF BAD PLAYZAFLOPPEN!
IN THOSE DAYS, THE BEST WAY TO DELIVER GOODIES FROM TOWN TO TOWN WAS BY PLANE!
THAT'S WHEN I FELL IN LOVE WITH FLYING AND BEGAN MY AIRPLANE COLLECTION!

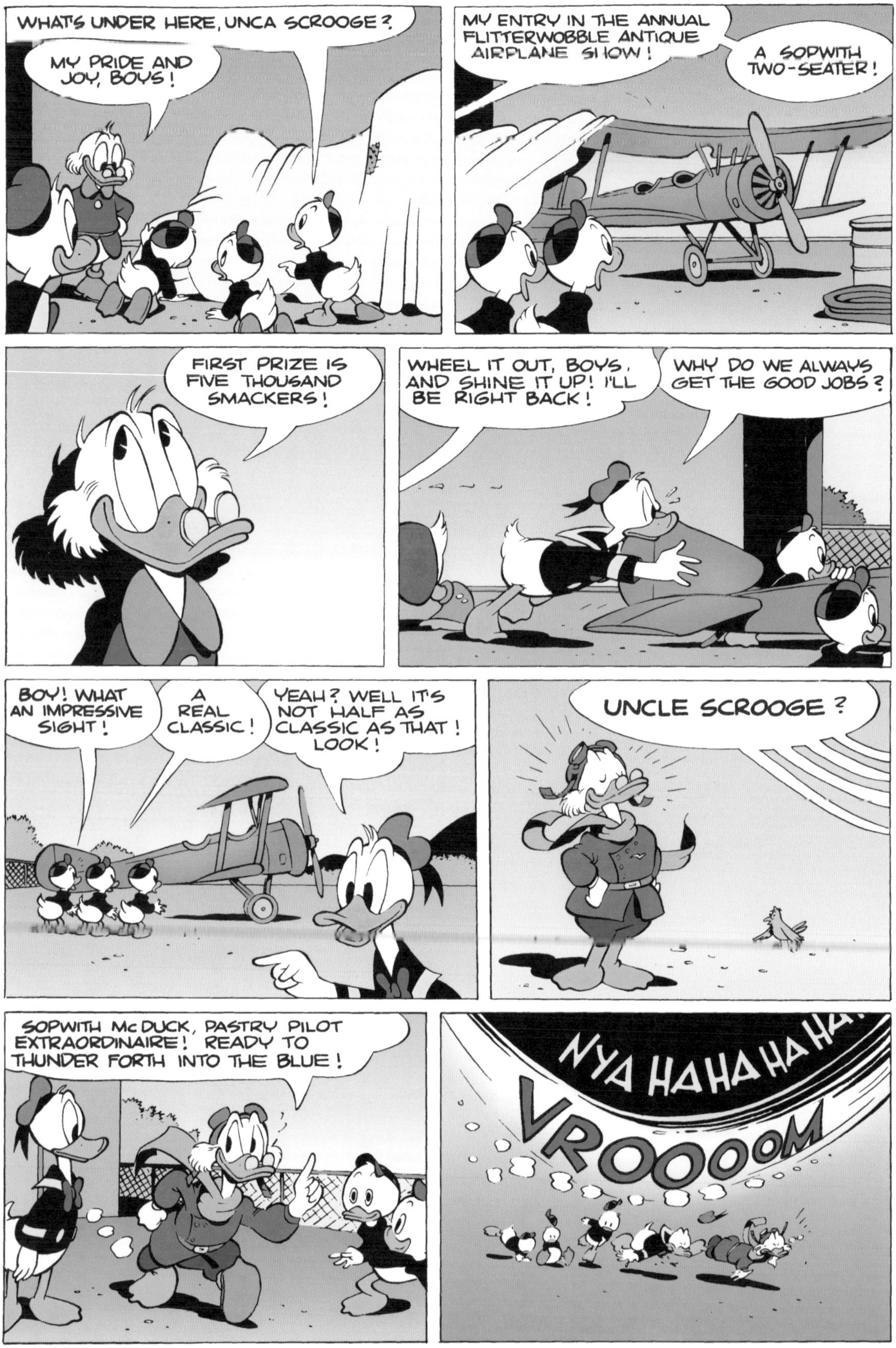

WHAT'S UNDER HERE, UNCA SCROOGE?
MY PRIDE AND JOY, BOYS!
MY ENTRY IN THE ANNUAL FLITTERWOBBLE ANTIQUE AIRPLANE SHOW!
A SOPWITH TWO-SEATER!
FIRST PRIZE IS FIVE THOUSAND SMACKERS!
WHEEL IT OUT, BOYS, AND SHINE IT UP! I'LL BE RIGHT BACK!
WHY DO WE ALWAYS GET THE GOOD JOBS?
BOY! WHAT AN IMPRESSIVE SIGHT!
A REAL CLASSIC!
YEAH? WELL IT'S NOT HALF AS CLASSIC AS THAT! LOOK!
UNCLE SCROOGE?
SOPWITH McDUCK, PASTRY PILOT EXTRAORDINAIRE! READY TO THUNDER FORTH INTO THE BLUE!
NYA HAHAHAHA!
VROOOOM

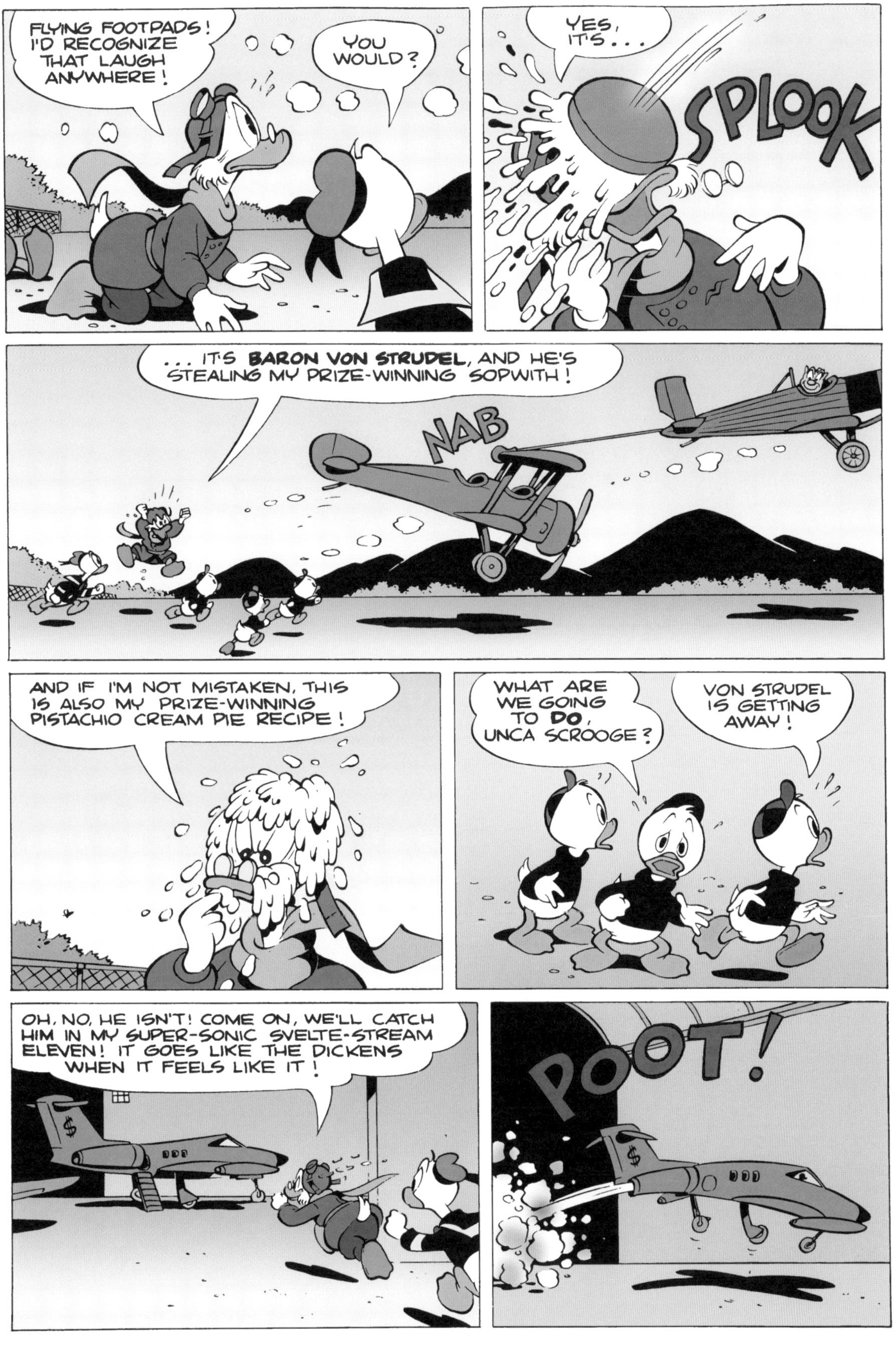
FLYING FOOTPADS! I'D RECOGNIZE THAT LAUGH ANYWHERE!
YOU WOULD?
YES, IT'S . . .
SPLOOK
. . . IT'S BARON VON STRUDEL, AND HE'S STEALING MY PRIZE-WINNING SOPWITH!
NAB
AND IF I'M NOT MISTAKEN, THIS IS ALSO MY PRIZE-WINNING PISTACHIO CREAM PIE RECIPE!
WHAT ARE WE GOING TO DO, UNCA SCROOGE?
VON STRUDEL IS GETTING AWAY!
OH, NO, HE ISN'T! COME ON, WE'LL CATCH HIM IN MY SUPER-SONIC SVELTE-STREAM ELEVEN! IT GOES LIKE THE DICKENS WHEN IT FEELS LIKE IT!
POOT!

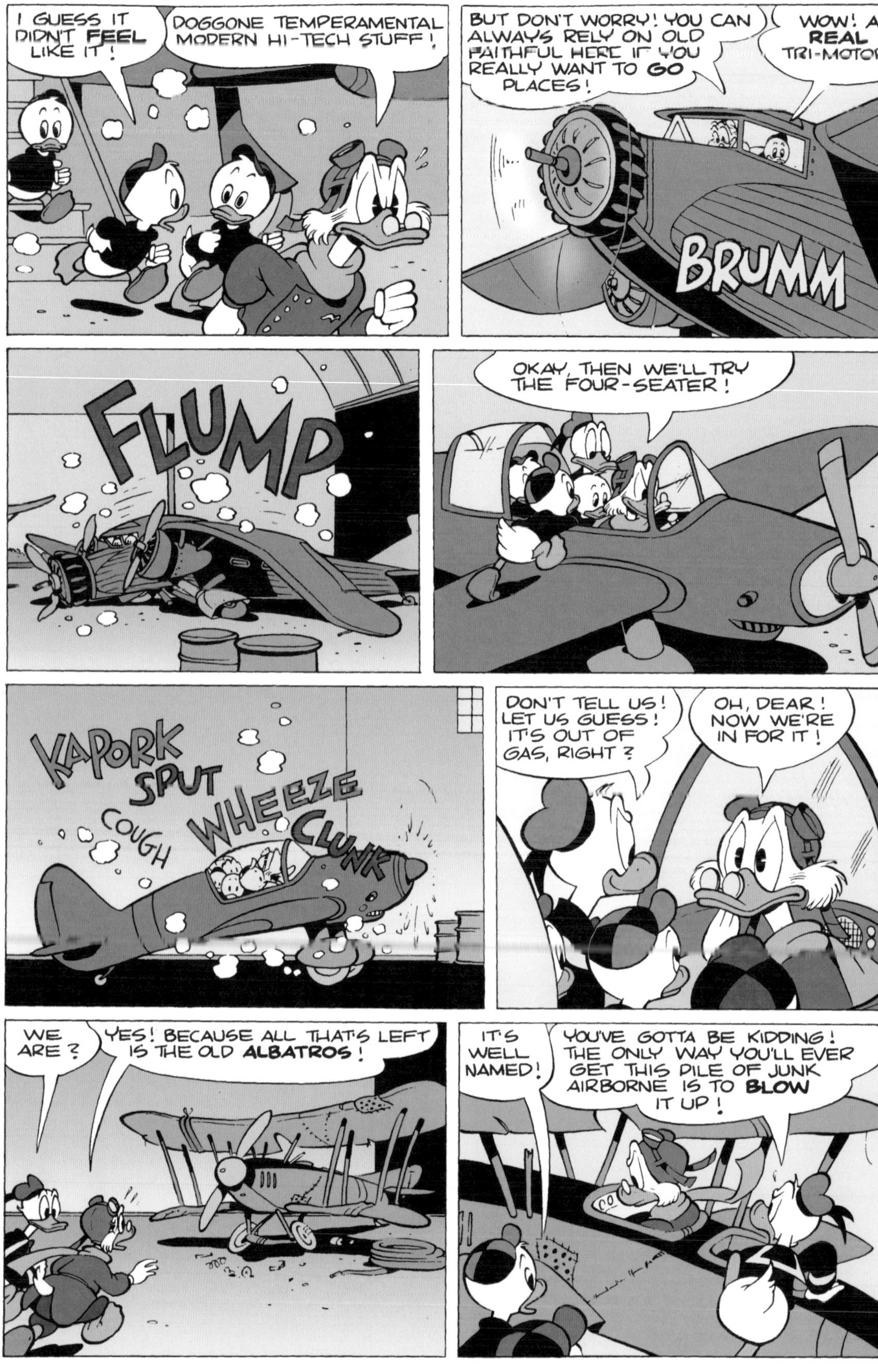
I GUESS IT DIDN'T FEEL LIKE IT!
DOGGONE TEMPERAMENTAL MODERN HI-TECH STUFF!
BUT DON'T WORRY! YOU CAN ALWAYS RELY ON OLD FAITHFUL HERE IF YOU REALLY WANT TO GO PLACES!
WOW! A REAL TRI-MOTOR!
BRUMM
FLUMP
OKAY, THEN WE'LL TRY THE FOUR-SEATER!
KAPORK
SPUT
COUGH
WHEEZE
CLUNK
DON'T TELL US! LET US GUESS! IT'S OUT OF GAS, RIGHT?
OH, DEAR! NOW WE'RE IN FOR IT!
WE ARE?
YES! BECAUSE ALL THAT'S LEFT IS THE OLD ALBATROS!
IT'S WELL NAMED!
YOU'VE GOTTA BE KIDDING! THE ONLY WAY YOU'LL EVER GET THIS PILE OF JUNK AIRBORNE IS TO BLOW IT UP!

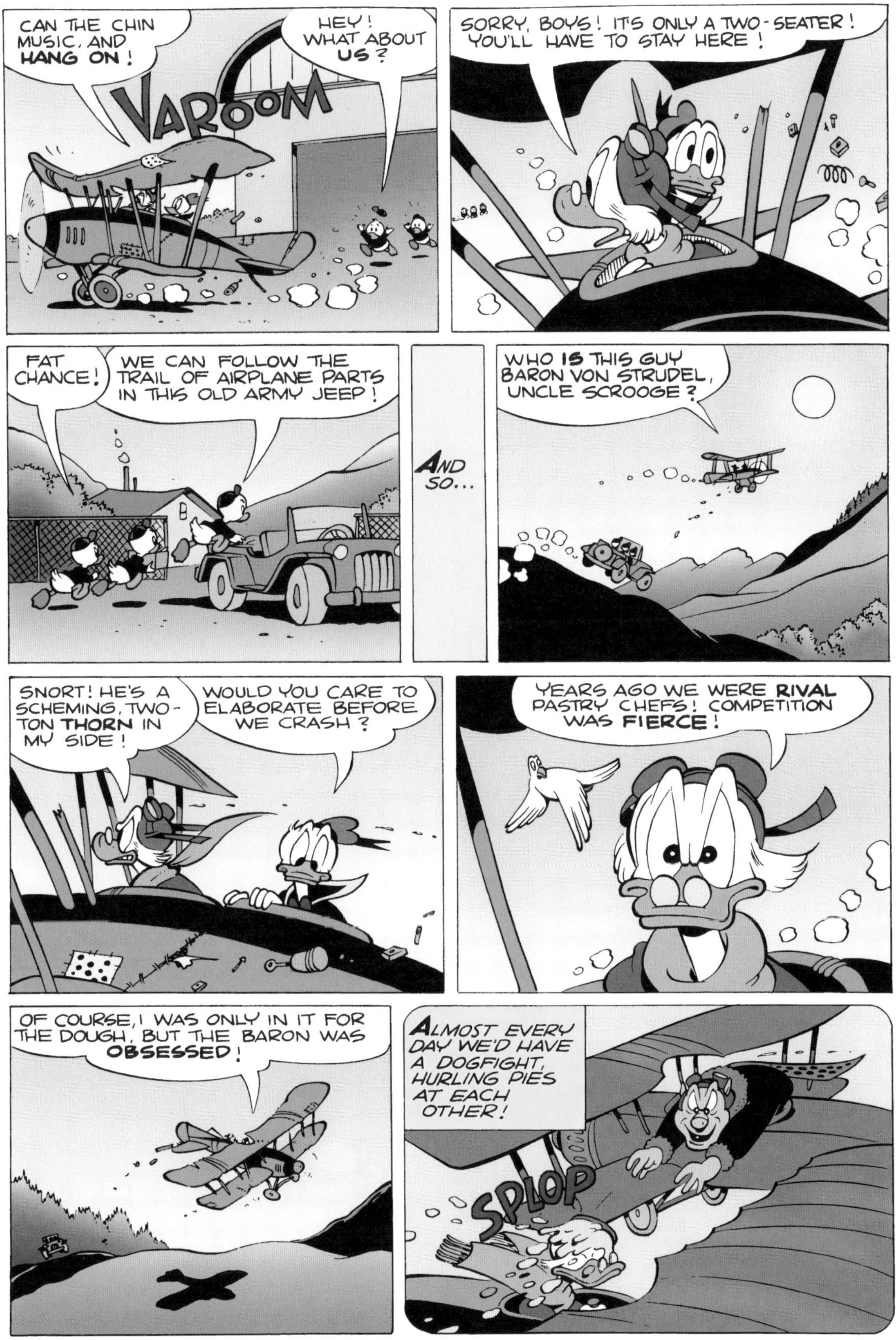
CAN THE CHIN MUSIC, AND HANG ON!
VAROOM
HEY! WHAT ABOUT US?
SORRY, BOYS! IT'S ONLY A TWO-SEATER! YOU'LL HAVE TO STAY HERE!
FAT CHANCE!
WE CAN FOLLOW THE TRAIL OF AIRPLANE PARTS IN THIS OLD ARMY JEEP!
AND SO...
WHO IS THIS GUY BARON VON STRUDEL, UNCLE SCROOGE?
SNORT! HE'S A SCHEMING, TWO-TON THORN IN MY SIDE!
WOULD YOU CARE TO ELABORATE BEFORE WE CRASH?
YEARS AGO WE WERE RIVAL PASTRY CHEFS! COMPETITION WAS FIERCE!
OF COURSE, I WAS ONLY IN IT FOR THE DOUGH, BUT THE BARON WAS OBSESSED!
ALMOST EVERY DAY WE'D HAVE A DOGFIGHT, HURLING PIES AT EACH OTHER!
SPLOP

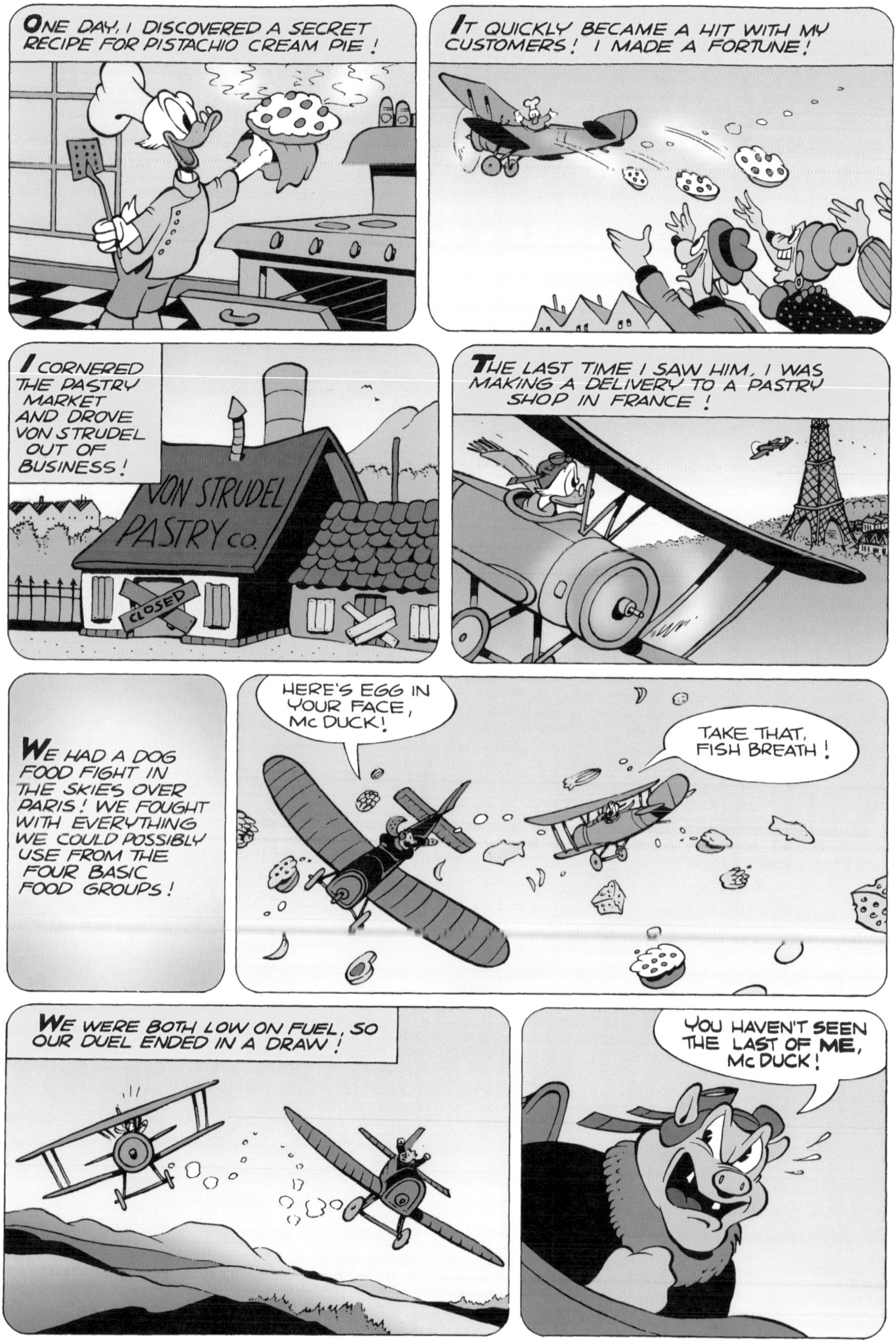
ONE DAY, I DISCOVERED A SECRET RECIPE FOR PISTACHIO CREAM PIE!
IT QUICKLY BECAME A HIT WITH MY CUSTOMERS! I MADE A FORTUNE!
I CORNERED THE PASTRY MARKET AND DROVE VON STRUDEL OUT OF BUSINESS!
VON STRUDEL PASTRY CO.
CLOSED
THE LAST TIME I SAW HIM, I WAS MAKING A DELIVERY TO A PASTRY SHOP IN FRANCE!
WE HAD A DOG FOOD FIGHT IN THE SKIES OVER PARIS! WE FOUGHT WITH EVERYTHING WE COULD POSSIBLY USE FROM THE FOUR BASIC FOOD GROUPS!
HERE'S EGG IN YOUR FACE, McDUCK!
TAKE THAT, FISH BREATH!
WE WERE BOTH LOW ON FUEL, SO OUR DUEL ENDED IN A DRAW!
YOU HAVEN'T SEEN THE LAST OF ME, McDUCK!

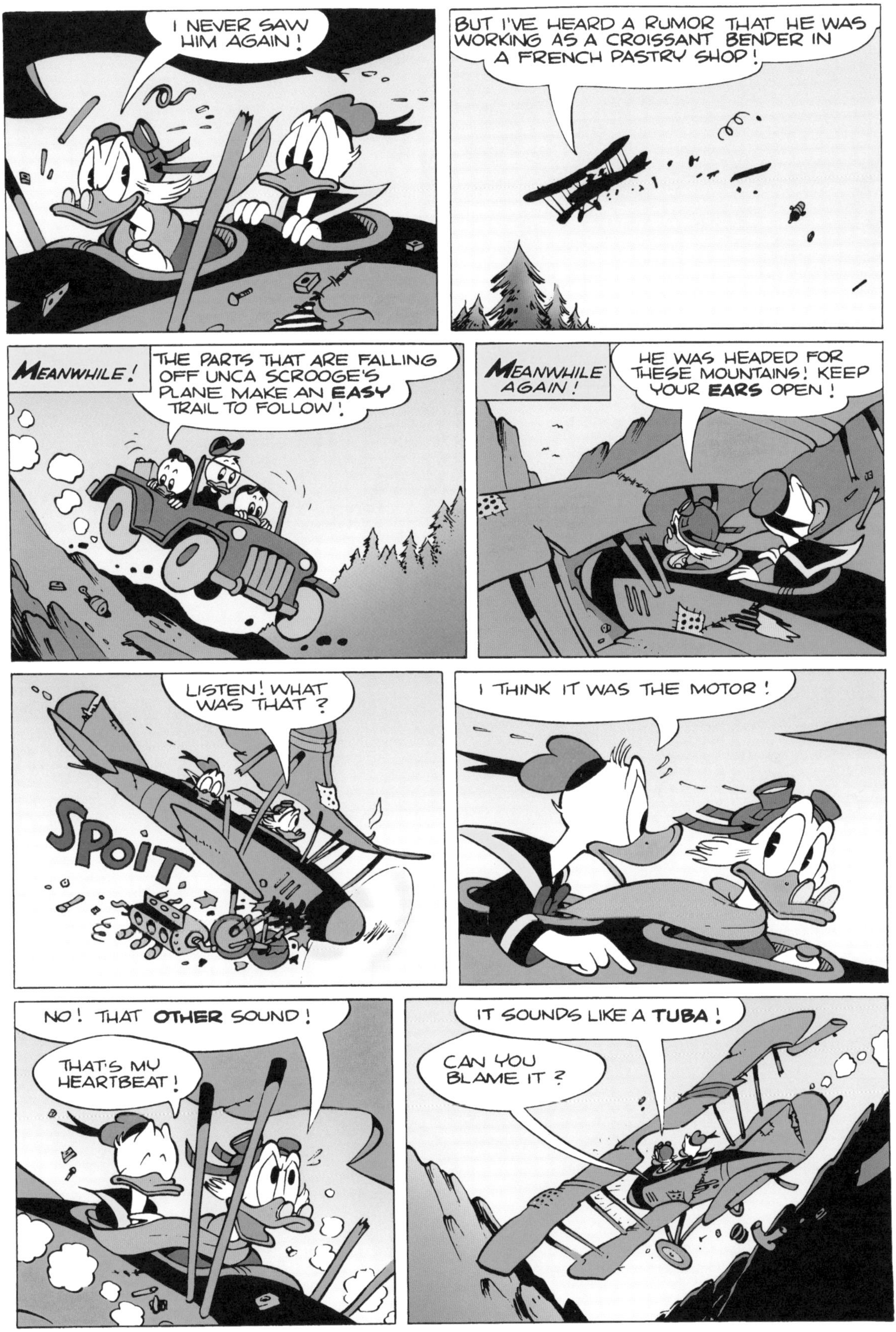
I NEVER SAW HIM AGAIN!
BUT I'VE HEARD A RUMOR THAT HE WAS WORKING AS A CROISSANT BENDER IN A FRENCH PASTRY SHOP!
MEANWHILE!
THE PARTS THAT ARE FALLING OFF UNCA SCROOGE'S PLANE MAKE AN EASY TRAIL TO FOLLOW!
MEANWHILE AGAIN!
HE WAS HEADED FOR THESE MOUNTAINS! KEEP YOUR EARS OPEN!
LISTEN! WHAT WAS THAT?
SPOIT
I THINK IT WAS THE MOTOR!
NO! THAT OTHER SOUND!
THAT'S MY HEARTBEAT!
IT SOUNDS LIKE A TUBA!
CAN YOU BLAME IT?

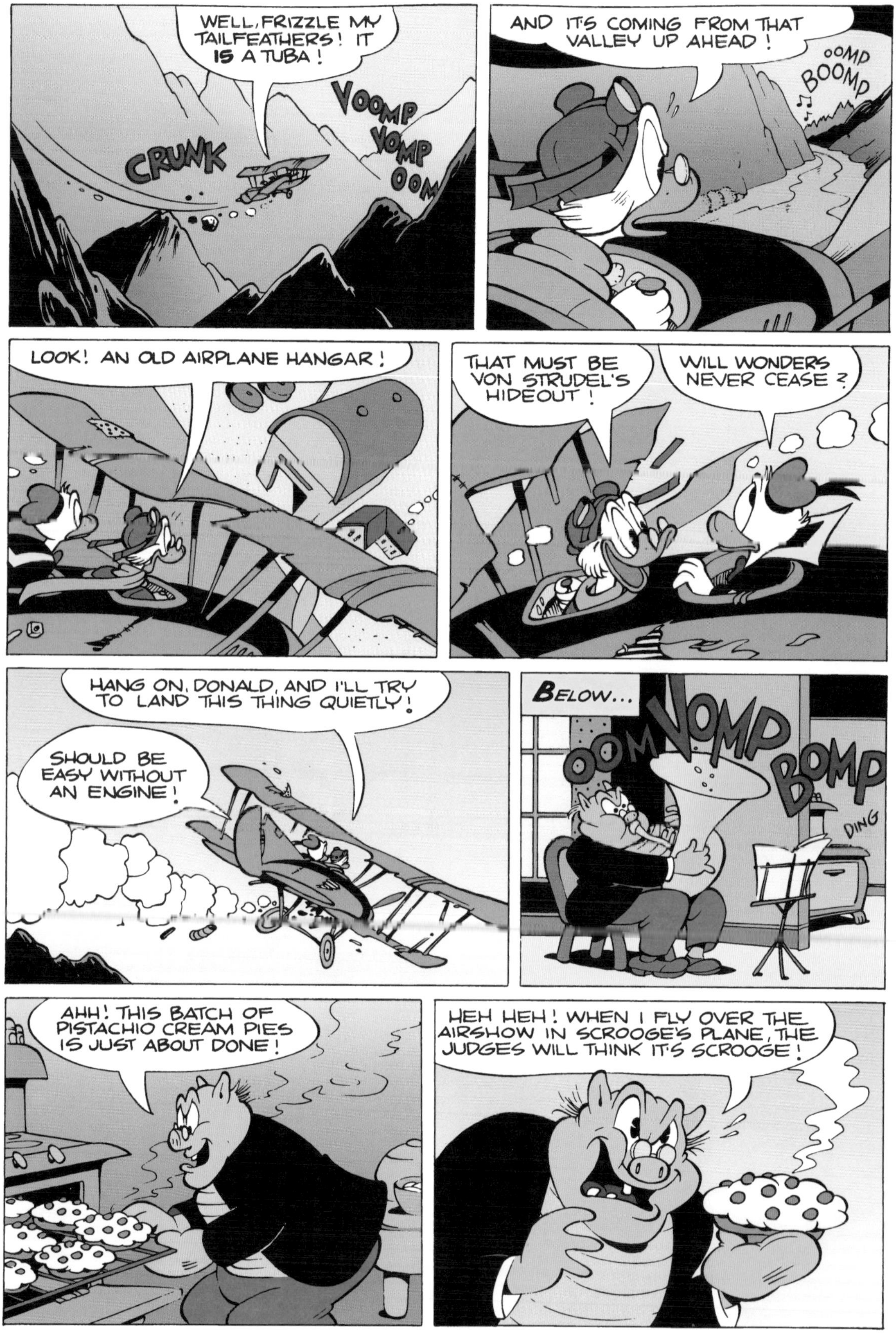
WELL, FRIZZLE MY TAILFEATHERS! IT IS A TUBA!
VOOMP YOMP OOM
CRUNK
AND IT'S COMING FROM THAT VALLEY UP AHEAD!
OOMP BOOMP
LOOK! AN OLD AIRPLANE HANGAR!
THAT MUST BE VON STRUDEL'S HIDEOUT!
WILL WONDERS NEVER CEASE?
HANG ON, DONALD, AND I'LL TRY TO LAND THIS THING QUIETLY!
SHOULD BE EASY WITHOUT AN ENGINE!
BELOW...
OOM VOMP BOMP
DING
AHH! THIS BATCH OF PISTACHIO CREAM PIES IS JUST ABOUT DONE!
HEH HEH! WHEN I FLY OVER THE AIRSHOW IN SCROOGE'S PLANE, THE JUDGES WILL THINK IT'S SCROOGE!

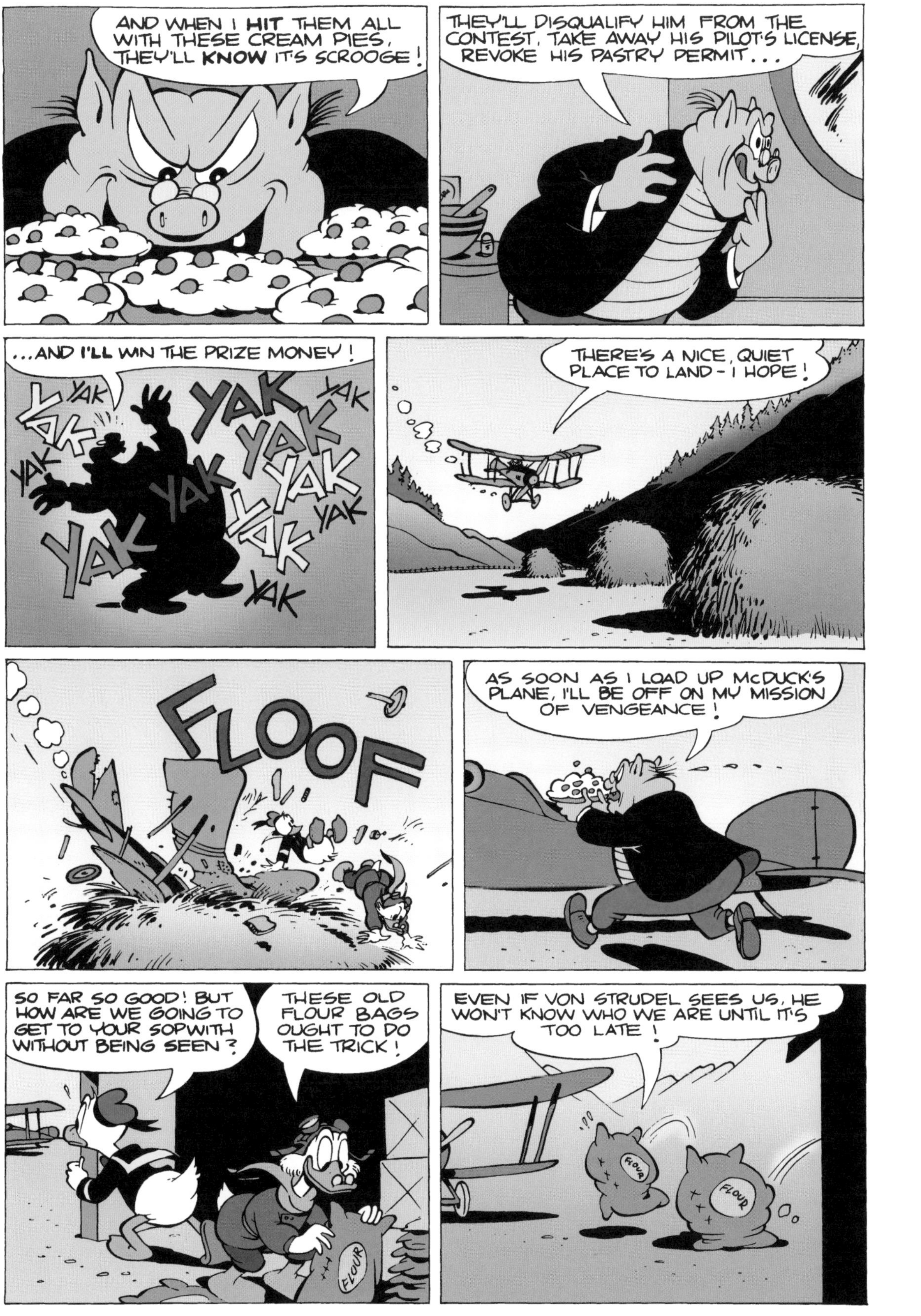
AND WHEN I HIT THEM ALL WITH THESE CREAM PIES, THEY'LL KNOW IT'S SCROOGE!
THEY'LL DISQUALIFY HIM FROM THE CONTEST, TAKE AWAY HIS PILOT'S LICENSE, REVOKE HIS PASTRY PERMIT...
...AND I'LL WIN THE PRIZE MONEY!
YAK YAK YAK YAK YAK YAK YAK YAK YAK YAK YAK YAK
THERE'S A NICE, QUIET PLACE TO LAND - I HOPE!
FLOOF
AS SOON AS I LOAD UP McDUCK'S PLANE, I'LL BE OFF ON MY MISSION OF VENGEANCE!
SO FAR SO GOOD! BUT HOW ARE WE GOING TO GET TO YOUR SOPWITH WITHOUT BEING SEEN?
THESE OLD FLOUR BAGS OUGHT TO DO THE TRICK!
FLOUR
EVEN IF VON STRUDEL SEES US, HE WON'T KNOW WHO WE ARE UNTIL IT'S TOO LATE!
FLOUR
FLOUR

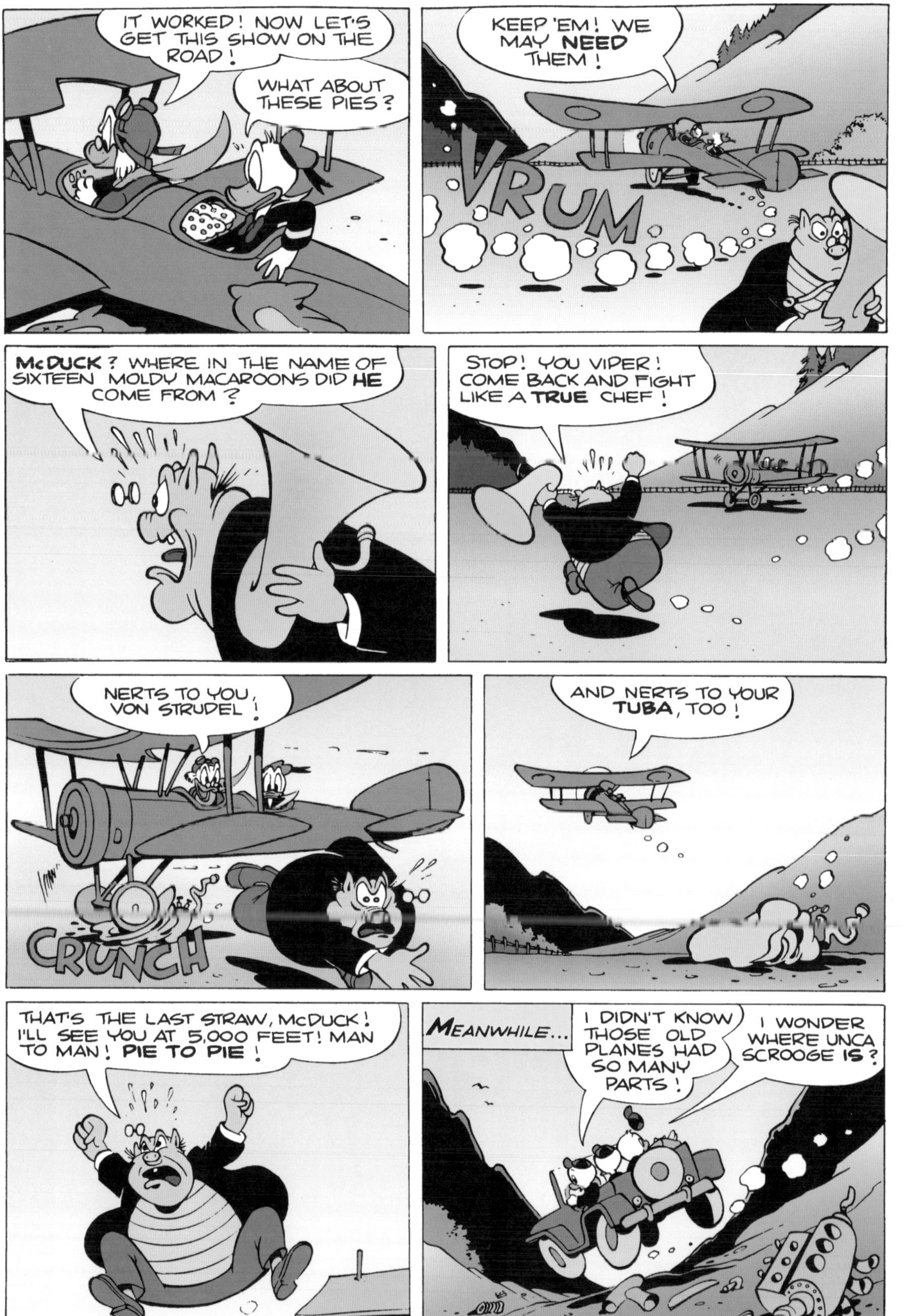
IT WORKED! NOW LET'S GET THIS SHOW ON THE ROAD!
WHAT ABOUT THESE PIES?
KEEP 'EM! WE MAY NEED THEM!
VRUM
McDUCK? WHERE IN THE NAME OF SIXTEEN MOLDY MACAROONS DID HE COME FROM?
STOP! YOU VIPER! COME BACK AND FIGHT LIKE A TRUE CHEF!
NERTS TO YOU, VON STRUDEL!
CRUNCH
AND NERTS TO YOUR TUBA, TOO!
THAT'S THE LAST STRAW, McDUCK! I'LL SEE YOU AT 5,000 FEET! MAN TO MAN! PIE TO PIE!
MEANWHILE...
I DIDN'T KNOW THOSE OLD PLANES HAD SO MANY PARTS!
I WONDER WHERE UNCA SCROOGE IS?

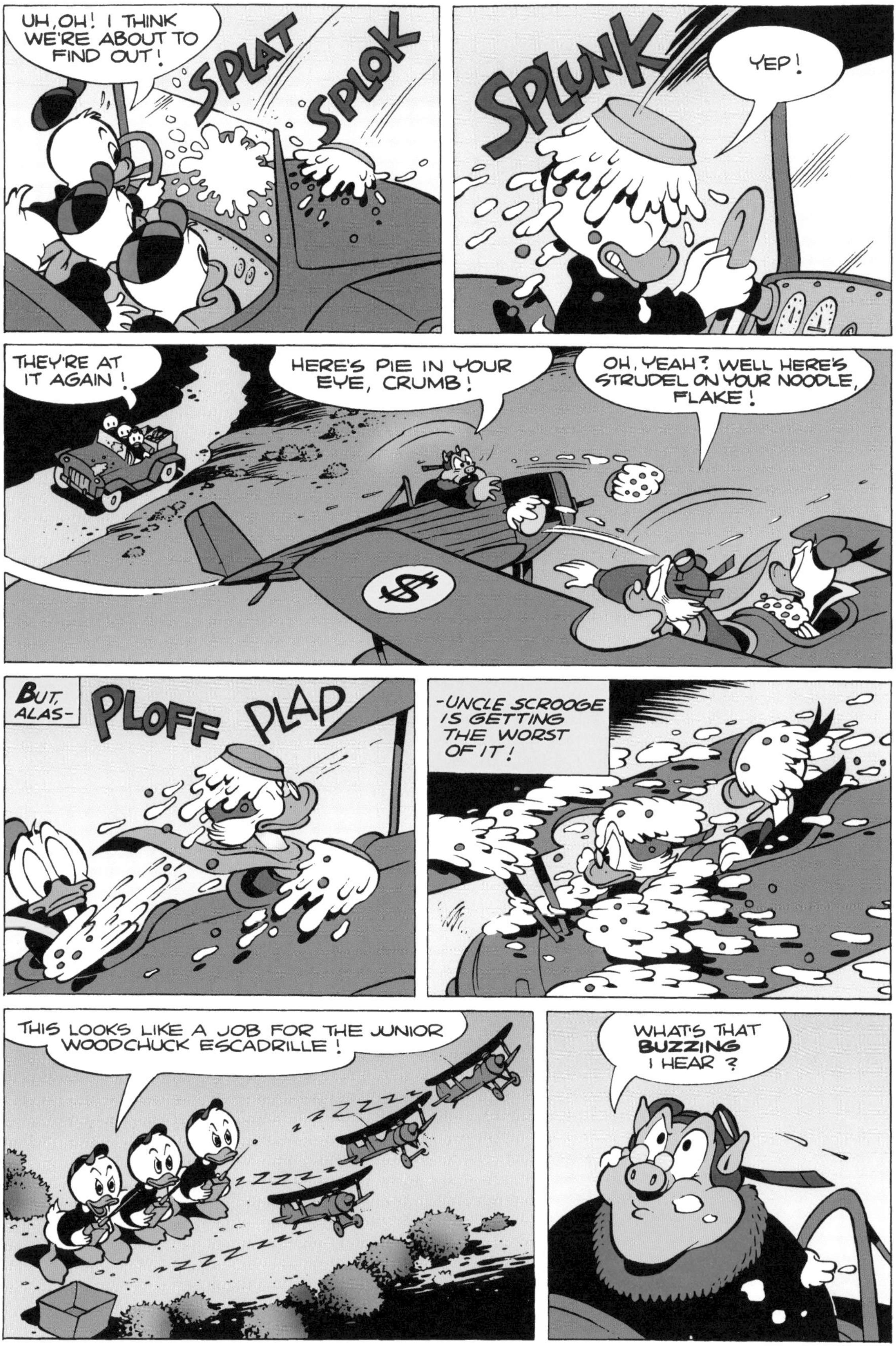

UH, OH! I THINK WE'RE ABOUT TO FIND OUT!
SPLAT
SPLOK
SPLUNK
YEP!
THEY'RE AT IT AGAIN!
HERE'S PIE IN YOUR EYE, CRUMB!
OH, YEAH? WELL HERE'S STRUDEL ON YOUR NOODLE, FLAKE!
BUT, ALAS-
PLOFF
PLAP
-UNCLE SCROOGE IS GETTING THE WORST OF IT!
THIS LOOKS LIKE A JOB FOR THE JUNIOR WOODCHUCK ESCADRILLE!
WHAT'S THAT **BUZZING** I HEAR?

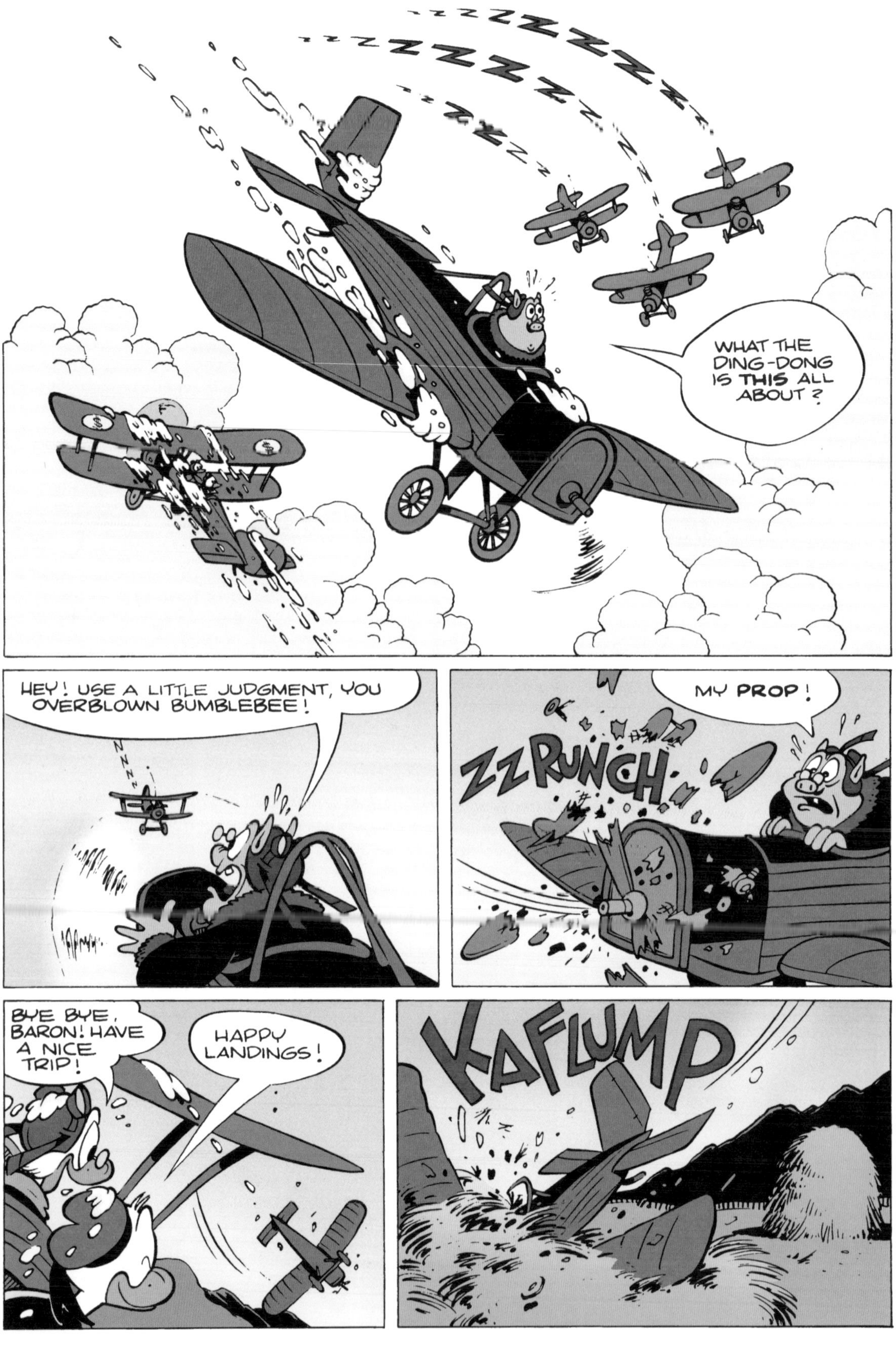
WHAT THE DING-DONG IS THIS ALL ABOUT?
HEY! USE A LITTLE JUDGMENT, YOU OVERBLOWN BUMBLEBEE!
MY PROP!
ZZRUNCH
BYE BYE, BARON! HAVE A NICE TRIP!
HAPPY LANDINGS!
KAFLUMP

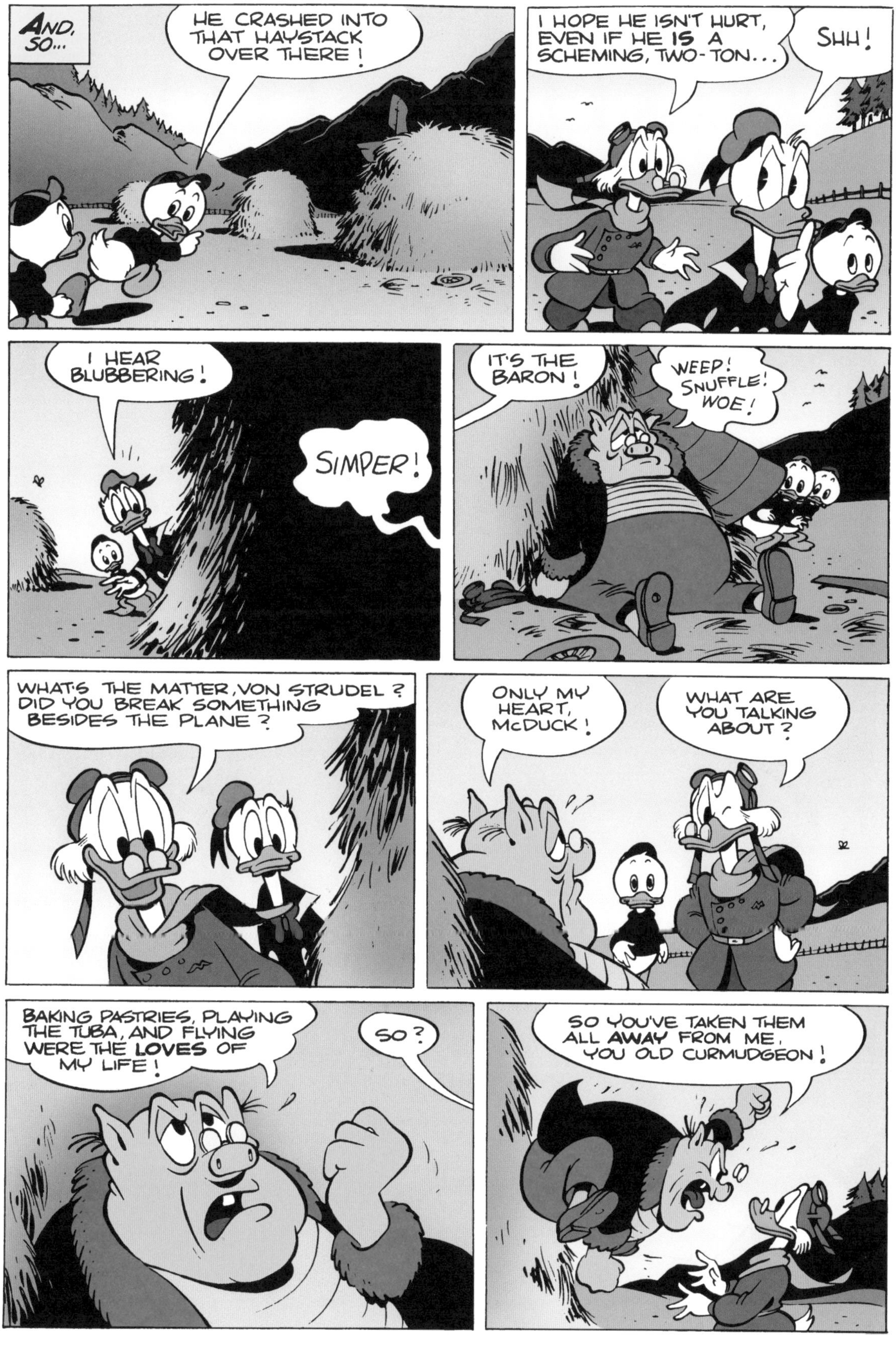
AND, SO...
HE CRASHED INTO THAT HAYSTACK OVER THERE!
I HOPE HE ISN'T HURT, EVEN IF HE IS A SCHEMING, TWO-TON...
SHH!
I HEAR BLUBBERING!
SIMPER!
IT'S THE BARON!
WEEP! SNUFFLE! WOE!
WHAT'S THE MATTER, VON STRUDEL? DID YOU BREAK SOMETHING BESIDES THE PLANE?
ONLY MY HEART, McDUCK!
WHAT ARE YOU TALKING ABOUT?
BAKING PASTRIES, PLAYING THE TUBA, AND FLYING WERE THE LOVES OF MY LIFE!
SO?
SO YOU'VE TAKEN THEM ALL AWAY FROM ME, YOU OLD CURMUDGEON!

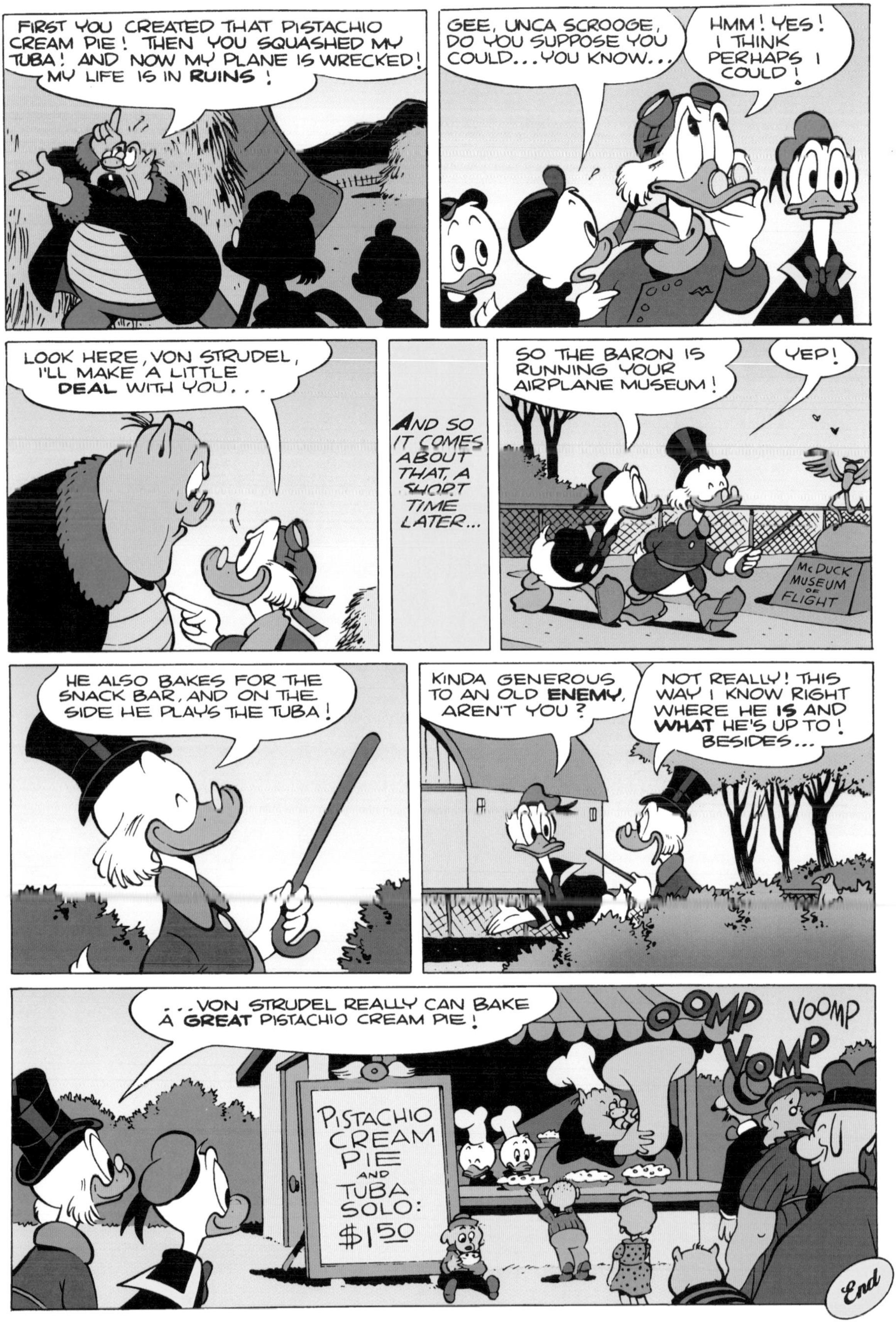
FIRST YOU CREATED THAT PISTACHIO CREAM PIE! THEN YOU SQUASHED MY TUBA! AND NOW MY PLANE IS WRECKED! MY LIFE IS IN RUINS!
GEE, UNCA SCROOGE, DO YOU SUPPOSE YOU COULD...YOU KNOW...
HMM! YES! I THINK PERHAPS I COULD!
LOOK HERE, VON STRUDEL, I'LL MAKE A LITTLE DEAL WITH YOU...
AND SO IT COMES ABOUT THAT, A SHORT TIME LATER...
SO THE BARON IS RUNNING YOUR AIRPLANE MUSEUM!
YEP!
McDUCK MUSEUM OF FLIGHT
HE ALSO BAKES FOR THE SNACK BAR, AND ON THE SIDE HE PLAYS THE TUBA!
KINDA GENEROUS TO AN OLD ENEMY, AREN'T YOU?
NOT REALLY! THIS WAY I KNOW RIGHT WHERE HE IS AND WHAT HE'S UP TO! BESIDES...
...VON STRUDEL REALLY CAN BAKE A GREAT PISTACHIO CREAM PIE!
OOMP
VOOMP
VOMP
PISTACHIO CREAM PIE AND TUBA SOLO: $1.50
End

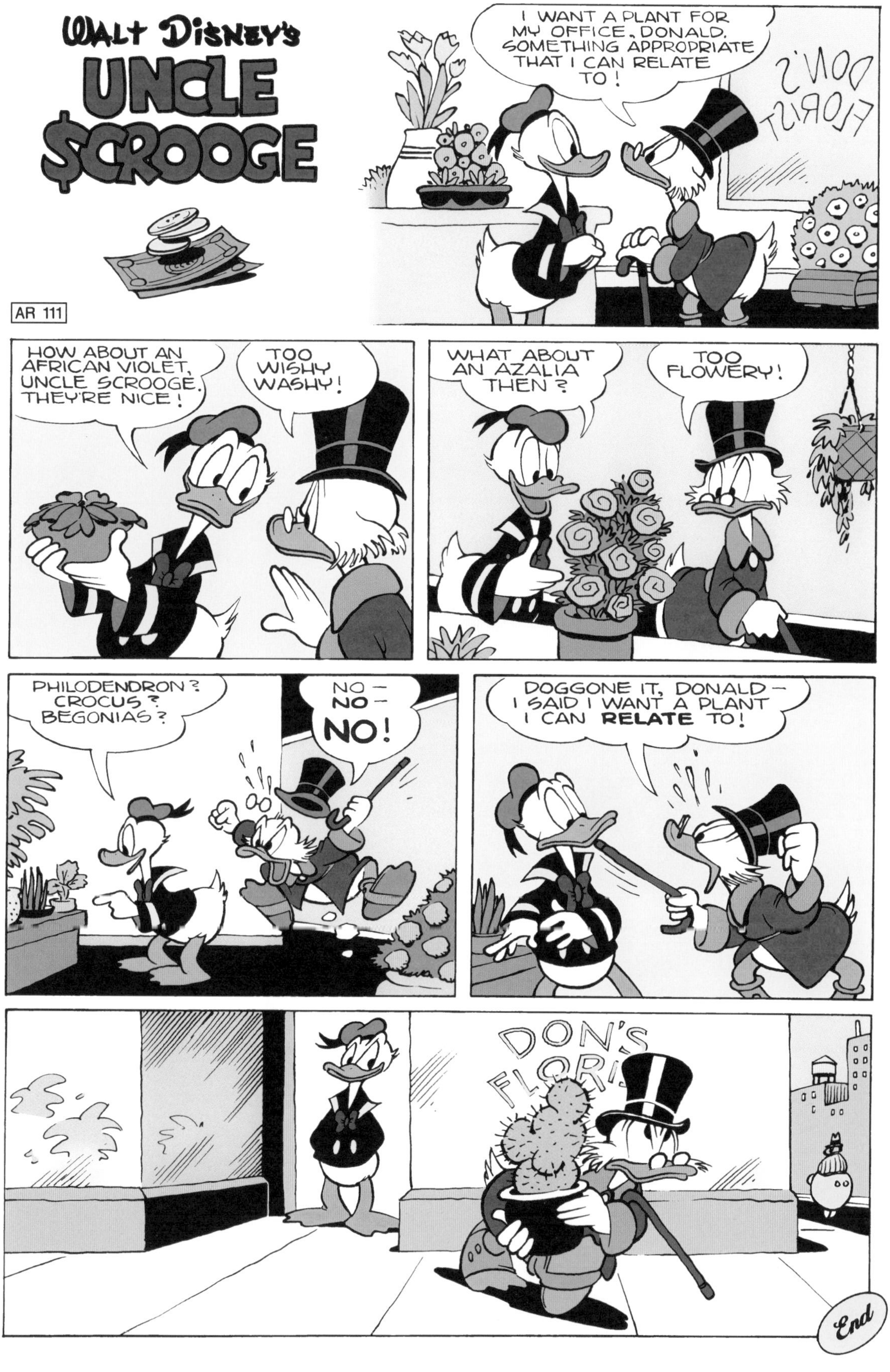
WALT DISNEY'S
UNCLE $CROOGE
AR 111
I WANT A PLANT FOR MY OFFICE, DONALD. SOMETHING APPROPRIATE THAT I CAN RELATE TO!
DON'S FLORIST
HOW ABOUT AN AFRICAN VIOLET, UNCLE SCROOGE. THEY'RE NICE!
TOO WISHY WASHY!
WHAT ABOUT AN AZALIA THEN?
TOO FLOWERY!
PHILODENDRON? CROCUS? BEGONIAS?
NO— NO— NO!
DOGGONE IT, DONALD— I SAID I WANT A PLANT I CAN RELATE TO!
DON'S FLORI
End

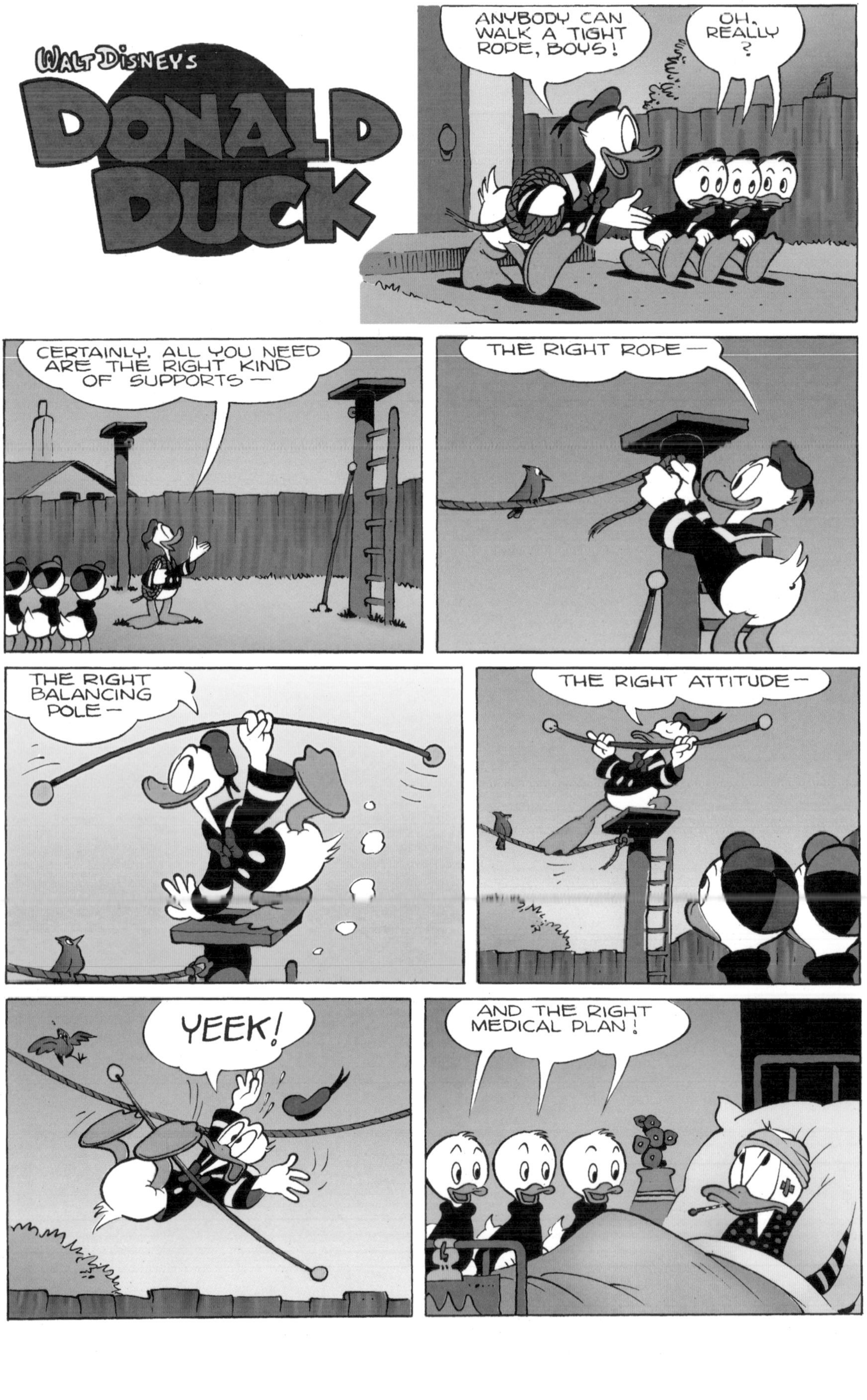

WALT DISNEY'S
DONALD DUCK
ANYBODY CAN WALK A TIGHT ROPE, BOYS!
OH, REALLY?
CERTAINLY. ALL YOU NEED ARE THE RIGHT KIND OF SUPPORTS —
THE RIGHT ROPE —
THE RIGHT BALANCING POLE —
THE RIGHT ATTITUDE —
YEEK!
AND THE RIGHT MEDICAL PLAN!

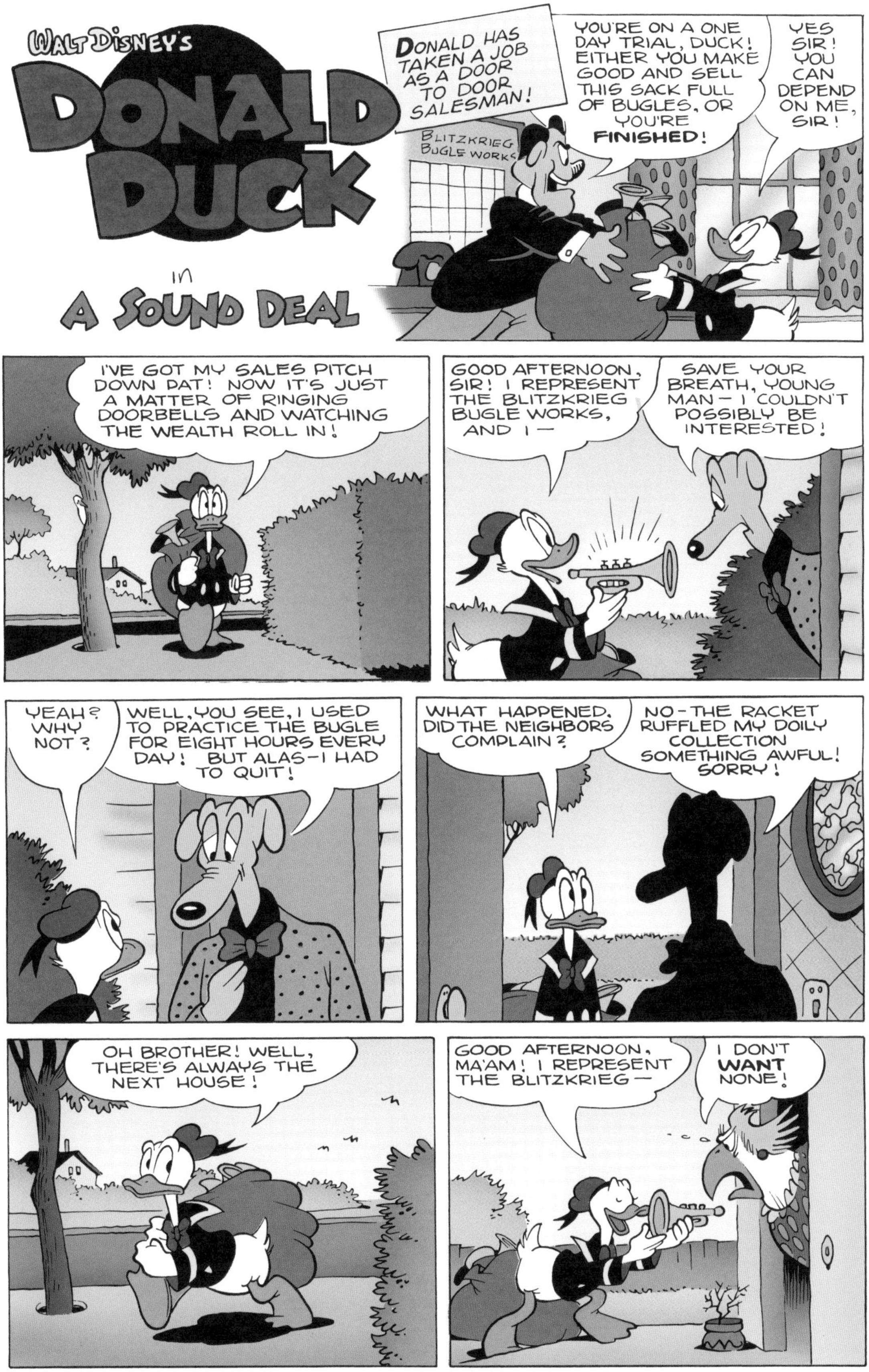
WALT DISNEY'S
DONALD DUCK
in
A SOUND DEAL
DONALD HAS TAKEN A JOB AS A DOOR TO DOOR SALESMAN!
BLITZKRIEG BUGLE WORKS
YOU'RE ON A ONE DAY TRIAL, DUCK! EITHER YOU MAKE GOOD AND SELL THIS SACK FULL OF BUGLES, OR YOU'RE **FINISHED**!
YES SIR! YOU CAN DEPEND ON ME, SIR!
I'VE GOT MY SALES PITCH DOWN PAT! NOW IT'S JUST A MATTER OF RINGING DOORBELLS AND WATCHING THE WEALTH ROLL IN!
GOOD AFTERNOON, SIR! I REPRESENT THE BLITZKRIEG BUGLE WORKS, AND I—
SAVE YOUR BREATH, YOUNG MAN— I COULDN'T POSSIBLY BE INTERESTED!
YEAH? WHY NOT?
WELL, YOU SEE, I USED TO PRACTICE THE BUGLE FOR EIGHT HOURS EVERY DAY! BUT ALAS—I HAD TO QUIT!
WHAT HAPPENED, DID THE NEIGHBORS COMPLAIN?
NO—THE RACKET RUFFLED MY DOILY COLLECTION SOMETHING AWFUL! **SORRY**!
OH BROTHER! WELL, THERE'S ALWAYS THE NEXT HOUSE!
GOOD AFTERNOON, MA'AM! I REPRESENT THE BLITZKRIEG—
I DON'T **WANT** NONE!

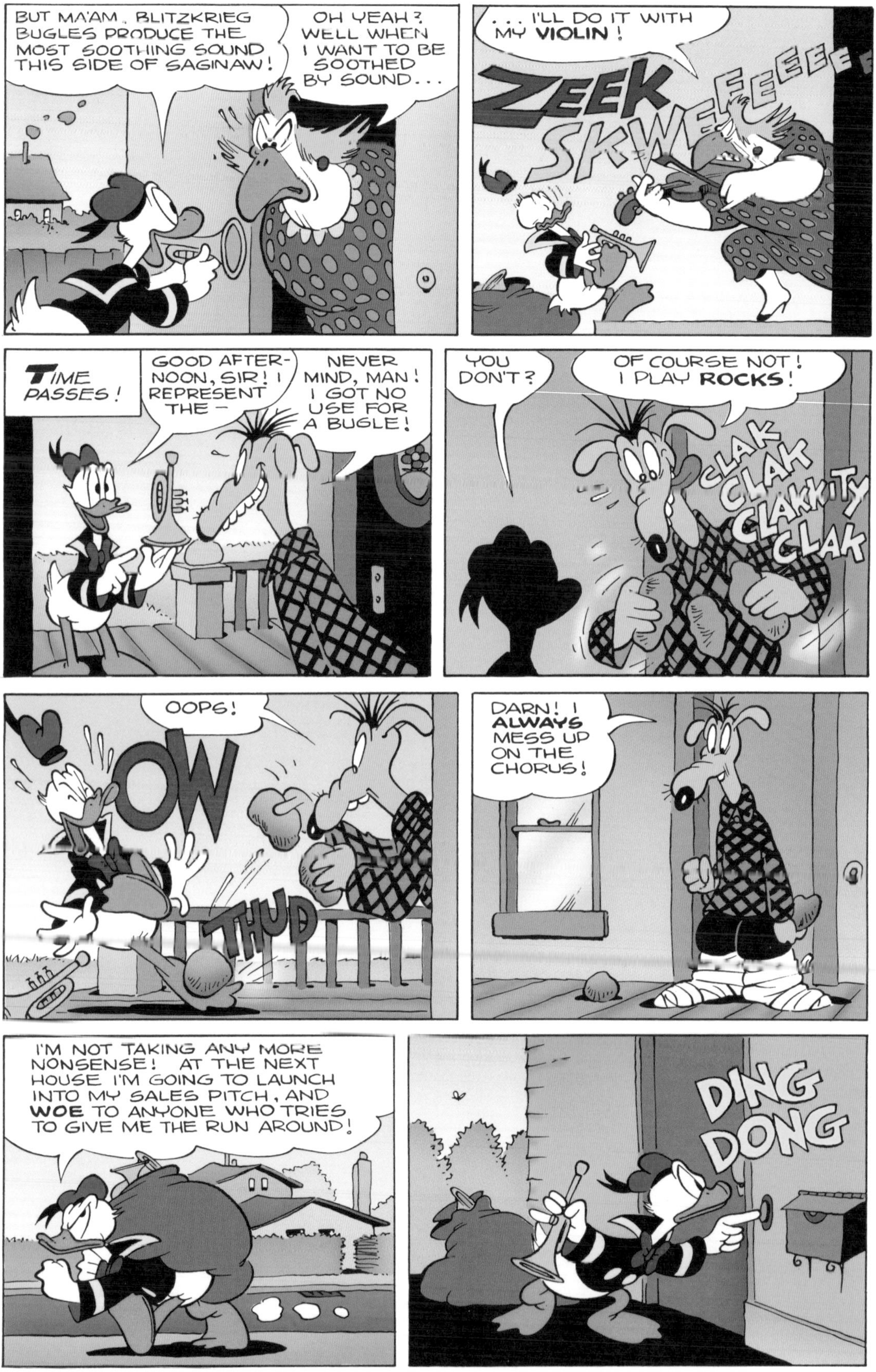
BUT MA'AM, BLITZKRIEG BUGLES PRODUCE THE MOST SOOTHING SOUND THIS SIDE OF SAGINAW!
OH YEAH? WELL WHEN I WANT TO BE SOOTHED BY SOUND...
... I'LL DO IT WITH MY **VIOLIN**!
ZEEK
SKWEEEEEEE
TIME PASSES!
GOOD AFTER-NOON, SIR! I REPRESENT THE—
NEVER MIND, MAN! I GOT NO USE FOR A BUGLE!
YOU DON'T?
OF COURSE NOT! I PLAY **ROCKS**!
CLAK CLAK CLAKKITY CLAK
OOPS!
OW
THUD
DARN! I **ALWAYS** MESS UP ON THE CHORUS!
I'M NOT TAKING ANY MORE NONSENSE! AT THE NEXT HOUSE I'M GOING TO LAUNCH INTO MY SALES PITCH, AND **WOE** TO ANYONE WHO TRIES TO GIVE ME THE RUN AROUND!
DING DONG

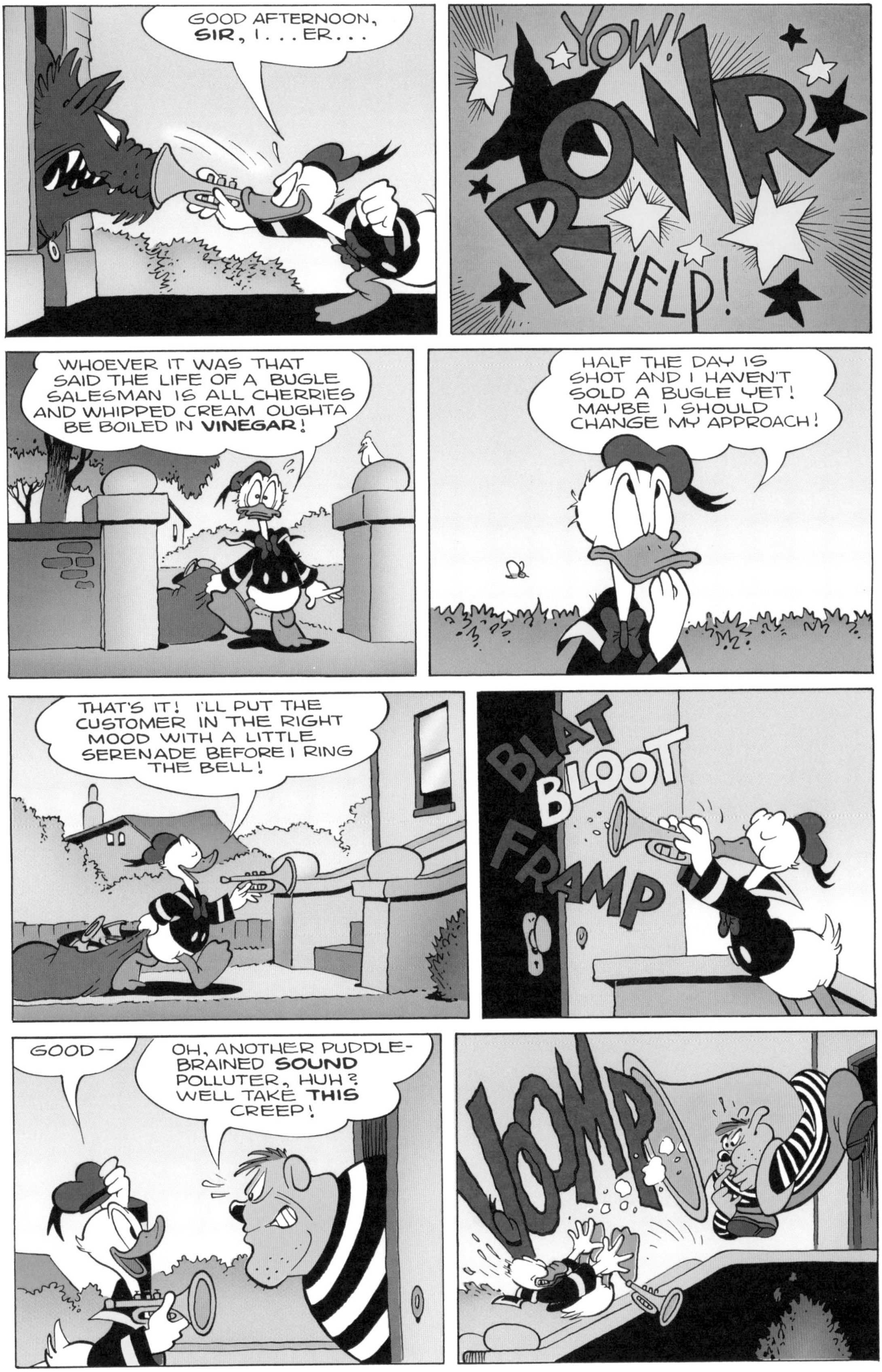
GOOD AFTERNOON, SIR, I . . . ER . . .
YOW!
ROWR
HELP!
WHOEVER IT WAS THAT SAID THE LIFE OF A BUGLE SALESMAN IS ALL CHERRIES AND WHIPPED CREAM OUGHTA BE BOILED IN VINEGAR!
HALF THE DAY IS SHOT AND I HAVEN'T SOLD A BUGLE YET! MAYBE I SHOULD CHANGE MY APPROACH!
THAT'S IT! I'LL PUT THE CUSTOMER IN THE RIGHT MOOD WITH A LITTLE SERENADE BEFORE I RING THE BELL!
BLAT
BLOOT
FRAMP
GOOD—
OH, ANOTHER PUDDLE-BRAINED SOUND POLLUTER, HUH? WELL TAKE THIS CREEP!
VOOMP

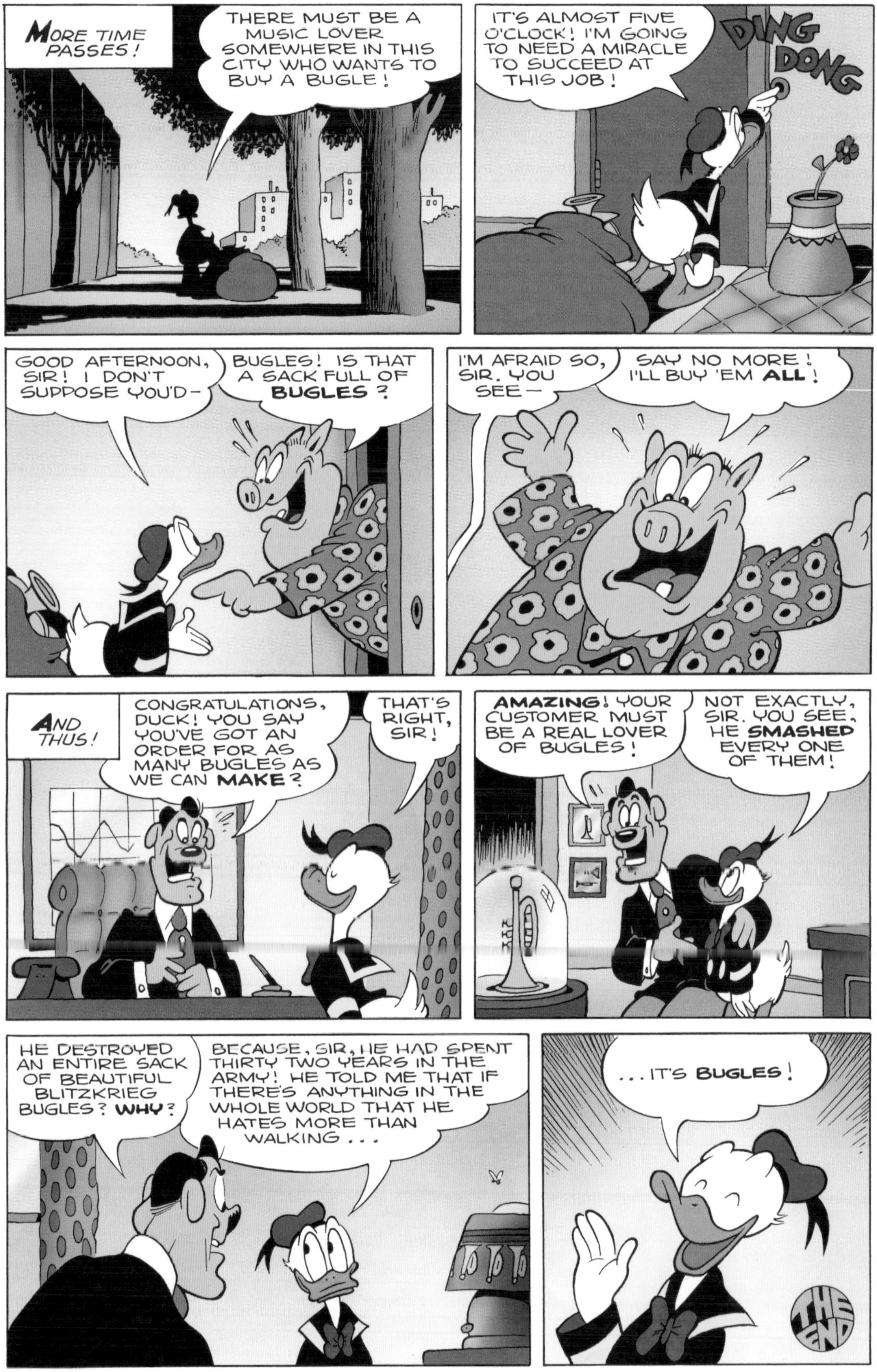
MORE TIME PASSES!
THERE MUST BE A MUSIC LOVER SOMEWHERE IN THIS CITY WHO WANTS TO BUY A BUGLE!
IT'S ALMOST FIVE O'CLOCK! I'M GOING TO NEED A MIRACLE TO SUCCEED AT THIS JOB!
DING DONG
GOOD AFTERNOON, SIR! I DON'T SUPPOSE YOU'D—
BUGLES! IS THAT A SACK FULL OF BUGLES?
I'M AFRAID SO, SIR. YOU SEE—
SAY NO MORE! I'LL BUY 'EM ALL!
AND THUS!
CONGRATULATIONS, DUCK! YOU SAY YOU'VE GOT AN ORDER FOR AS MANY BUGLES AS WE CAN MAKE?
THAT'S RIGHT, SIR!
AMAZING! YOUR CUSTOMER MUST BE A REAL LOVER OF BUGLES!
NOT EXACTLY, SIR. YOU SEE, HE SMASHED EVERY ONE OF THEM!
HE DESTROYED AN ENTIRE SACK OF BEAUTIFUL BLITZKRIEG BUGLES? WHY?
BECAUSE, SIR, HE HAD SPENT THIRTY TWO YEARS IN THE ARMY! HE TOLD ME THAT IF THERE'S ANYTHING IN THE WHOLE WORLD THAT HE HATES MORE THAN WALKING...
...IT'S BUGLES!
THE END

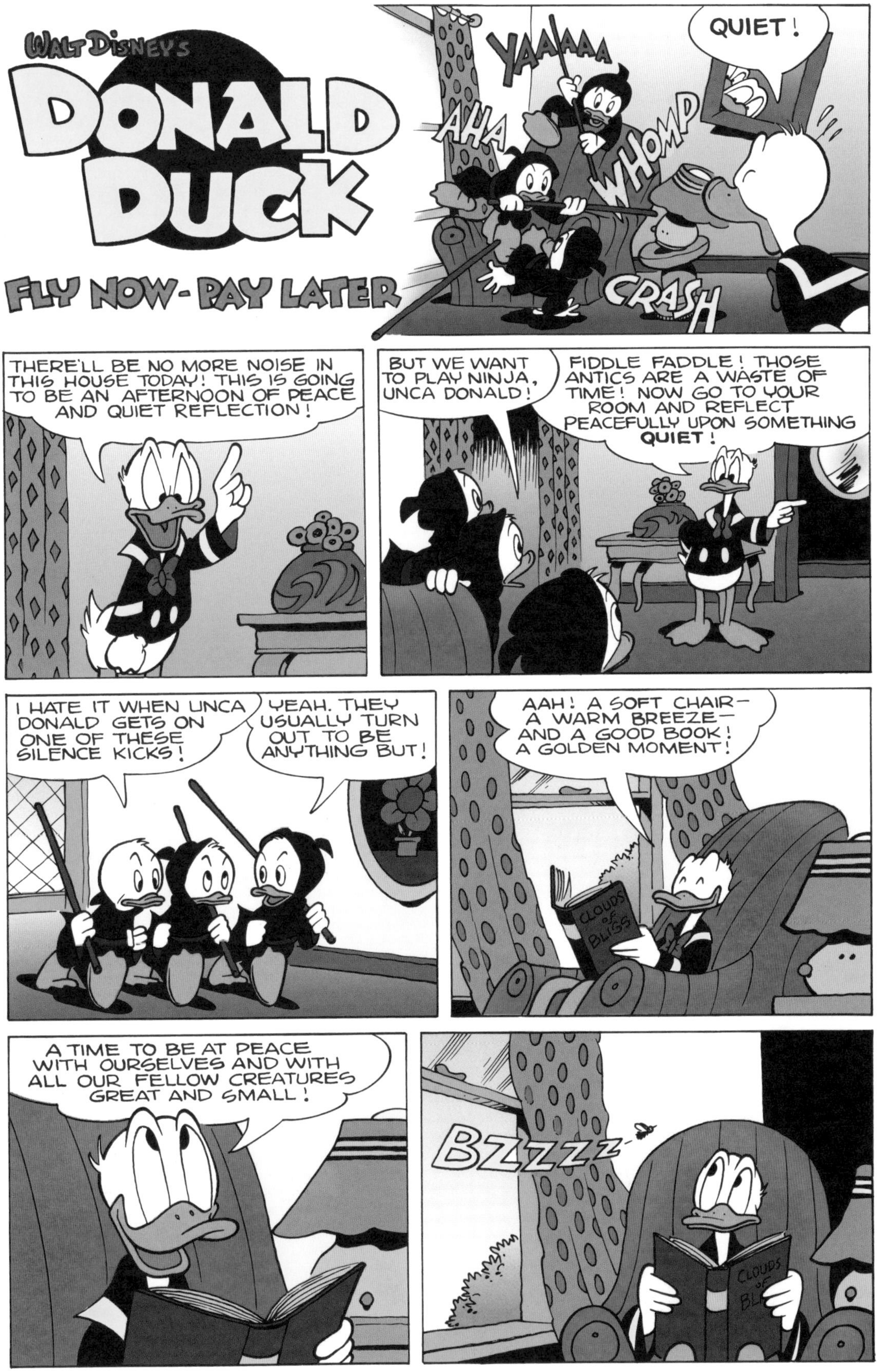
Walt Disney's
DONALD DUCK
FLY NOW - PAY LATER
YAAAAA
AHA
WHOMP
CRASH
QUIET!
THERE'LL BE NO MORE NOISE IN THIS HOUSE TODAY! THIS IS GOING TO BE AN AFTERNOON OF PEACE AND QUIET REFLECTION!
BUT WE WANT TO PLAY NINJA, UNCA DONALD!
FIDDLE FADDLE! THOSE ANTICS ARE A WASTE OF TIME! NOW GO TO YOUR ROOM AND REFLECT PEACEFULLY UPON SOMETHING QUIET!
I HATE IT WHEN UNCA DONALD GETS ON ONE OF THESE SILENCE KICKS!
YEAH. THEY USUALLY TURN OUT TO BE ANYTHING BUT!
AAH! A SOFT CHAIR— A WARM BREEZE— AND A GOOD BOOK! A GOLDEN MOMENT!
CLOUDS OF BLISS
A TIME TO BE AT PEACE WITH OURSELVES AND WITH ALL OUR FELLOW CREATURES GREAT AND SMALL!
BZZZZZ

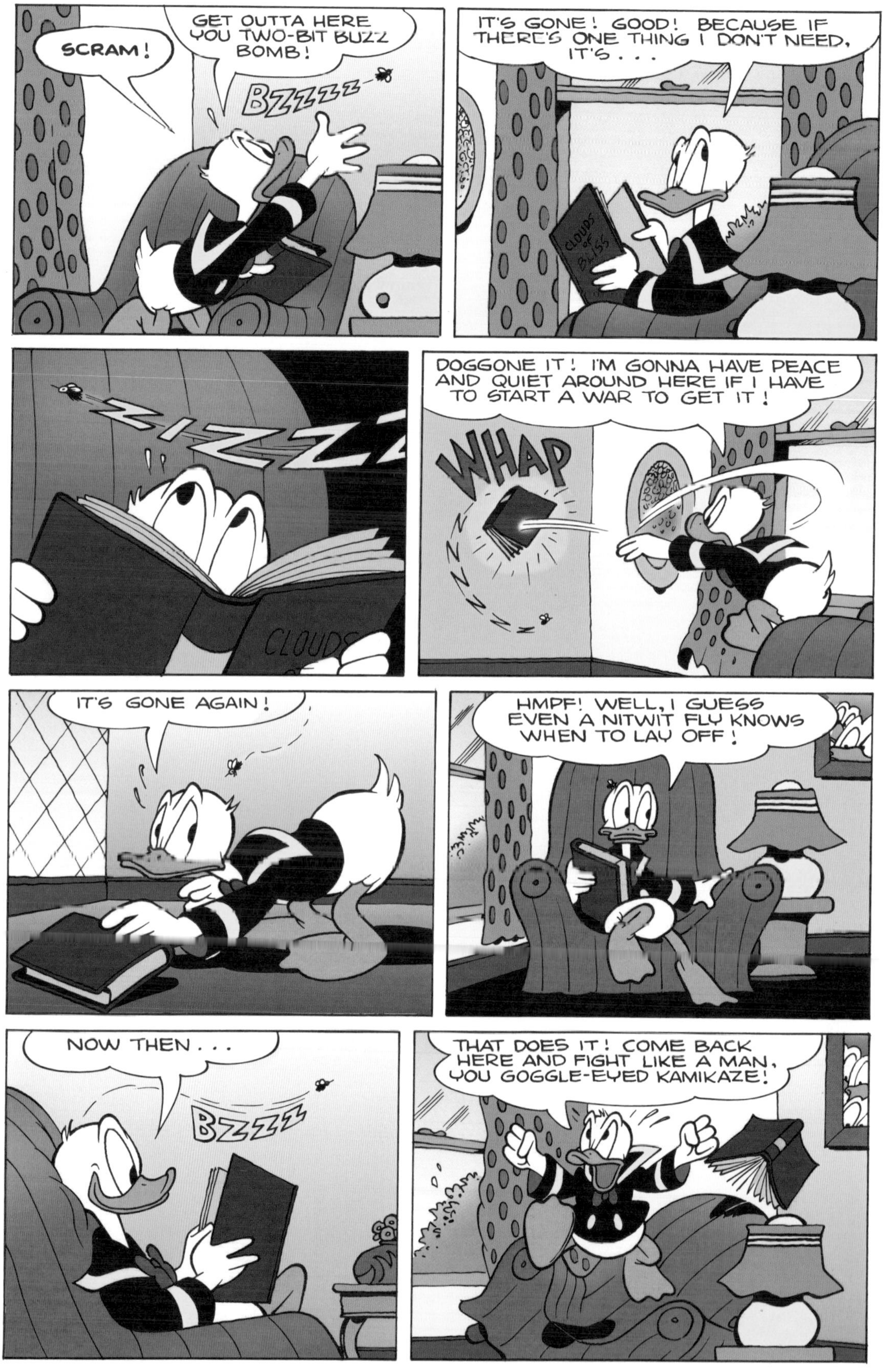
SCRAM!
GET OUTTA HERE YOU TWO-BIT BUZZ BOMB!
BZZZZZ
IT'S GONE! GOOD! BECAUSE IF THERE'S ONE THING I DON'T NEED, IT'S . . .
CLOUDS OF BLISS
ZIZZZ
CLOUDS
DOGGONE IT! I'M GONNA HAVE PEACE AND QUIET AROUND HERE IF I HAVE TO START A WAR TO GET IT!
WHAP
IT'S GONE AGAIN!
HMPF! WELL, I GUESS EVEN A NITWIT FLY KNOWS WHEN TO LAY OFF!
NOW THEN . . .
BZZZ
THAT DOES IT! COME BACK HERE AND FIGHT LIKE A MAN, YOU GOGGLE-EYED KAMIKAZE!

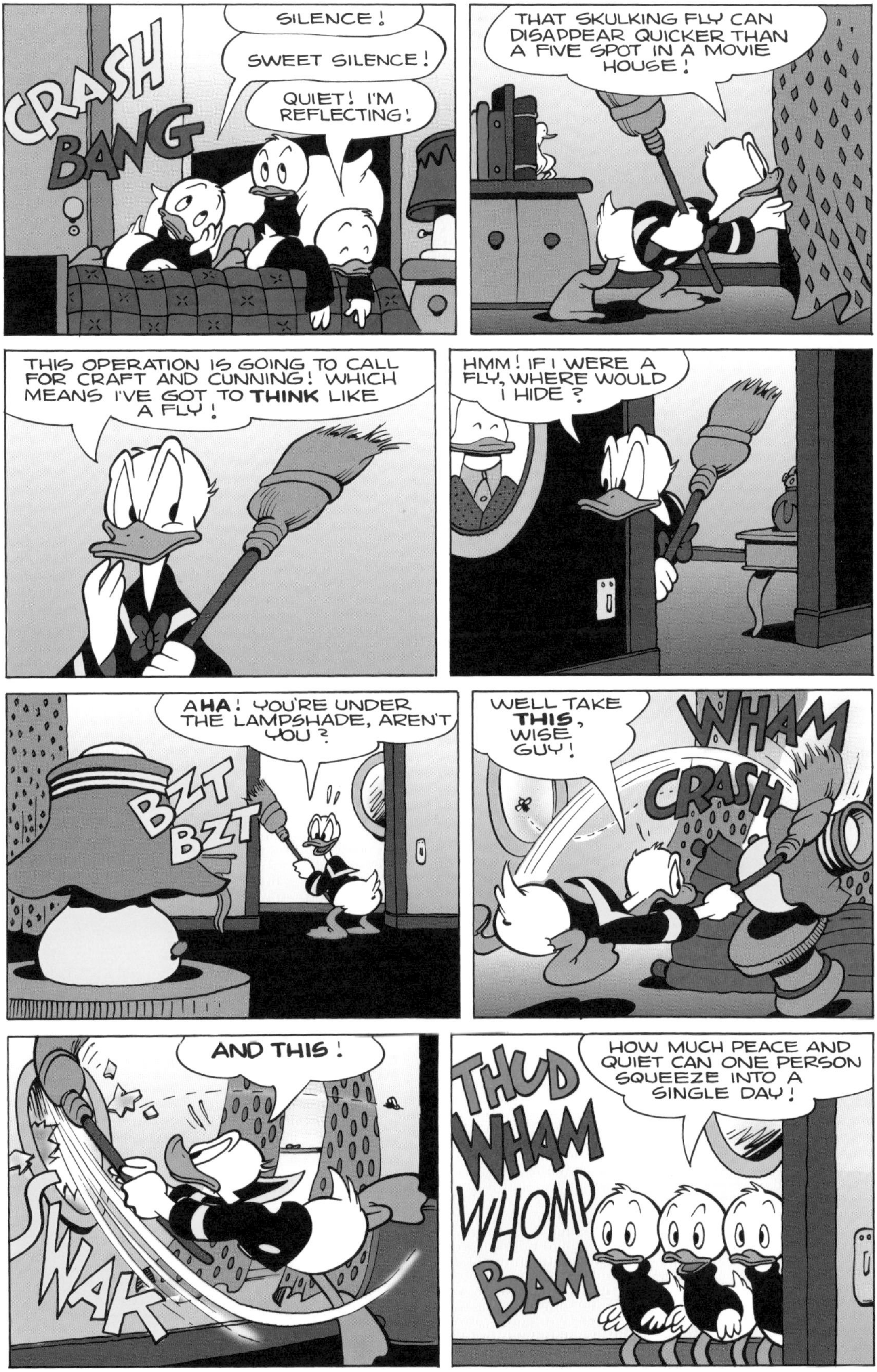

CRASH
BANG
SILENCE!
SWEET SILENCE!
QUIET! I'M REFLECTING!
THAT SKULKING FLY CAN DISAPPEAR QUICKER THAN A FIVE SPOT IN A MOVIE HOUSE!
THIS OPERATION IS GOING TO CALL FOR CRAFT AND CUNNING! WHICH MEANS I'VE GOT TO **THINK** LIKE A FLY!
HMM! IF I WERE A FLY, WHERE WOULD I HIDE?
AHA! YOU'RE UNDER THE LAMPSHADE, AREN'T YOU?
BZT BZT
WELL TAKE **THIS**, WISE GUY!
WHAM
CRASH
AND THIS!
SWAK
THUD
WHAM
WHOMP
BAM
HOW MUCH PEACE AND QUIET CAN ONE PERSON SQUEEZE INTO A SINGLE DAY!

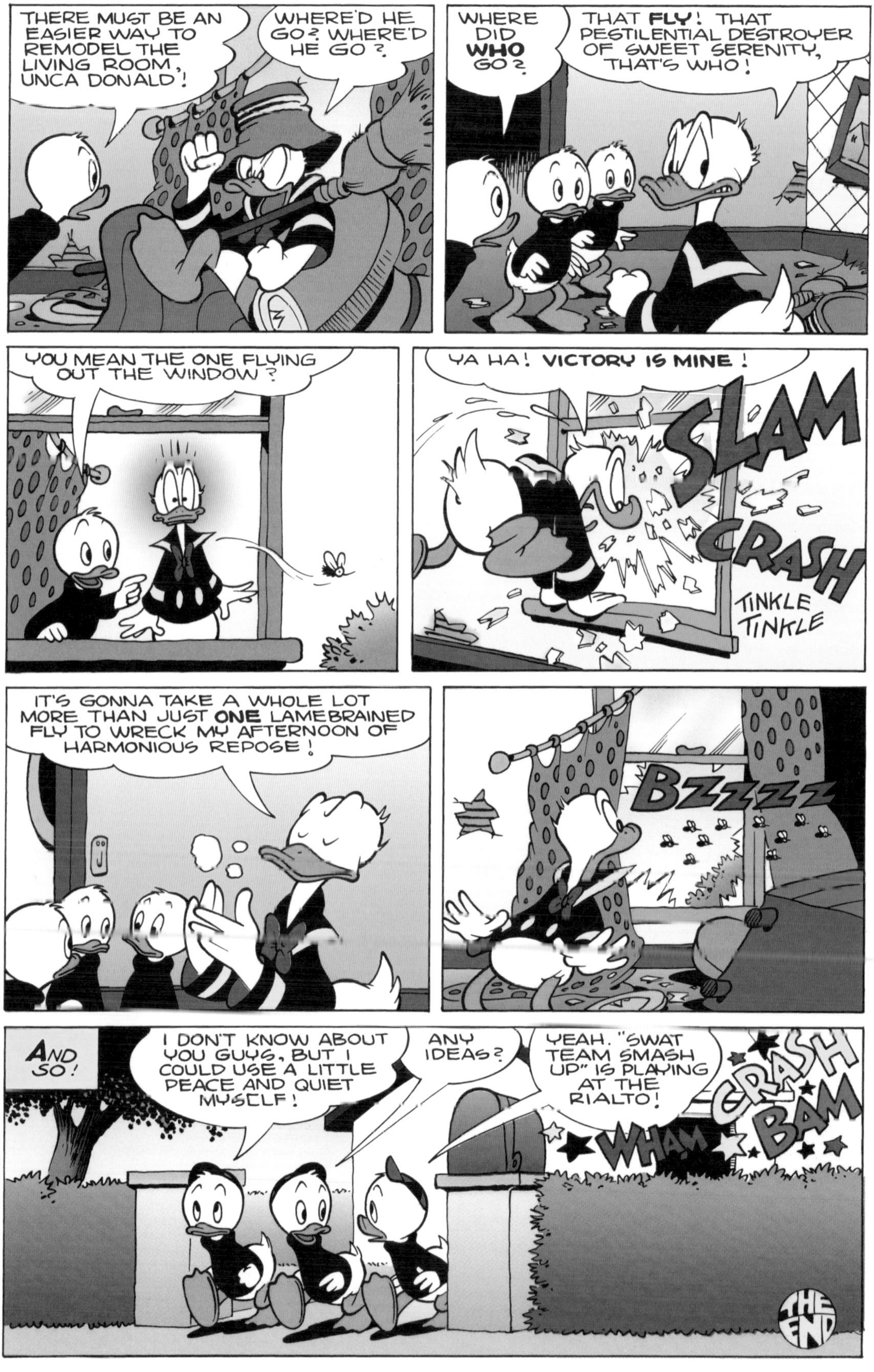

THERE MUST BE AN EASIER WAY TO REMODEL THE LIVING ROOM, UNCA DONALD!
WHERE'D HE GO? WHERE'D HE GO?
WHERE DID WHO GO?
THAT FLY! THAT PESTILENTIAL DESTROYER OF SWEET SERENITY, THAT'S WHO!
YOU MEAN THE ONE FLYING OUT THE WINDOW?
YA HA! VICTORY IS MINE!
SLAM
CRASH
TINKLE TINKLE
IT'S GONNA TAKE A WHOLE LOT MORE THAN JUST ONE LAMEBRAINED FLY TO WRECK MY AFTERNOON OF HARMONIOUS REPOSE!
BZZZZZ
AND SO!
I DON'T KNOW ABOUT YOU GUYS, BUT I COULD USE A LITTLE PEACE AND QUIET MYSELF!
ANY IDEAS?
YEAH. "SWAT TEAM SMASH UP" IS PLAYING AT THE RIALTO!
CRASH
WHAM
BAM
THE END

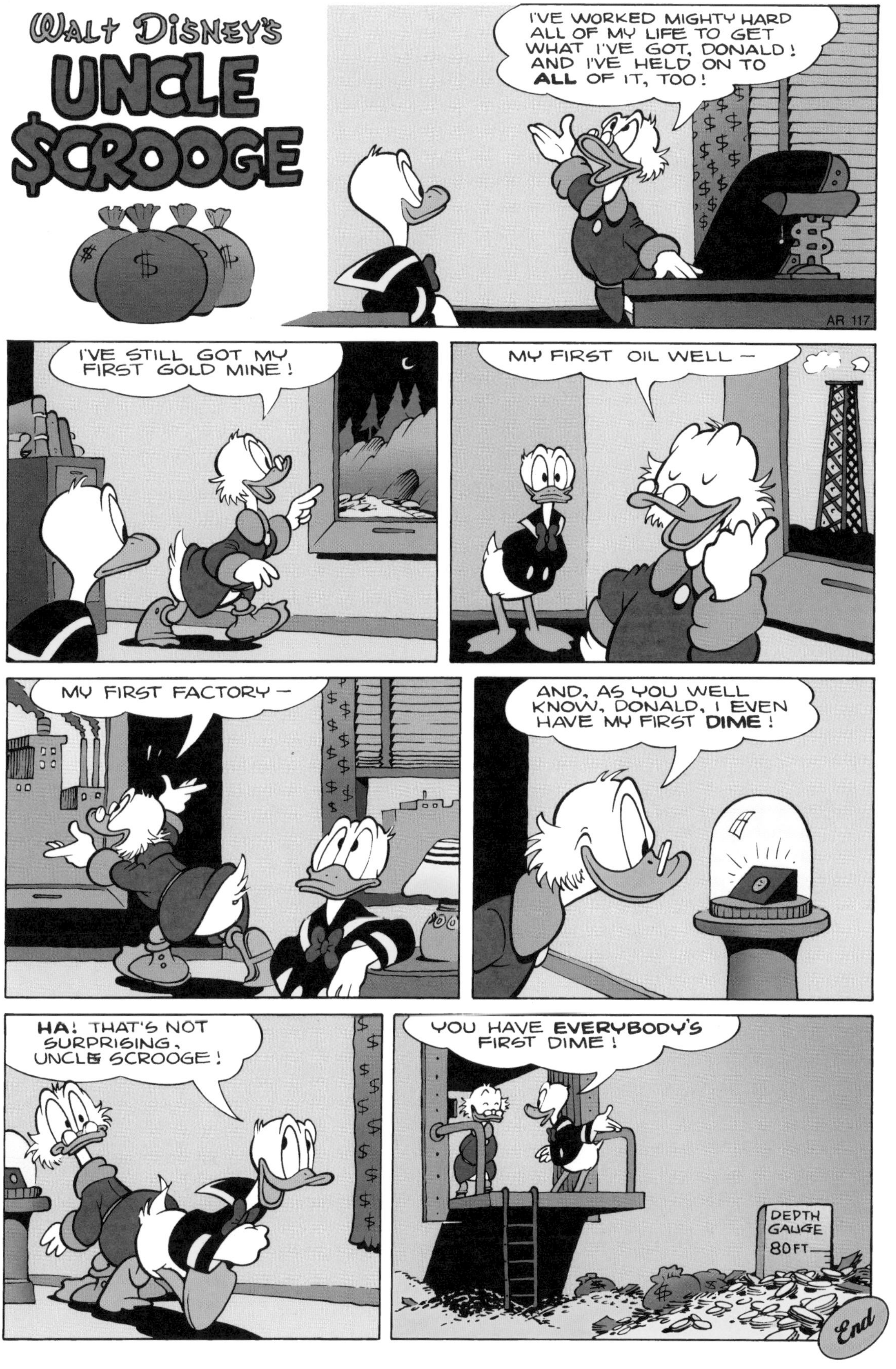
WALT DISNEY'S
UNCLE $CROOGE
I'VE WORKED MIGHTY HARD ALL OF MY LIFE TO GET WHAT I'VE GOT, DONALD! AND I'VE HELD ON TO **ALL** OF IT, TOO!
AR 117
I'VE STILL GOT MY FIRST GOLD MINE!
MY FIRST OIL WELL —
MY FIRST FACTORY —
AND, AS YOU WELL KNOW, DONALD, I EVEN HAVE MY FIRST **DIME**!
HA! THAT'S NOT SURPRISING, UNCLE SCROOGE!
YOU HAVE **EVERYBODY'S** FIRST DIME!
DEPTH GAUGE 80 FT.
End

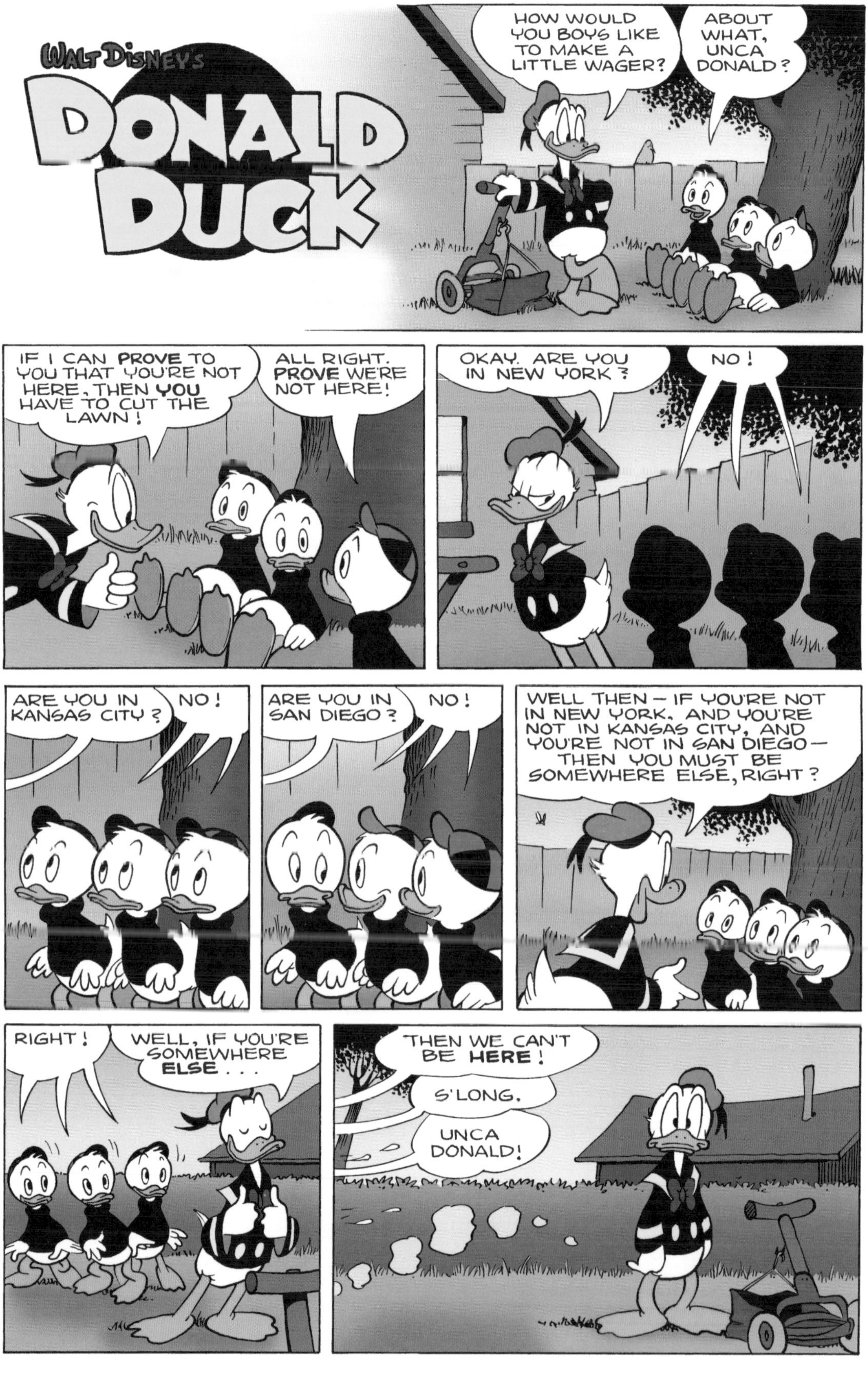
WALT DISNEY'S
DONALD DUCK
HOW WOULD YOU BOYS LIKE TO MAKE A LITTLE WAGER?
ABOUT WHAT, UNCA DONALD?
IF I CAN PROVE TO YOU THAT YOU'RE NOT HERE, THEN YOU HAVE TO CUT THE LAWN!
ALL RIGHT. PROVE WE'RE NOT HERE!
OKAY. ARE YOU IN NEW YORK?
NO!
ARE YOU IN KANSAS CITY?
NO!
ARE YOU IN SAN DIEGO?
NO!
WELL THEN — IF YOU'RE NOT IN NEW YORK, AND YOU'RE NOT IN KANSAS CITY, AND YOU'RE NOT IN SAN DIEGO — THEN YOU MUST BE SOMEWHERE ELSE, RIGHT?
RIGHT!
WELL, IF YOU'RE SOMEWHERE ELSE . . .
THEN WE CAN'T BE HERE!
S'LONG.
UNCA DONALD!

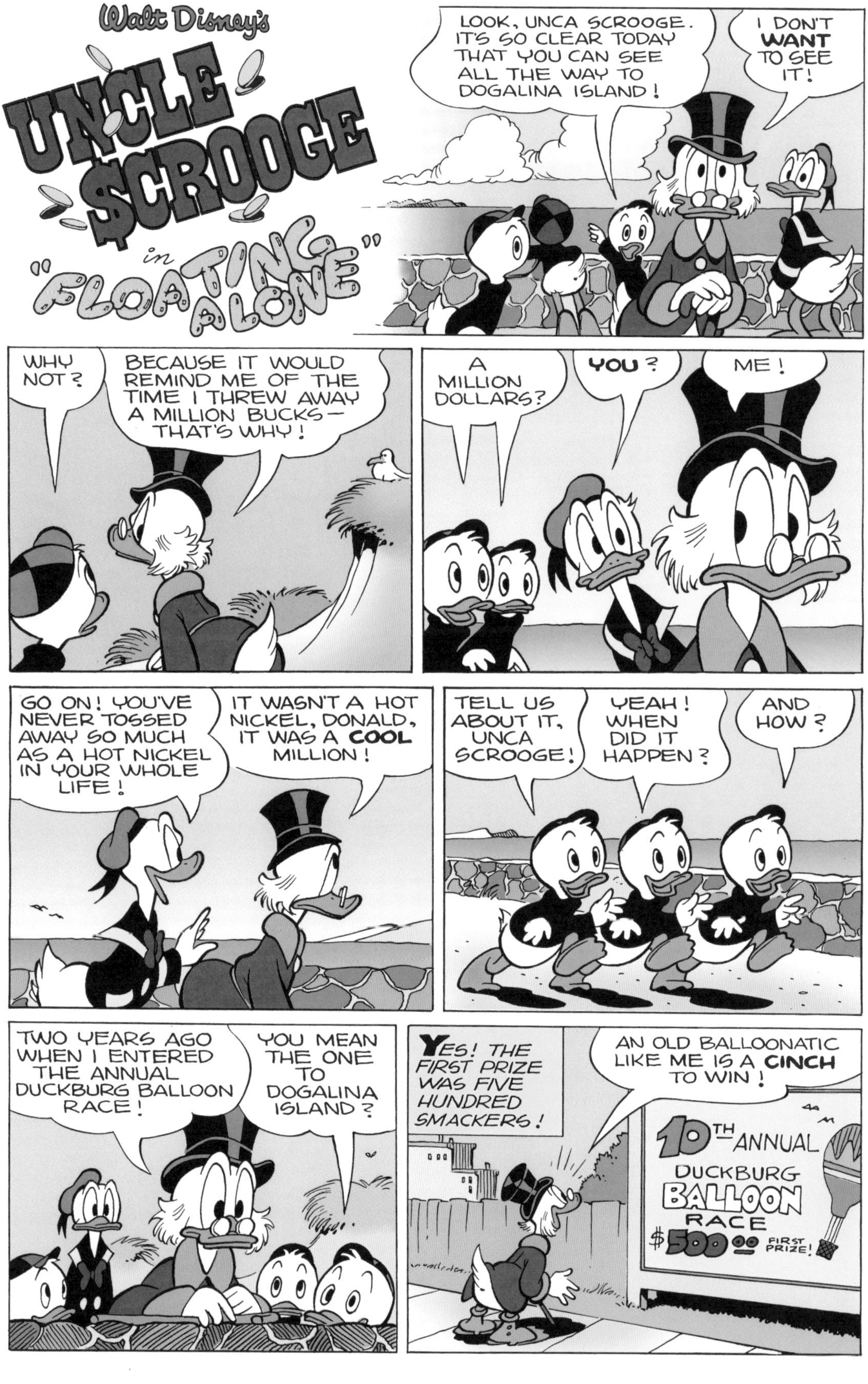
Walt Disney's
UNCLE $CROOGE
in
"FLOATING ALONE"
LOOK, UNCA SCROOGE. IT'S SO CLEAR TODAY THAT YOU CAN SEE ALL THE WAY TO DOGALINA ISLAND!
I DON'T WANT TO SEE IT!
WHY NOT?
BECAUSE IT WOULD REMIND ME OF THE TIME I THREW AWAY A MILLION BUCKS — THAT'S WHY!
A MILLION DOLLARS?
YOU?
ME!
GO ON! YOU'VE NEVER TOSSED AWAY SO MUCH AS A HOT NICKEL IN YOUR WHOLE LIFE!
IT WASN'T A HOT NICKEL, DONALD, IT WAS A COOL MILLION!
TELL US ABOUT IT, UNCA SCROOGE!
YEAH! WHEN DID IT HAPPEN?
AND HOW?
TWO YEARS AGO WHEN I ENTERED THE ANNUAL DUCKBURG BALLOON RACE!
YOU MEAN THE ONE TO DOGALINA ISLAND?
YES! THE FIRST PRIZE WAS FIVE HUNDRED SMACKERS!
AN OLD BALLOONATIC LIKE ME IS A CINCH TO WIN!
10TH ANNUAL
DUCKBURG
BALLOON
RACE
$500.00 FIRST PRIZE!

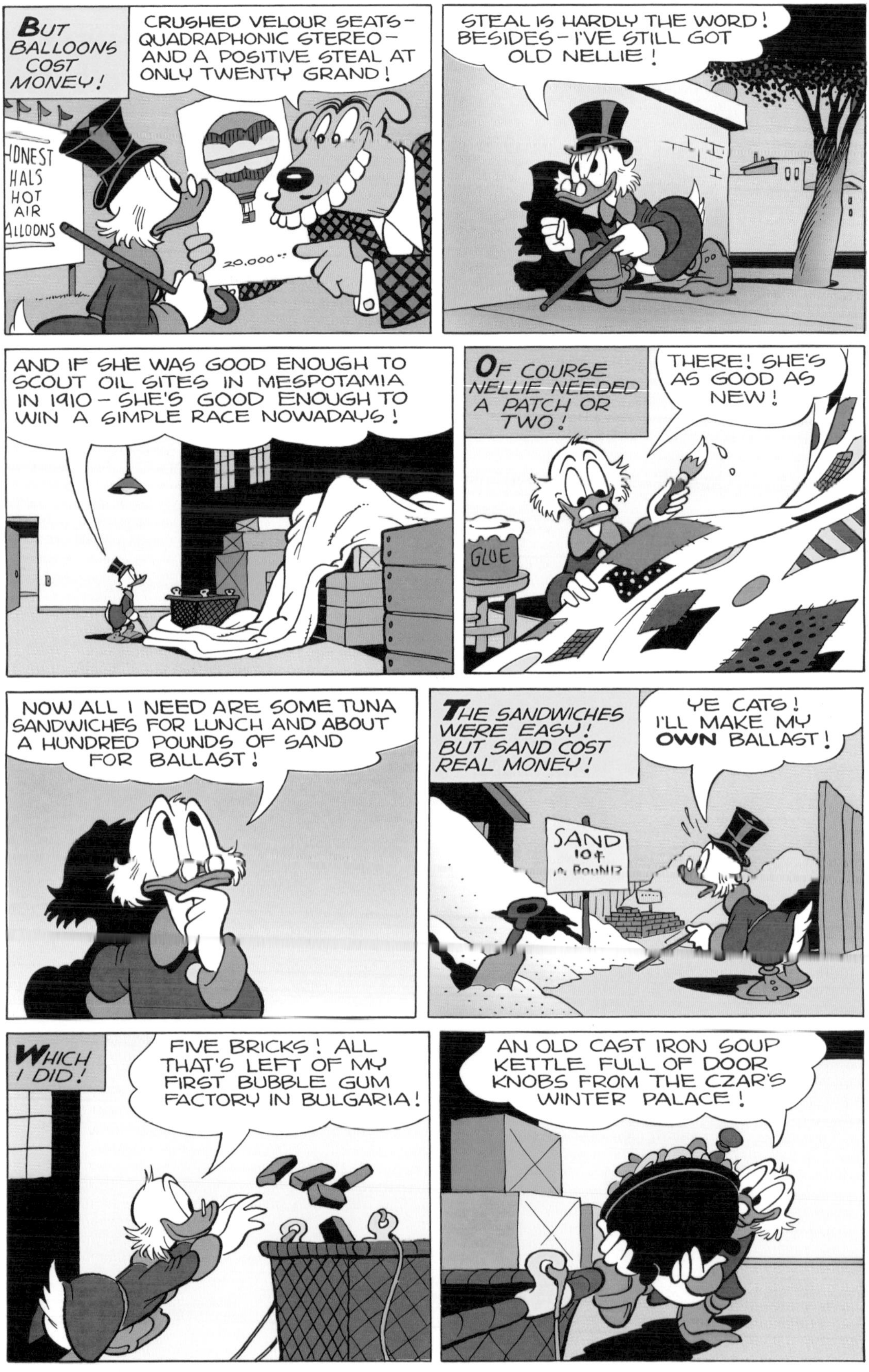

BUT BALLOONS COST MONEY!
CRUSHED VELOUR SEATS—QUADRAPHONIC STEREO—AND A POSITIVE STEAL AT ONLY TWENTY GRAND!
HONEST HALS HOT AIR ALLOONS
20,000
STEAL IS HARDLY THE WORD! BESIDES—I'VE STILL GOT OLD NELLIE!
AND IF SHE WAS GOOD ENOUGH TO SCOUT OIL SITES IN MESPOTAMIA IN 1910—SHE'S GOOD ENOUGH TO WIN A SIMPLE RACE NOWADAYS!
OF COURSE NELLIE NEEDED A PATCH OR TWO!
THERE! SHE'S AS GOOD AS NEW!
GLUE
NOW ALL I NEED ARE SOME TUNA SANDWICHES FOR LUNCH AND ABOUT A HUNDRED POUNDS OF SAND FOR BALLAST!
THE SANDWICHES WERE EASY! BUT SAND COST REAL MONEY!
YE CATS! I'LL MAKE MY **OWN** BALLAST!
SAND 10¢
WHICH I DID!
FIVE BRICKS! ALL THAT'S LEFT OF MY FIRST BUBBLE GUM FACTORY IN BULGARIA!
AN OLD CAST IRON SOUP KETTLE FULL OF DOOR KNOBS FROM THE CZAR'S WINTER PALACE!

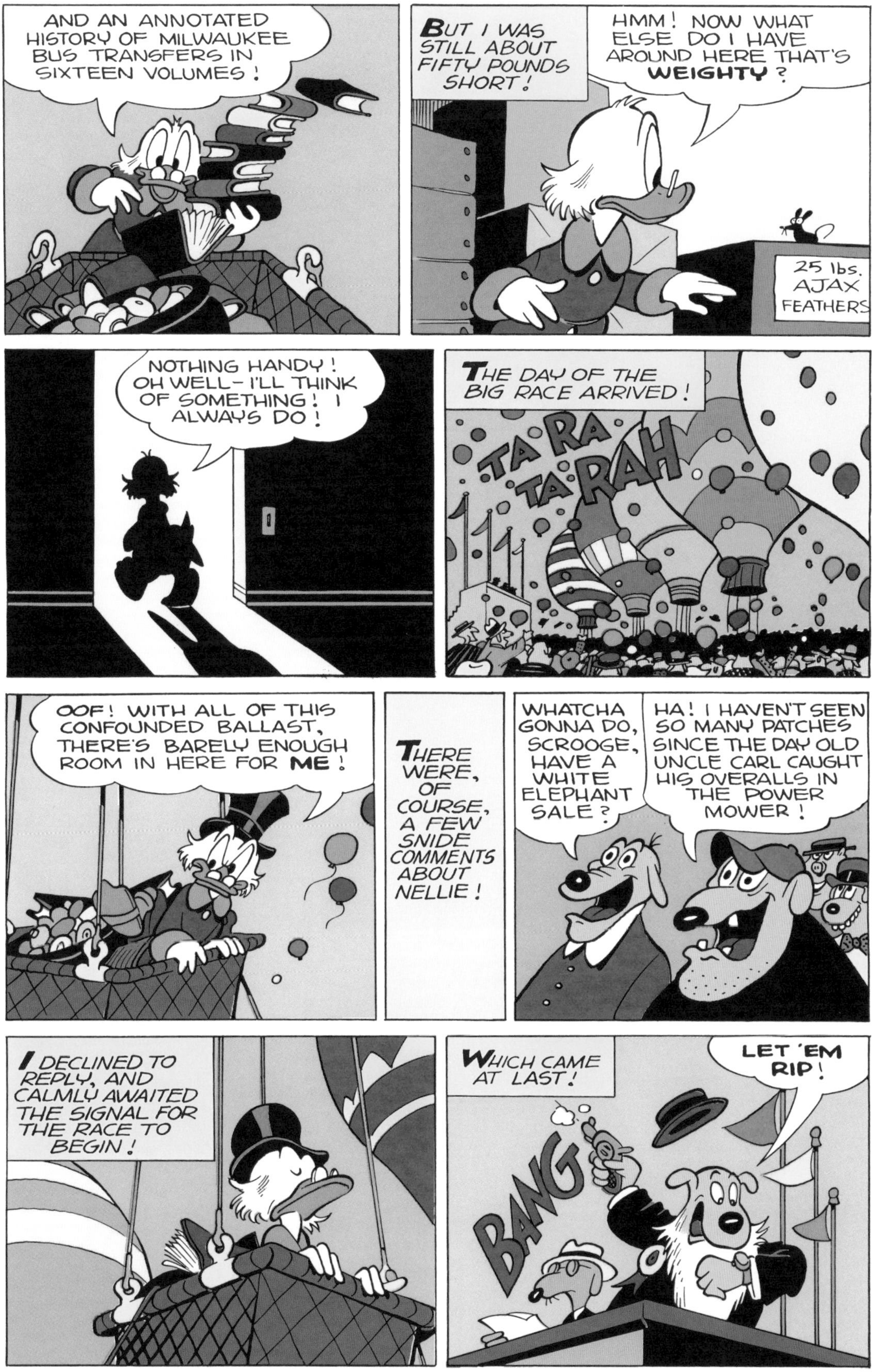
AND AN ANNOTATED HISTORY OF MILWAUKEE BUS TRANSFERS IN SIXTEEN VOLUMES!
BUT I WAS STILL ABOUT FIFTY POUNDS SHORT!
HMM! NOW WHAT ELSE DO I HAVE AROUND HERE THAT'S WEIGHTY?
25 lbs. AJAX FEATHERS
NOTHING HANDY! OH WELL- I'LL THINK OF SOMETHING! I ALWAYS DO!
THE DAY OF THE BIG RACE ARRIVED!
TA RA TA RA TA RAH
OOF! WITH ALL OF THIS CONFOUNDED BALLAST, THERE'S BARELY ENOUGH ROOM IN HERE FOR ME!
THERE WERE, OF COURSE, A FEW SNIDE COMMENTS ABOUT NELLIE!
WHATCHA GONNA DO, SCROOGE, HAVE A WHITE ELEPHANT SALE?
HA! I HAVEN'T SEEN SO MANY PATCHES SINCE THE DAY OLD UNCLE CARL CAUGHT HIS OVERALLS IN THE POWER MOWER!
I DECLINED TO REPLY, AND CALMLY AWAITED THE SIGNAL FOR THE RACE TO BEGIN!
WHICH CAME AT LAST!
LET 'EM RIP!
BANG

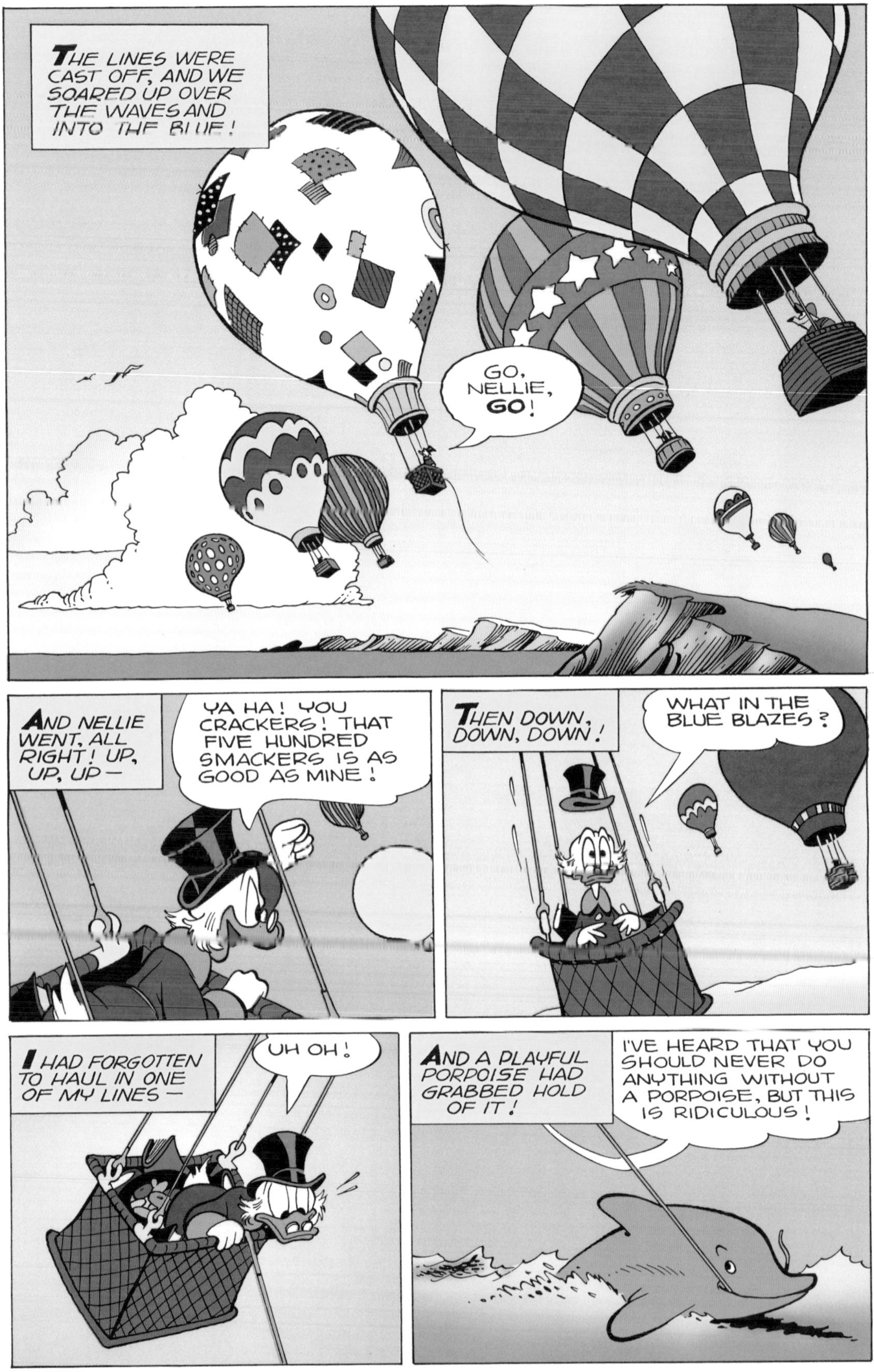
THE LINES WERE CAST OFF, AND WE SOARED UP OVER THE WAVES AND INTO THE BLUE!
GO, NELLIE, GO!
AND NELLIE WENT, ALL RIGHT! UP, UP, UP—
YA HA! YOU CRACKERS! THAT FIVE HUNDRED SMACKERS IS AS GOOD AS MINE!
THEN DOWN, DOWN, DOWN!
WHAT IN THE BLUE BLAZES?
I HAD FORGOTTEN TO HAUL IN ONE OF MY LINES—
UH OH!
AND A PLAYFUL PORPOISE HAD GRABBED HOLD OF IT!
I'VE HEARD THAT YOU SHOULD NEVER DO ANYTHING WITHOUT A PORPOISE, BUT THIS IS RIDICULOUS!

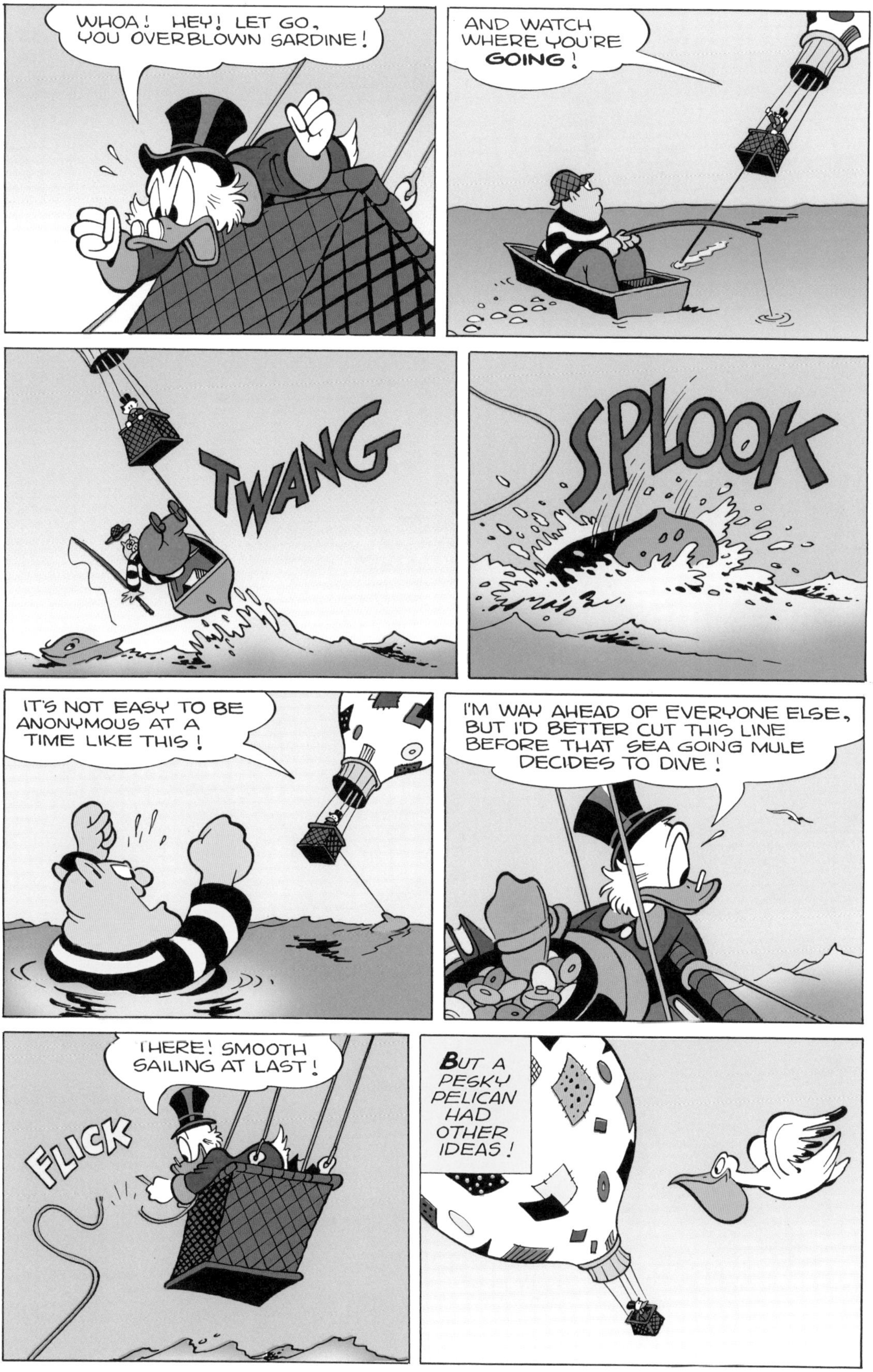
WHOA! HEY! LET GO, YOU OVERBLOWN SARDINE!
AND WATCH WHERE YOU'RE GOING!
TWANG
SPLOOK
IT'S NOT EASY TO BE ANONYMOUS AT A TIME LIKE THIS!
I'M WAY AHEAD OF EVERYONE ELSE, BUT I'D BETTER CUT THIS LINE BEFORE THAT SEA GOING MULE DECIDES TO DIVE!
THERE! SMOOTH SAILING AT LAST!
FLICK
BUT A PESKY PELICAN HAD OTHER IDEAS!

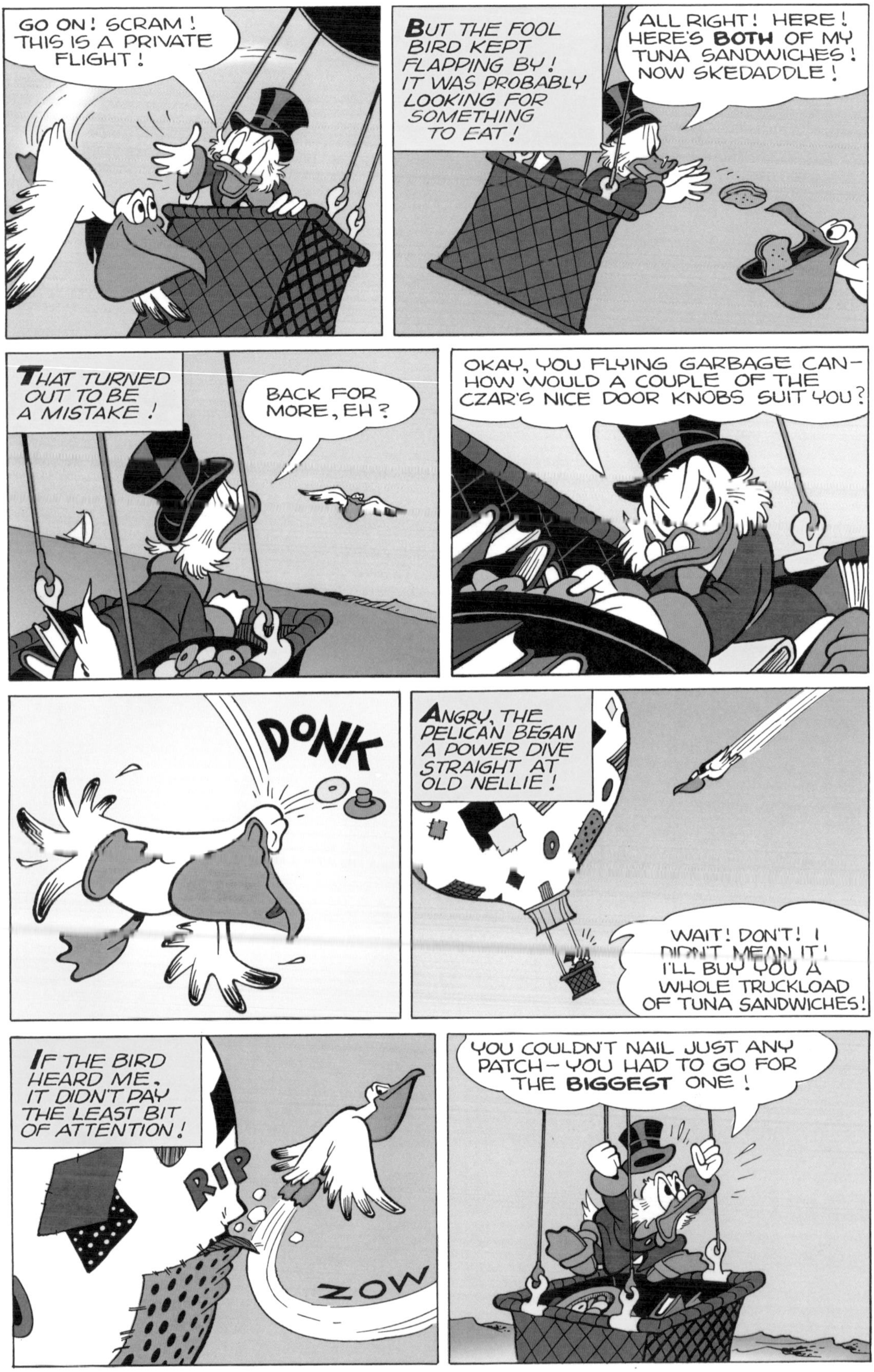
GO ON! SCRAM! THIS IS A PRIVATE FLIGHT!
BUT THE FOOL BIRD KEPT FLAPPING BY! IT WAS PROBABLY LOOKING FOR SOMETHING TO EAT!
ALL RIGHT! HERE! HERE'S BOTH OF MY TUNA SANDWICHES! NOW SKEDADDLE!
THAT TURNED OUT TO BE A MISTAKE!
BACK FOR MORE, EH?
OKAY, YOU FLYING GARBAGE CAN-HOW WOULD A COUPLE OF THE CZAR'S NICE DOOR KNOBS SUIT YOU?
DONK
ANGRY, THE PELICAN BEGAN A POWER DIVE STRAIGHT AT OLD NELLIE!
WAIT! DON'T! I DIDN'T MEAN IT! I'LL BUY YOU A WHOLE TRUCKLOAD OF TUNA SANDWICHES!
IF THE BIRD HEARD ME, IT DIDN'T PAY THE LEAST BIT OF ATTENTION!
RIP
ZOW
YOU COULDN'T NAIL JUST ANY PATCH-YOU HAD TO GO FOR THE BIGGEST ONE!

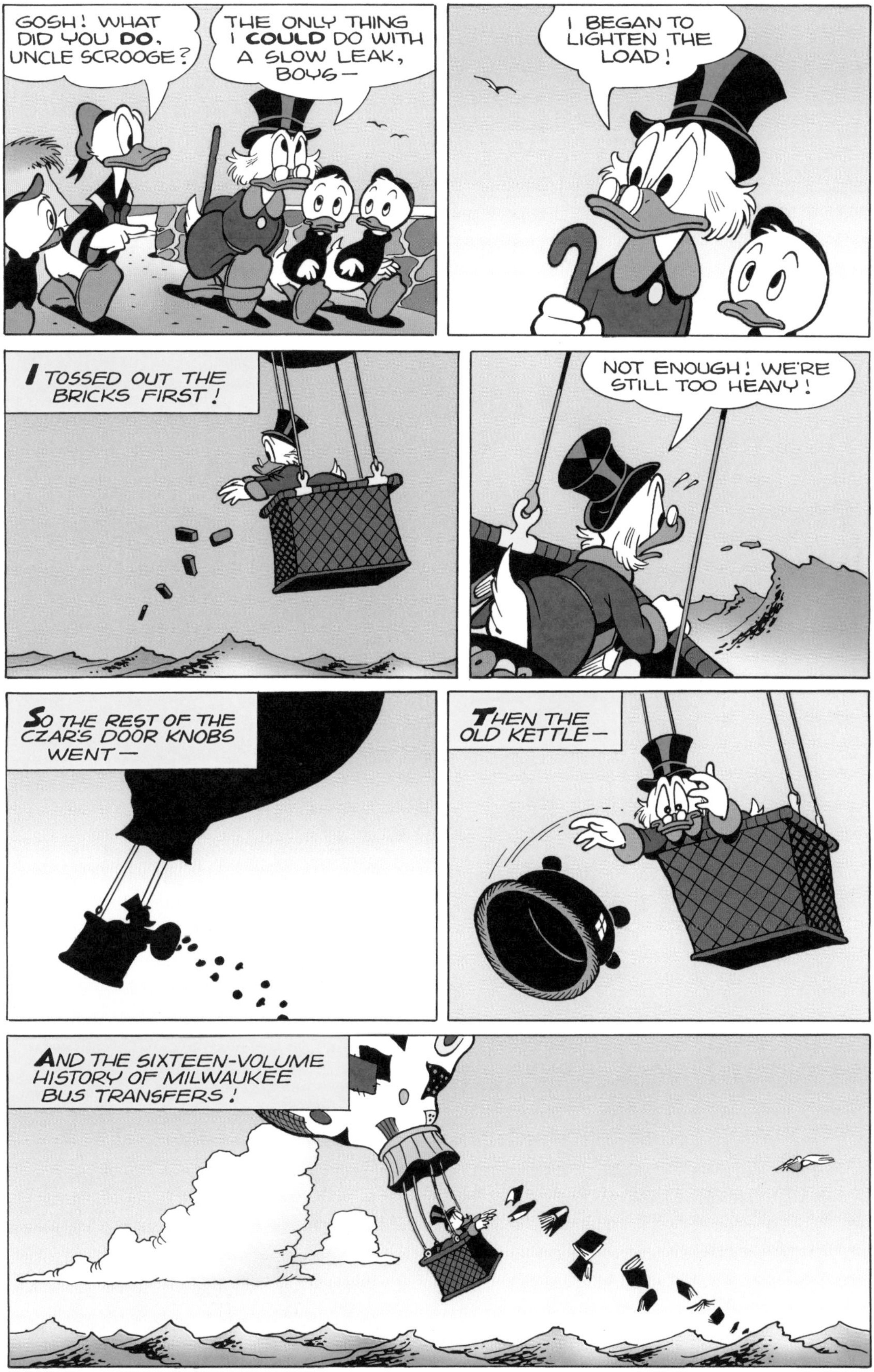
GOSH! WHAT DID YOU DO, UNCLE SCROOGE?
THE ONLY THING I COULD DO WITH A SLOW LEAK, BOYS—
I BEGAN TO LIGHTEN THE LOAD!
I TOSSED OUT THE BRICKS FIRST!
NOT ENOUGH! WE'RE STILL TOO HEAVY!
SO THE REST OF THE CZAR'S DOOR KNOBS WENT—
THEN THE OLD KETTLE—
AND THE SIXTEEN-VOLUME HISTORY OF MILWAUKEE BUS TRANSFERS!

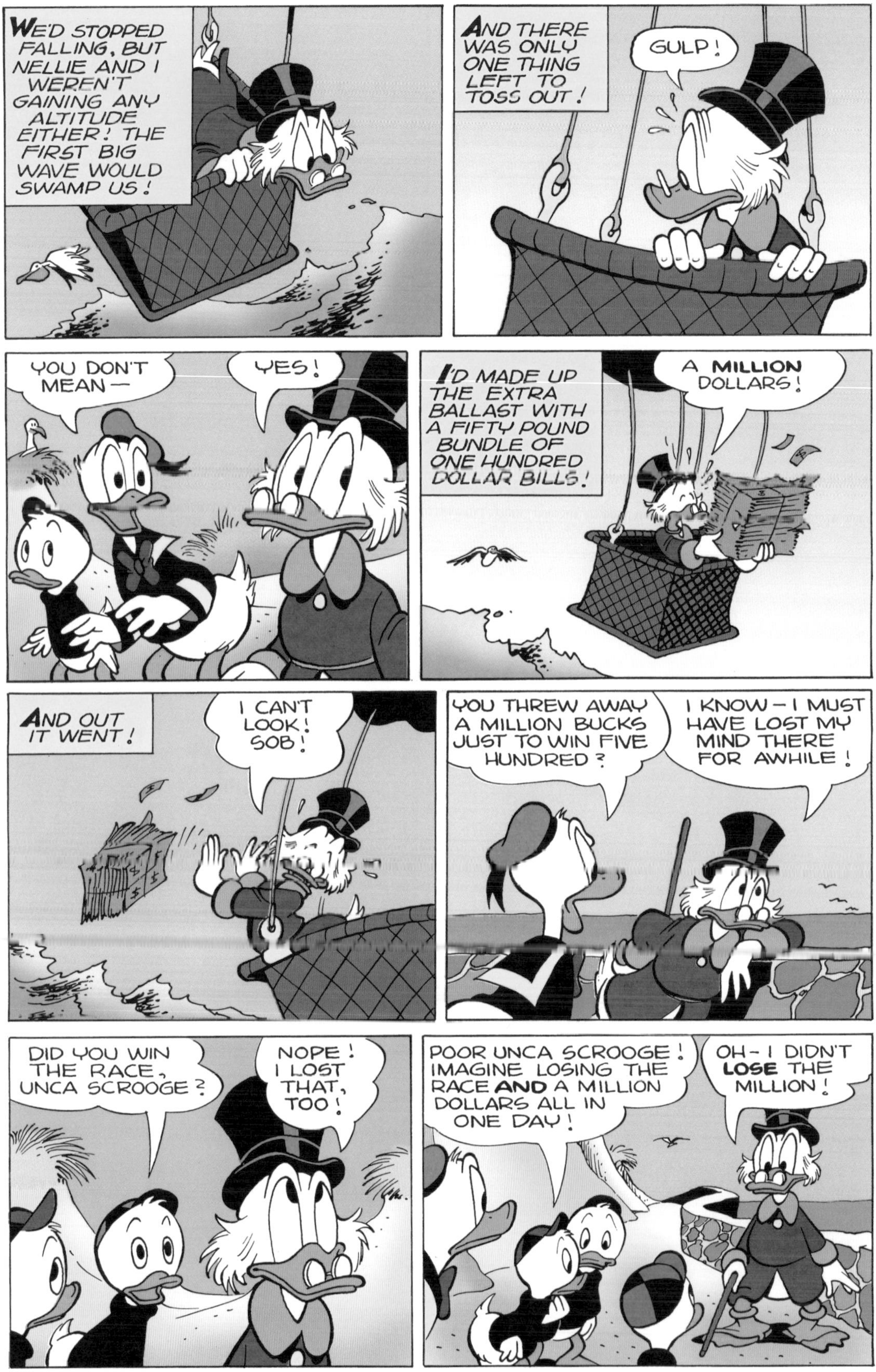
WE'D STOPPED FALLING, BUT NELLIE AND I WEREN'T GAINING ANY ALTITUDE EITHER! THE FIRST BIG WAVE WOULD SWAMP US!
AND THERE WAS ONLY ONE THING LEFT TO TOSS OUT!
GULP!
YOU DON'T MEAN—
YES!
I'D MADE UP THE EXTRA BALLAST WITH A FIFTY POUND BUNDLE OF ONE HUNDRED DOLLAR BILLS!
A MILLION DOLLARS!
AND OUT IT WENT!
I CAN'T LOOK! SOB!
YOU THREW AWAY A MILLION BUCKS JUST TO WIN FIVE HUNDRED?
I KNOW—I MUST HAVE LOST MY MIND THERE FOR AWHILE!
DID YOU WIN THE RACE, UNCA SCROOGE?
NOPE! I LOST THAT, TOO!
POOR UNCA SCROOGE! IMAGINE LOSING THE RACE AND A MILLION DOLLARS ALL IN ONE DAY!
OH—I DIDN'T LOSE THE MILLION!

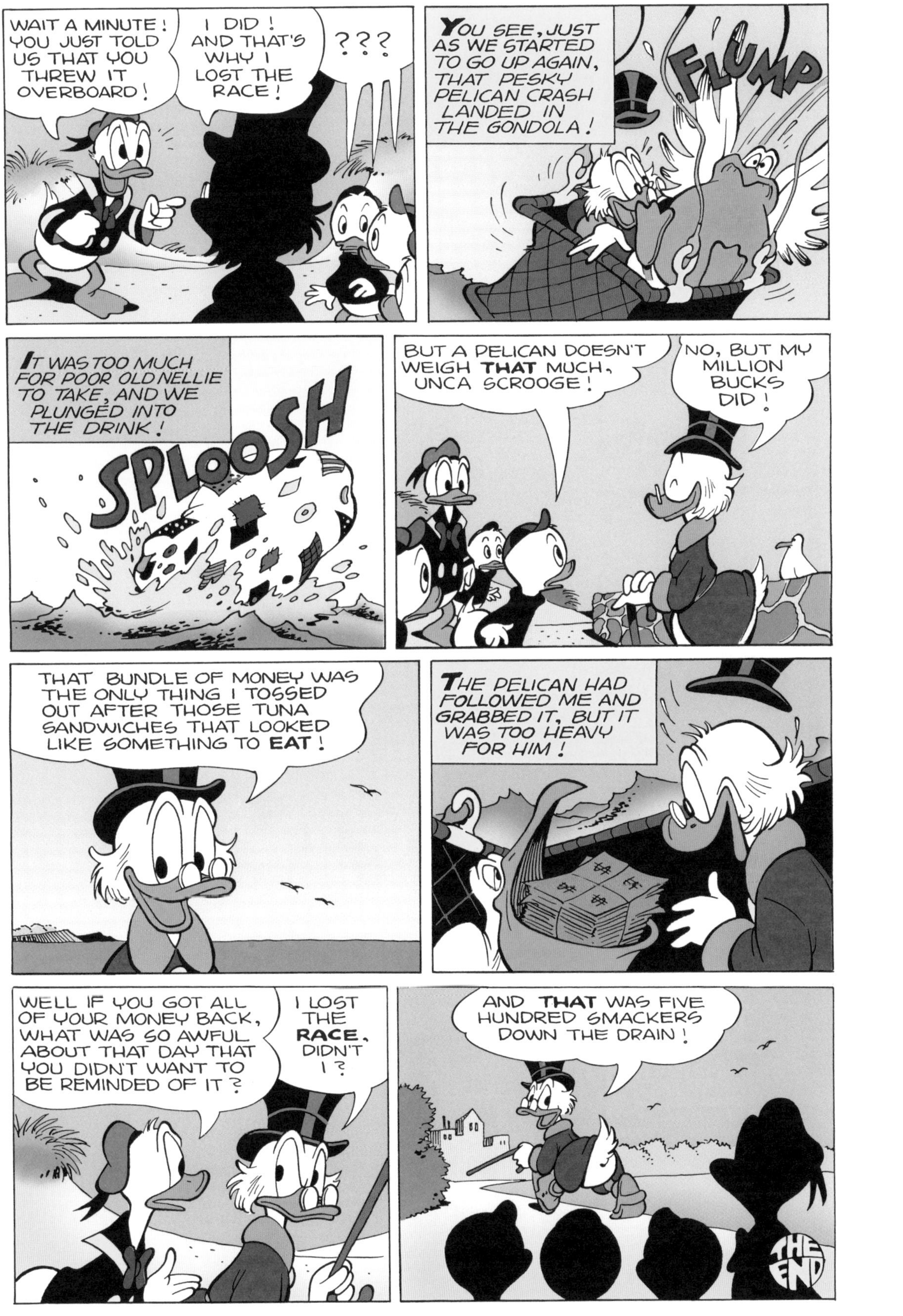
WAIT A MINUTE! YOU JUST TOLD US THAT YOU THREW IT OVERBOARD!
I DID! AND THAT'S WHY I LOST THE RACE!
???
YOU SEE, JUST AS WE STARTED TO GO UP AGAIN, THAT PESKY PELICAN CRASH LANDED IN THE GONDOLA!
FLUMP
IT WAS TOO MUCH FOR POOR OLD NELLIE TO TAKE, AND WE PLUNGED INTO THE DRINK!
SPLOOSH
BUT A PELICAN DOESN'T WEIGH THAT MUCH, UNCA SCROOGE!
NO, BUT MY MILLION BUCKS DID!
THAT BUNDLE OF MONEY WAS THE ONLY THING I TOSSED OUT AFTER THOSE TUNA SANDWICHES THAT LOOKED LIKE SOMETHING TO EAT!
THE PELICAN HAD FOLLOWED ME AND GRABBED IT, BUT IT WAS TOO HEAVY FOR HIM!
WELL IF YOU GOT ALL OF YOUR MONEY BACK, WHAT WAS SO AWFUL ABOUT THAT DAY THAT YOU DIDN'T WANT TO BE REMINDED OF IT?
I LOST THE RACE, DIDN'T I?
AND THAT WAS FIVE HUNDRED SMACKERS DOWN THE DRAIN!
THE END

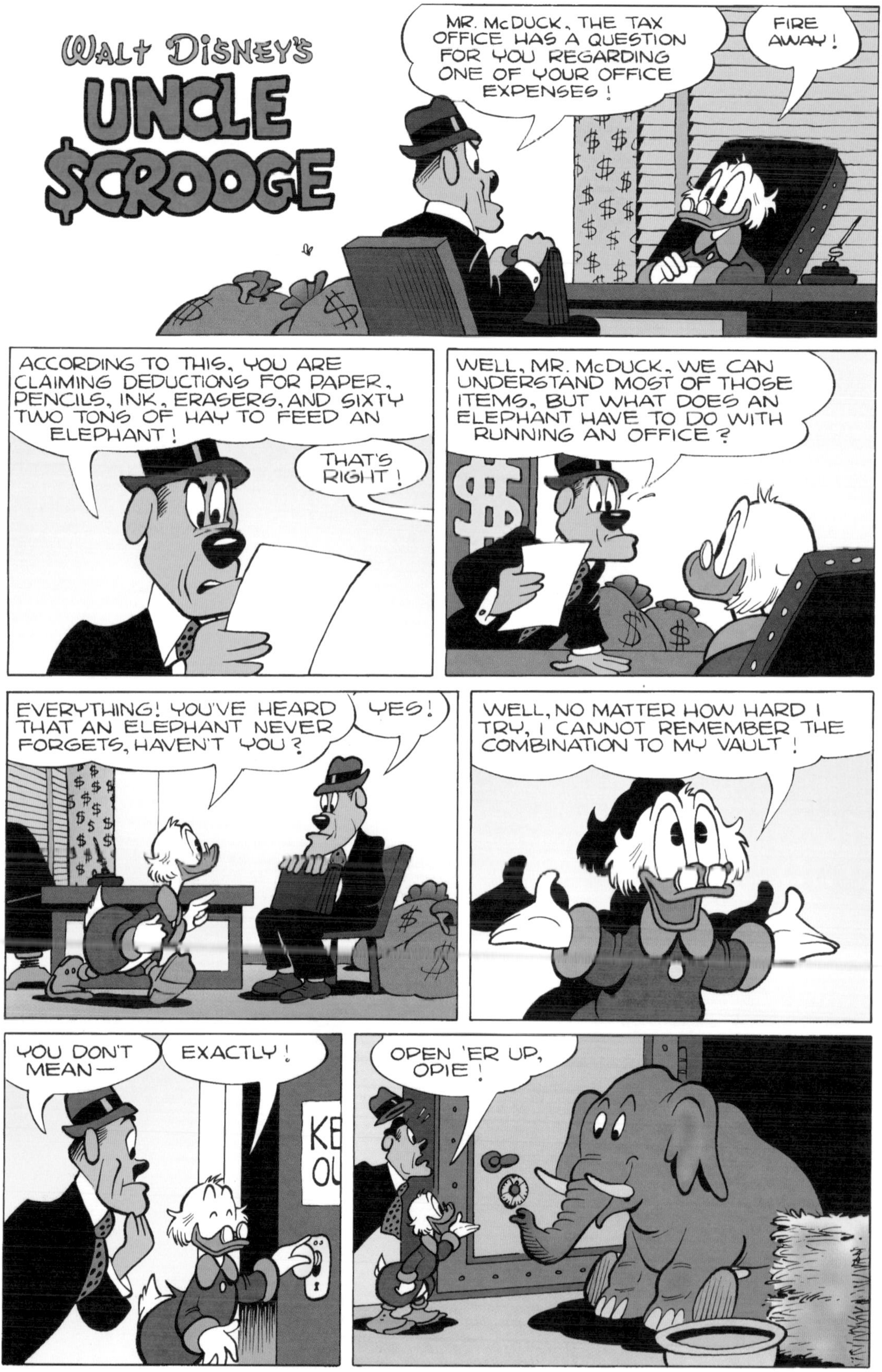
WALT DISNEY'S
UNCLE $CROOGE
MR. McDUCK, THE TAX OFFICE HAS A QUESTION FOR YOU REGARDING ONE OF YOUR OFFICE EXPENSES!
FIRE AWAY!
ACCORDING TO THIS, YOU ARE CLAIMING DEDUCTIONS FOR PAPER, PENCILS, INK, ERASERS, AND SIXTY TWO TONS OF HAY TO FEED AN ELEPHANT!
THAT'S RIGHT!
WELL, MR. McDUCK, WE CAN UNDERSTAND MOST OF THOSE ITEMS, BUT WHAT DOES AN ELEPHANT HAVE TO DO WITH RUNNING AN OFFICE?
EVERYTHING! YOU'VE HEARD THAT AN ELEPHANT NEVER FORGETS, HAVEN'T YOU?
YES!
WELL, NO MATTER HOW HARD I TRY, I CANNOT REMEMBER THE COMBINATION TO MY VAULT!
YOU DON'T MEAN—
EXACTLY!
OPEN 'ER UP, OPIE!

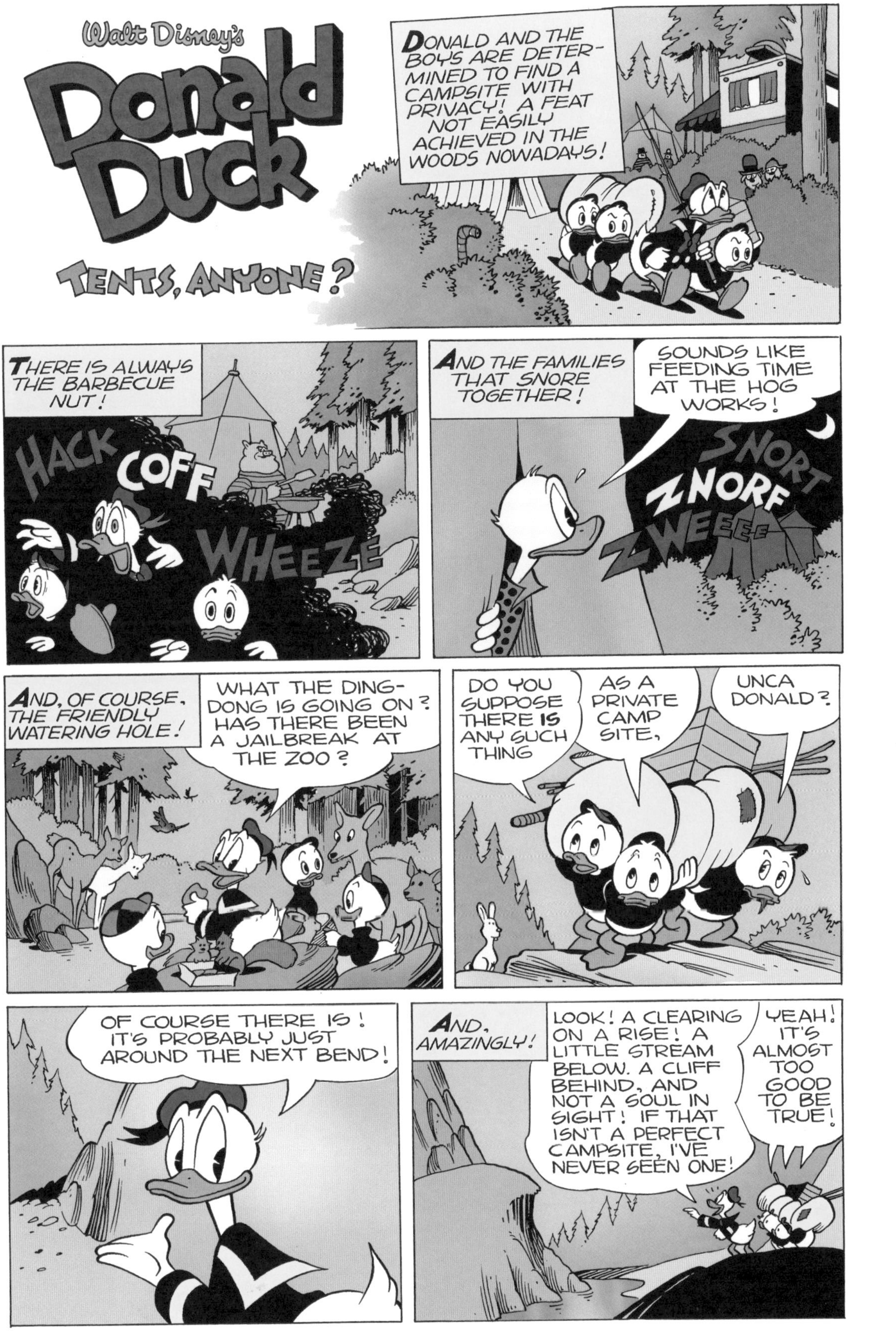
Walt Disney's
Donald Duck
TENTS, ANYONE?
DONALD AND THE BOYS ARE DETERMINED TO FIND A CAMPSITE WITH PRIVACY! A FEAT NOT EASILY ACHIEVED IN THE WOODS NOWADAYS!
THERE IS ALWAYS THE BARBECUE NUT!
HACK
COFF
WHEEZE
AND THE FAMILIES THAT SNORE TOGETHER!
SOUNDS LIKE FEEDING TIME AT THE HOG WORKS!
SNORT
ZNORF
ZWEEEE
AND, OF COURSE, THE FRIENDLY WATERING HOLE!
WHAT THE DING-DONG IS GOING ON? HAS THERE BEEN A JAILBREAK AT THE ZOO?
DO YOU SUPPOSE THERE IS ANY SUCH THING
AS A PRIVATE CAMP SITE,
UNCA DONALD?
OF COURSE THERE IS! IT'S PROBABLY JUST AROUND THE NEXT BEND!
AND, AMAZINGLY!
LOOK! A CLEARING ON A RISE! A LITTLE STREAM BELOW. A CLIFF BEHIND, AND NOT A SOUL IN SIGHT! IF THAT ISN'T A PERFECT CAMPSITE, I'VE NEVER SEEN ONE!
YEAH! IT'S ALMOST TOO GOOD TO BE TRUE!

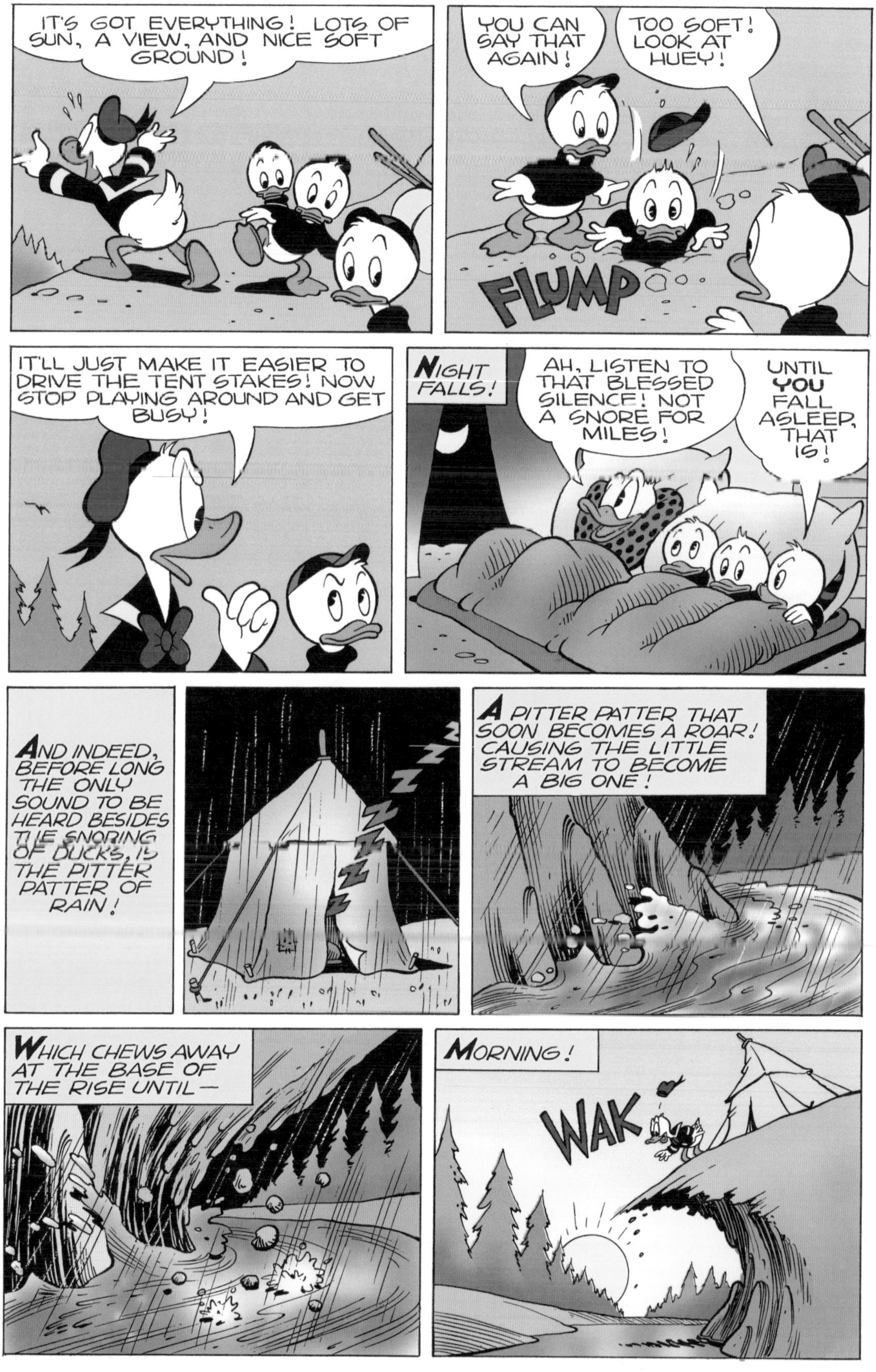

IT'S GOT EVERYTHING! LOTS OF SUN, A VIEW, AND NICE SOFT GROUND!
YOU CAN SAY THAT AGAIN!
TOO SOFT! LOOK AT HUEY!
FLUMP
IT'LL JUST MAKE IT EASIER TO DRIVE THE TENT STAKES! NOW STOP PLAYING AROUND AND GET BUSY!
NIGHT FALLS!
AH, LISTEN TO THAT BLESSED SILENCE! NOT A SNORE FOR MILES!
UNTIL YOU FALL ASLEEP, THAT IS!
AND INDEED, BEFORE LONG THE ONLY SOUND TO BE HEARD BESIDES THE SNORING OF DUCKS, IS THE PITTER PATTER OF RAIN!
A PITTER PATTER THAT SOON BECOMES A ROAR! CAUSING THE LITTLE STREAM TO BECOME A BIG ONE!
WHICH CHEWS AWAY AT THE BASE OF THE RISE UNTIL—
MORNING!
WAK

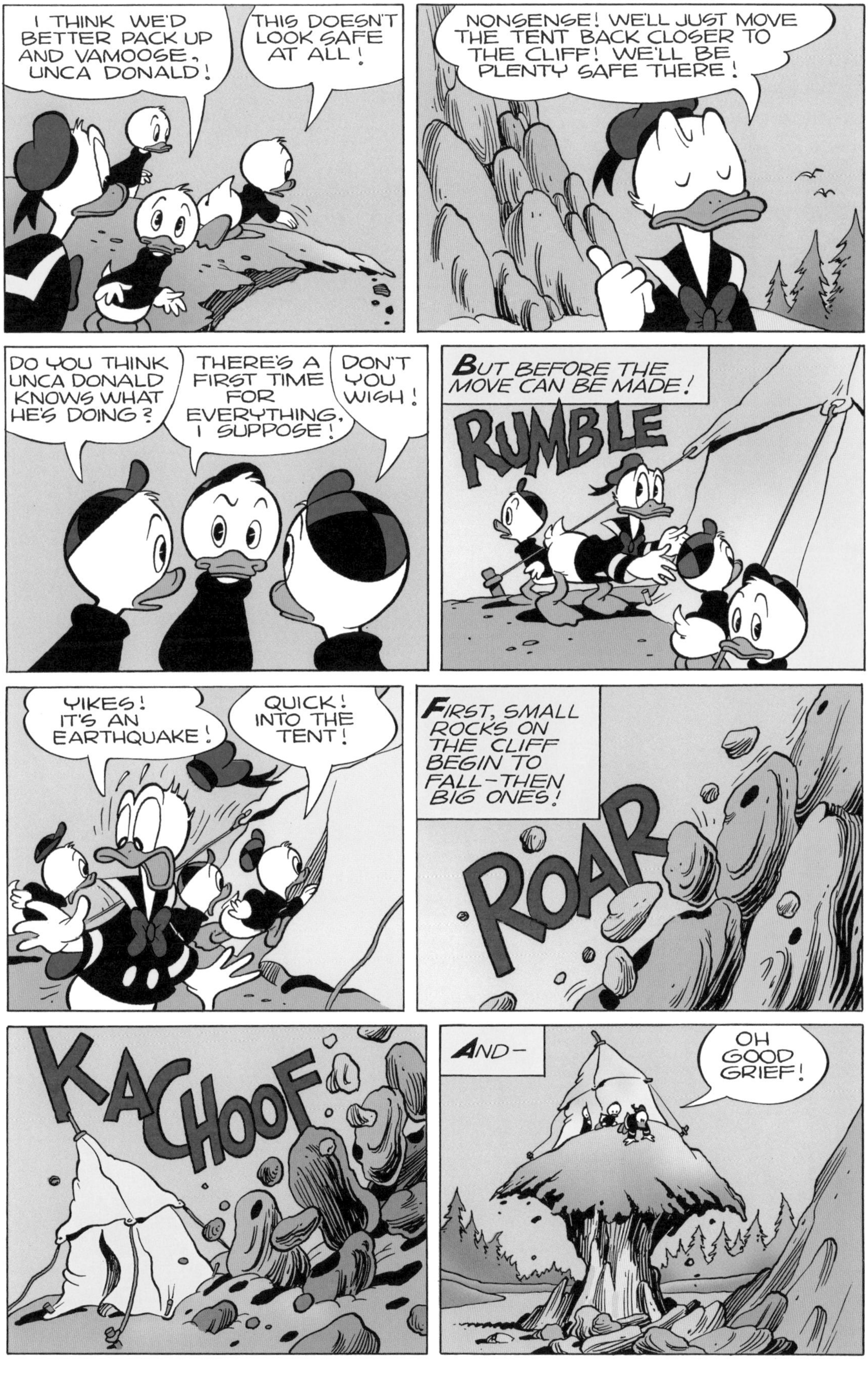
I THINK WE'D BETTER PACK UP AND VAMOOSE, UNCA DONALD!
THIS DOESN'T LOOK SAFE AT ALL!
NONSENSE! WE'LL JUST MOVE THE TENT BACK CLOSER TO THE CLIFF! WE'LL BE PLENTY SAFE THERE!
DO YOU THINK UNCA DONALD KNOWS WHAT HE'S DOING?
THERE'S A FIRST TIME FOR EVERYTHING, I SUPPOSE!
DON'T YOU WISH!
BUT BEFORE THE MOVE CAN BE MADE!
RUMBLE
YIKES! IT'S AN EARTHQUAKE!
QUICK! INTO THE TENT!
FIRST, SMALL ROCKS ON THE CLIFF BEGIN TO FALL–THEN BIG ONES!
ROAR
KACHOOF
AND–
OH GOOD GRIEF!

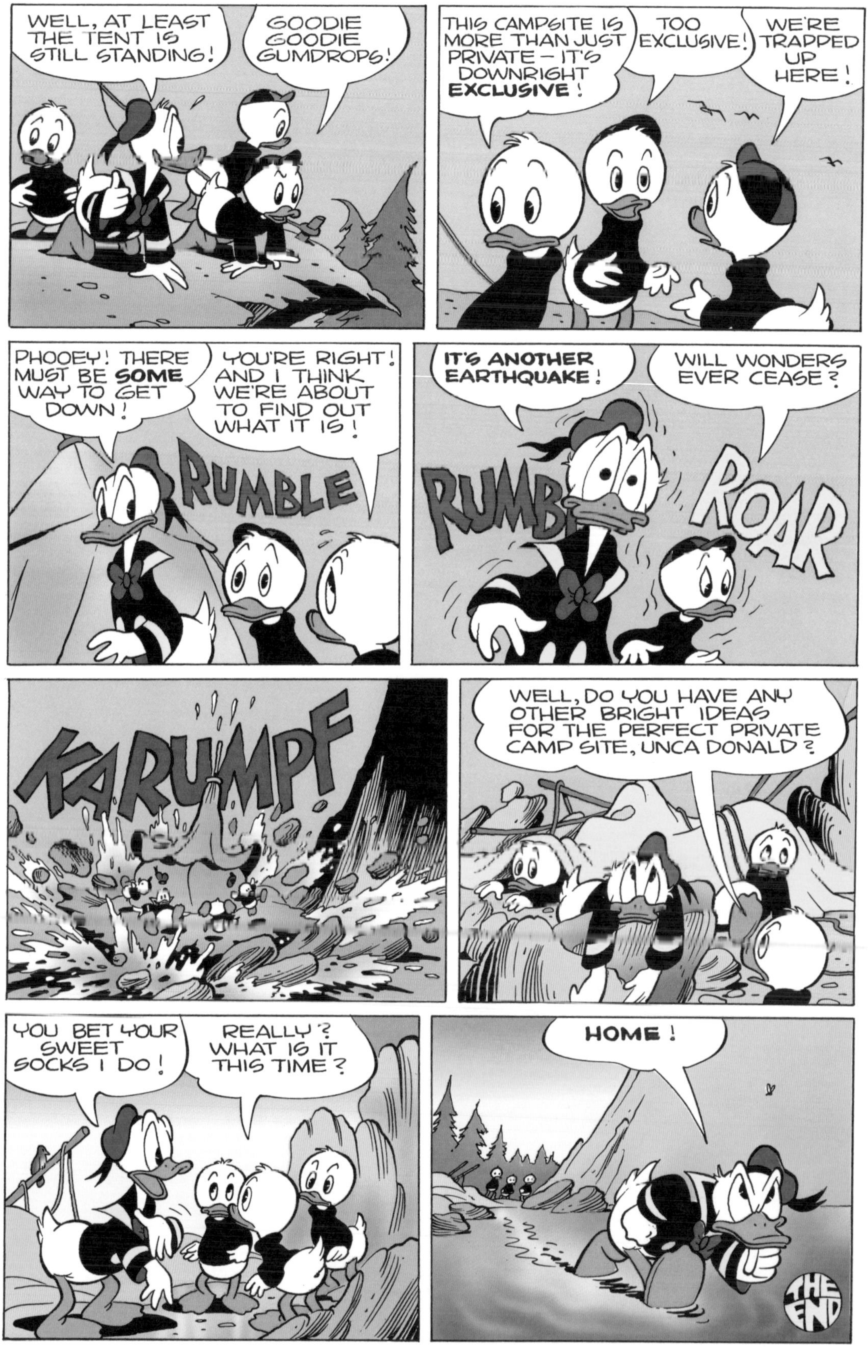
WELL, AT LEAST THE TENT IS STILL STANDING!
GOODIE GOODIE GUMDROPS!
THIS CAMPSITE IS MORE THAN JUST PRIVATE – IT'S DOWNRIGHT **EXCLUSIVE**!
TOO EXCLUSIVE!
WE'RE TRAPPED UP HERE!
PHOOEY! THERE MUST BE **SOME** WAY TO GET DOWN!
YOU'RE RIGHT! AND I THINK WE'RE ABOUT TO FIND OUT WHAT IT IS!
RUMBLE
IT'S ANOTHER EARTHQUAKE!
WILL WONDERS EVER CEASE?
RUMB
ROAR
KARUMPF
WELL, DO YOU HAVE ANY OTHER BRIGHT IDEAS FOR THE PERFECT PRIVATE CAMP SITE, UNCA DONALD?
YOU BET YOUR SWEET SOCKS I DO!
REALLY? WHAT IS IT THIS TIME?
HOME!
THE END

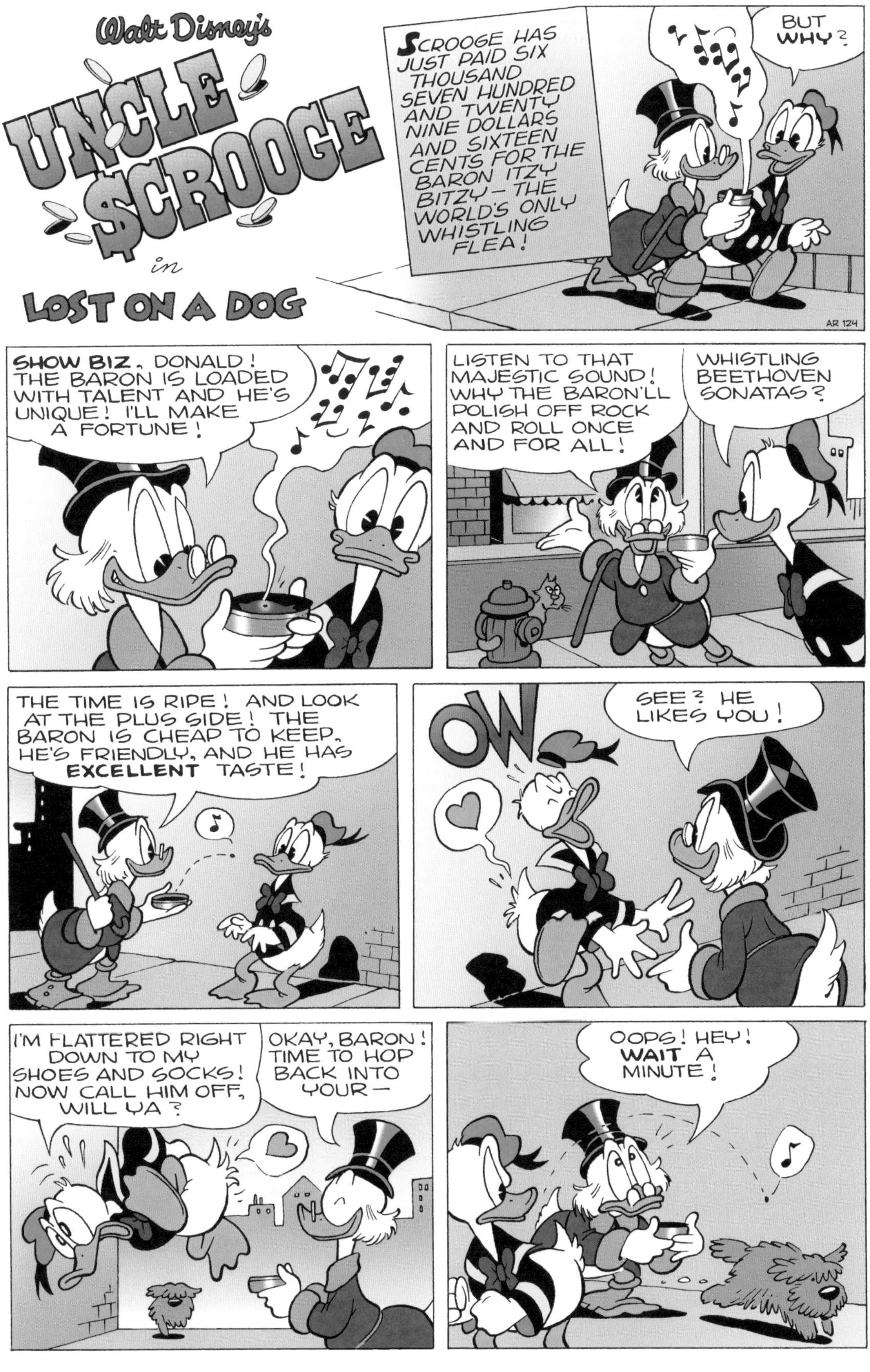
Walt Disney's
UNCLE $CROOGE
in
LOST ON A DOG
SCROOGE HAS JUST PAID SIX THOUSAND SEVEN HUNDRED AND TWENTY NINE DOLLARS AND SIXTEEN CENTS FOR THE BARON ITZY BITZY — THE WORLD'S ONLY WHISTLING FLEA!
BUT WHY?
AR 124
SHOW BIZ, DONALD! THE BARON IS LOADED WITH TALENT AND HE'S UNIQUE! I'LL MAKE A FORTUNE!
LISTEN TO THAT MAJESTIC SOUND! WHY THE BARON'LL POLISH OFF ROCK AND ROLL ONCE AND FOR ALL!
WHISTLING BEETHOVEN SONATAS?
THE TIME IS RIPE! AND LOOK AT THE PLUS SIDE! THE BARON IS CHEAP TO KEEP, HE'S FRIENDLY, AND HE HAS EXCELLENT TASTE!
OW
SEE? HE LIKES YOU!
I'M FLATTERED RIGHT DOWN TO MY SHOES AND SOCKS! NOW CALL HIM OFF, WILL YA?
OKAY, BARON! TIME TO HOP BACK INTO YOUR —
OOPS! HEY! WAIT A MINUTE!

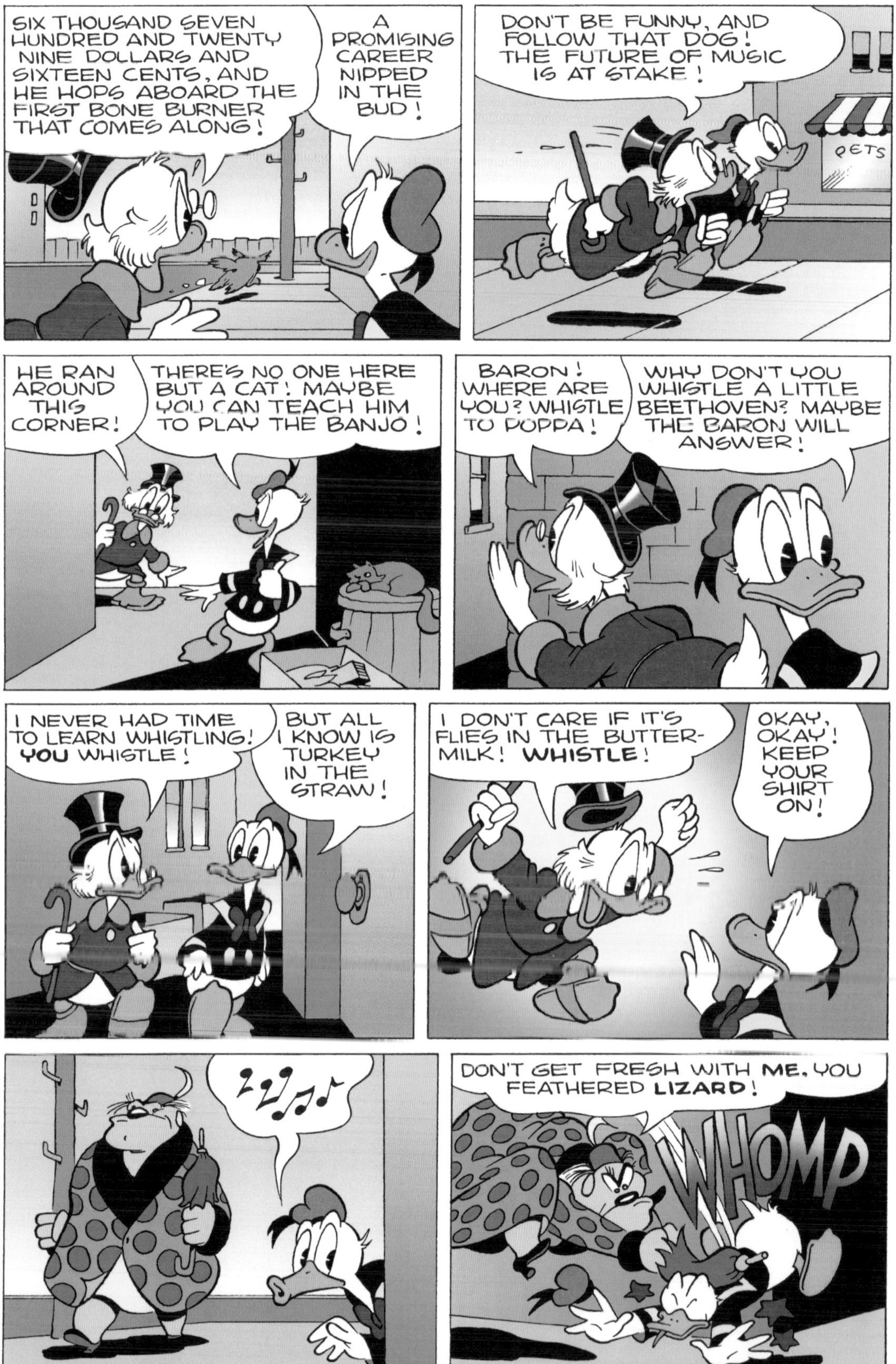

SIX THOUSAND SEVEN HUNDRED AND TWENTY NINE DOLLARS AND SIXTEEN CENTS, AND HE HOPS ABOARD THE FIRST BONE BURNER THAT COMES ALONG!
A PROMISING CAREER NIPPED IN THE BUD!
DON'T BE FUNNY, AND FOLLOW THAT DOG! THE FUTURE OF MUSIC IS AT STAKE!
PETS
HE RAN AROUND THIS CORNER!
THERE'S NO ONE HERE BUT A CAT! MAYBE YOU CAN TEACH HIM TO PLAY THE BANJO!
BARON! WHERE ARE YOU? WHISTLE TO POPPA!
WHY DON'T YOU WHISTLE A LITTLE BEETHOVEN? MAYBE THE BARON WILL ANSWER!
I NEVER HAD TIME TO LEARN WHISTLING! **YOU** WHISTLE!
BUT ALL I KNOW IS TURKEY IN THE STRAW!
I DON'T CARE IF IT'S FLIES IN THE BUTTER-MILK! **WHISTLE**!
OKAY, OKAY! KEEP YOUR SHIRT ON!
DON'T GET FRESH WITH **ME**, YOU FEATHERED **LIZARD**!
WHOMP

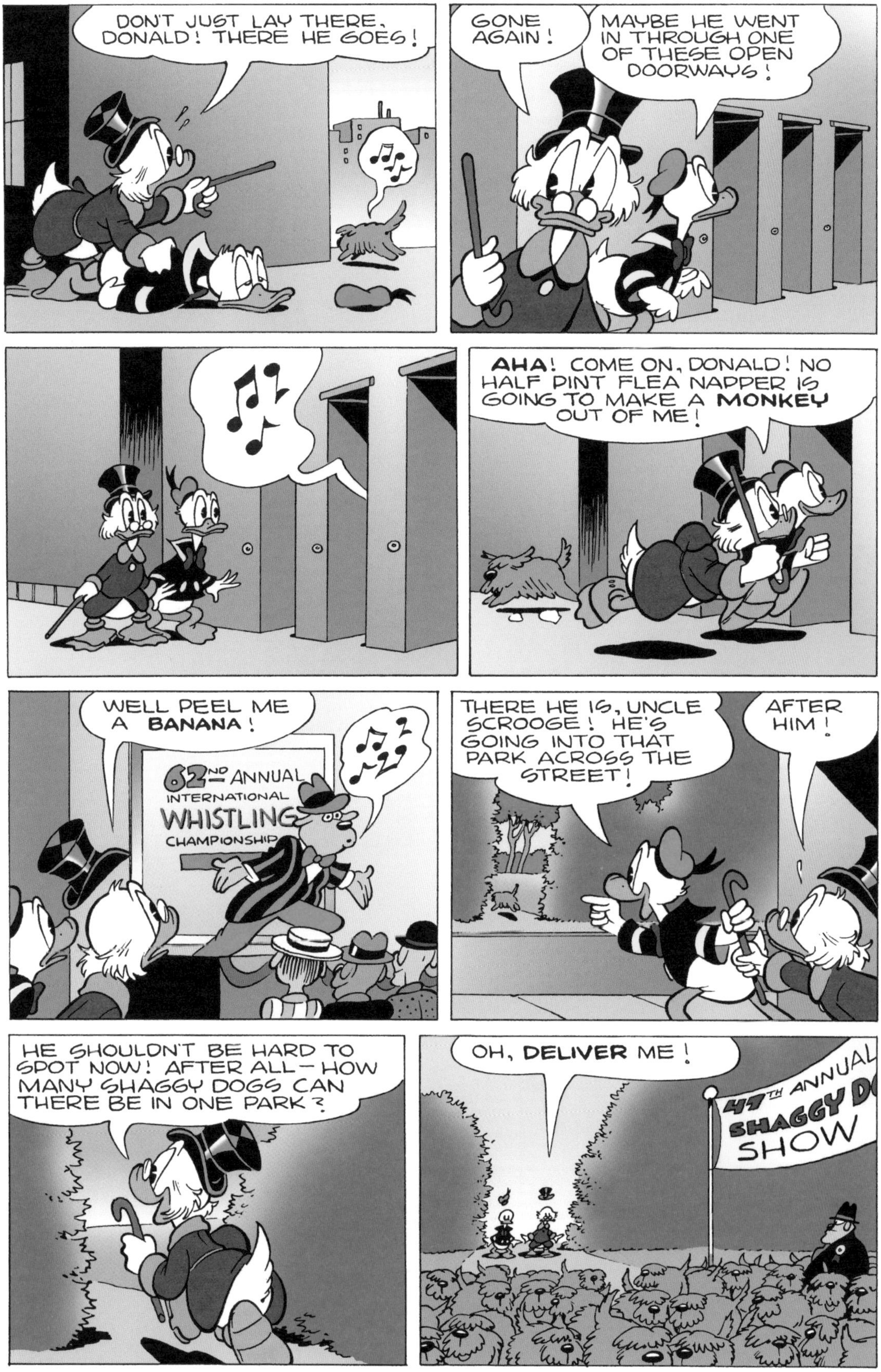
DON'T JUST LAY THERE, DONALD! THERE HE GOES!
GONE AGAIN!
MAYBE HE WENT IN THROUGH ONE OF THESE OPEN DOORWAYS!
AHA! COME ON, DONALD! NO HALF PINT FLEA NAPPER IS GOING TO MAKE A MONKEY OUT OF ME!
WELL PEEL ME A BANANA!
62ND ANNUAL INTERNATIONAL WHISTLING CHAMPIONSHIP
THERE HE IS, UNCLE SCROOGE! HE'S GOING INTO THAT PARK ACROSS THE STREET!
AFTER HIM!
HE SHOULDN'T BE HARD TO SPOT NOW! AFTER ALL—HOW MANY SHAGGY DOGS CAN THERE BE IN ONE PARK?
OH, DELIVER ME!
47TH ANNUAL SHAGGY DO SHOW

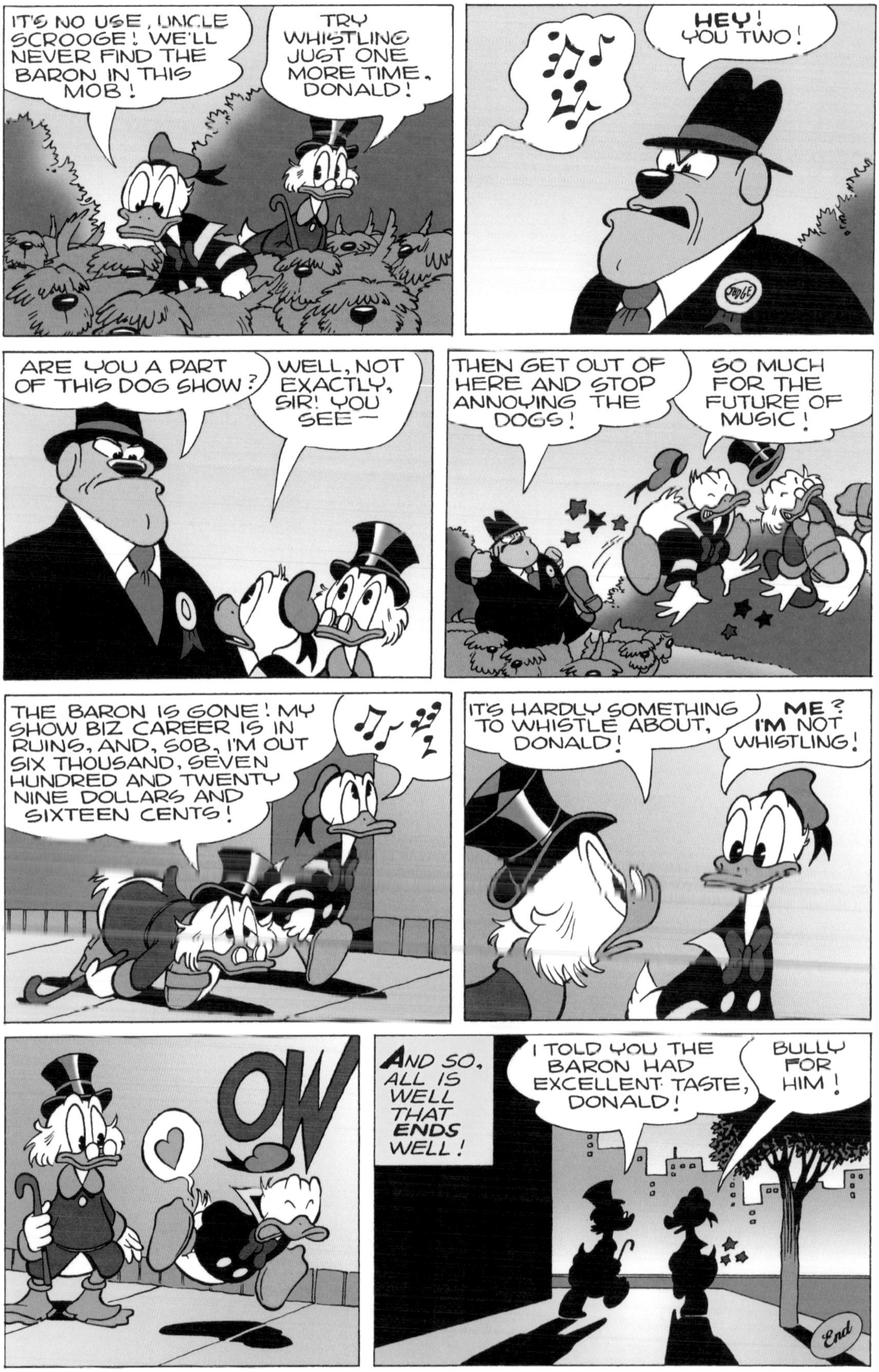

IT'S NO USE, UNCLE SCROOGE! WE'LL NEVER FIND THE BARON IN THIS MOB!
TRY WHISTLING JUST ONE MORE TIME, DONALD!
HEY! YOU TWO!
JUDGE
ARE YOU A PART OF THIS DOG SHOW?
WELL, NOT EXACTLY, SIR! YOU SEE—
THEN GET OUT OF HERE AND STOP ANNOYING THE DOGS!
SO MUCH FOR THE FUTURE OF MUSIC!
THE BARON IS GONE! MY SHOW BIZ CAREER IS IN RUINS, AND, SOB, I'M OUT SIX THOUSAND, SEVEN HUNDRED AND TWENTY NINE DOLLARS AND SIXTEEN CENTS!
IT'S HARDLY SOMETHING TO WHISTLE ABOUT, DONALD!
ME? I'M NOT WHISTLING!
OW
AND SO, ALL IS WELL THAT ENDS WELL!
I TOLD YOU THE BARON HAD EXCELLENT TASTE, DONALD!
BULLY FOR HIM!
End

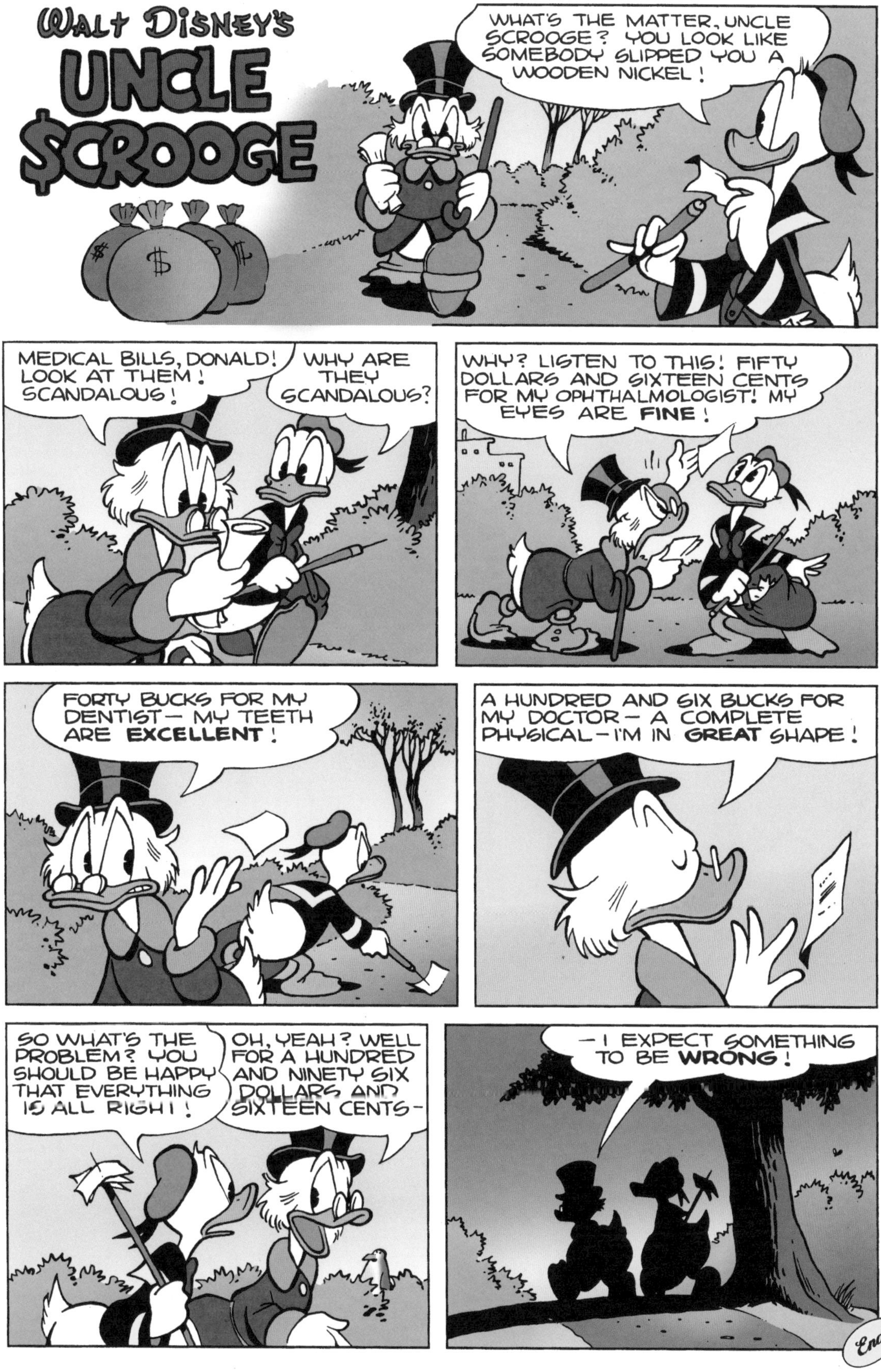
WALT DISNEY'S
UNCLE $CROOGE
WHAT'S THE MATTER, UNCLE SCROOGE? YOU LOOK LIKE SOMEBODY SLIPPED YOU A WOODEN NICKEL!
MEDICAL BILLS, DONALD! LOOK AT THEM! SCANDALOUS!
WHY ARE THEY SCANDALOUS?
WHY? LISTEN TO THIS! FIFTY DOLLARS AND SIXTEEN CENTS FOR MY OPHTHALMOLOGIST! MY EYES ARE **FINE**!
FORTY BUCKS FOR MY DENTIST— MY TEETH ARE **EXCELLENT**!
A HUNDRED AND SIX BUCKS FOR MY DOCTOR— A COMPLETE PHYSICAL—I'M IN **GREAT** SHAPE!
SO WHAT'S THE PROBLEM? YOU SHOULD BE HAPPY THAT EVERYTHING IS ALL RIGHT!
OH, YEAH? WELL FOR A HUNDRED AND NINETY SIX DOLLARS AND SIXTEEN CENTS—
—I EXPECT SOMETHING TO BE **WRONG**!
End

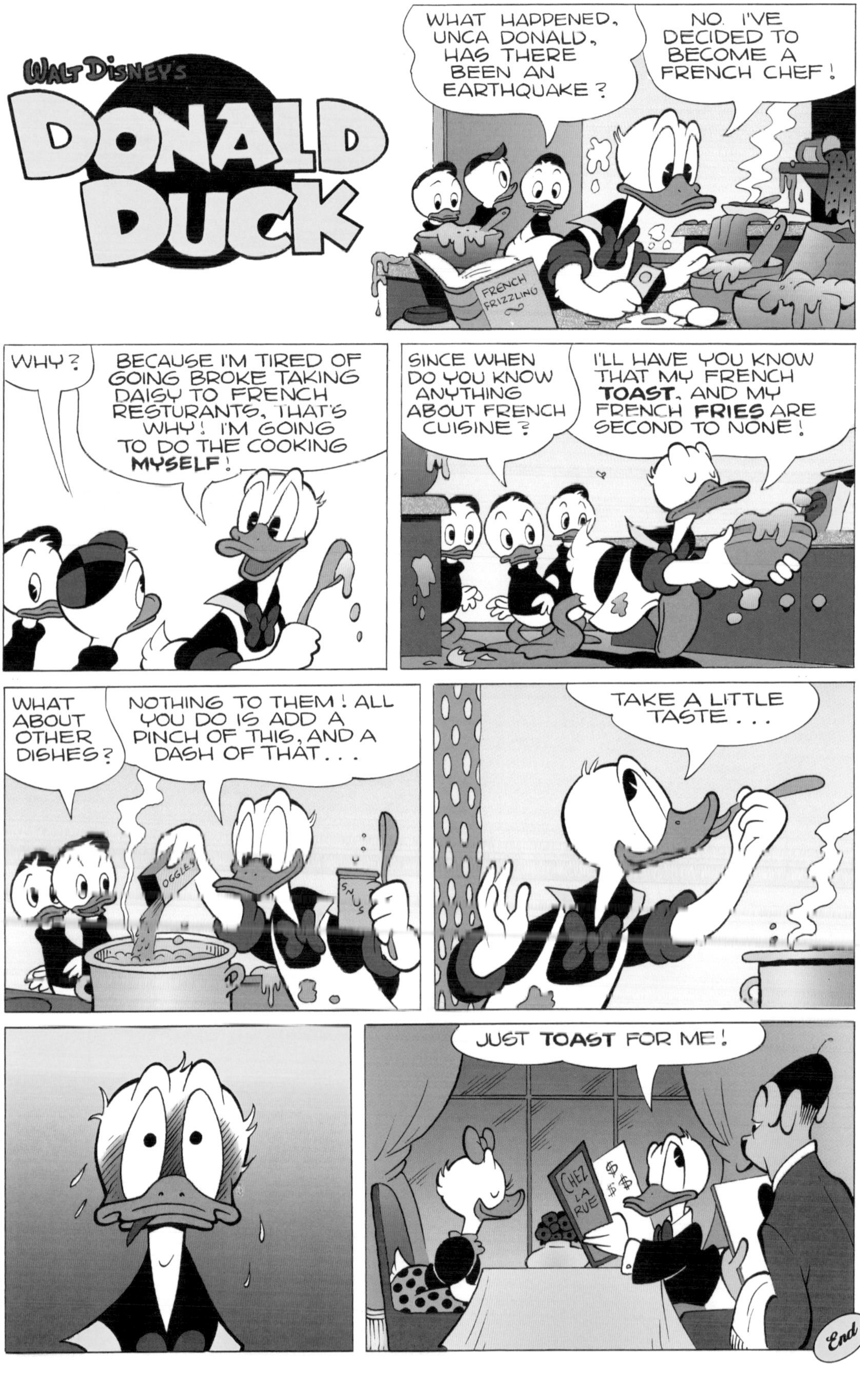
WALT DISNEY'S
DONALD DUCK
WHAT HAPPENED, UNCA DONALD, HAS THERE BEEN AN EARTHQUAKE?
NO. I'VE DECIDED TO BECOME A FRENCH CHEF!
FRENCH FRIZZLING
WHY?
BECAUSE I'M TIRED OF GOING BROKE TAKING DAISY TO FRENCH RESTURANTS, THAT'S WHY! I'M GOING TO DO THE COOKING **MYSELF**!
SINCE WHEN DO YOU KNOW ANYTHING ABOUT FRENCH CUISINE?
I'LL HAVE YOU KNOW THAT MY FRENCH **TOAST**, AND MY FRENCH **FRIES** ARE SECOND TO NONE!
WHAT ABOUT OTHER DISHES?
NOTHING TO THEM! ALL YOU DO IS ADD A PINCH OF THIS, AND A DASH OF THAT...
OGGLES
SNUS
TAKE A LITTLE TASTE...
JUST **TOAST** FOR ME!
CHEZ LA RUE
End

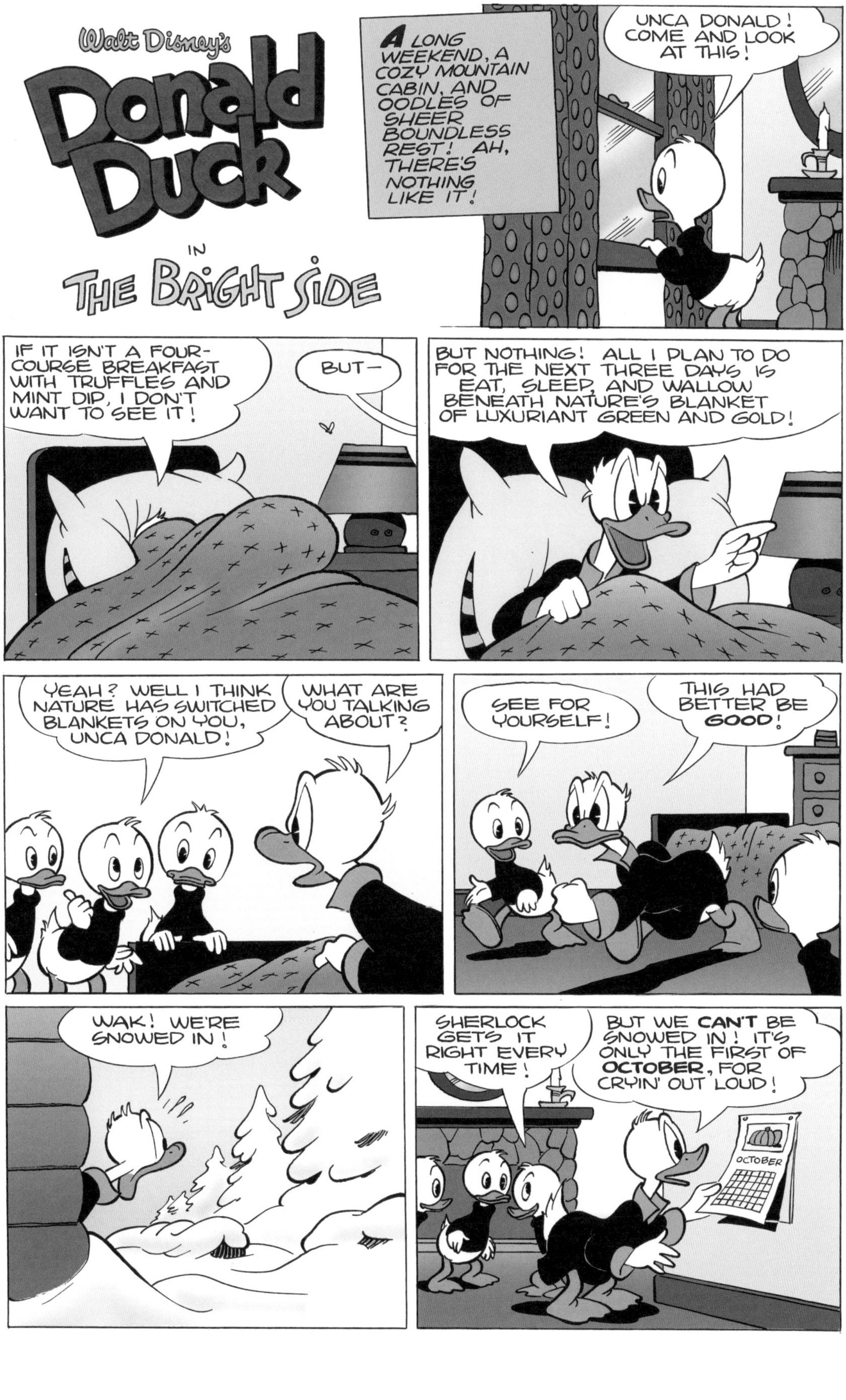
Walt Disney's
Donald Duck
IN
THE BRIGHT SIDE
A LONG WEEKEND, A COZY MOUNTAIN CABIN, AND OODLES OF SHEER BOUNDLESS REST! AH, THERE'S NOTHING LIKE IT!
UNCA DONALD! COME AND LOOK AT THIS!
IF IT ISN'T A FOUR-COURSE BREAKFAST WITH TRUFFLES AND MINT DIP, I DON'T WANT TO SEE IT!
BUT—
BUT NOTHING! ALL I PLAN TO DO FOR THE NEXT THREE DAYS IS EAT, SLEEP, AND WALLOW BENEATH NATURE'S BLANKET OF LUXURIANT GREEN AND GOLD!
YEAH? WELL I THINK NATURE HAS SWITCHED BLANKETS ON YOU, UNCA DONALD!
WHAT ARE YOU TALKING ABOUT?
SEE FOR YOURSELF!
THIS HAD BETTER BE GOOD!
WAK! WE'RE SNOWED IN!
SHERLOCK GETS IT RIGHT EVERY TIME!
BUT WE CAN'T BE SNOWED IN! IT'S ONLY THE FIRST OF OCTOBER, FOR CRYIN' OUT LOUD!
OCTOBER

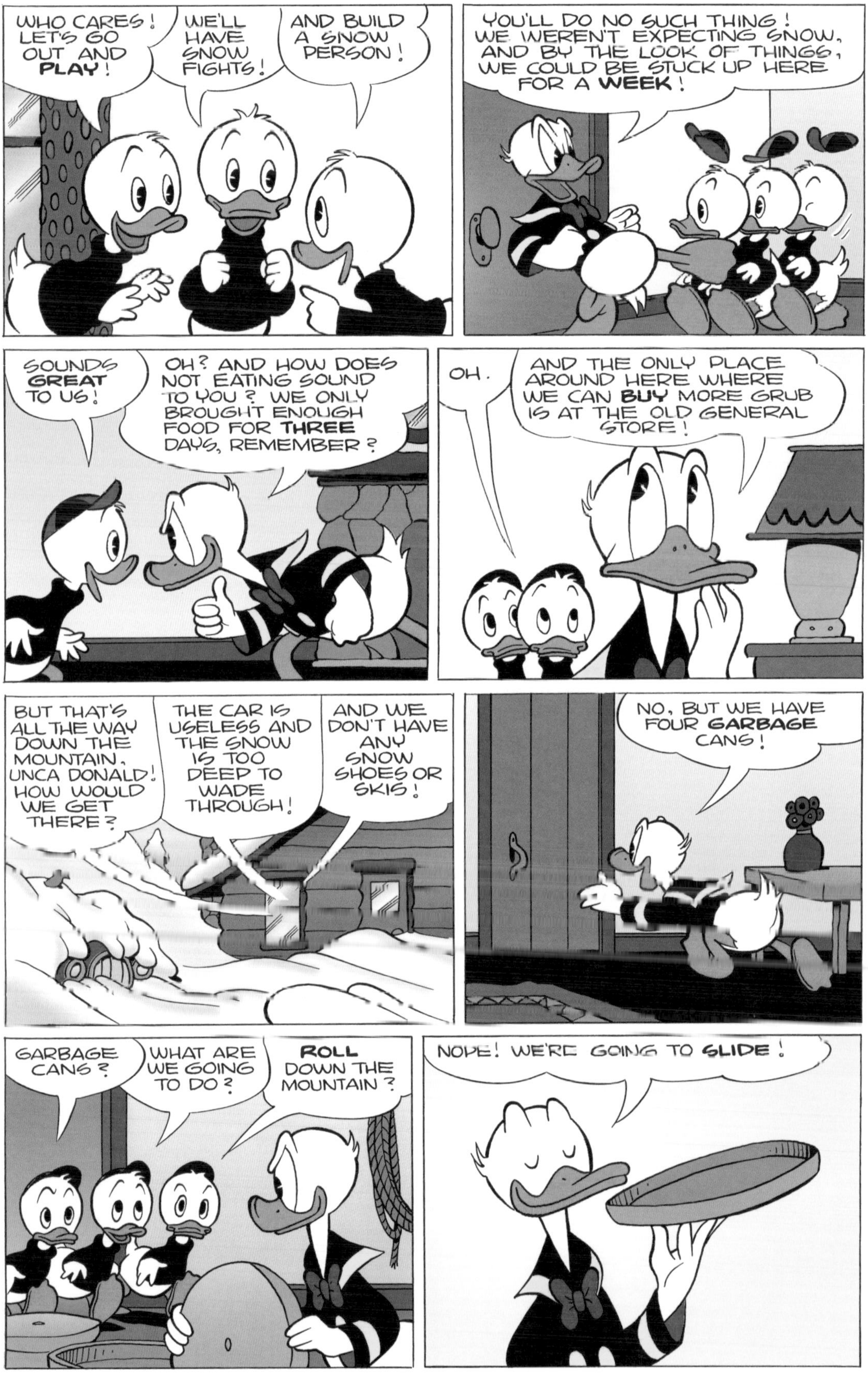
WHO CARES! LET'S GO OUT AND **PLAY**!
WE'LL HAVE SNOW FIGHTS!
AND BUILD A SNOW PERSON!
YOU'LL DO NO SUCH THING! WE WEREN'T EXPECTING SNOW, AND BY THE LOOK OF THINGS, WE COULD BE STUCK UP HERE FOR A **WEEK**!
SOUNDS **GREAT** TO US!
OH? AND HOW DOES NOT EATING SOUND TO YOU? WE ONLY BROUGHT ENOUGH FOOD FOR **THREE** DAYS, REMEMBER?
OH.
AND THE ONLY PLACE AROUND HERE WHERE WE CAN **BUY** MORE GRUB IS AT THE OLD GENERAL STORE!
BUT THAT'S ALL THE WAY DOWN THE MOUNTAIN, UNCA DONALD! HOW WOULD WE GET THERE?
THE CAR IS USELESS AND THE SNOW IS TOO DEEP TO WADE THROUGH!
AND WE DON'T HAVE ANY SNOW SHOES OR SKIS!
NO, BUT WE HAVE FOUR **GARBAGE** CANS!
GARBAGE CANS?
WHAT ARE WE GOING TO DO?
ROLL DOWN THE MOUNTAIN?
NOPE! WE'RE GOING TO **SLIDE**!

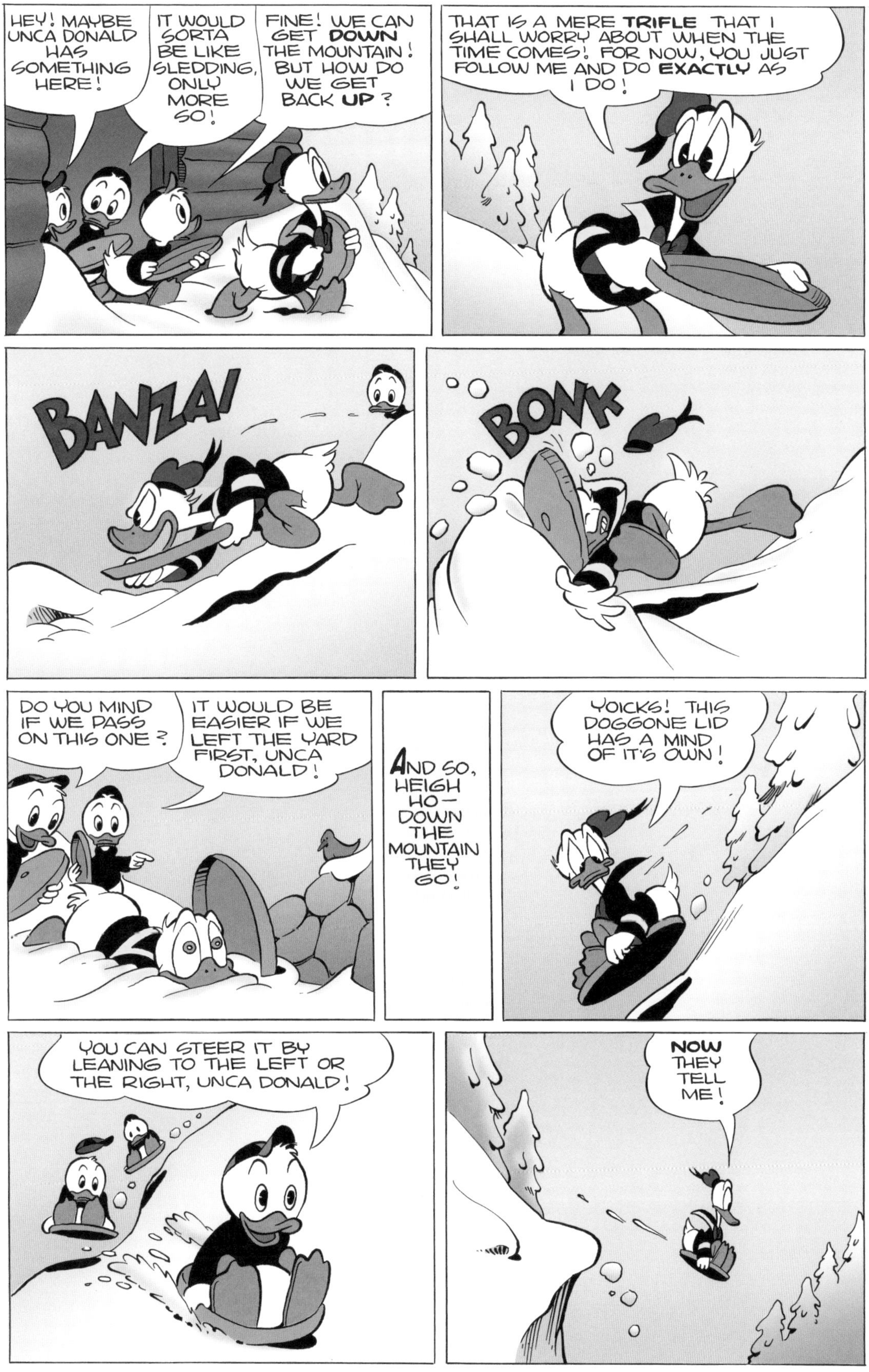
HEY! MAYBE UNCA DONALD HAS SOMETHING HERE!
IT WOULD SORTA BE LIKE SLEDDING, ONLY MORE SO!
FINE! WE CAN GET **DOWN** THE MOUNTAIN! BUT HOW DO WE GET BACK **UP**?
THAT IS A MERE **TRIFLE** THAT I SHALL WORRY ABOUT WHEN THE TIME COMES! FOR NOW, YOU JUST FOLLOW ME AND DO **EXACTLY** AS I DO!
BANZAI
BONK
DO YOU MIND IF WE PASS ON THIS ONE?
IT WOULD BE EASIER IF WE LEFT THE YARD FIRST, UNCA DONALD!
AND SO, HEIGH HO—DOWN THE MOUNTAIN THEY GO!
YOICKS! THIS DOGGONE LID HAS A MIND OF IT'S OWN!
YOU CAN STEER IT BY LEANING TO THE LEFT OR THE RIGHT, UNCA DONALD!
NOW THEY TELL ME!

I THINK I'VE FINALLY GOT THE HANG OF THIS! NOW YOU'RE GOING TO SEE SOME **REAL** SLEDDING!

SLEDDING? WELL, MAYBE!

CUT BETWEEN THOSE TREES, BOYS!

NO, UNCA DONALD! VEER TO THE RIGHT! IT'S A MORE CONTROLLABLE SLOPE!

PHOOEY! STRAIGHT AHEAD IS **QUICKER**! AND THE SOONER I GET DOWN OFF THIS OVER BLOWN SNOW CONE, THE BETTER!

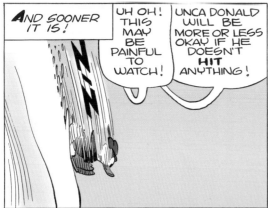

AND SOONER IT IS!

UH OH! THIS MAY BE PAINFUL TO WATCH!

UNCA DONALD WILL BE MORE OR LESS OKAY IF HE DOESN'T **HIT** ANYTHING!

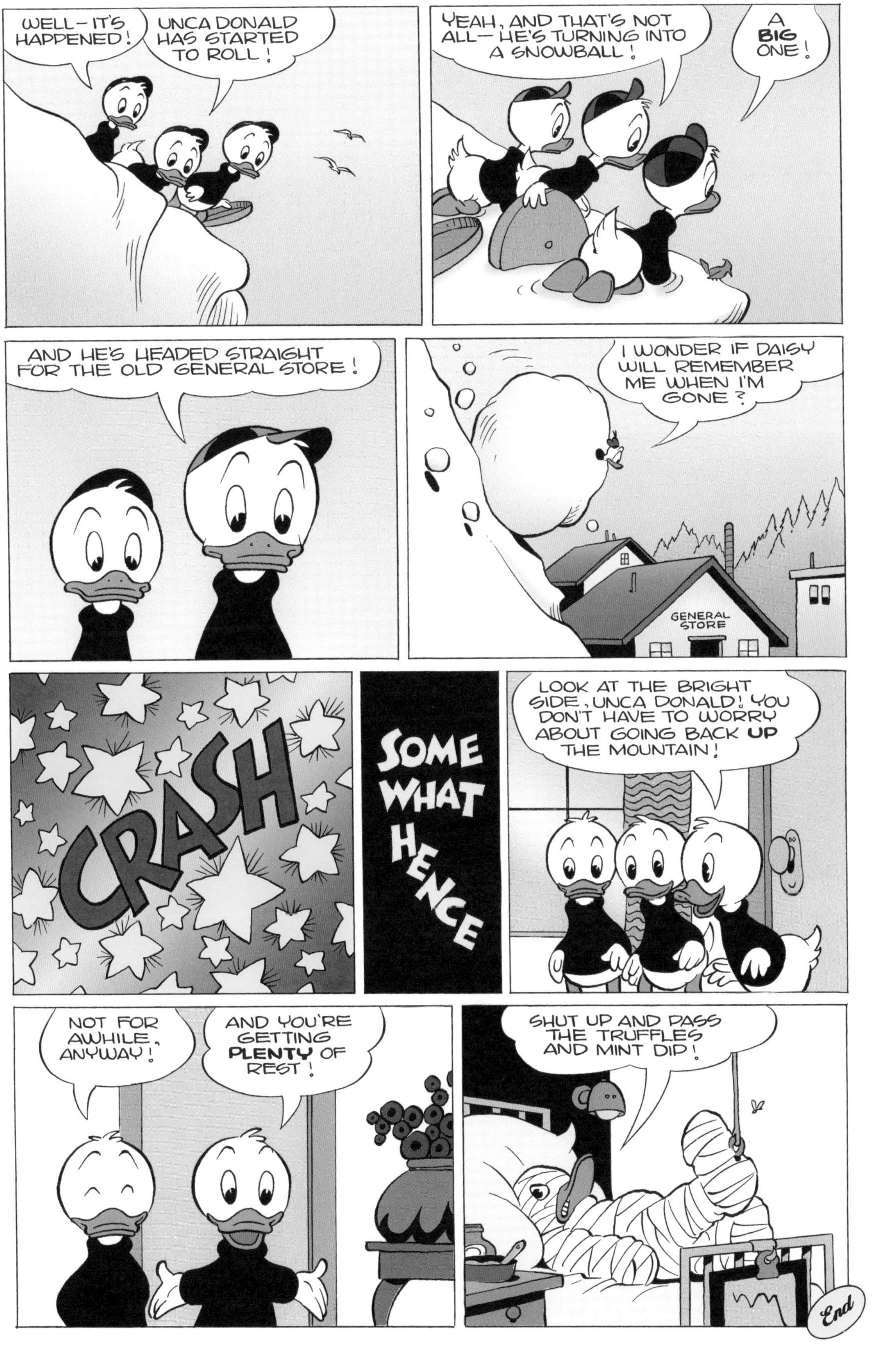
WELL—IT'S HAPPENED!
UNCA DONALD HAS STARTED TO ROLL!
YEAH, AND THAT'S NOT ALL—HE'S TURNING INTO A SNOWBALL!
A BIG ONE!
AND HE'S HEADED STRAIGHT FOR THE OLD GENERAL STORE!
I WONDER IF DAISY WILL REMEMBER ME WHEN I'M GONE?
GENERAL STORE
CRASH
SOME WHAT HENCE
LOOK AT THE BRIGHT SIDE, UNCA DONALD! YOU DON'T HAVE TO WORRY ABOUT GOING BACK UP THE MOUNTAIN!
NOT FOR AWHILE, ANYWAY!
AND YOU'RE GETTING PLENTY OF REST!
SHUT UP AND PASS THE TRUFFLES AND MINT DIP!
End

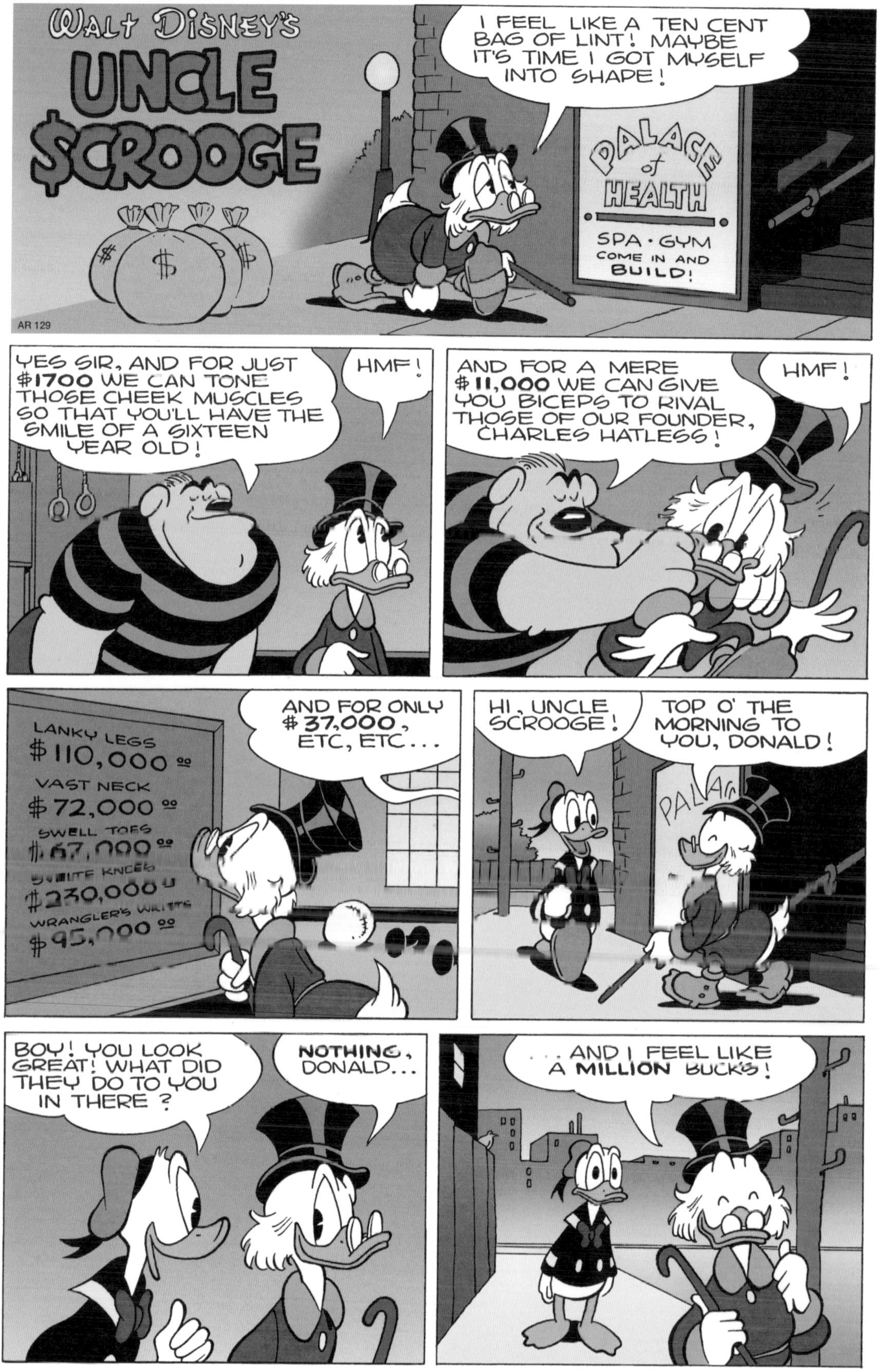
WALT DISNEY'S
UNCLE $CROOGE
I FEEL LIKE A TEN CENT BAG OF LINT! MAYBE IT'S TIME I GOT MYSELF INTO SHAPE!
PALACE of HEALTH
SPA • GYM COME IN AND BUILD!
AR 129
YES SIR, AND FOR JUST $1700 WE CAN TONE THOSE CHEEK MUSCLES SO THAT YOU'LL HAVE THE SMILE OF A SIXTEEN YEAR OLD!
HMF!
AND FOR A MERE $11,000 WE CAN GIVE YOU BICEPS TO RIVAL THOSE OF OUR FOUNDER, CHARLES HATLESS!
HMF!
LANKY LEGS $110,000
VAST NECK $72,000
SWELL TOES $67,000
$230,000
WRANGLER'S WRISTS $95,000
AND FOR ONLY $37,000, ETC, ETC...
HI, UNCLE SCROOGE!
TOP O' THE MORNING TO YOU, DONALD!
BOY! YOU LOOK GREAT! WHAT DID THEY DO TO YOU IN THERE?
NOTHING, DONALD...
...AND I FEEL LIKE A MILLION BUCKS!

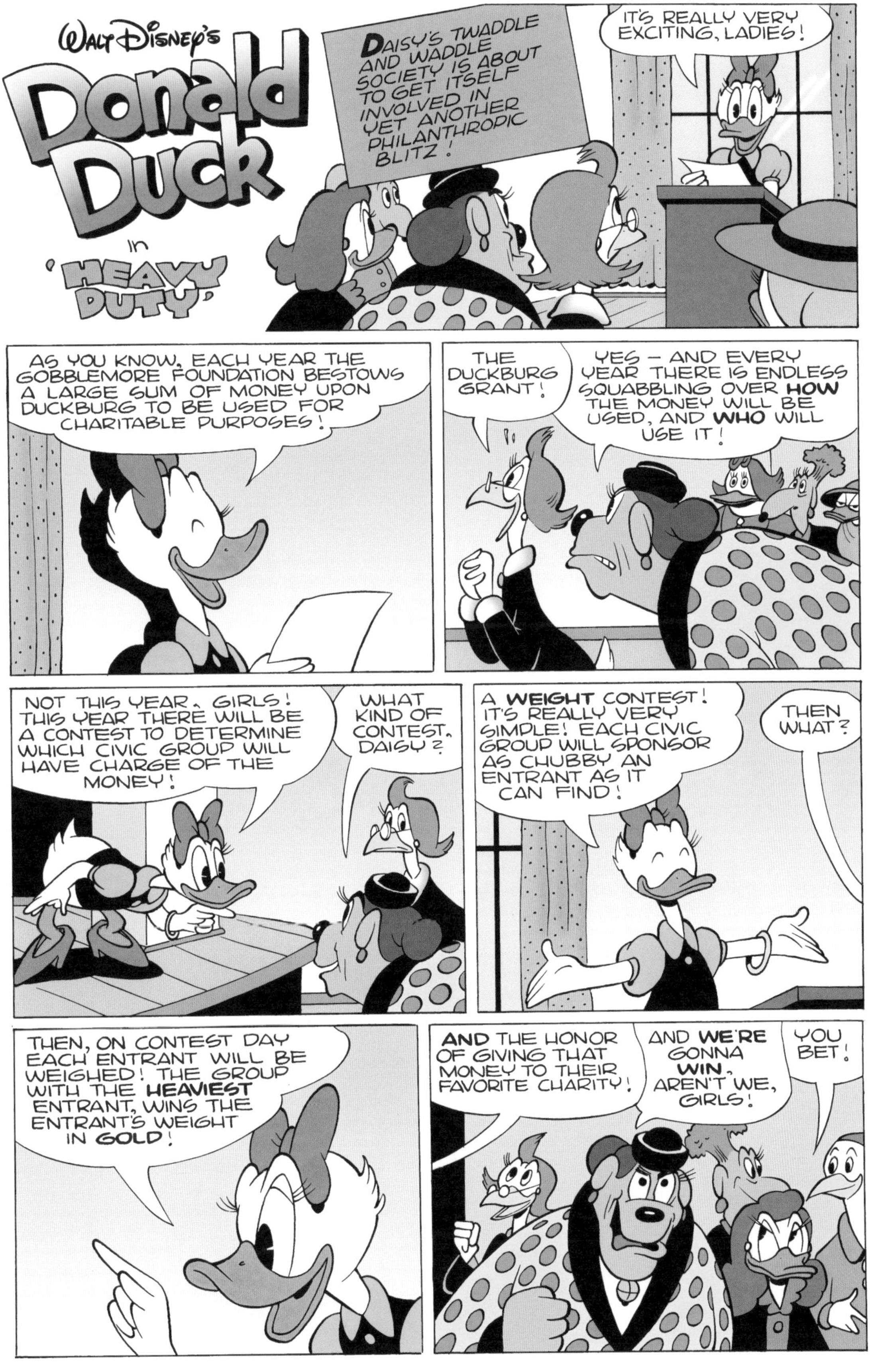

WALT DISNEY'S
Donald Duck
in
'HEAVY DUTY'
DAISY'S TWADDLE AND WADDLE SOCIETY IS ABOUT TO GET ITSELF INVOLVED IN YET ANOTHER PHILANTHROPIC BLITZ!
IT'S REALLY VERY EXCITING, LADIES!
AS YOU KNOW, EACH YEAR THE GOBBLEMORE FOUNDATION BESTOWS A LARGE SUM OF MONEY UPON DUCKBURG TO BE USED FOR CHARITABLE PURPOSES!
THE DUCKBURG GRANT!
YES – AND EVERY YEAR THERE IS ENDLESS SQUABBLING OVER HOW THE MONEY WILL BE USED, AND WHO WILL USE IT!
NOT THIS YEAR, GIRLS! THIS YEAR THERE WILL BE A CONTEST TO DETERMINE WHICH CIVIC GROUP WILL HAVE CHARGE OF THE MONEY!
WHAT KIND OF CONTEST, DAISY?
A WEIGHT CONTEST! IT'S REALLY VERY SIMPLE! EACH CIVIC GROUP WILL SPONSOR AS CHUBBY AN ENTRANT AS IT CAN FIND!
THEN WHAT?
THEN, ON CONTEST DAY EACH ENTRANT WILL BE WEIGHED! THE GROUP WITH THE HEAVIEST ENTRANT, WINS THE ENTRANT'S WEIGHT IN GOLD!
AND THE HONOR OF GIVING THAT MONEY TO THEIR FAVORITE CHARITY!
AND WE'RE GONNA WIN, AREN'T WE, GIRLS!
YOU BET!

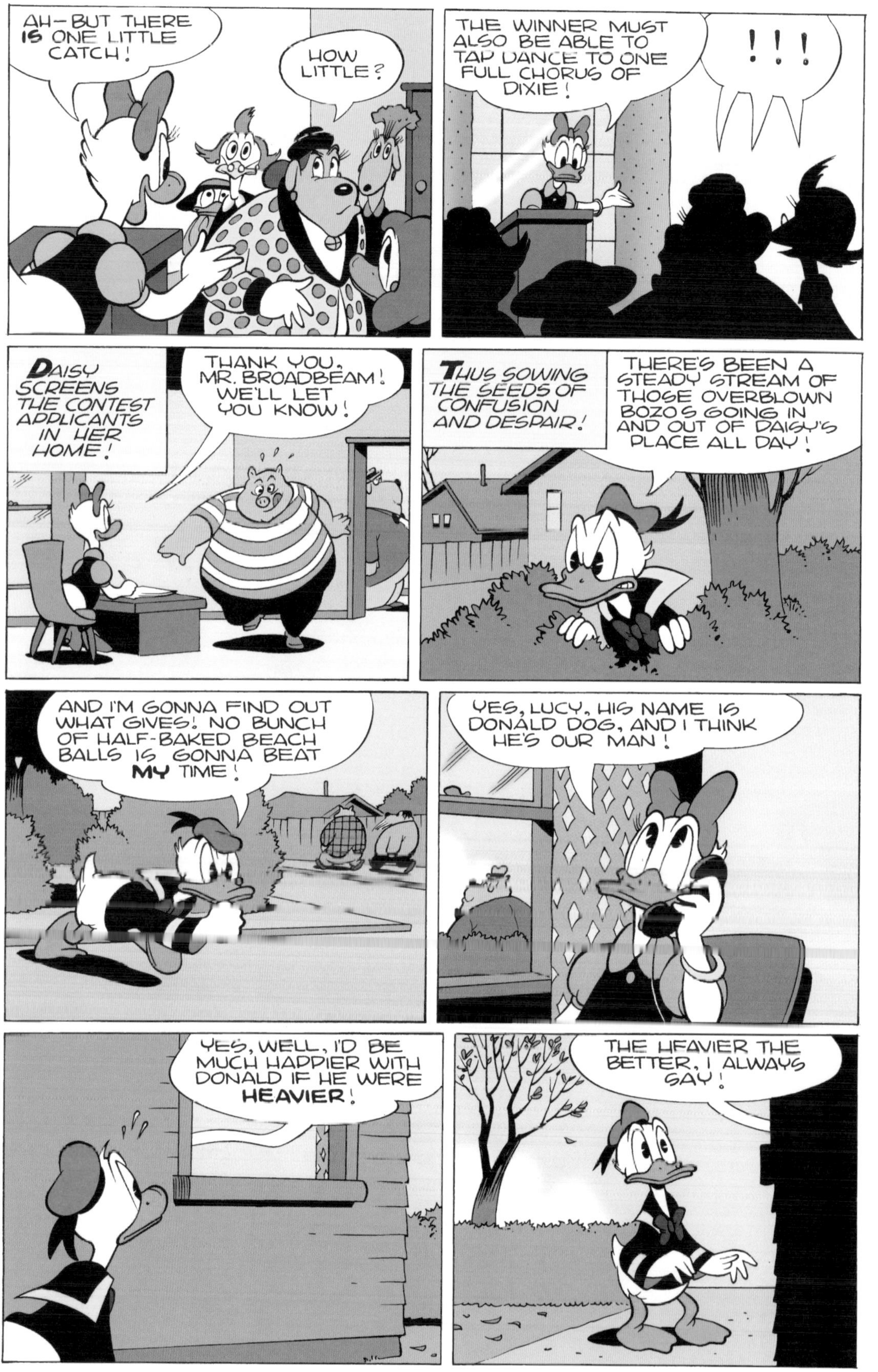
AH—BUT THERE IS ONE LITTLE CATCH!
HOW LITTLE?
THE WINNER MUST ALSO BE ABLE TO TAP DANCE TO ONE FULL CHORUS OF DIXIE!
! ! !
DAISY SCREENS THE CONTEST APPLICANTS IN HER HOME!
THANK YOU, MR. BROADBEAM! WE'LL LET YOU KNOW!
THUS SOWING THE SEEDS OF CONFUSION AND DESPAIR!
THERE'S BEEN A STEADY STREAM OF THOSE OVERBLOWN BOZOS GOING IN AND OUT OF DAISY'S PLACE ALL DAY!
AND I'M GONNA FIND OUT WHAT GIVES! NO BUNCH OF HALF-BAKED BEACH BALLS IS GONNA BEAT MY TIME!
YES, LUCY, HIS NAME IS DONALD DOG, AND I THINK HE'S OUR MAN!
YES, WELL, I'D BE MUCH HAPPIER WITH DONALD IF HE WERE HEAVIER!
THE HEAVIER THE BETTER, I ALWAYS SAY!

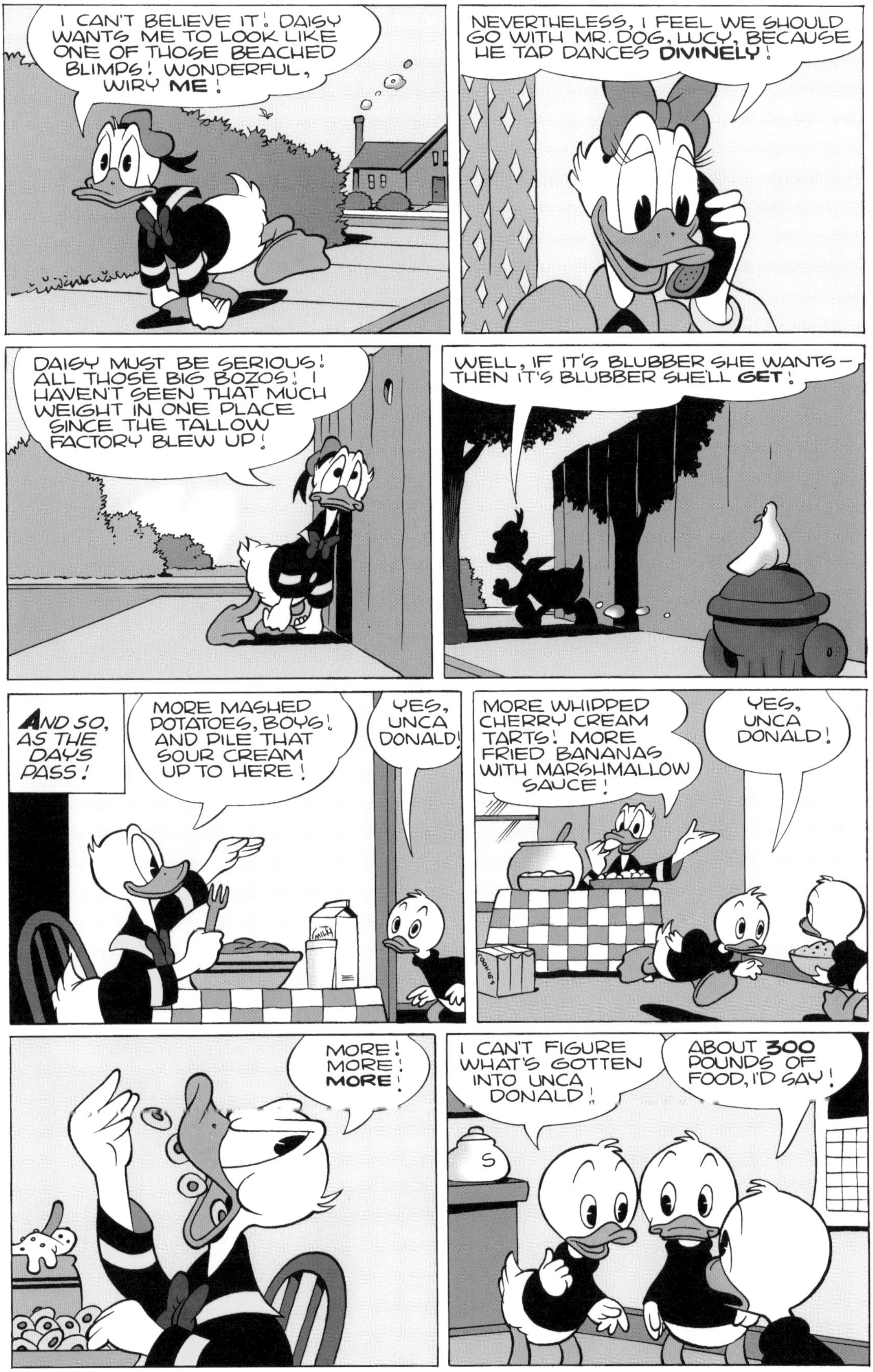
I CAN'T BELIEVE IT! DAISY WANTS ME TO LOOK LIKE ONE OF THOSE BEACHED BLIMPS! WONDERFUL, WIRY **ME**!
NEVERTHELESS, I FEEL WE SHOULD GO WITH MR. DOG, LUCY, BECAUSE HE TAP DANCES **DIVINELY**!
DAISY MUST BE SERIOUS! ALL THOSE BIG BOZOS! I HAVEN'T SEEN THAT MUCH WEIGHT IN ONE PLACE SINCE THE TALLOW FACTORY BLEW UP!
WELL, IF IT'S BLUBBER SHE WANTS— THEN IT'S BLUBBER SHE'LL **GET**!
AND SO, AS THE DAYS PASS!
MORE MASHED POTATOES, BOYS! AND PILE THAT SOUR CREAM UP TO HERE!
YES, UNCA DONALD!
MILK
MORE WHIPPED CHERRY CREAM TARTS! MORE FRIED BANANAS WITH MARSHMALLOW SAUCE!
YES, UNCA DONALD!
COOKIES
MORE! MORE! **MORE**!
I CAN'T FIGURE WHAT'S GOTTEN INTO UNCA DONALD!
ABOUT **300** POUNDS OF FOOD, I'D SAY!
S

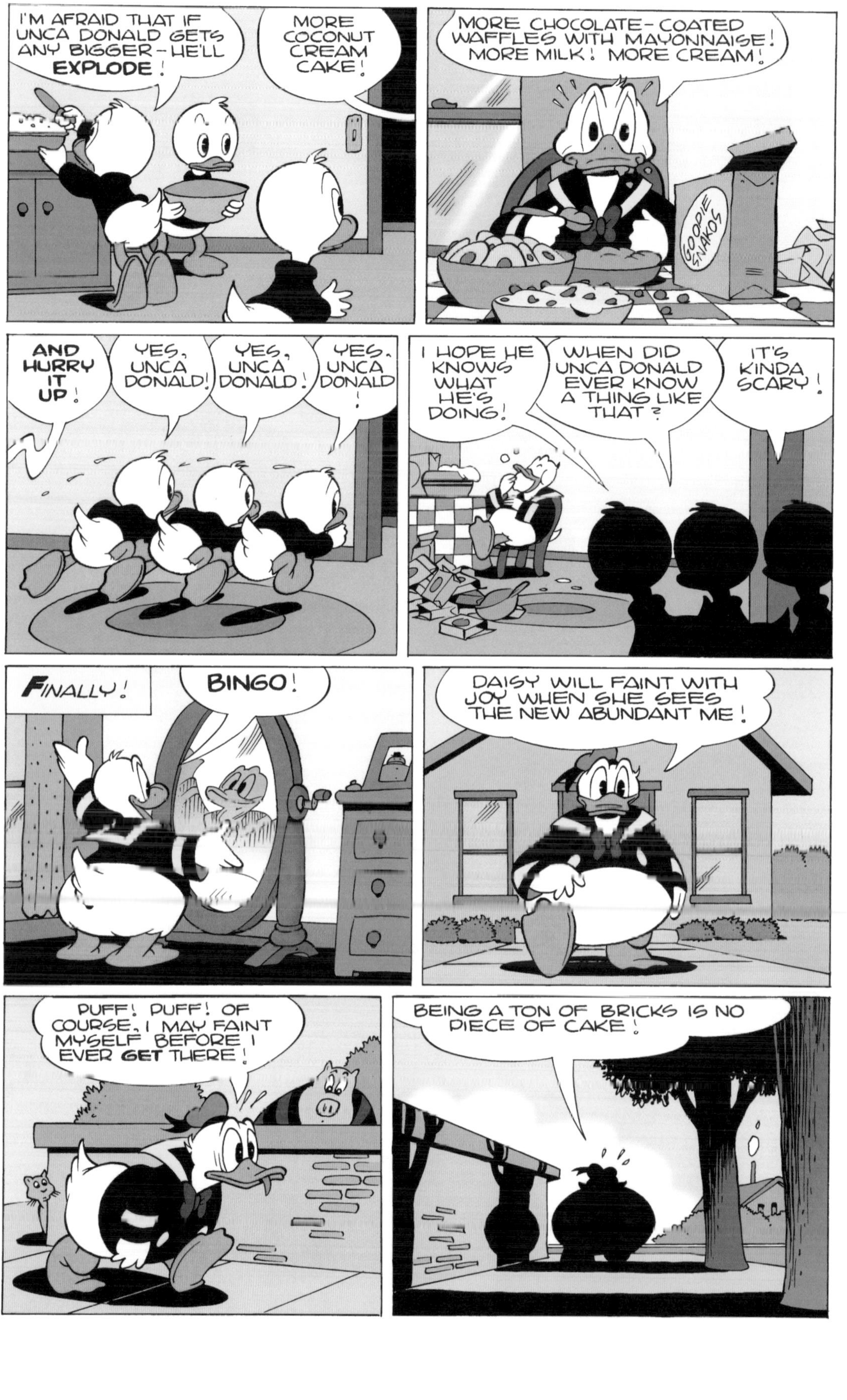
I'M AFRAID THAT IF UNCA DONALD GETS ANY BIGGER—HE'LL **EXPLODE**!
MORE COCONUT CREAM CAKE!
MORE CHOCOLATE-COATED WAFFLES WITH MAYONNAISE! MORE MILK! MORE CREAM!
GOOPIE SNAKOS
AND HURRY IT UP!
YES, UNCA DONALD!
YES, UNCA DONALD!
YES, UNCA DONALD!
I HOPE HE KNOWS WHAT HE'S DOING!
WHEN DID UNCA DONALD EVER KNOW A THING LIKE THAT?
IT'S KINDA SCARY!
FINALLY!
BINGO!
DAISY WILL FAINT WITH JOY WHEN SHE SEES THE NEW ABUNDANT ME!
PUFF! PUFF! OF COURSE, I MAY FAINT MYSELF BEFORE I EVER **GET** THERE!
BEING A TON OF BRICKS IS NO PIECE OF CAKE!

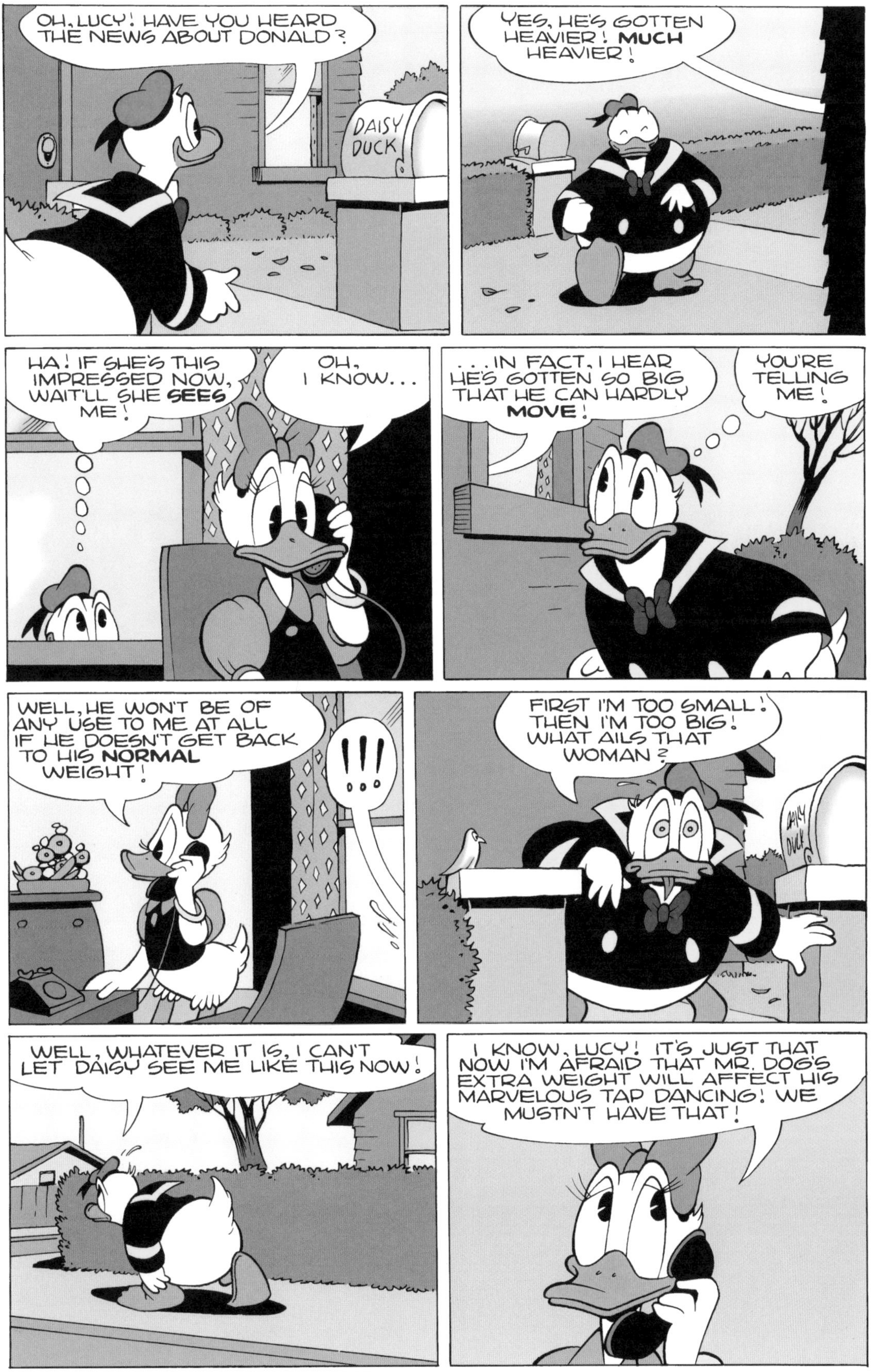

OH, LUCY! HAVE YOU HEARD THE NEWS ABOUT DONALD?
DAISY DUCK
YES, HE'S GOTTEN HEAVIER! **MUCH** HEAVIER!
HA! IF SHE'S THIS IMPRESSED NOW, WAIT'LL SHE **SEES** ME!
OH, I KNOW...
...IN FACT, I HEAR HE'S GOTTEN SO BIG THAT HE CAN HARDLY **MOVE**!
YOU'RE TELLING ME!
WELL, HE WON'T BE OF ANY USE TO ME AT ALL IF HE DOESN'T GET BACK TO HIS **NORMAL** WEIGHT!
!!!
FIRST I'M TOO SMALL! THEN I'M TOO BIG! WHAT AILS THAT WOMAN?
DAISY DUCK
WELL, WHATEVER IT IS, I CAN'T LET DAISY SEE ME LIKE THIS NOW!
I KNOW, LUCY! IT'S JUST THAT NOW I'M AFRAID THAT MR. DOG'S EXTRA WEIGHT WILL AFFECT HIS MARVELOUS TAP DANCING! WE MUSTN'T HAVE THAT!

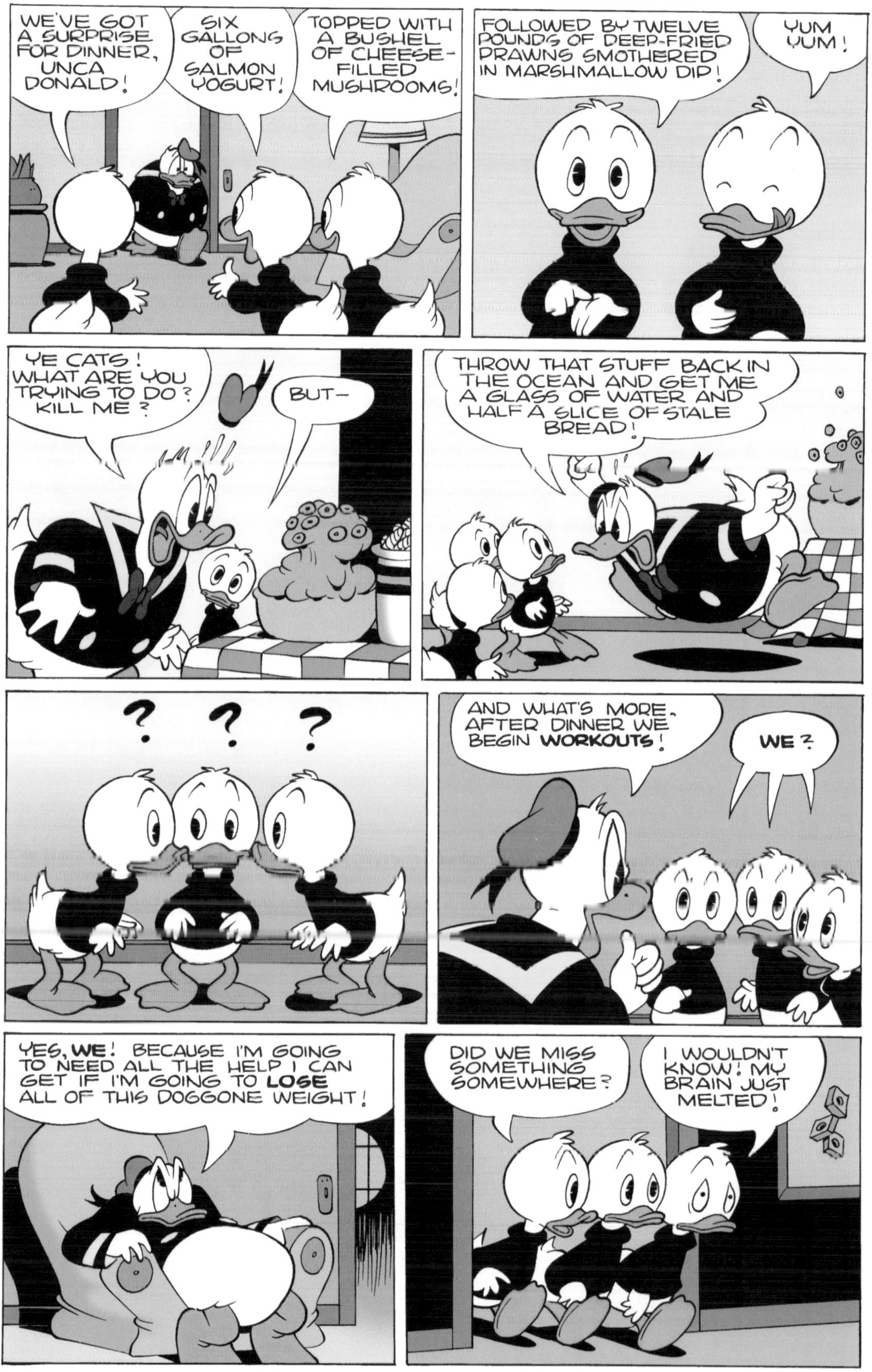
WE'VE GOT A SURPRISE FOR DINNER, UNCA DONALD!
SIX GALLONS OF SALMON YOGURT!
TOPPED WITH A BUSHEL OF CHEESE-FILLED MUSHROOMS!
FOLLOWED BY TWELVE POUNDS OF DEEP-FRIED PRAWNS SMOTHERED IN MARSHMALLOW DIP!
YUM YUM!
YE CATS! WHAT ARE YOU TRYING TO DO? KILL ME?
BUT—
THROW THAT STUFF BACK IN THE OCEAN AND GET ME A GLASS OF WATER AND HALF A SLICE OF STALE BREAD!
? ? ?
AND WHAT'S MORE, AFTER DINNER WE BEGIN WORKOUTS!
WE?
YES, WE! BECAUSE I'M GOING TO NEED ALL THE HELP I CAN GET IF I'M GOING TO LOSE ALL OF THIS DOGGONE WEIGHT!
DID WE MISS SOMETHING SOMEWHERE?
I WOULDN'T KNOW! MY BRAIN JUST MELTED!

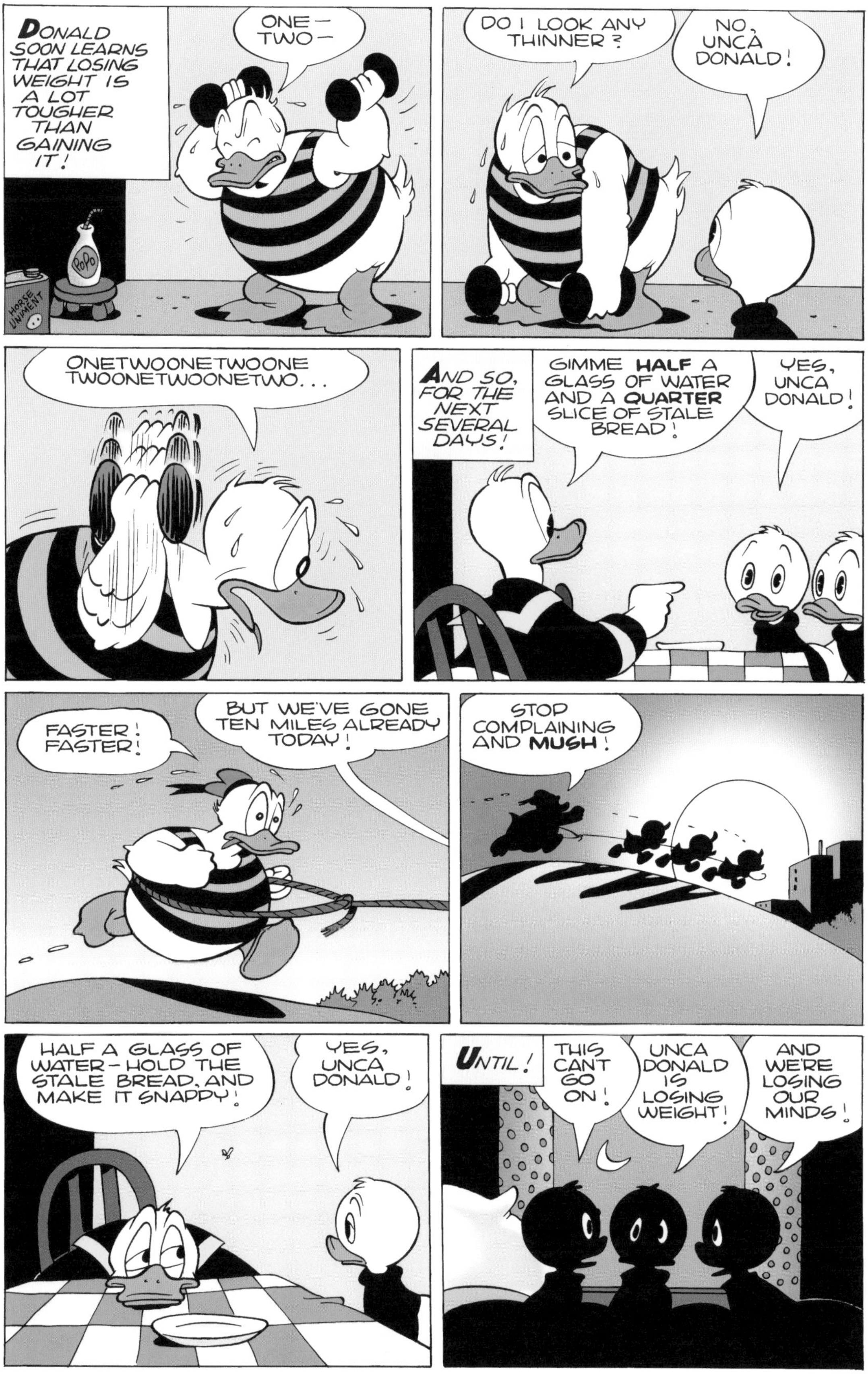
DONALD SOON LEARNS THAT LOSING WEIGHT IS A LOT TOUGHER THAN GAINING IT!
ONE— TWO—
POPO
HORSE LINIMENT
DO I LOOK ANY THINNER?
NO, UNCA DONALD!
ONETWOONETWOONE TWOONETWOONETWO...
AND SO, FOR THE NEXT SEVERAL DAYS!
GIMME **HALF** A GLASS OF WATER AND A **QUARTER** SLICE OF STALE BREAD!
YES, UNCA DONALD!
FASTER! FASTER!
BUT WE'VE GONE TEN MILES ALREADY TODAY!
STOP COMPLAINING AND **MUSH**!
HALF A GLASS OF WATER—HOLD THE STALE BREAD, AND MAKE IT SNAPPY!
YES, UNCA DONALD!
UNTIL!
THIS CAN'T GO ON!
UNCA DONALD IS LOSING WEIGHT!
AND WE'RE LOSING OUR MINDS!

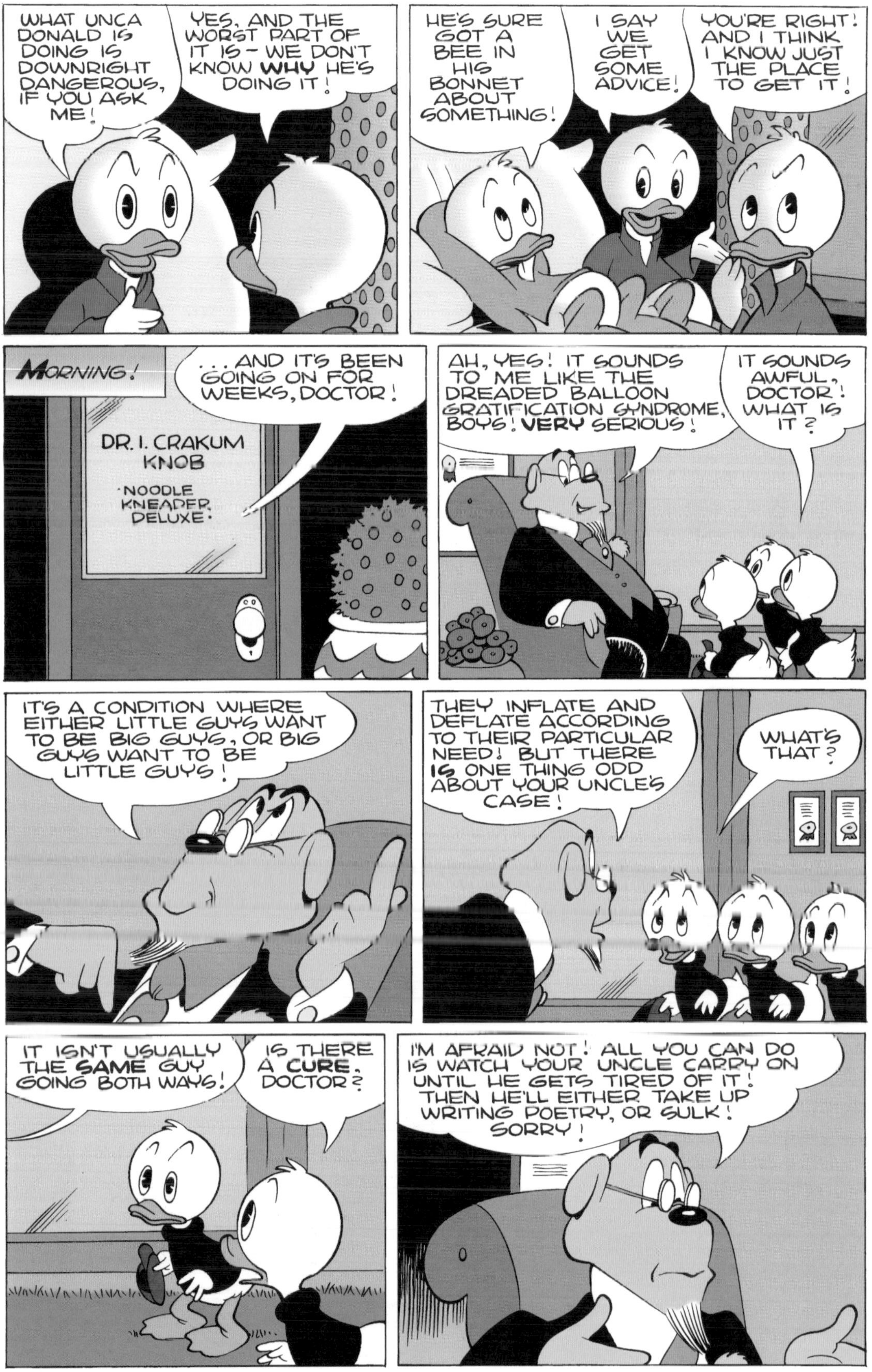
WHAT UNCA DONALD IS DOING IS DOWNRIGHT DANGEROUS, IF YOU ASK ME!
YES, AND THE WORST PART OF IT IS – WE DON'T KNOW **WHY** HE'S DOING IT!
HE'S SURE GOT A BEE IN HIS BONNET ABOUT SOMETHING!
I SAY WE GET SOME ADVICE!
YOU'RE RIGHT! AND I THINK I KNOW JUST THE PLACE TO GET IT!
MORNING!
. . . AND IT'S BEEN GOING ON FOR WEEKS, DOCTOR!
DR. I. CRAKUM KNOB
·NOODLE KNEADER DELUXE·
AH, YES! IT SOUNDS TO ME LIKE THE DREADED BALLOON GRATIFICATION SYNDROME, BOYS! **VERY** SERIOUS!
IT SOUNDS AWFUL, DOCTOR! WHAT IS IT?
IT'S A CONDITION WHERE EITHER LITTLE GUYS WANT TO BE BIG GUYS, OR BIG GUYS WANT TO BE LITTLE GUYS!
THEY INFLATE AND DEFLATE ACCORDING TO THEIR PARTICULAR NEED! BUT THERE **IS** ONE THING ODD ABOUT YOUR UNCLE'S CASE!
WHAT'S THAT?
IT ISN'T USUALLY THE **SAME** GUY GOING BOTH WAYS!
IS THERE A **CURE**, DOCTOR?
I'M AFRAID NOT! ALL YOU CAN DO IS WATCH YOUR UNCLE CARRY ON UNTIL HE GETS TIRED OF IT! THEN HE'LL EITHER TAKE UP WRITING POETRY, OR SULK! SORRY!

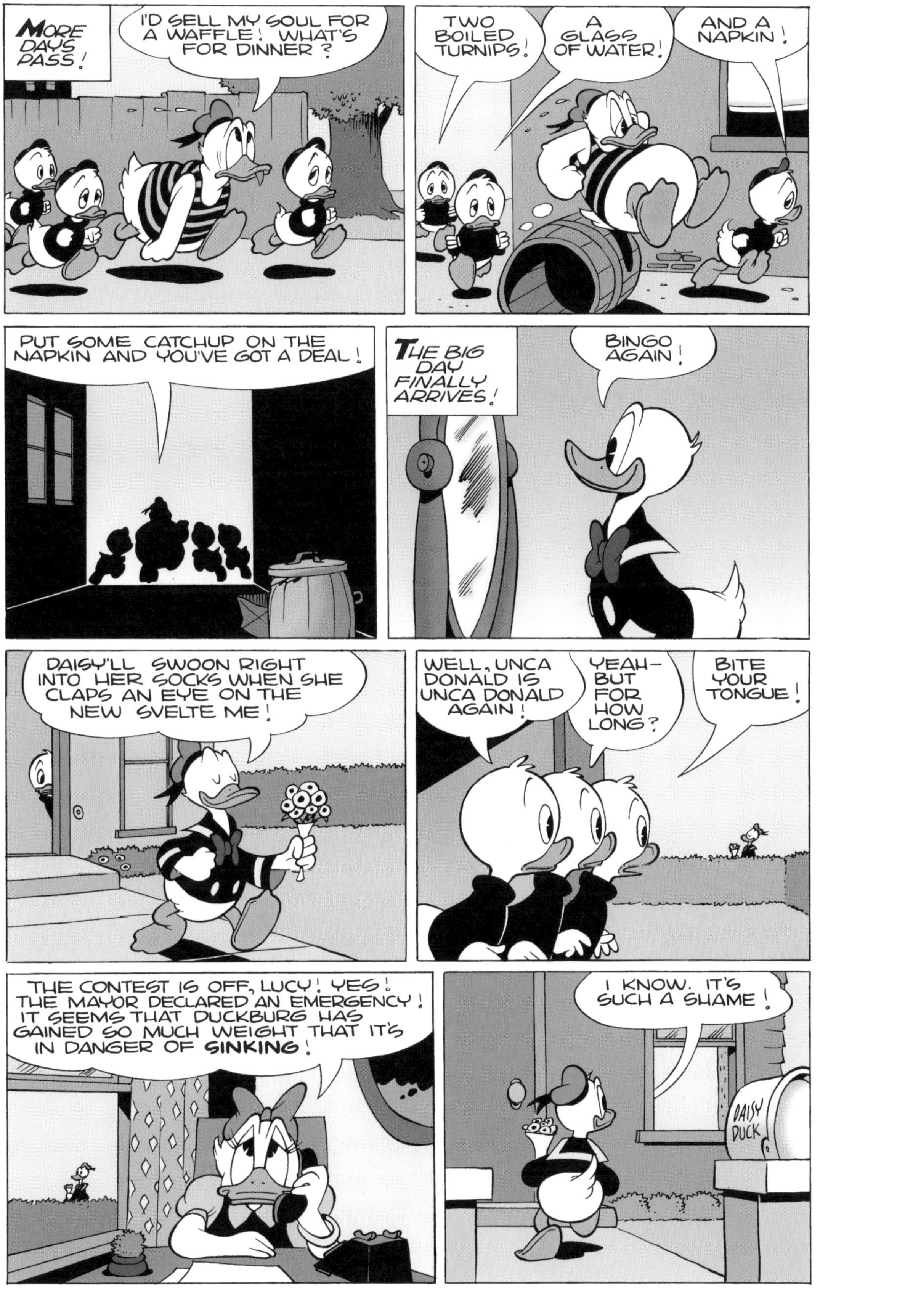
MORE DAYS PASS!
I'D SELL MY SOUL FOR A WAFFLE! WHAT'S FOR DINNER?
TWO BOILED TURNIPS!
A GLASS OF WATER!
AND A NAPKIN!
PUT SOME CATCHUP ON THE NAPKIN AND YOU'VE GOT A DEAL!
THE BIG DAY FINALLY ARRIVES!
BINGO AGAIN!
DAISY'LL SWOON RIGHT INTO HER SOCKS WHEN SHE CLAPS AN EYE ON THE NEW SVELTE ME!
WELL, UNCA DONALD IS UNCA DONALD AGAIN!
YEAH— BUT FOR HOW LONG?
BITE YOUR TONGUE!
THE CONTEST IS OFF, LUCY! YES! THE MAYOR DECLARED AN EMERGENCY! IT SEEMS THAT DUCKBURG HAS GAINED SO MUCH WEIGHT THAT IT'S IN DANGER OF **SINKING**!
I KNOW. IT'S SUCH A SHAME!
DAISY DUCK

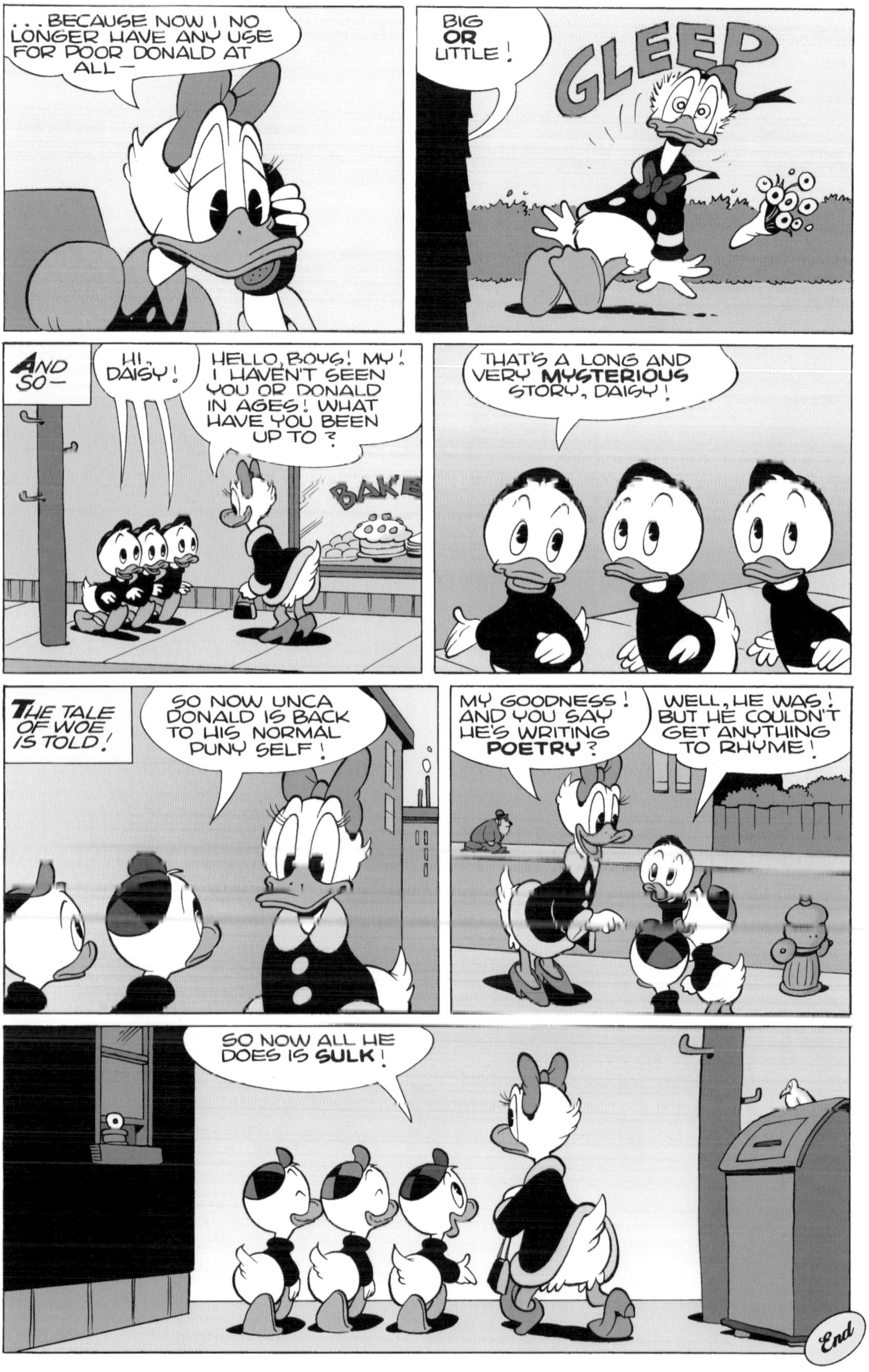

. . . BECAUSE NOW I NO LONGER HAVE ANY USE FOR POOR DONALD AT ALL—
BIG **OR** LITTLE!
GLEEP
AND SO—
HI, DAISY!
HELLO, BOYS! MY! I HAVEN'T SEEN YOU OR DONALD IN AGES! WHAT HAVE YOU BEEN UP TO?
BAKE
THAT'S A LONG AND VERY **MYSTERIOUS** STORY, DAISY!
THE TALE OF WOE IS TOLD!
SO NOW UNCA DONALD IS BACK TO HIS NORMAL PUNY SELF!
MY GOODNESS! AND YOU SAY HE'S WRITING **POETRY**?
WELL, HE WAS! BUT HE COULDN'T GET ANYTHING TO RHYME!
SO NOW ALL HE DOES IS **SULK**!
End

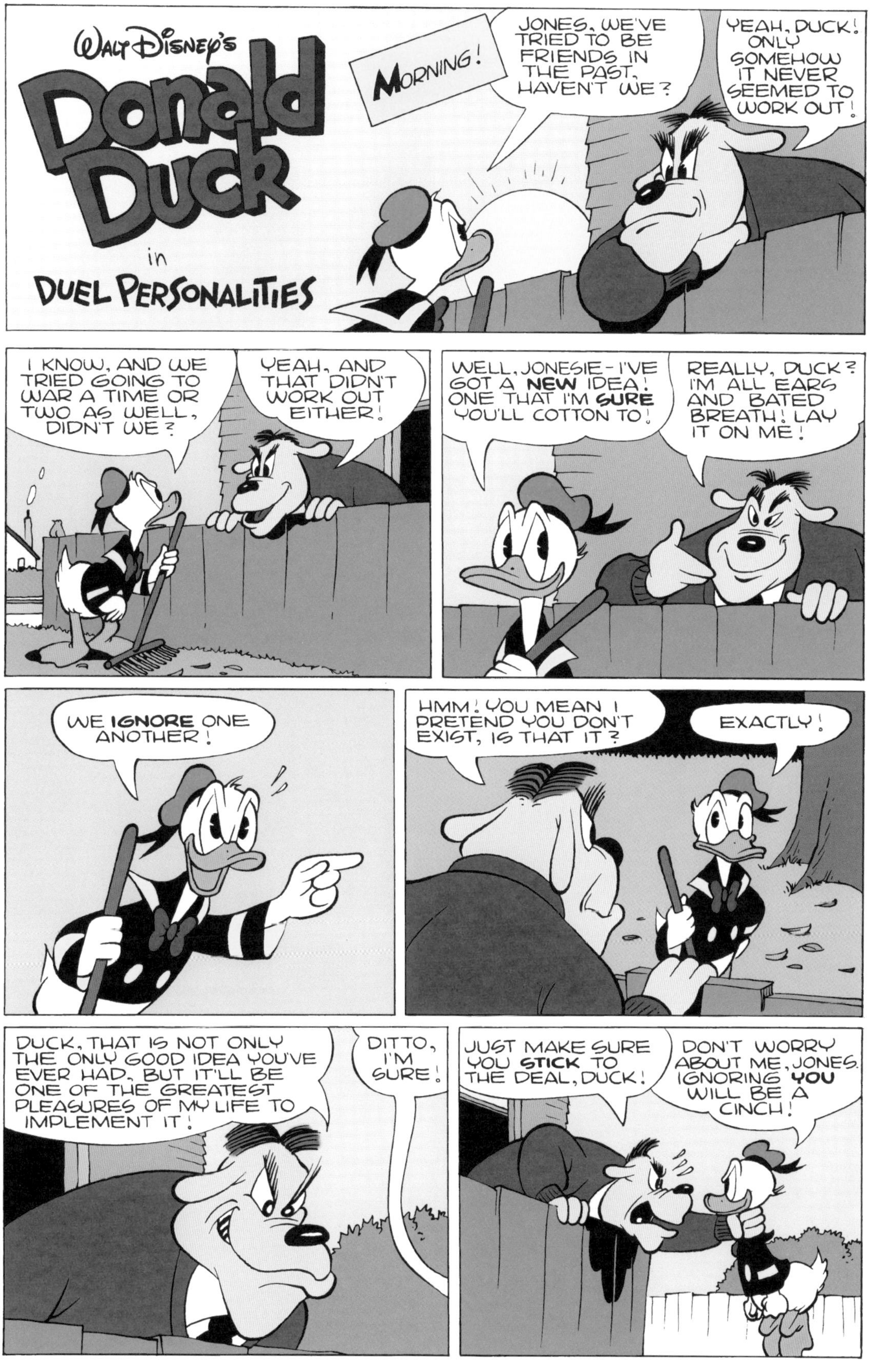
WALT DISNEY'S
Donald Duck
in
DUEL PERSONALITIES
MORNING!
JONES, WE'VE TRIED TO BE FRIENDS IN THE PAST, HAVEN'T WE?
YEAH, DUCK! ONLY SOMEHOW IT NEVER SEEMED TO WORK OUT!
I KNOW, AND WE TRIED GOING TO WAR A TIME OR TWO AS WELL, DIDN'T WE?
YEAH, AND THAT DIDN'T WORK OUT EITHER!
WELL, JONESIE - I'VE GOT A NEW IDEA! ONE THAT I'M SURE YOU'LL COTTON TO!
REALLY, DUCK? I'M ALL EARS AND BATED BREATH! LAY IT ON ME!
WE IGNORE ONE ANOTHER!
HMM! YOU MEAN I PRETEND YOU DON'T EXIST, IS THAT IT?
EXACTLY!
DUCK, THAT IS NOT ONLY THE ONLY GOOD IDEA YOU'VE EVER HAD, BUT IT'LL BE ONE OF THE GREATEST PLEASURES OF MY LIFE TO IMPLEMENT IT!
DITTO, I'M SURE!
JUST MAKE SURE YOU STICK TO THE DEAL, DUCK!
DON'T WORRY ABOUT ME, JONES. IGNORING YOU WILL BE A CINCH!

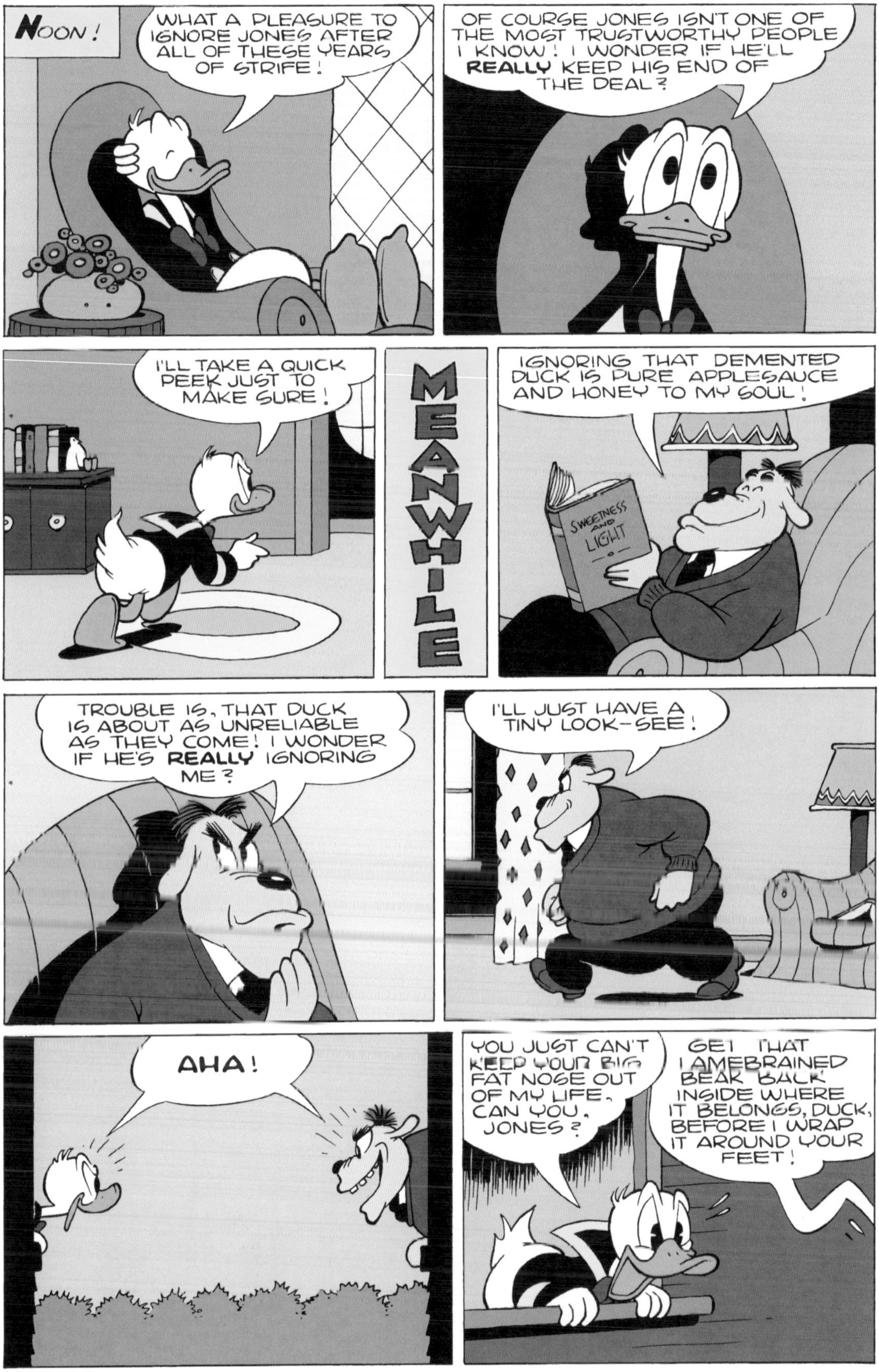
NOON!
WHAT A PLEASURE TO IGNORE JONES AFTER ALL OF THESE YEARS OF STRIFE!
OF COURSE JONES ISN'T ONE OF THE MOST TRUSTWORTHY PEOPLE I KNOW! I WONDER IF HE'LL REALLY KEEP HIS END OF THE DEAL?
I'LL TAKE A QUICK PEEK JUST TO MAKE SURE!
MEANWHILE
IGNORING THAT DEMENTED DUCK IS PURE APPLESAUCE AND HONEY TO MY SOUL!
SWEETNESS AND LIGHT
TROUBLE IS, THAT DUCK IS ABOUT AS UNRELIABLE AS THEY COME! I WONDER IF HE'S REALLY IGNORING ME?
I'LL JUST HAVE A TINY LOOK-SEE!
AHA!
YOU JUST CAN'T KEEP YOUR BIG FAT NOSE OUT OF MY LIFE, CAN YOU, JONES?
GET THAT LAMEBRAINED BEAK BACK INSIDE WHERE IT BELONGS, DUCK, BEFORE I WRAP IT AROUND YOUR FEET!

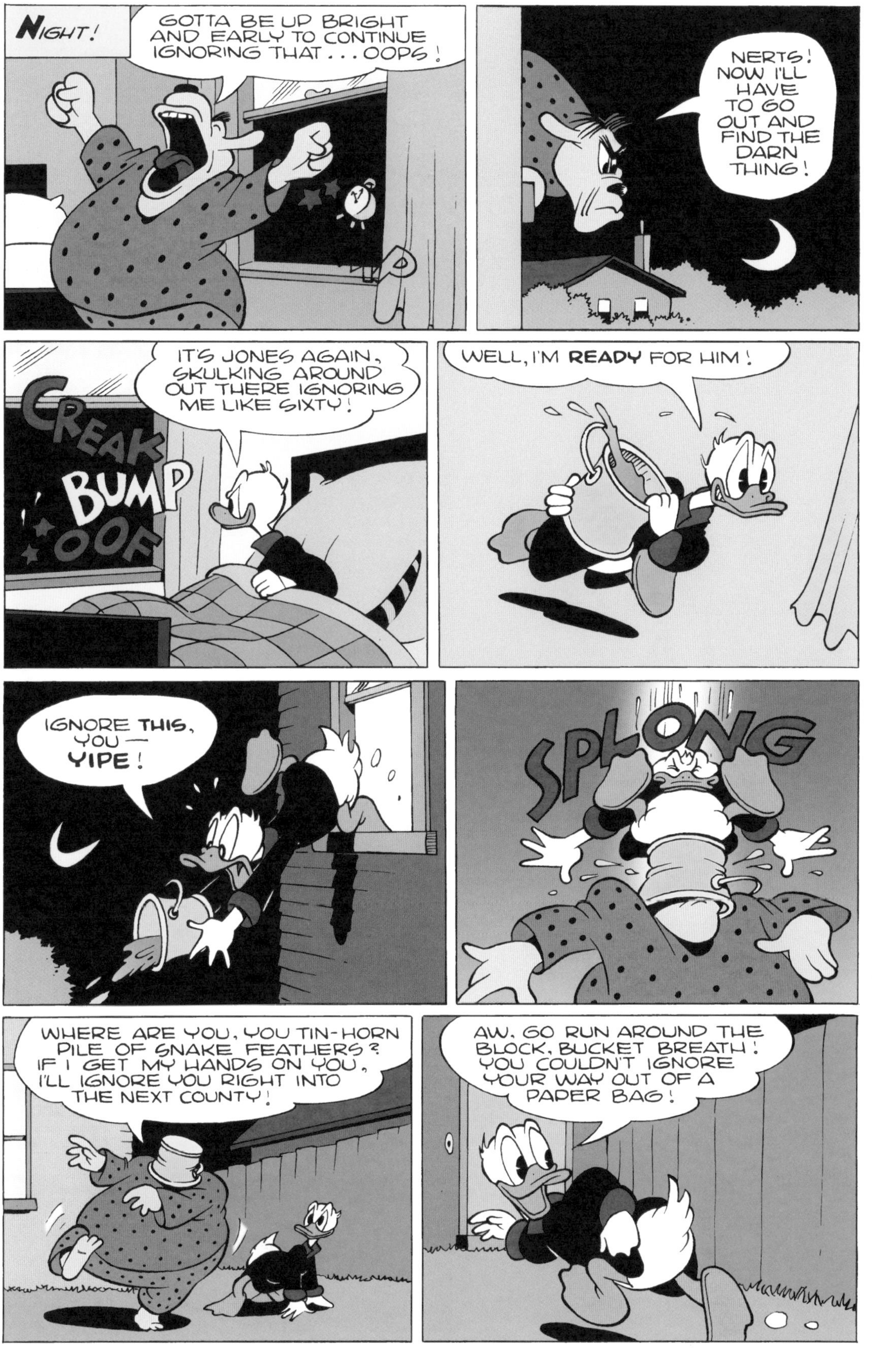
NIGHT!
GOTTA BE UP BRIGHT AND EARLY TO CONTINUE IGNORING THAT . . . OOPS!
NERTS! NOW I'LL HAVE TO GO OUT AND FIND THE DARN THING!
IT'S JONES AGAIN, SKULKING AROUND OUT THERE IGNORING ME LIKE SIXTY!
CREAK
BUMP
OOF
WELL, I'M **READY** FOR HIM!
IGNORE **THIS**, YOU— **YIPE**!
SPLONG
WHERE ARE YOU, YOU TIN-HORN PILE OF SNAKE FEATHERS? IF I GET MY HANDS ON YOU, I'LL IGNORE YOU RIGHT INTO THE NEXT COUNTY!
AW, GO RUN AROUND THE BLOCK, BUCKET BREATH! YOU COULDN'T IGNORE YOUR WAY OUT OF A PAPER BAG!

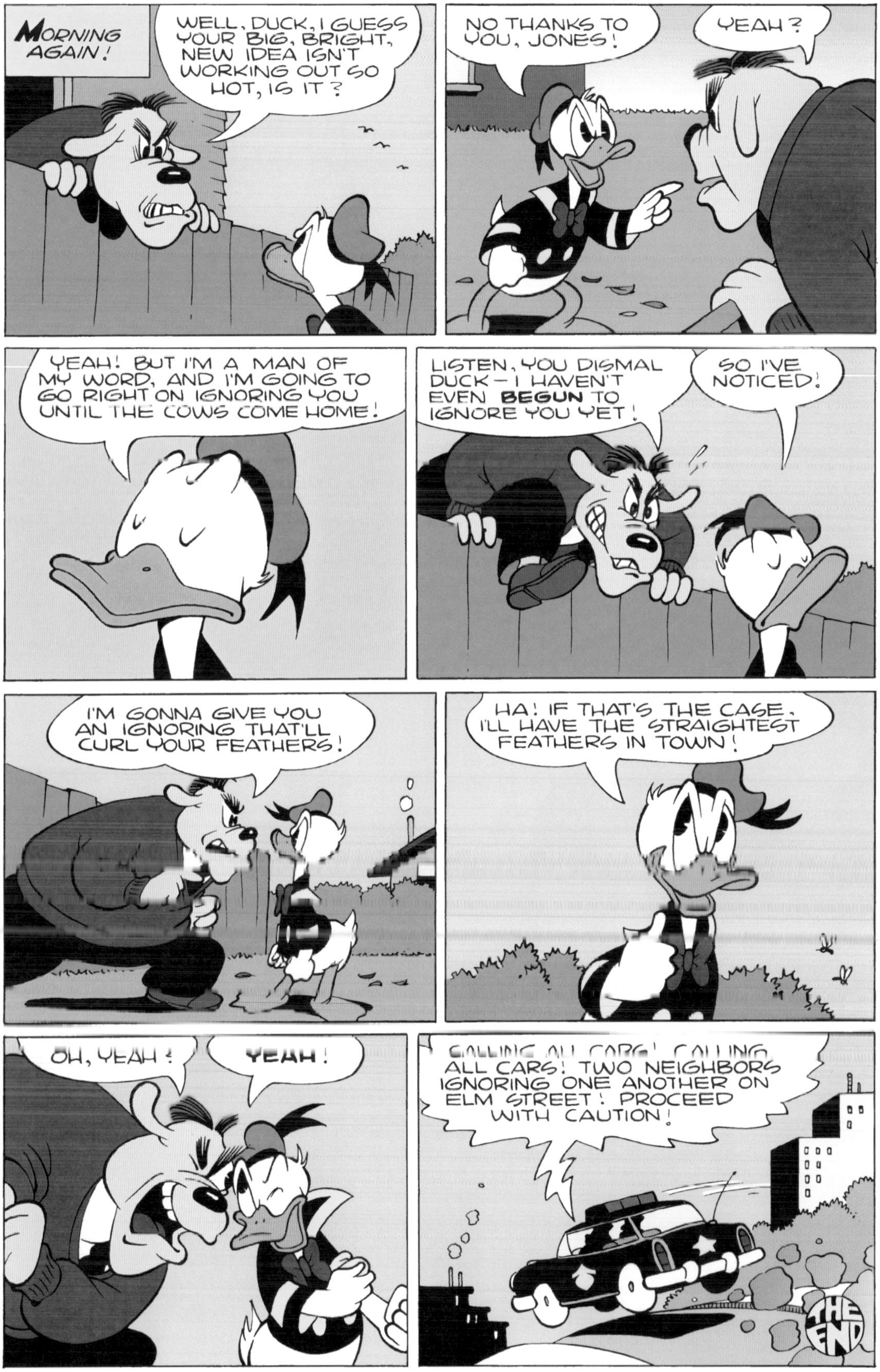
MORNING AGAIN!
WELL, DUCK, I GUESS YOUR BIG, BRIGHT, NEW IDEA ISN'T WORKING OUT SO HOT, IS IT?
NO THANKS TO YOU, JONES!
YEAH?
YEAH! BUT I'M A MAN OF MY WORD, AND I'M GOING TO GO RIGHT ON IGNORING YOU UNTIL THE COWS COME HOME!
LISTEN, YOU DISMAL DUCK — I HAVEN'T EVEN BEGUN TO IGNORE YOU YET!
SO I'VE NOTICED!
I'M GONNA GIVE YOU AN IGNORING THAT'LL CURL YOUR FEATHERS!
HA! IF THAT'S THE CASE, I'LL HAVE THE STRAIGHTEST FEATHERS IN TOWN!
OH, YEAH!
YEAH!
CALLING ALL CARS! CALLING ALL CARS! TWO NEIGHBORS IGNORING ONE ANOTHER ON ELM STREET! PROCEED WITH CAUTION!
THE END

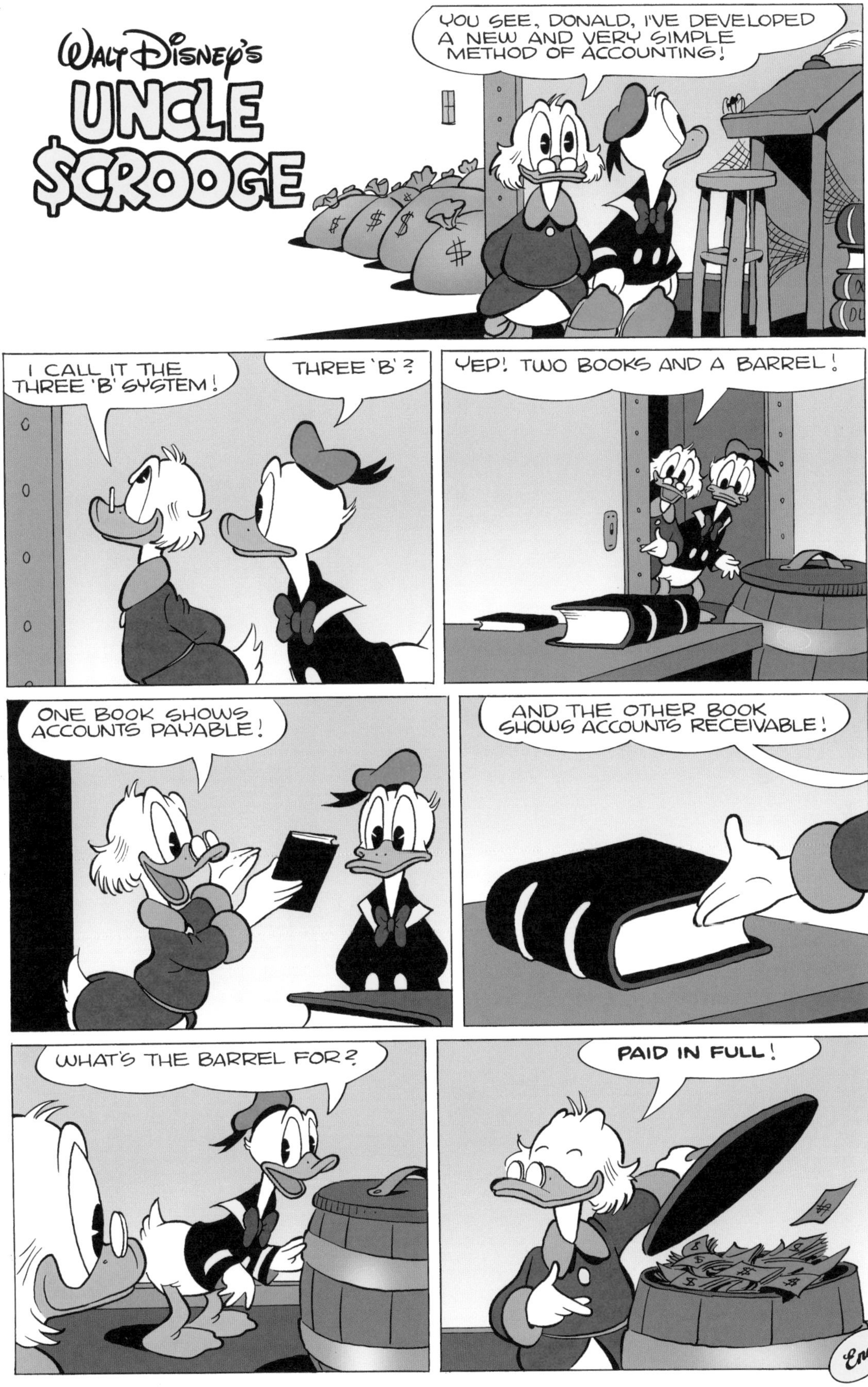
WALT DISNEY'S
UNCLE $CROOGE
YOU SEE, DONALD, I'VE DEVELOPED A NEW AND VERY SIMPLE METHOD OF ACCOUNTING!
I CALL IT THE THREE 'B' SYSTEM!
THREE 'B'?
YEP! TWO BOOKS AND A BARREL!
ONE BOOK SHOWS ACCOUNTS PAYABLE!
AND THE OTHER BOOK SHOWS ACCOUNTS RECEIVABLE!
WHAT'S THE BARREL FOR?
PAID IN FULL!
End

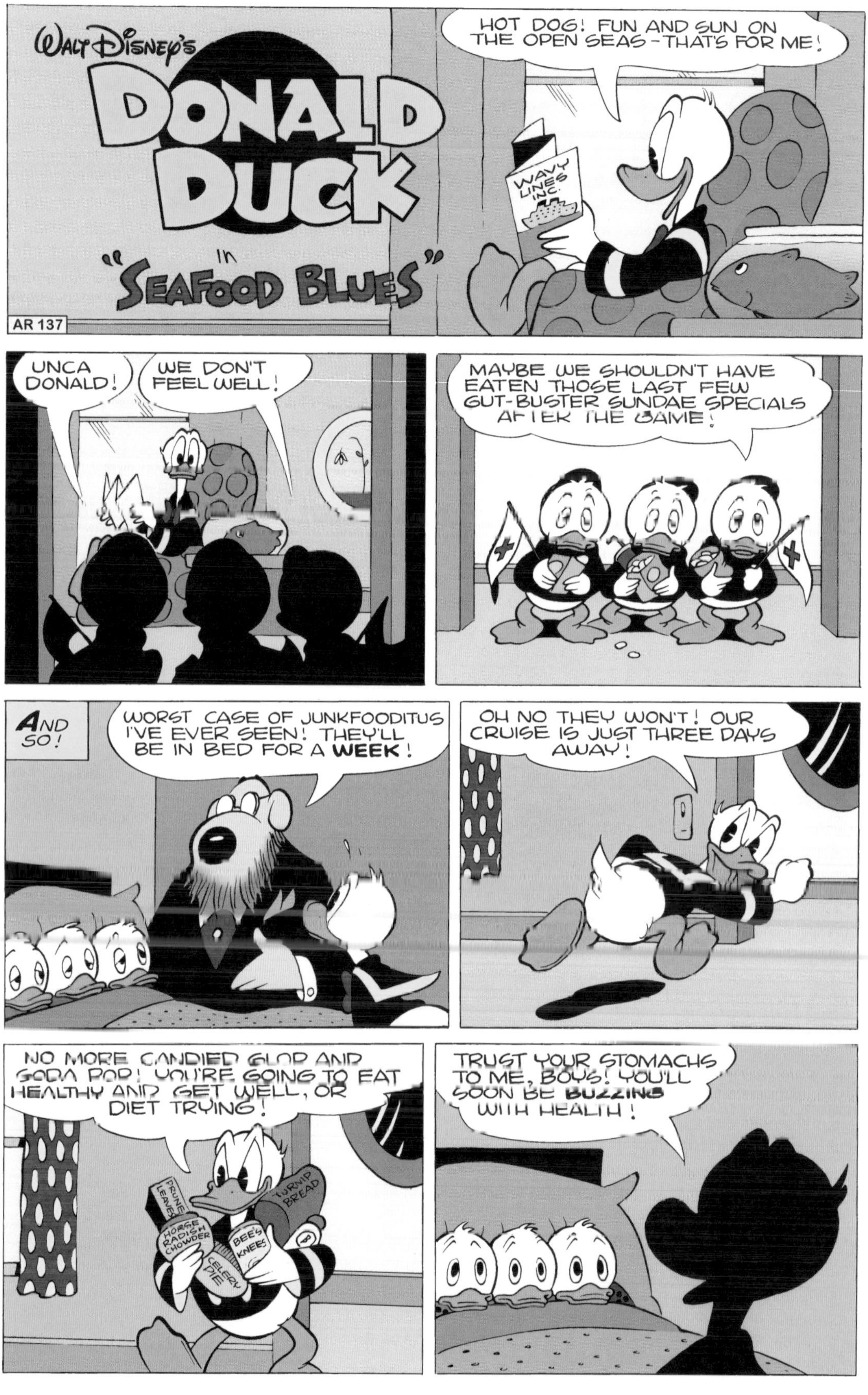
Walt Disney's
DONALD DUCK
in
"SEAFOOD BLUES"
AR 137
HOT DOG! FUN AND SUN ON THE OPEN SEAS - THAT'S FOR ME!
WAVY LINES INC.
UNCA DONALD!
WE DON'T FEEL WELL!
MAYBE WE SHOULDN'T HAVE EATEN THOSE LAST FEW GUT-BUSTER SUNDAE SPECIALS AFTER THE GAME!
AND SO!
WORST CASE OF JUNKFOODITUS I'VE EVER SEEN! THEY'LL BE IN BED FOR A WEEK!
OH NO THEY WON'T! OUR CRUISE IS JUST THREE DAYS AWAY!
NO MORE CANDIED GLOP AND SODA POP! YOU'RE GOING TO EAT HEALTHY AND GET WELL, OR DIET TRYING!
PRUNE LEAVES
TURNIP BREAD
HORSE RADISH CHOWDER
BEE'S KNEES
CELERY PIE
TRUST YOUR STOMACHS TO ME, BOYS! YOU'LL SOON BE BUZZING WITH HEALTH!

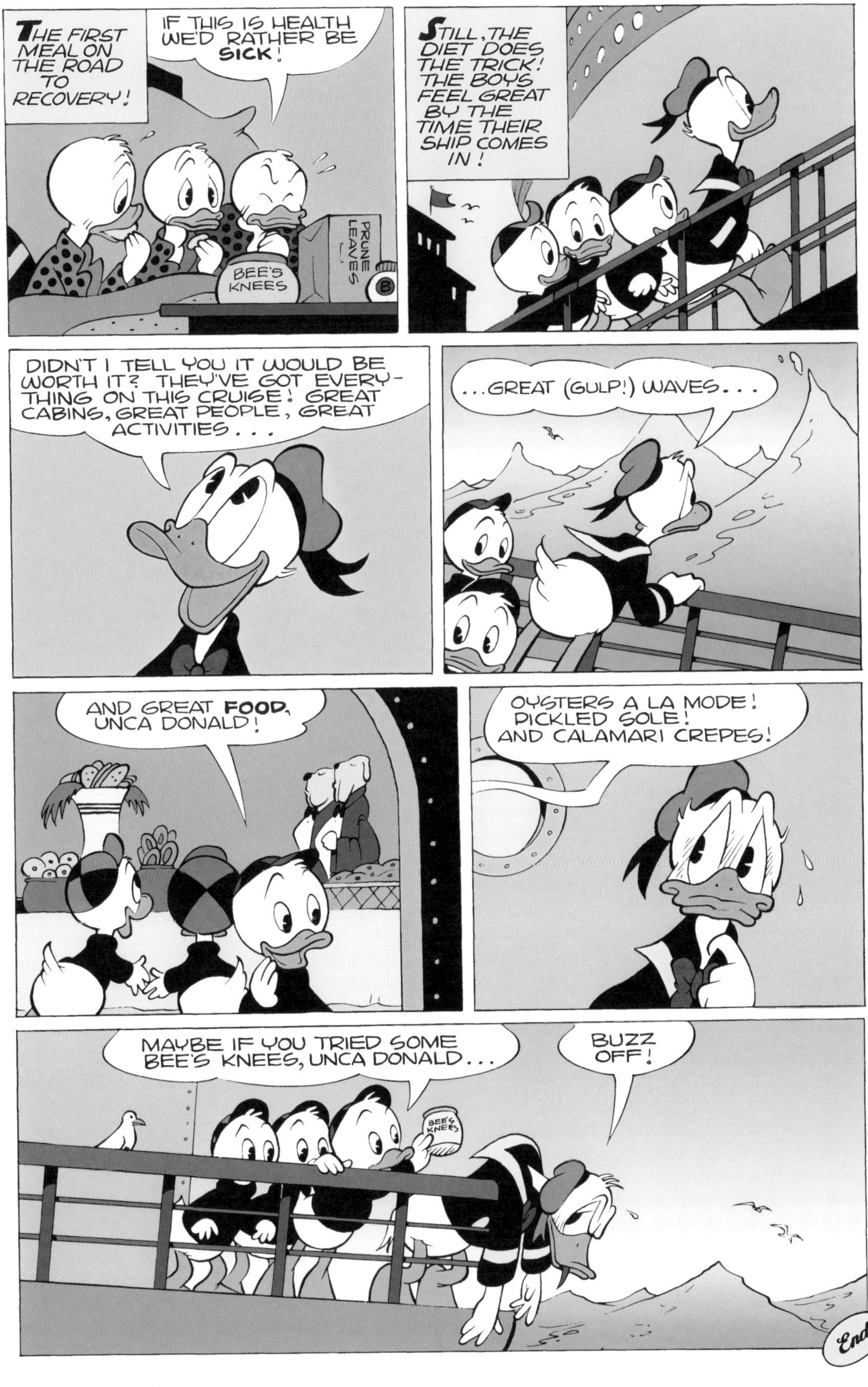
THE FIRST MEAL ON THE ROAD TO RECOVERY!
IF THIS IS HEALTH WE'D RATHER BE SICK!
PRUNE LEAVES
BEE'S KNEES
STILL, THE DIET DOES THE TRICK! THE BOYS FEEL GREAT BY THE TIME THEIR SHIP COMES IN!
DIDN'T I TELL YOU IT WOULD BE WORTH IT? THEY'VE GOT EVERY-THING ON THIS CRUISE! GREAT CABINS, GREAT PEOPLE, GREAT ACTIVITIES . . .
. . . GREAT (GULP!) WAVES . . .
AND GREAT FOOD, UNCA DONALD!
OYSTERS A LA MODE! PICKLED SOLE! AND CALAMARI CREPES!
MAYBE IF YOU TRIED SOME BEE'S KNEES, UNCA DONALD . . .
BEE'S KNEES
BUZZ OFF!
End

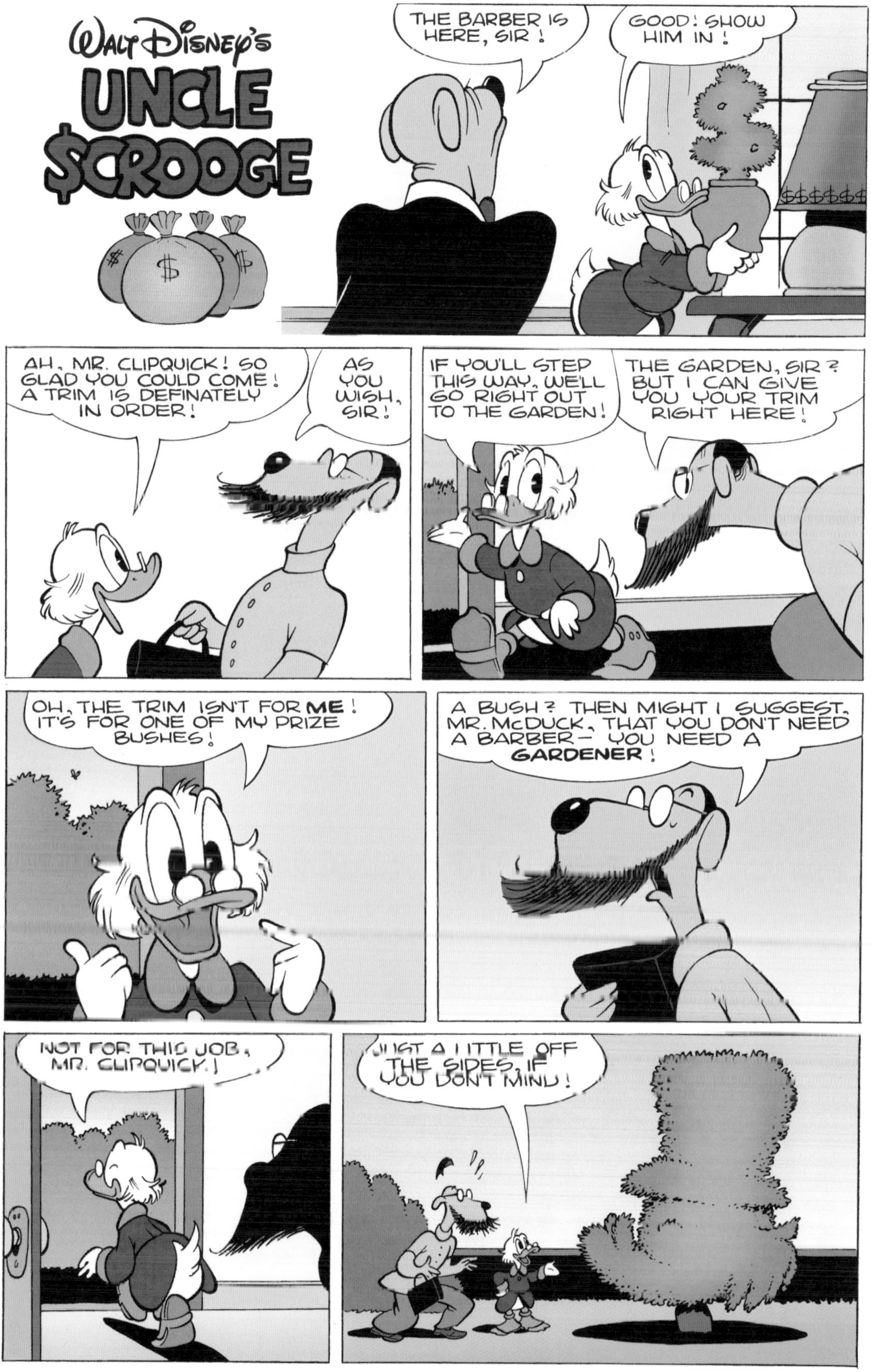
WALT DISNEY'S
UNCLE $CROOGE
THE BARBER IS HERE, SIR!
GOOD! SHOW HIM IN!
AH, MR. CLIPQUICK! SO GLAD YOU COULD COME! A TRIM IS DEFINATELY IN ORDER!
AS YOU WISH, SIR!
IF YOU'LL STEP THIS WAY, WE'LL GO RIGHT OUT TO THE GARDEN!
THE GARDEN, SIR? BUT I CAN GIVE YOU YOUR TRIM RIGHT HERE!
OH, THE TRIM ISN'T FOR ME! IT'S FOR ONE OF MY PRIZE BUSHES!
A BUSH? THEN MIGHT I SUGGEST, MR. McDUCK, THAT YOU DON'T NEED A BARBER— YOU NEED A GARDENER!
NOT FOR THIS JOB, MR. CLIPQUICK!
JUST A LITTLE OFF THE SIDES, IF YOU DON'T MIND!

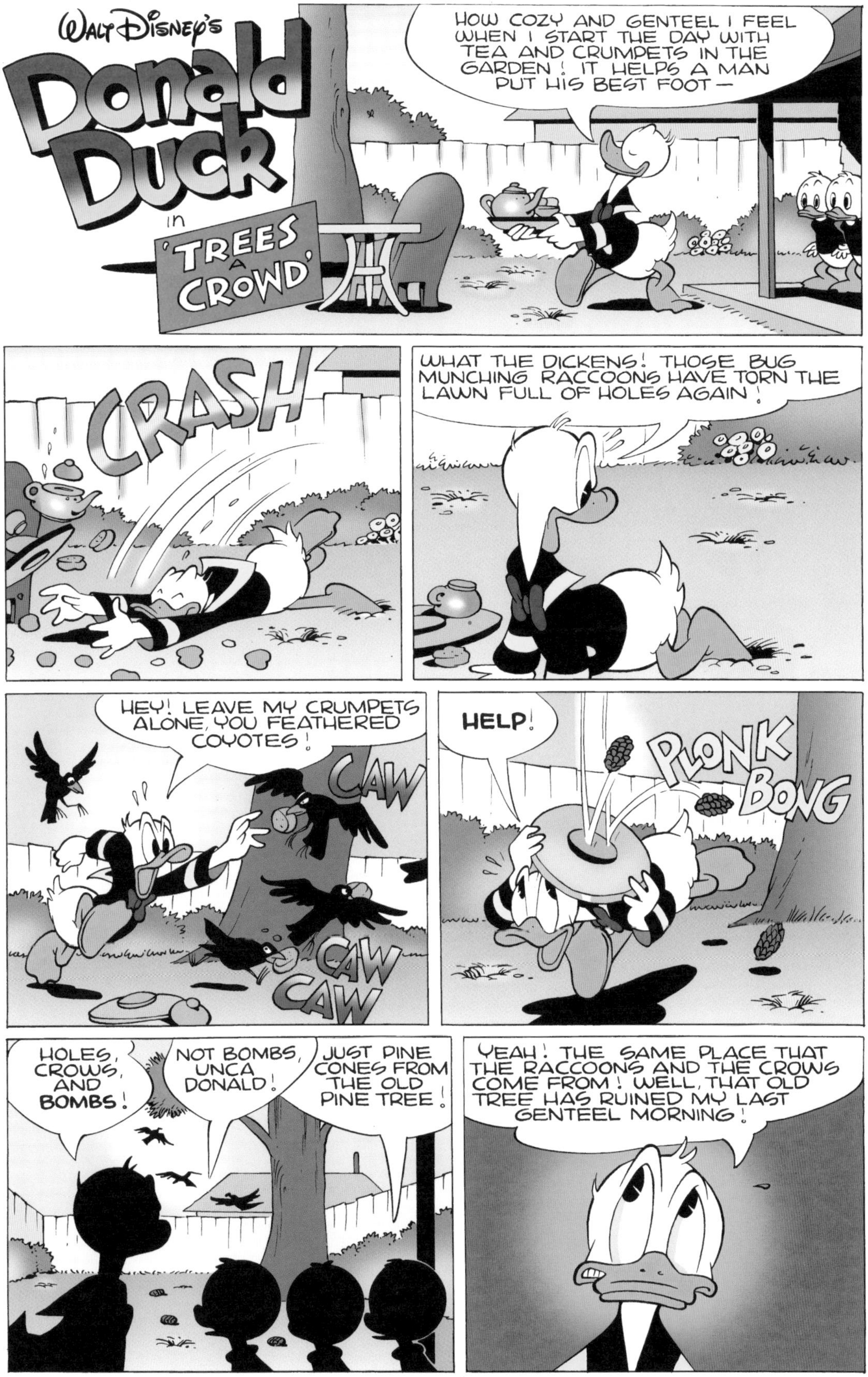
WALT DISNEY'S
Donald Duck
in
'TREES A CROWD'
HOW COZY AND GENTEEL I FEEL WHEN I START THE DAY WITH TEA AND CRUMPETS IN THE GARDEN! IT HELPS A MAN PUT HIS BEST FOOT—
CRASH
WHAT THE DICKENS! THOSE BUG MUNCHING RACCOONS HAVE TORN THE LAWN FULL OF HOLES AGAIN!
HEY! LEAVE MY CRUMPETS ALONE, YOU FEATHERED COYOTES!
CAW
CAW CAW
HELP!
PLONK
BONG
HOLES, CROWS, AND BOMBS!
NOT BOMBS, UNCA DONALD!
JUST PINE CONES FROM THE OLD PINE TREE!
YEAH! THE SAME PLACE THAT THE RACCOONS AND THE CROWS COME FROM! WELL, THAT OLD TREE HAS RUINED MY LAST GENTEEL MORNING!

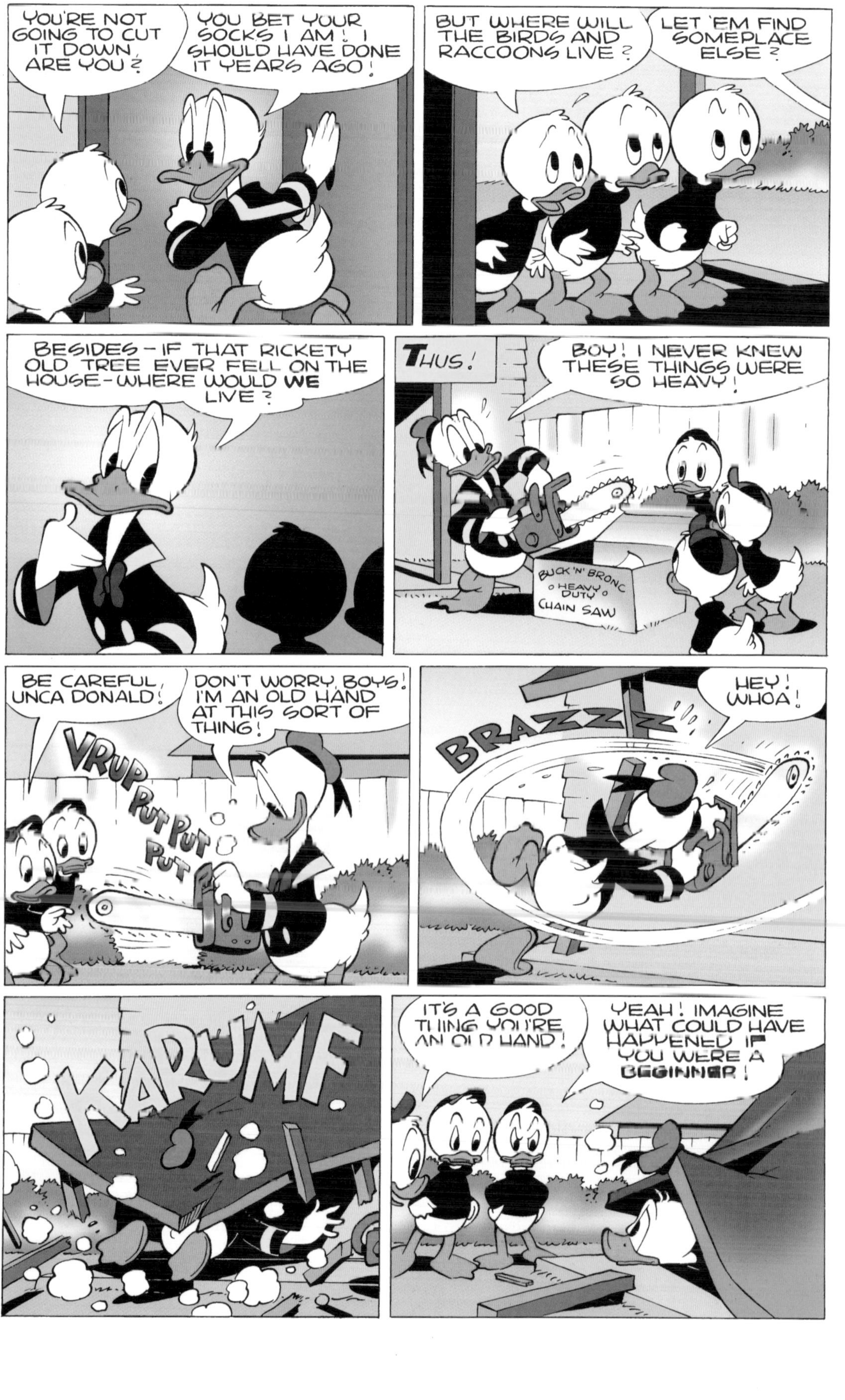
YOU'RE NOT GOING TO CUT IT DOWN, ARE YOU?
YOU BET YOUR SOCKS I AM! I SHOULD HAVE DONE IT YEARS AGO!
BUT WHERE WILL THE BIRDS AND RACCOONS LIVE?
LET 'EM FIND SOMEPLACE ELSE!
BESIDES-IF THAT RICKETY OLD TREE EVER FELL ON THE HOUSE-WHERE WOULD WE LIVE?
THUS!
BOY! I NEVER KNEW THESE THINGS WERE SO HEAVY!
BUCK 'N' BRONC HEAVY DUTY CHAIN SAW
BE CAREFUL, UNCA DONALD!
DON'T WORRY, BOYS! I'M AN OLD HAND AT THIS SORT OF THING!
VRUP PUT PUT PUT
BRAZZZZ
HEY! WHOA!
KARUMF
IT'S A GOOD THING YOU'RE AN OLD HAND!
YEAH! IMAGINE WHAT COULD HAVE HAPPENED IF YOU WERE A BEGINNER!

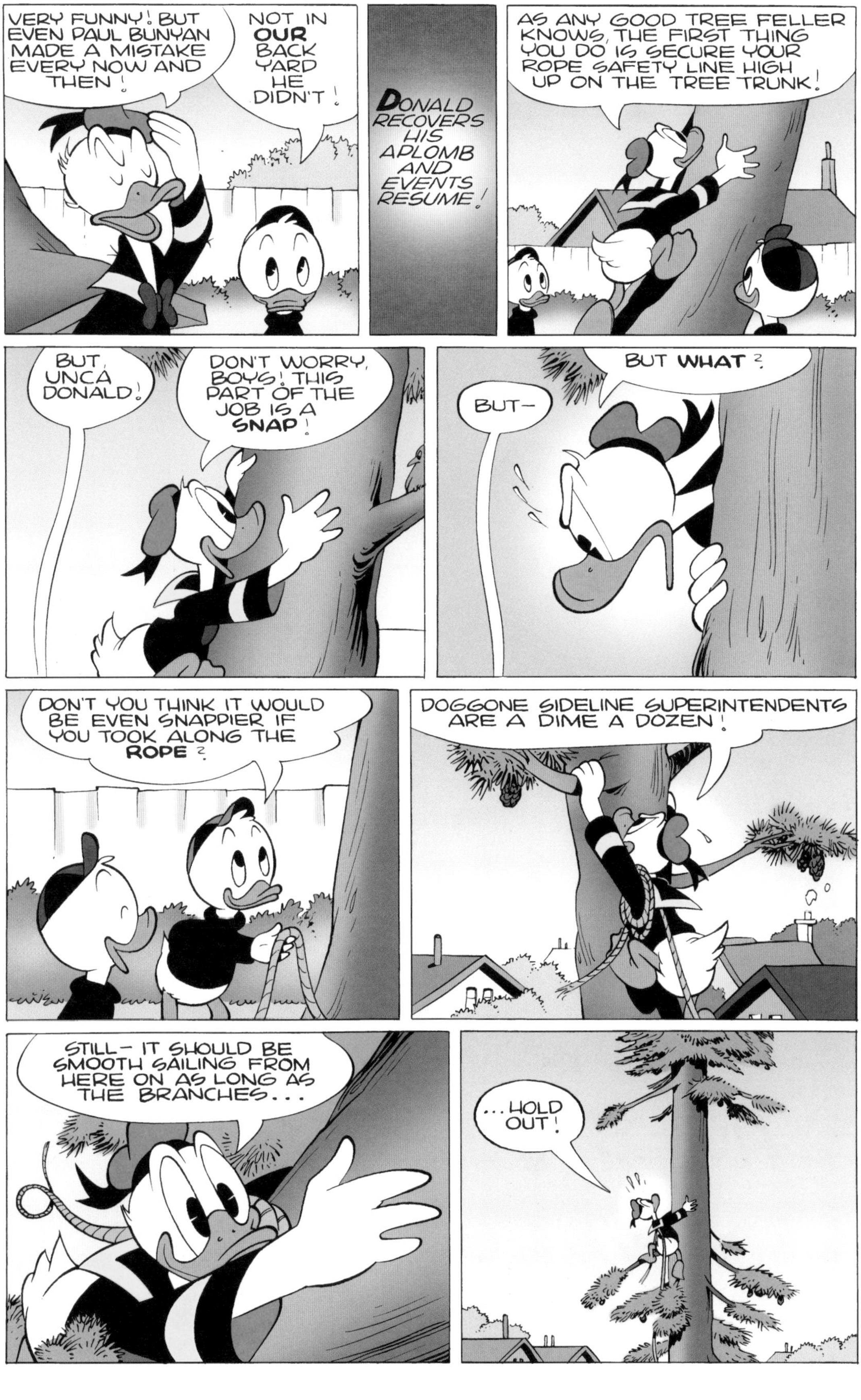
VERY FUNNY! BUT EVEN PAUL BUNYAN MADE A MISTAKE EVERY NOW AND THEN!
NOT IN **OUR** BACK YARD HE DIDN'T!
DONALD RECOVERS HIS APLOMB AND EVENTS RESUME!
AS ANY GOOD TREE FELLER KNOWS, THE FIRST THING YOU DO IS SECURE YOUR ROPE SAFETY LINE HIGH UP ON THE TREE TRUNK!
BUT, UNCA DONALD!
DON'T WORRY, BOYS! THIS PART OF THE JOB IS A **SNAP**!
BUT–
BUT **WHAT**?
DON'T YOU THINK IT WOULD BE EVEN SNAPPIER IF YOU TOOK ALONG THE **ROPE**?
DOGGONE SIDELINE SUPERINTENDENTS ARE A DIME A DOZEN!
STILL– IT SHOULD BE SMOOTH SAILING FROM HERE ON AS LONG AS THE BRANCHES...
...HOLD OUT!

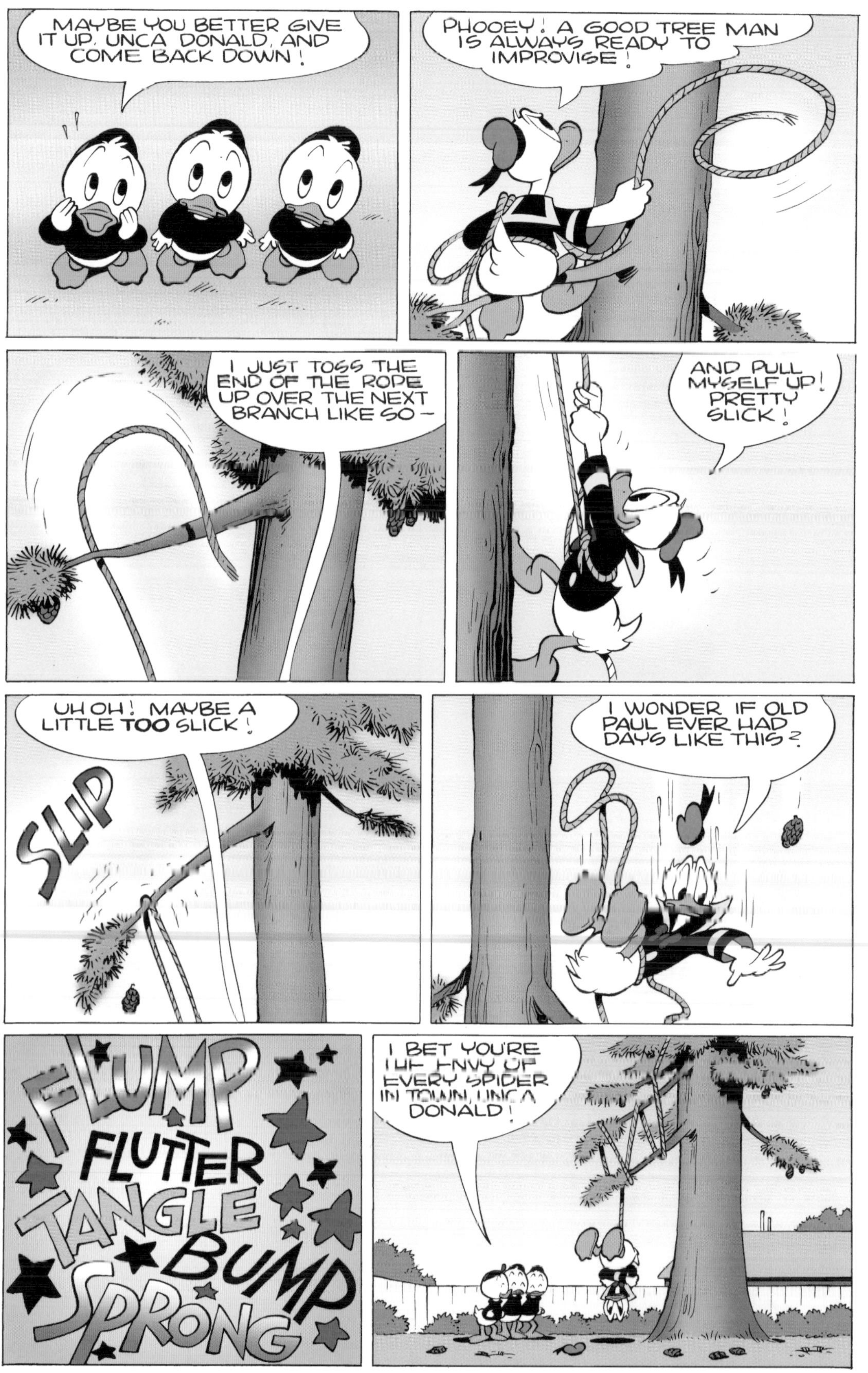
MAYBE YOU BETTER GIVE IT UP, UNCA DONALD, AND COME BACK DOWN!
PHOOEY! A GOOD TREE MAN IS ALWAYS READY TO IMPROVISE!
I JUST TOSS THE END OF THE ROPE UP OVER THE NEXT BRANCH LIKE SO —
AND PULL MYSELF UP! PRETTY SLICK!
UH OH! MAYBE A LITTLE TOO SLICK!
SLIP
I WONDER IF OLD PAUL EVER HAD DAYS LIKE THIS?
FLUMP
FLUTTER
TANGLE
BUMP
SPRONG
I BET YOU'RE THE ENVY OF EVERY SPIDER IN TOWN, UNCA DONALD!

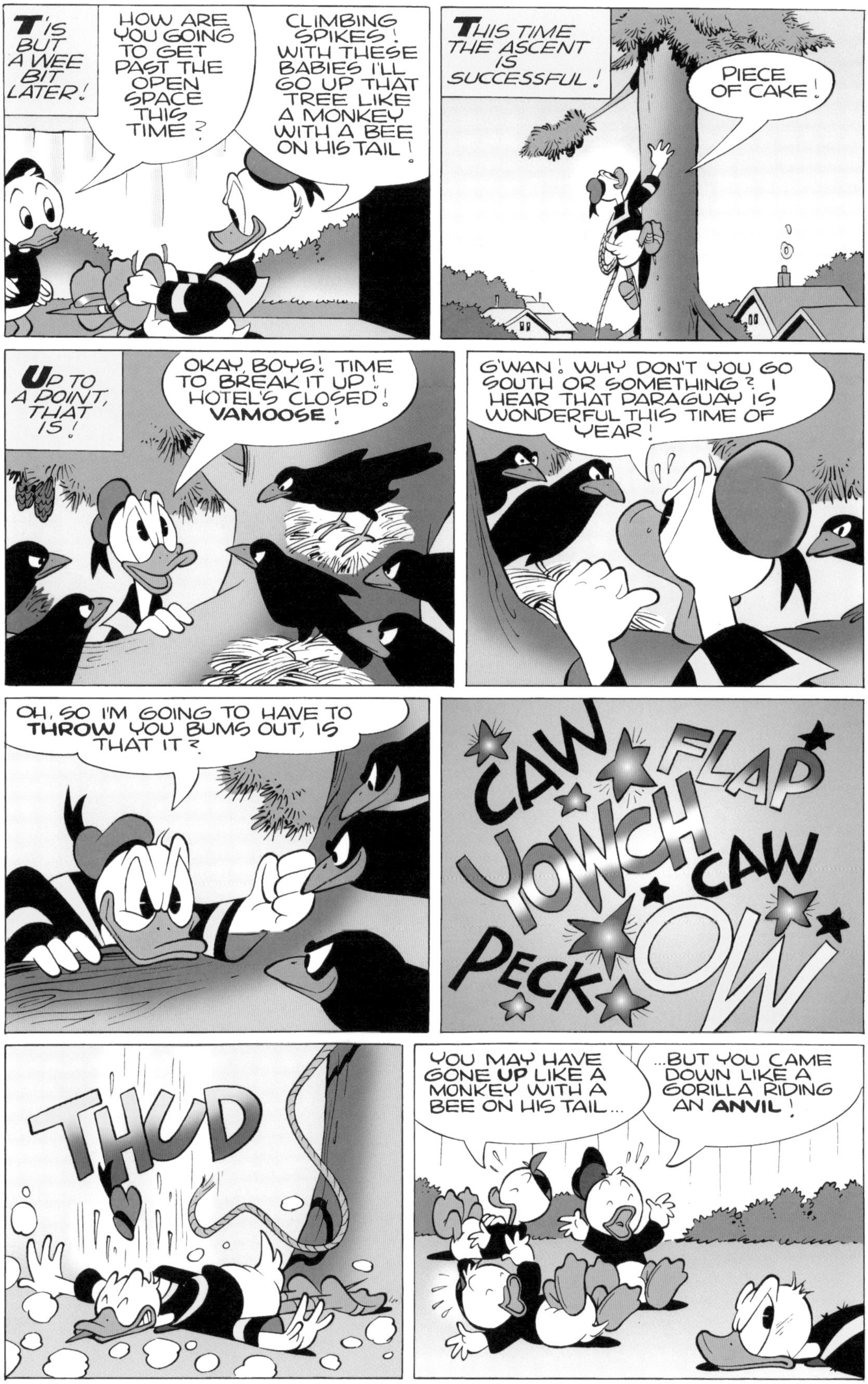
'TIS BUT A WEE BIT LATER!
HOW ARE YOU GOING TO GET PAST THE OPEN SPACE THIS TIME?
CLIMBING SPIKES! WITH THESE BABIES I'LL GO UP THAT TREE LIKE A MONKEY WITH A BEE ON HIS TAIL!
THIS TIME THE ASCENT IS SUCCESSFUL!
PIECE OF CAKE!
UP TO A POINT, THAT IS!
OKAY, BOYS! TIME TO BREAK IT UP! HOTEL'S CLOSED! VAMOOSE!
G'WAN! WHY DON'T YOU GO SOUTH OR SOMETHING? I HEAR THAT PARAGUAY IS WONDERFUL THIS TIME OF YEAR!
OH, SO I'M GOING TO HAVE TO THROW YOU BUMS OUT, IS THAT IT?
CAW
FLAP
YOWCH
CAW
PECK
OW
THUD
YOU MAY HAVE GONE UP LIKE A MONKEY WITH A BEE ON HIS TAIL...
...BUT YOU CAME DOWN LIKE A GORILLA RIDING AN ANVIL!

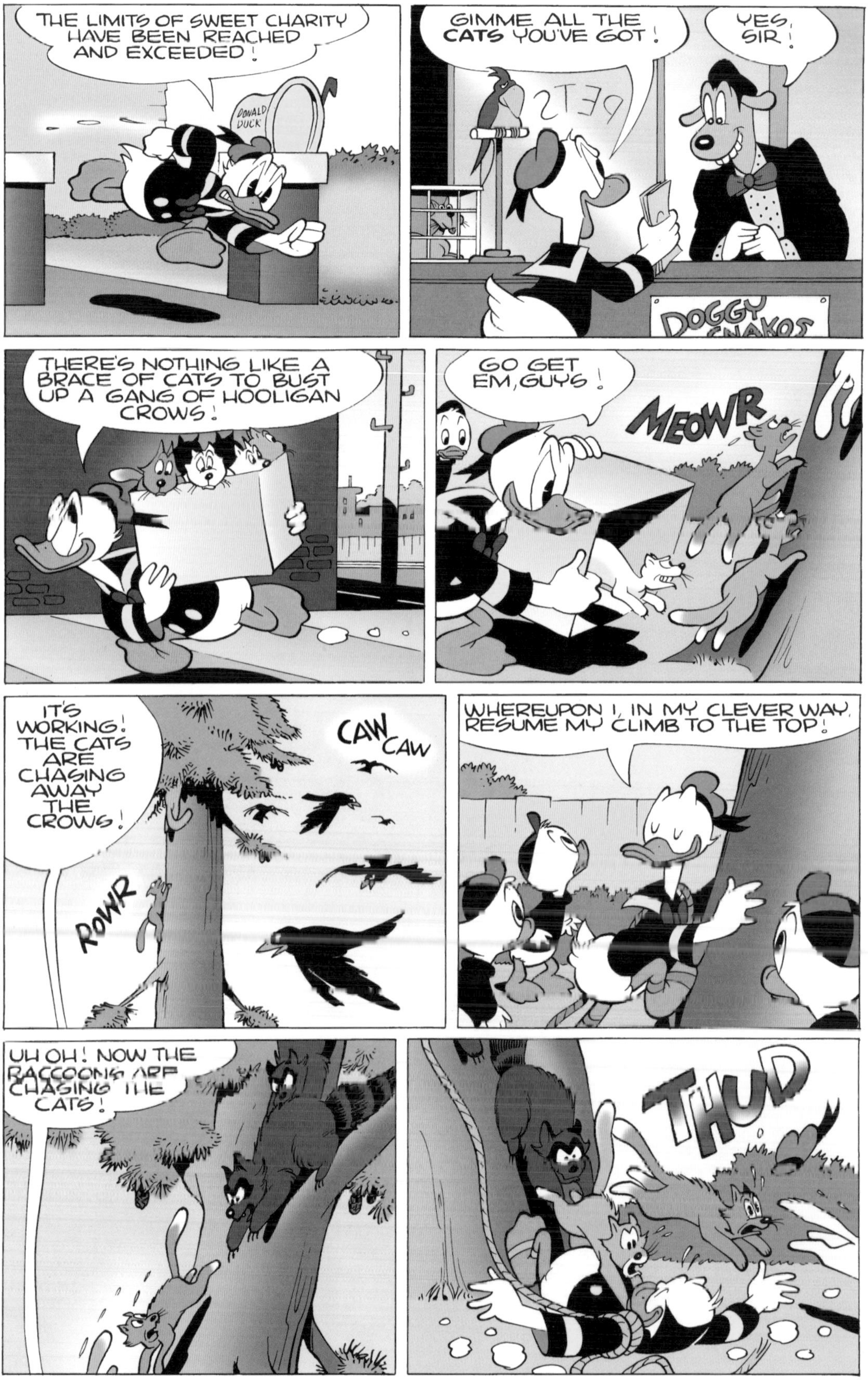
THE LIMITS OF SWEET CHARITY HAVE BEEN REACHED AND EXCEEDED!
DONALD DUCK
GIMME ALL THE CATS YOU'VE GOT!
YES, SIR!
DOGGY
THERE'S NOTHING LIKE A BRACE OF CATS TO BUST UP A GANG OF HOOLIGAN CROWS!
GO GET EM, GUYS!
MEOWR
IT'S WORKING! THE CATS ARE CHASING AWAY THE CROWS!
CAW CAW
ROWR
WHEREUPON I, IN MY CLEVER WAY, RESUME MY CLIMB TO THE TOP!
UH OH! NOW THE RACCOONS ARE CHASING THE CATS!
THUD

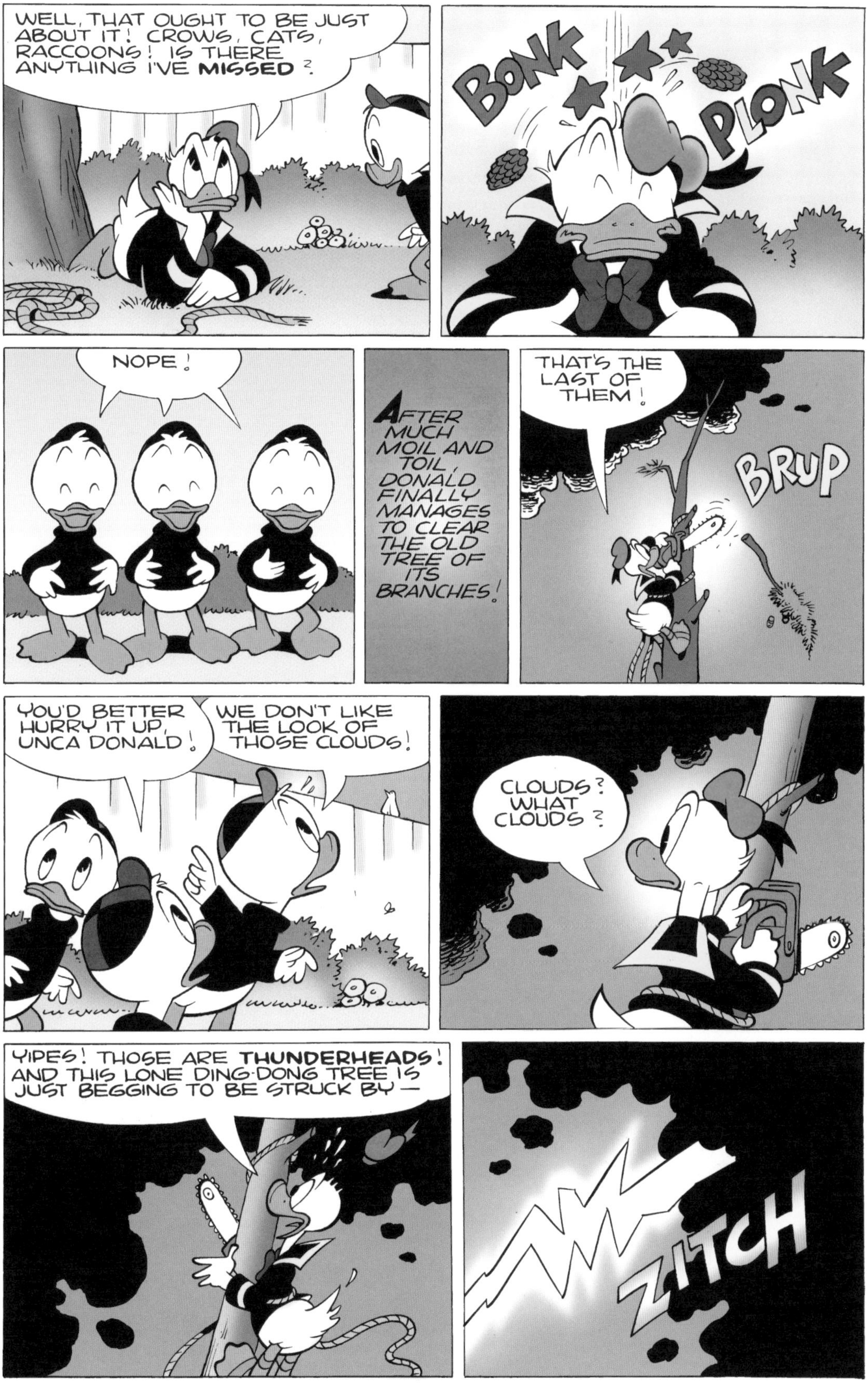
WELL, THAT OUGHT TO BE JUST ABOUT IT! CROWS, CATS, RACCOONS! IS THERE ANYTHING I'VE **MISSED**?
BONK
PLONK
NOPE!
AFTER MUCH MOIL AND TOIL, DONALD FINALLY MANAGES TO CLEAR THE OLD TREE OF ITS BRANCHES!
THAT'S THE LAST OF THEM!
BRUP
YOU'D BETTER HURRY IT UP, UNCA DONALD!
WE DON'T LIKE THE LOOK OF THOSE CLOUDS!
CLOUDS? WHAT CLOUDS?
YIPES! THOSE ARE **THUNDERHEADS**! AND THIS LONE DING-DONG TREE IS JUST BEGGING TO BE STRUCK BY—
ZITCH

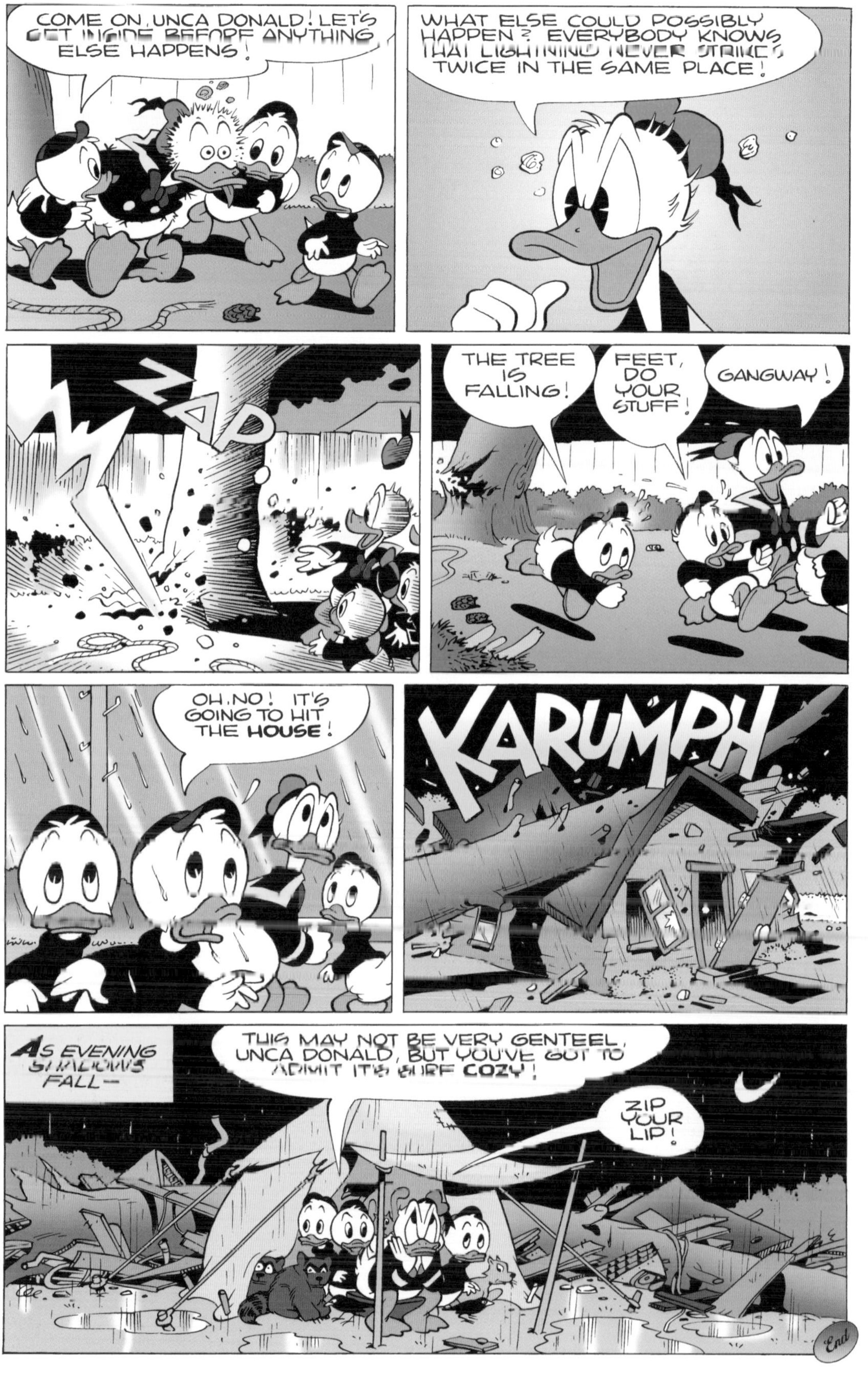

COME ON, UNCA DONALD! LET'S GET INSIDE BEFORE ANYTHING ELSE HAPPENS!
WHAT ELSE COULD POSSIBLY HAPPEN? EVERYBODY KNOWS THAT LIGHTNING NEVER STRIKES TWICE IN THE SAME PLACE!
ZAP
THE TREE IS FALLING!
FEET, DO YOUR STUFF!
GANGWAY!
OH, NO! IT'S GOING TO HIT THE **HOUSE**!
KARUMPH
AS EVENING SHADOWS FALL—
THIS MAY NOT BE VERY GENTEEL, UNCA DONALD, BUT YOU'VE GOT TO ADMIT IT'S SURE **COZY**!
ZIP YOUR LIP!
End

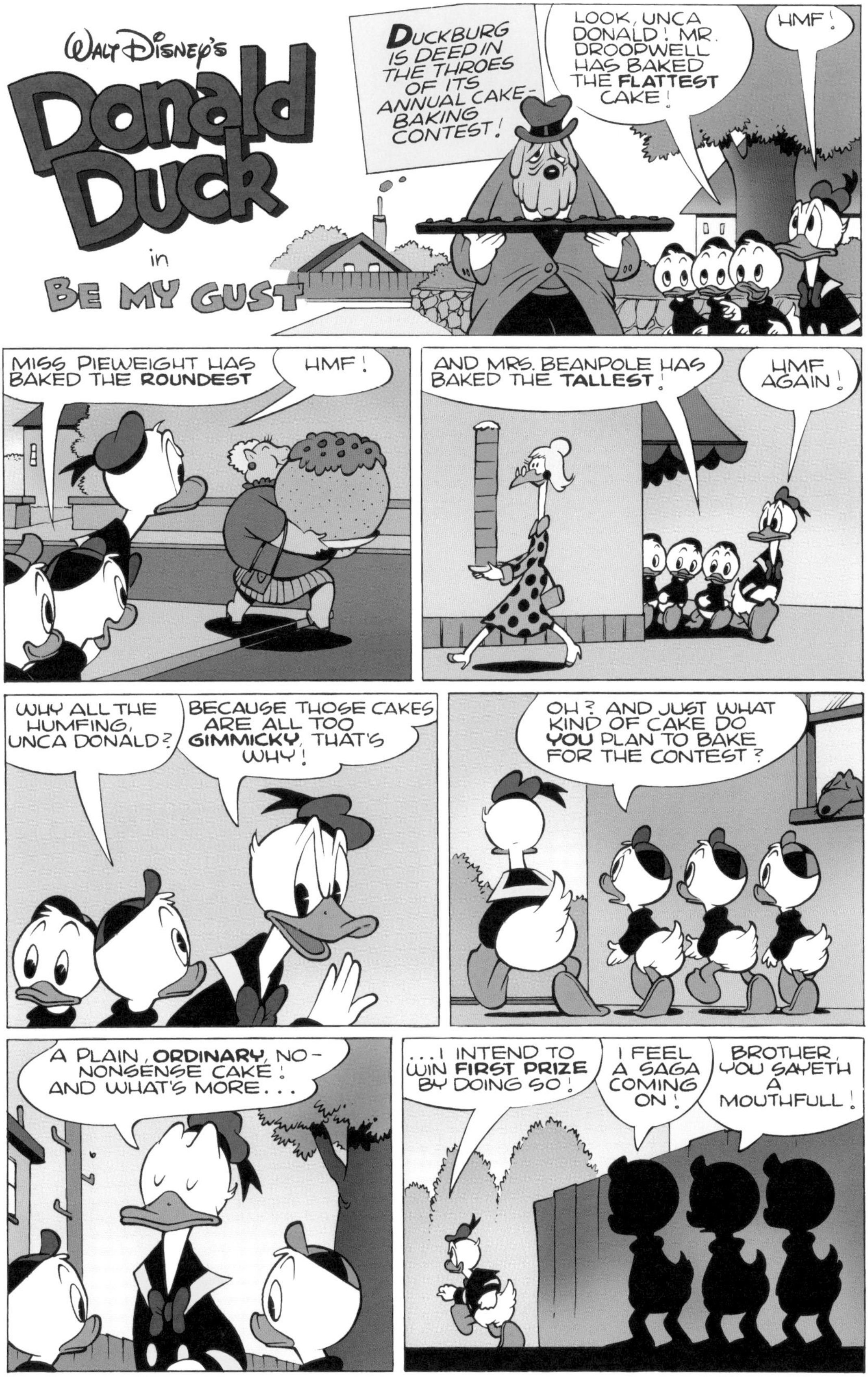
Walt Disney's
Donald Duck
in
BE MY GUST
DUCKBURG IS DEEP IN THE THROES OF ITS ANNUAL CAKE-BAKING CONTEST!
LOOK, UNCA DONALD! MR. DROOPWELL HAS BAKED THE **FLATTEST** CAKE!
HMF!
MISS PIEWEIGHT HAS BAKED THE **ROUNDEST**
HMF!
AND MRS. BEANPOLE HAS BAKED THE **TALLEST**!
HMF AGAIN!
WHY ALL THE HUMFING, UNCA DONALD?
BECAUSE THOSE CAKES ARE ALL TOO **GIMMICKY**, THAT'S WHY!
OH? AND JUST WHAT KIND OF CAKE DO **YOU** PLAN TO BAKE FOR THE CONTEST?
A PLAIN, **ORDINARY**, NO-NONSENSE CAKE! AND WHAT'S MORE...
...I INTEND TO WIN **FIRST PRIZE** BY DOING SO!
I FEEL A SAGA COMING ON!
BROTHER, YOU SAYETH A MOUTHFULL!

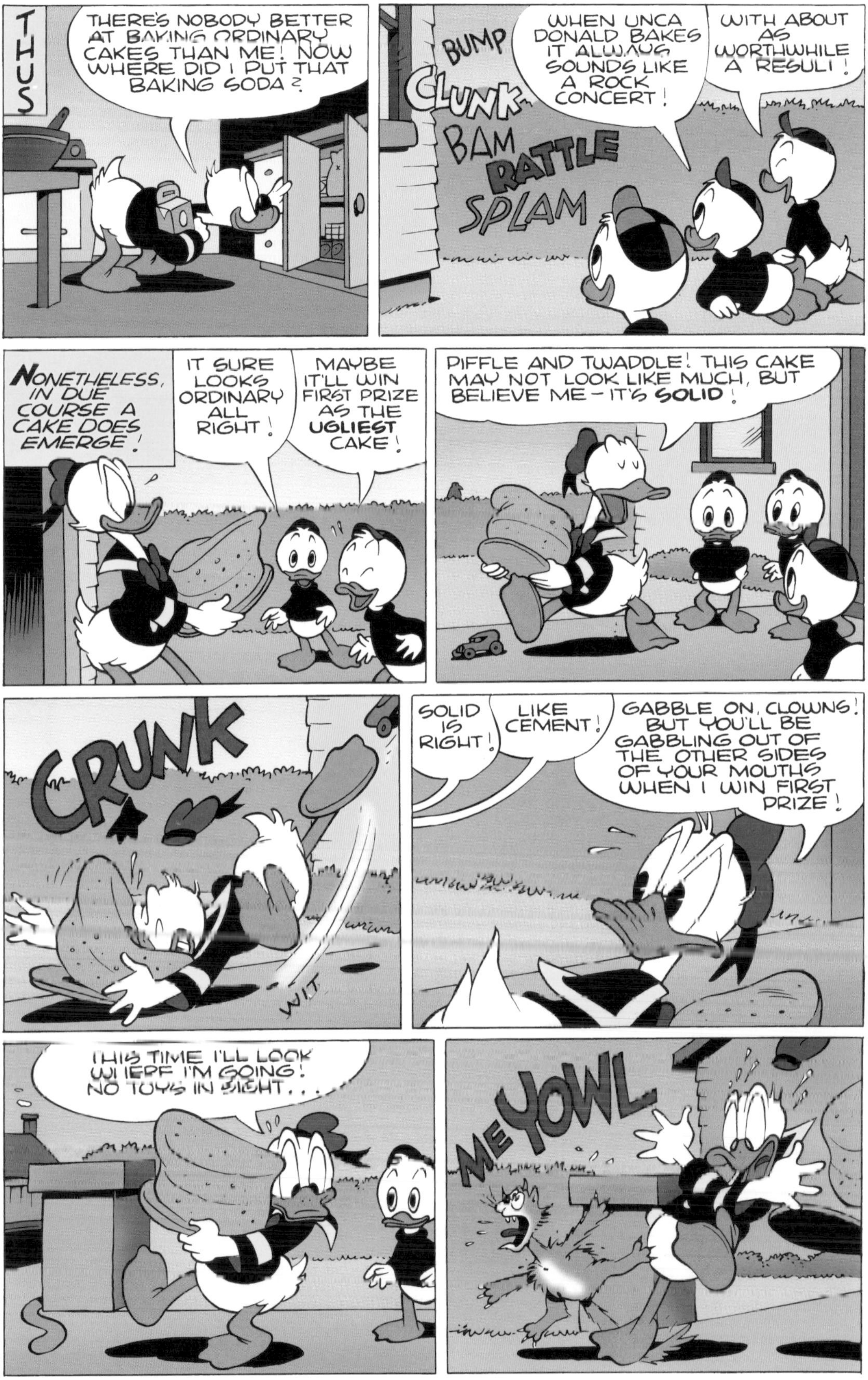
THUS
THERE'S NOBODY BETTER AT BAKING ORDINARY CAKES THAN ME! NOW WHERE DID I PUT THAT BAKING SODA?
BUMP
CLUNK
BAM
RATTLE
SPLAM
WHEN UNCA DONALD BAKES IT ALWAYS SOUNDS LIKE A ROCK CONCERT!
WITH ABOUT AS WORTHWHILE A RESULT!
NONETHELESS, IN DUE COURSE A CAKE DOES EMERGE!
IT SURE LOOKS ORDINARY ALL RIGHT!
MAYBE IT'LL WIN FIRST PRIZE AS THE UGLIEST CAKE!
PIFFLE AND TWADDLE! THIS CAKE MAY NOT LOOK LIKE MUCH, BUT BELIEVE ME—IT'S SOLID!
CRUNK
WIT
SOLID IS RIGHT!
LIKE CEMENT!
GABBLE ON, CLOWNS! BUT YOU'LL BE GABBLING OUT OF THE OTHER SIDES OF YOUR MOUTHS WHEN I WIN FIRST PRIZE!
THIS TIME I'LL LOOK WHERE I'M GOING! NO TOYS IN SIGHT...
MEYOWL

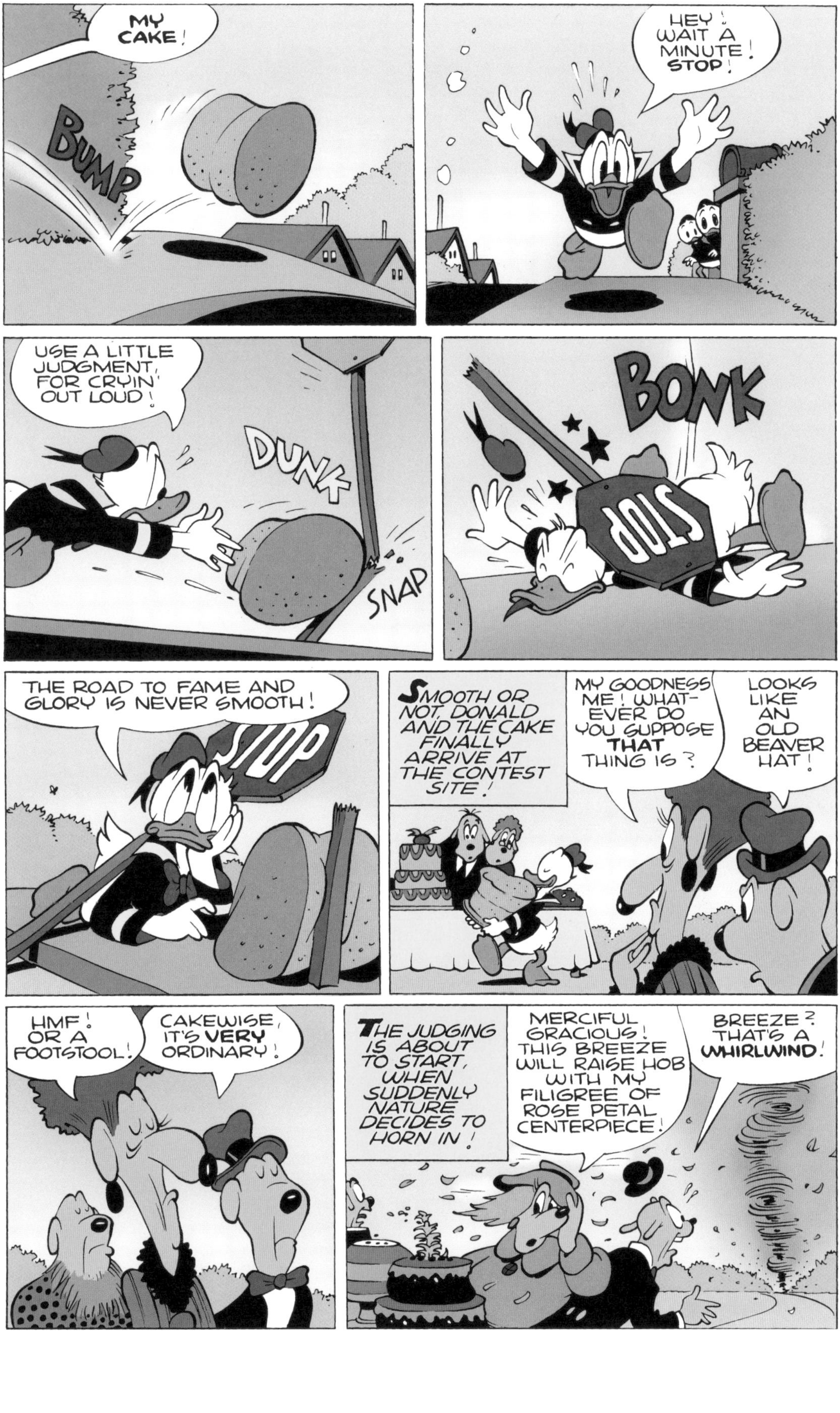

MY CAKE!
BUMP
HEY! WAIT A MINUTE! STOP!
USE A LITTLE JUDGMENT, FOR CRYIN' OUT LOUD!
DUNK
SNAP
BONK
STOP
THE ROAD TO FAME AND GLORY IS NEVER SMOOTH!
STOP
SMOOTH OR NOT, DONALD AND THE CAKE FINALLY ARRIVE AT THE CONTEST SITE!
MY GOODNESS ME! WHATEVER DO YOU SUPPOSE THAT THING IS?
LOOKS LIKE AN OLD BEAVER HAT!
HMF! OR A FOOTSTOOL!
CAKEWISE, IT'S VERY ORDINARY!
THE JUDGING IS ABOUT TO START, WHEN SUDDENLY NATURE DECIDES TO HORN IN!
MERCIFUL GRACIOUS! THIS BREEZE WILL RAISE HOB WITH MY FILIGREE OF ROSE PETAL CENTERPIECE!
BREEZE? THAT'S A WHIRLWIND!

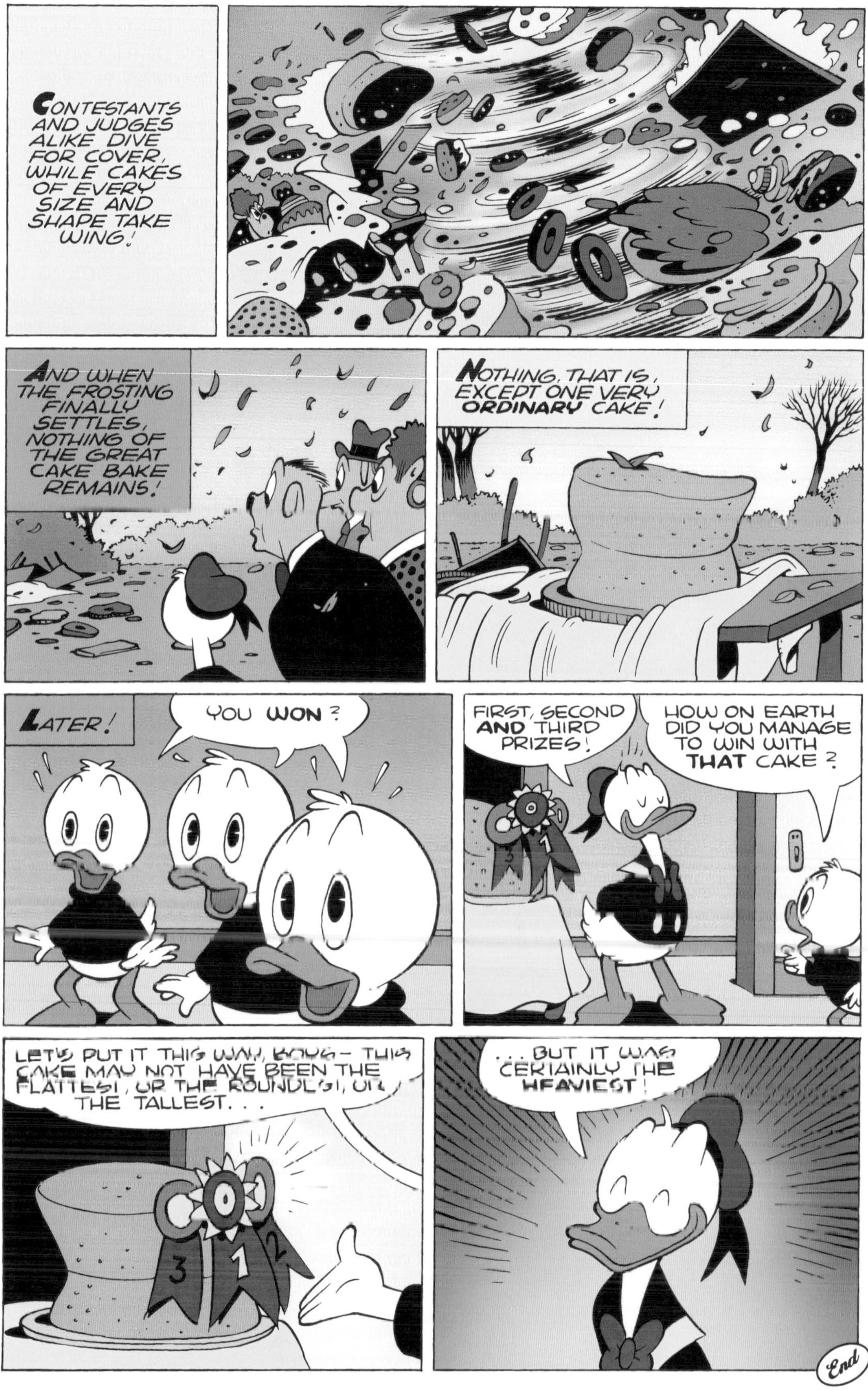

CONTESTANTS AND JUDGES ALIKE DIVE FOR COVER, WHILE CAKES OF EVERY SIZE AND SHAPE TAKE WING!
AND WHEN THE FROSTING FINALLY SETTLES, NOTHING OF THE GREAT CAKE BAKE REMAINS!
NOTHING, THAT IS, EXCEPT ONE VERY ORDINARY CAKE!
LATER!
YOU WON?
FIRST, SECOND AND THIRD PRIZES!
HOW ON EARTH DID YOU MANAGE TO WIN WITH THAT CAKE?
LET'S PUT IT THIS WAY, BOYS— THIS CAKE MAY NOT HAVE BEEN THE FLATTEST, OR THE ROUNDEST, OR THE TALLEST. . .
. . . BUT IT WAS CERTAINLY THE HEAVIEST!
End

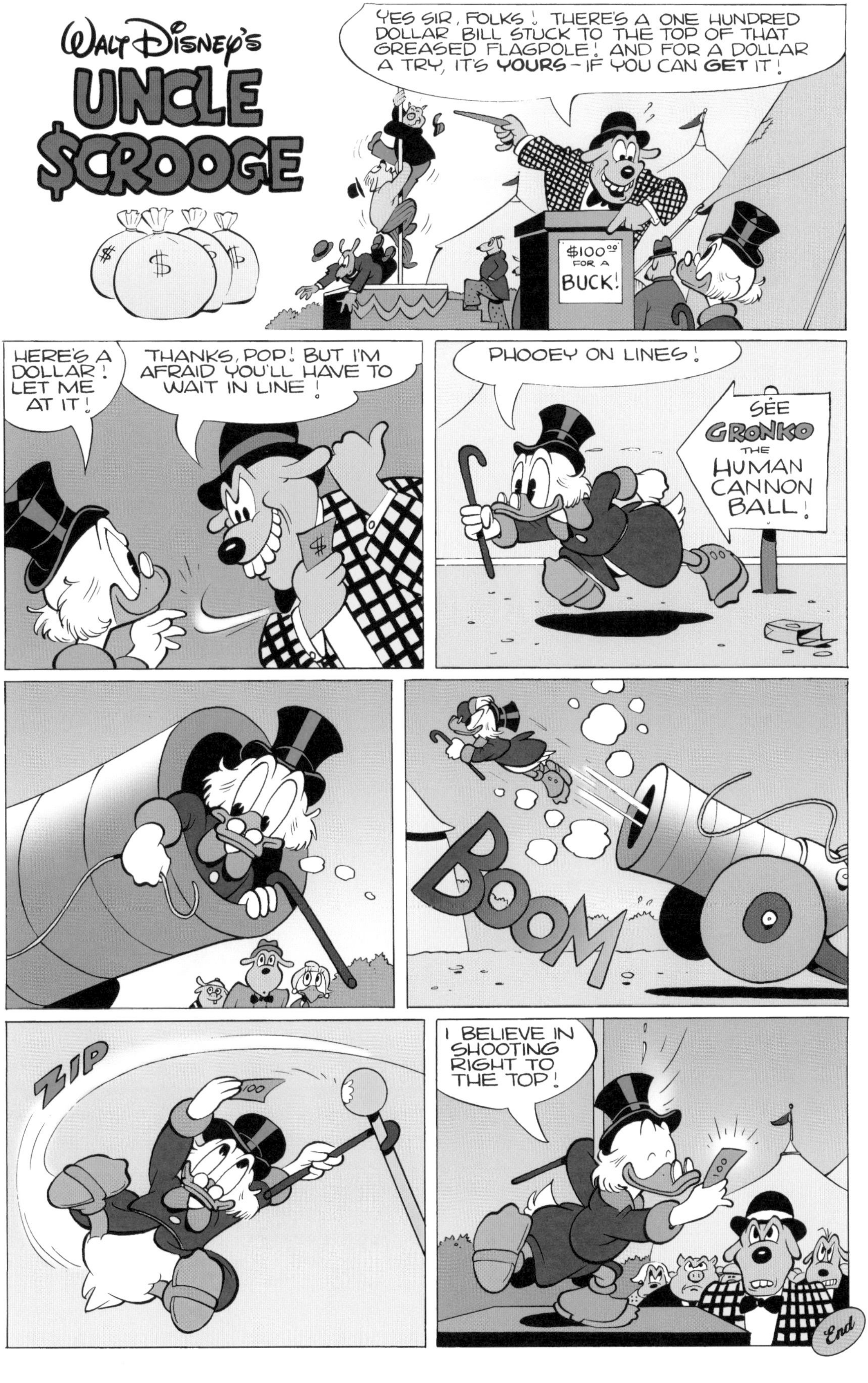
WALT DISNEY'S
UNCLE $CROOGE
YES SIR, FOLKS! THERE'S A ONE HUNDRED DOLLAR BILL STUCK TO THE TOP OF THAT GREASED FLAGPOLE! AND FOR A DOLLAR A TRY, IT'S YOURS - IF YOU CAN GET IT!
$100.00 FOR A BUCK!
HERE'S A DOLLAR! LET ME AT IT!
THANKS, POP! BUT I'M AFRAID YOU'LL HAVE TO WAIT IN LINE!
PHOOEY ON LINES!
SEE GRONKO THE HUMAN CANNON BALL!
BOOM
ZIP
100
I BELIEVE IN SHOOTING RIGHT TO THE TOP!
100
End

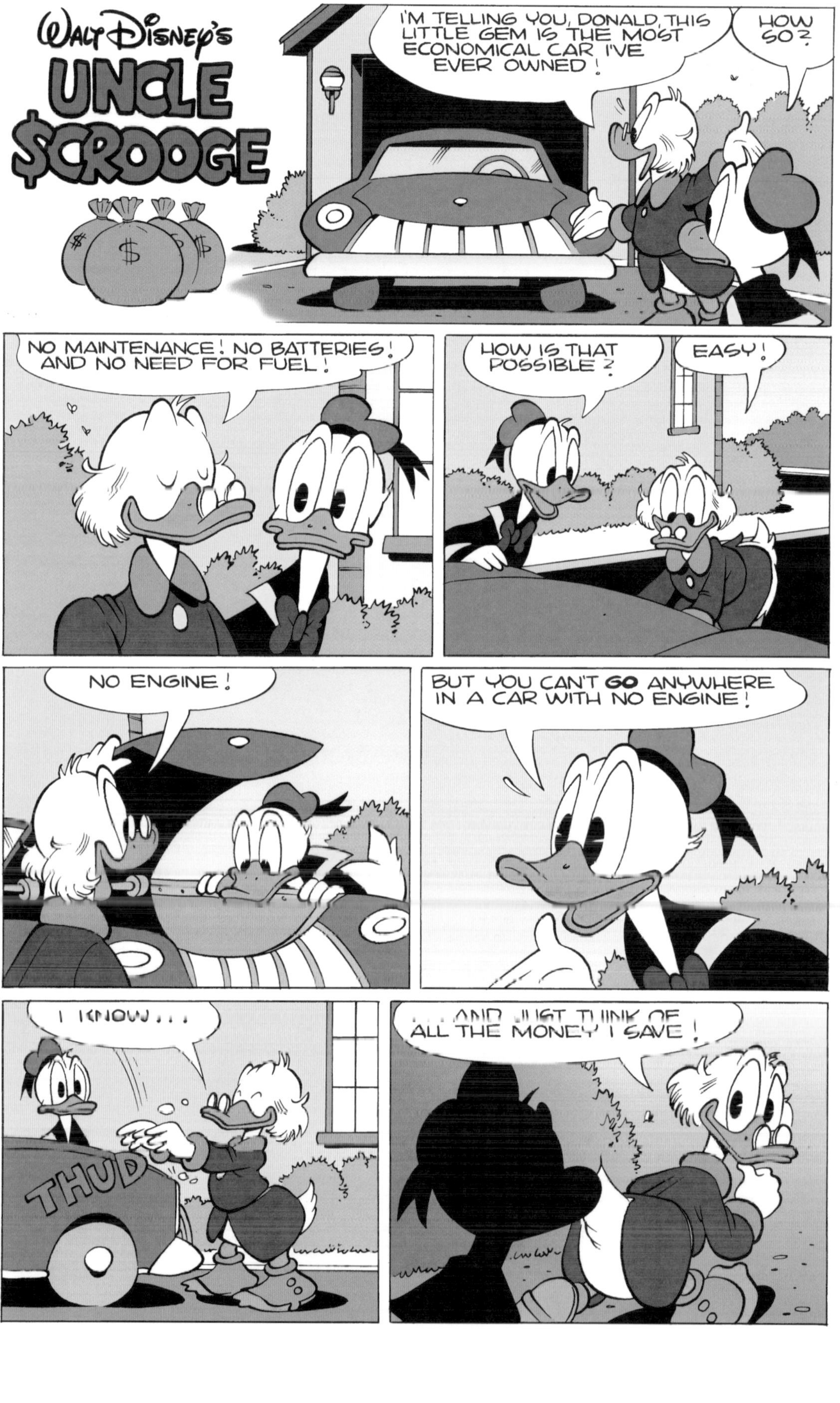
WALT DISNEY'S
UNCLE $CROOGE
I'M TELLING YOU, DONALD, THIS LITTLE GEM IS THE MOST ECONOMICAL CAR I'VE EVER OWNED!
HOW SO?
NO MAINTENANCE! NO BATTERIES! AND NO NEED FOR FUEL!
HOW IS THAT POSSIBLE?
EASY!
NO ENGINE!
BUT YOU CAN'T GO ANYWHERE IN A CAR WITH NO ENGINE!
I KNOW . . .
THUD
. . . AND JUST THINK OF ALL THE MONEY I SAVE!

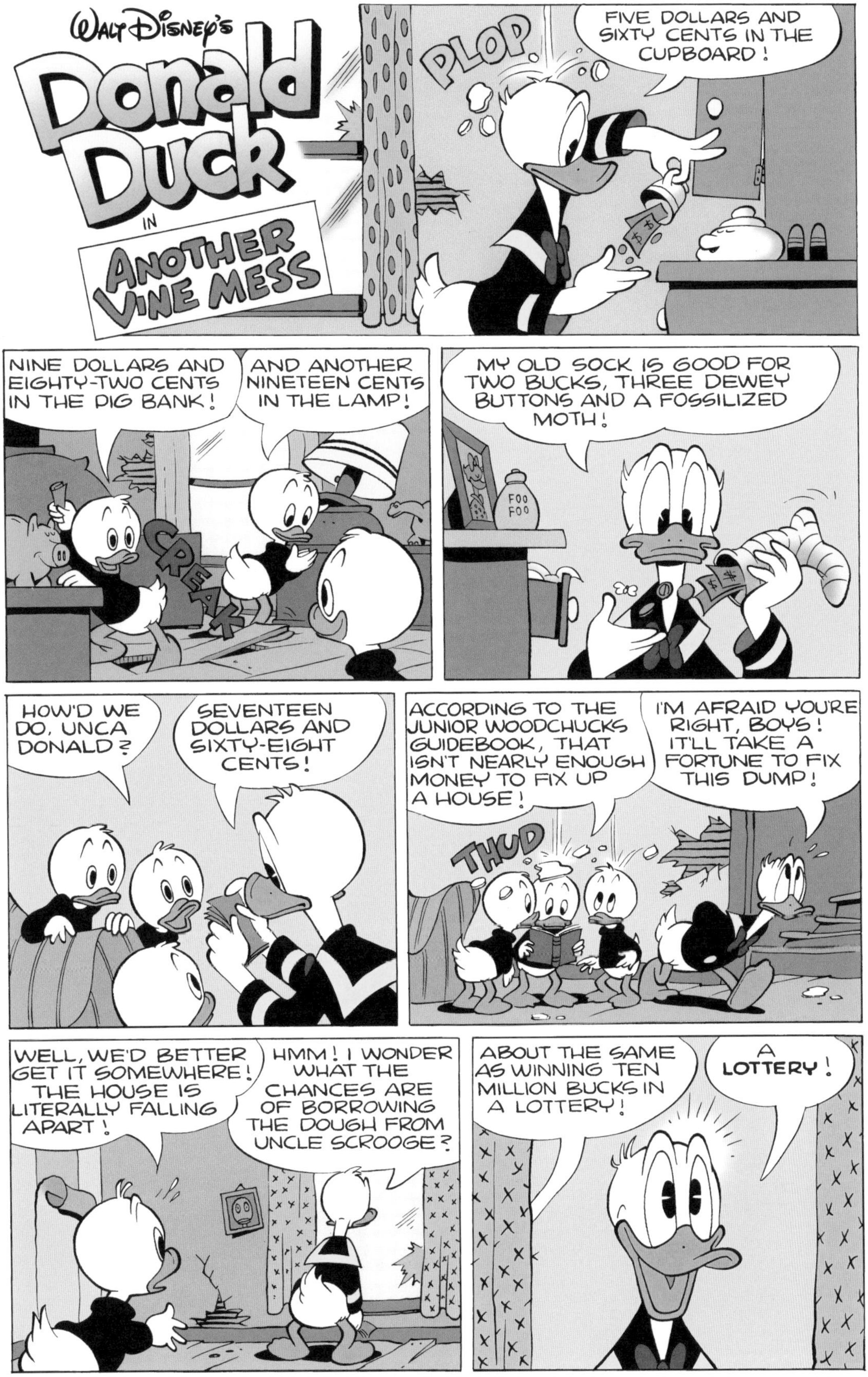

WALT DISNEY'S
Donald Duck
IN
ANOTHER VINE MESS
PLOP
FIVE DOLLARS AND SIXTY CENTS IN THE CUPBOARD!
NINE DOLLARS AND EIGHTY-TWO CENTS IN THE PIG BANK!
AND ANOTHER NINETEEN CENTS IN THE LAMP!
CREAK
MY OLD SOCK IS GOOD FOR TWO BUCKS, THREE DEWEY BUTTONS AND A FOSSILIZED MOTH!
FOO FOO
HOW'D WE DO, UNCA DONALD?
SEVENTEEN DOLLARS AND SIXTY-EIGHT CENTS!
ACCORDING TO THE JUNIOR WOODCHUCKS GUIDEBOOK, THAT ISN'T NEARLY ENOUGH MONEY TO FIX UP A HOUSE!
I'M AFRAID YOU'RE RIGHT, BOYS! IT'LL TAKE A FORTUNE TO FIX THIS DUMP!
THUD
WELL, WE'D BETTER GET IT SOMEWHERE! THE HOUSE IS LITERALLY FALLING APART!
HMM! I WONDER WHAT THE CHANCES ARE OF BORROWING THE DOUGH FROM UNCLE SCROOGE?
ABOUT THE SAME AS WINNING TEN MILLION BUCKS IN A LOTTERY!
A **LOTTERY**!

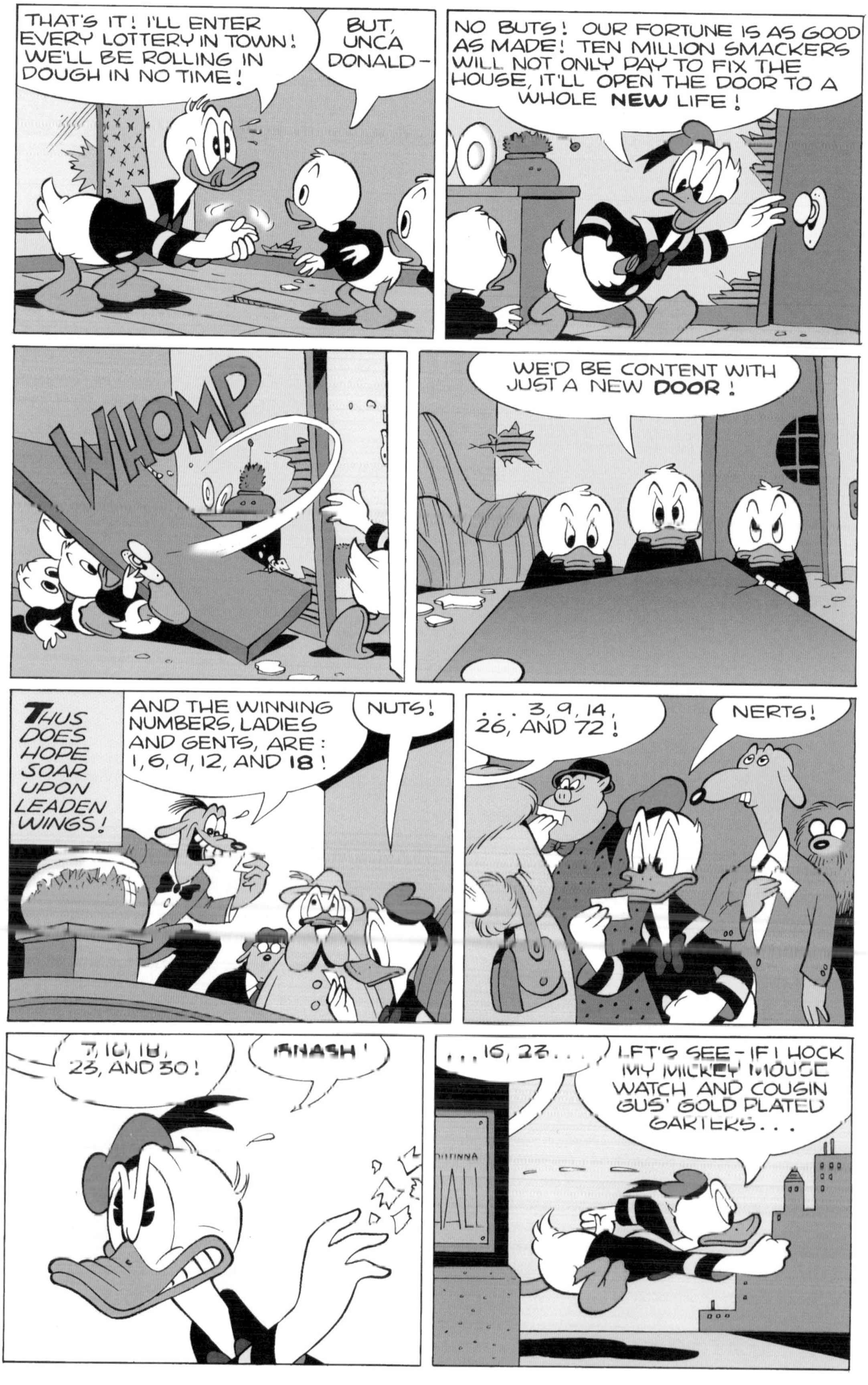
THAT'S IT! I'LL ENTER EVERY LOTTERY IN TOWN! WE'LL BE ROLLING IN DOUGH IN NO TIME!
BUT, UNCA DONALD–
NO BUTS! OUR FORTUNE IS AS GOOD AS MADE! TEN MILLION SMACKERS WILL NOT ONLY PAY TO FIX THE HOUSE, IT'LL OPEN THE DOOR TO A WHOLE **NEW** LIFE!
WHOMP
WE'D BE CONTENT WITH JUST A NEW **DOOR**!
THUS DOES HOPE SOAR UPON LEADEN WINGS!
AND THE WINNING NUMBERS, LADIES AND GENTS, ARE: 1, 6, 9, 12, AND **18**!
NUTS!
. . . 3, 9, 14, 26, AND 72!
NERTS!
7, 10, 18, 23, AND 30!
GNASH!
. . . 16, 23 . . .
LET'S SEE – IF I HOCK MY MICKEY MOUSE WATCH AND COUSIN GUS' GOLD PLATED GARTERS . . .
HALL

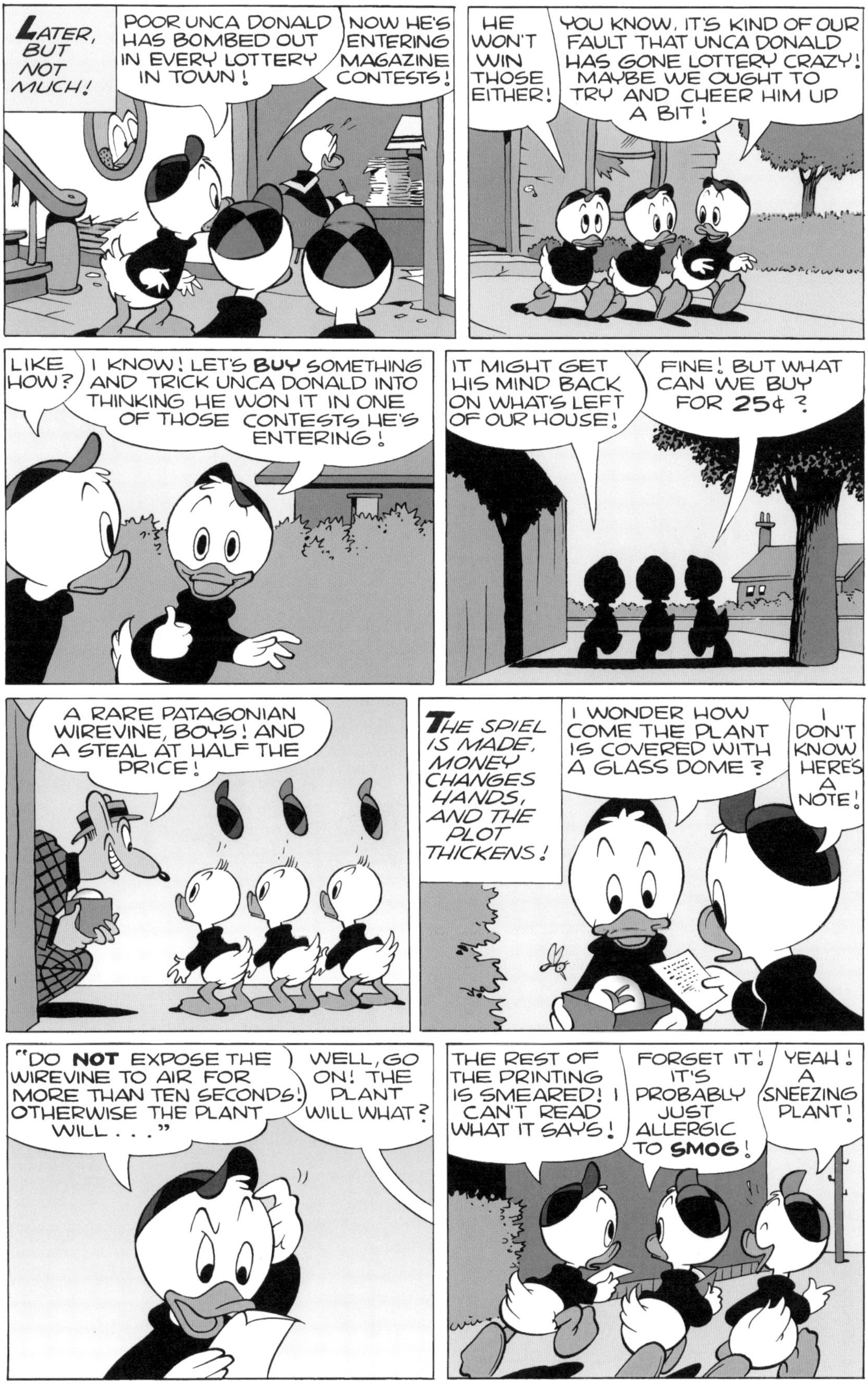
LATER, BUT NOT MUCH!
POOR UNCA DONALD HAS BOMBED OUT IN EVERY LOTTERY IN TOWN!
NOW HE'S ENTERING MAGAZINE CONTESTS!
HE WON'T WIN THOSE EITHER!
YOU KNOW, IT'S KIND OF OUR FAULT THAT UNCA DONALD HAS GONE LOTTERY CRAZY! MAYBE WE OUGHT TO TRY AND CHEER HIM UP A BIT!
LIKE HOW?
I KNOW! LET'S BUY SOMETHING AND TRICK UNCA DONALD INTO THINKING HE WON IT IN ONE OF THOSE CONTESTS HE'S ENTERING!
IT MIGHT GET HIS MIND BACK ON WHAT'S LEFT OF OUR HOUSE!
FINE! BUT WHAT CAN WE BUY FOR 25¢?
A RARE PATAGONIAN WIREVINE, BOYS! AND A STEAL AT HALF THE PRICE!
THE SPIEL IS MADE, MONEY CHANGES HANDS, AND THE PLOT THICKENS!
I WONDER HOW COME THE PLANT IS COVERED WITH A GLASS DOME?
I DON'T KNOW. HERE'S A NOTE!
"DO NOT EXPOSE THE WIREVINE TO AIR FOR MORE THAN TEN SECONDS! OTHERWISE THE PLANT WILL . . ."
WELL, GO ON! THE PLANT WILL WHAT?
THE REST OF THE PRINTING IS SMEARED! I CAN'T READ WHAT IT SAYS!
FORGET IT! IT'S PROBABLY JUST ALLERGIC TO SMOG!
YEAH! A SNEEZING PLANT!

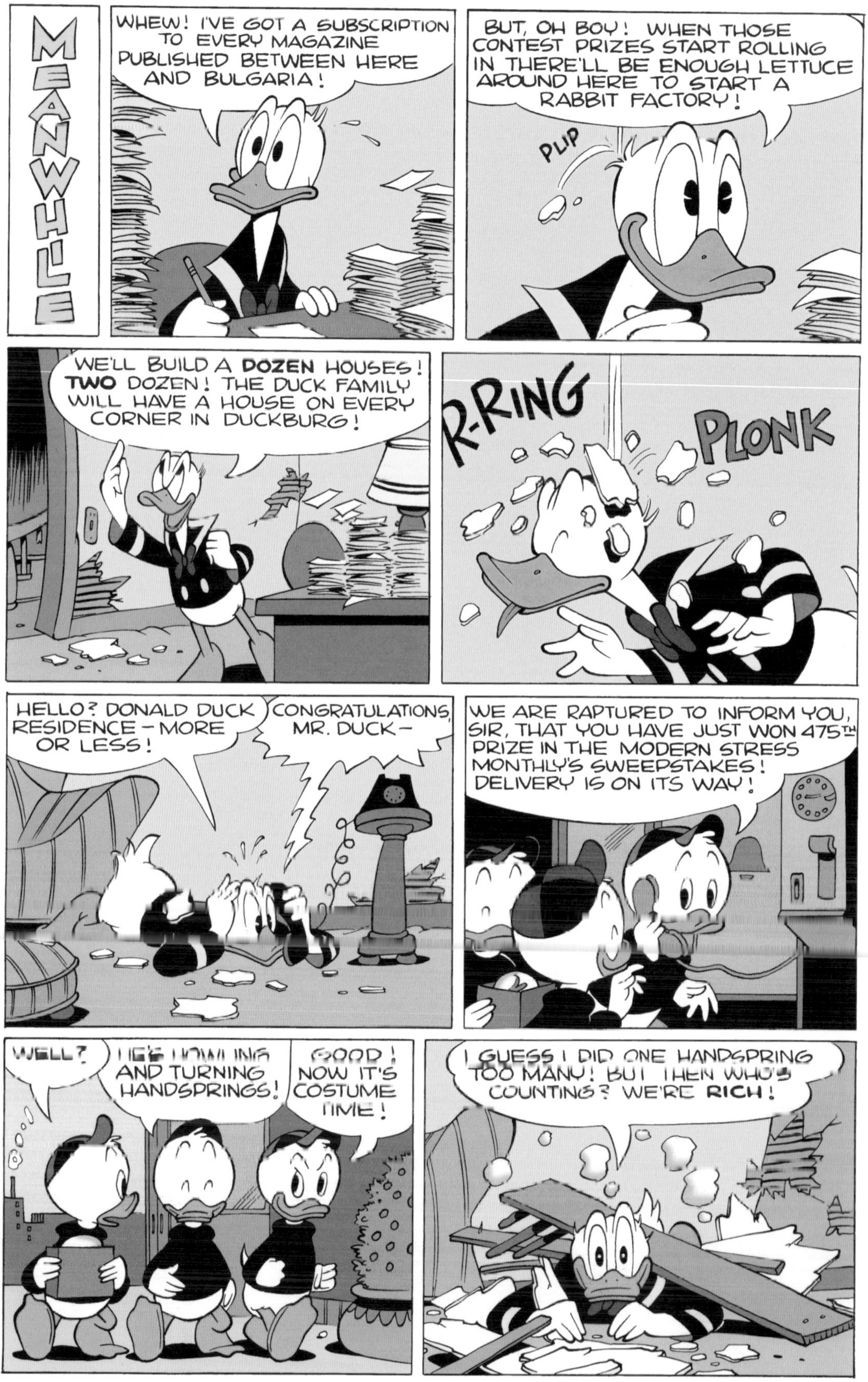
MEANWHILE
WHEW! I'VE GOT A SUBSCRIPTION TO EVERY MAGAZINE PUBLISHED BETWEEN HERE AND BULGARIA!
BUT, OH BOY! WHEN THOSE CONTEST PRIZES START ROLLING IN THERE'LL BE ENOUGH LETTUCE AROUND HERE TO START A RABBIT FACTORY!
PLIP
WE'LL BUILD A **DOZEN** HOUSES! **TWO** DOZEN! THE DUCK FAMILY WILL HAVE A HOUSE ON EVERY CORNER IN DUCKBURG!
R-RING
PLONK
HELLO? DONALD DUCK RESIDENCE—MORE OR LESS!
CONGRATULATIONS, MR. DUCK—
WE ARE RAPTURED TO INFORM YOU, SIR, THAT YOU HAVE JUST WON 475TH PRIZE IN THE MODERN STRESS MONTHLY'S SWEEPSTAKES! DELIVERY IS ON ITS WAY!
WELL?
HE'S HOWLING AND TURNING HANDSPRINGS!
GOOD! NOW IT'S COSTUME TIME!
I GUESS I DID ONE HANDSPRING TOO MANY! BUT THEN WHO'S COUNTING? WE'RE **RICH**!

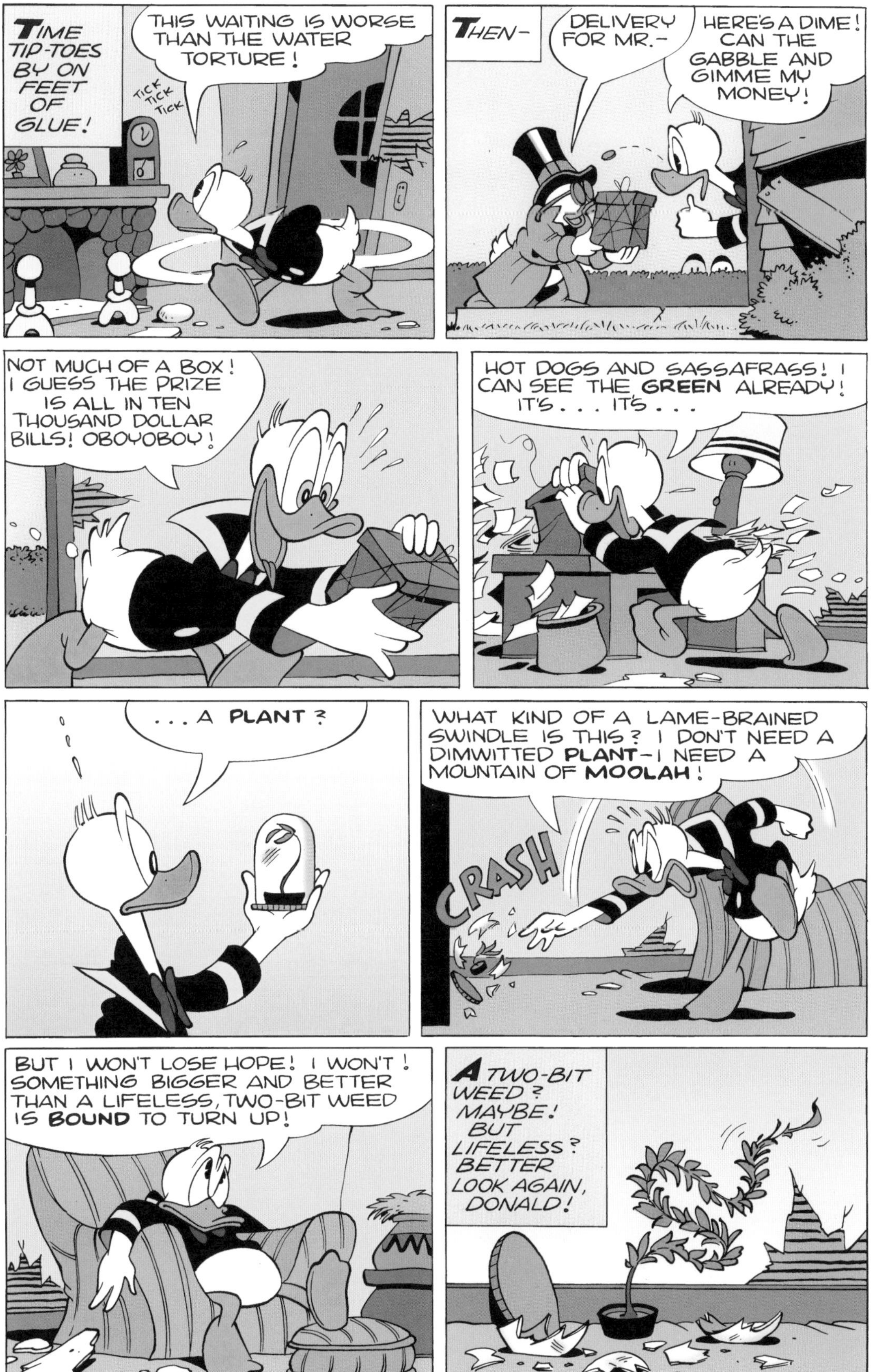
TIME TIP-TOES BY ON FEET OF GLUE!
THIS WAITING IS WORSE THAN THE WATER TORTURE!
TICK TICK TICK
THEN-
DELIVERY FOR MR.-
HERE'S A DIME! CAN THE GABBLE AND GIMME MY MONEY!
NOT MUCH OF A BOX! I GUESS THE PRIZE IS ALL IN TEN THOUSAND DOLLAR BILLS! OBOYOBOY!
HOT DOGS AND SASSAFRASS! I CAN SEE THE GREEN ALREADY! IT'S . . . IT'S . . .
. . . A PLANT?
WHAT KIND OF A LAME-BRAINED SWINDLE IS THIS? I DON'T NEED A DIMWITTED PLANT-I NEED A MOUNTAIN OF MOOLAH!
CRASH
BUT I WON'T LOSE HOPE! I WON'T! SOMETHING BIGGER AND BETTER THAN A LIFELESS, TWO-BIT WEED IS BOUND TO TURN UP!
A TWO-BIT WEED? MAYBE! BUT LIFELESS? BETTER LOOK AGAIN, DONALD!

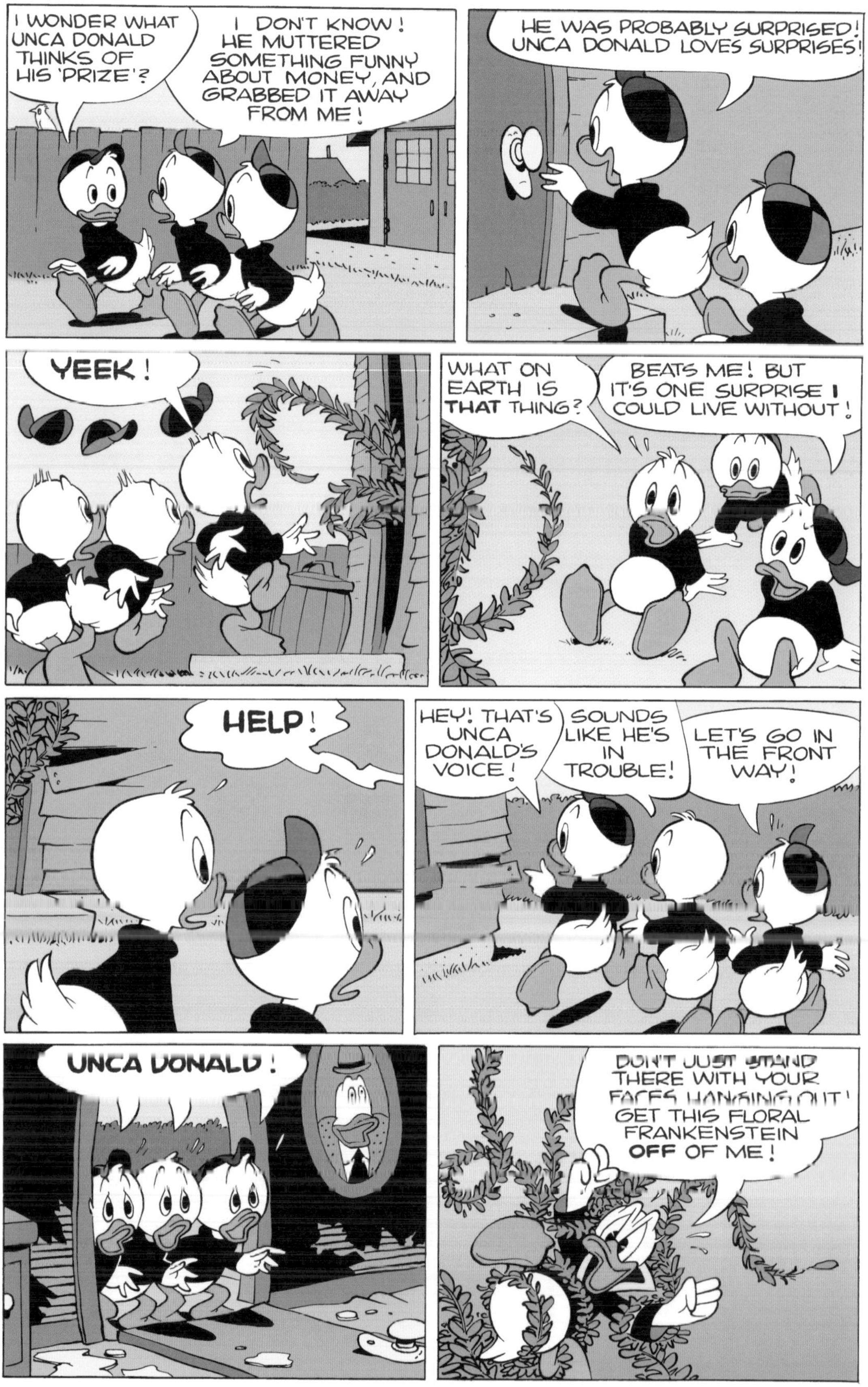
I WONDER WHAT UNCA DONALD THINKS OF HIS 'PRIZE'?
I DON'T KNOW! HE MUTTERED SOMETHING FUNNY ABOUT MONEY, AND GRABBED IT AWAY FROM ME!
HE WAS PROBABLY SURPRISED! UNCA DONALD LOVES SURPRISES!
YEEK!
WHAT ON EARTH IS **THAT** THING?
BEATS ME! BUT IT'S ONE SURPRISE **I** COULD LIVE WITHOUT!
HELP!
HEY! THAT'S UNCA DONALD'S VOICE!
SOUNDS LIKE HE'S IN TROUBLE!
LET'S GO IN THE FRONT WAY!
UNCA DONALD!
DON'T JUST STAND THERE WITH YOUR FACES HANGING OUT! GET THIS FLORAL FRANKENSTEIN **OFF** OF ME!

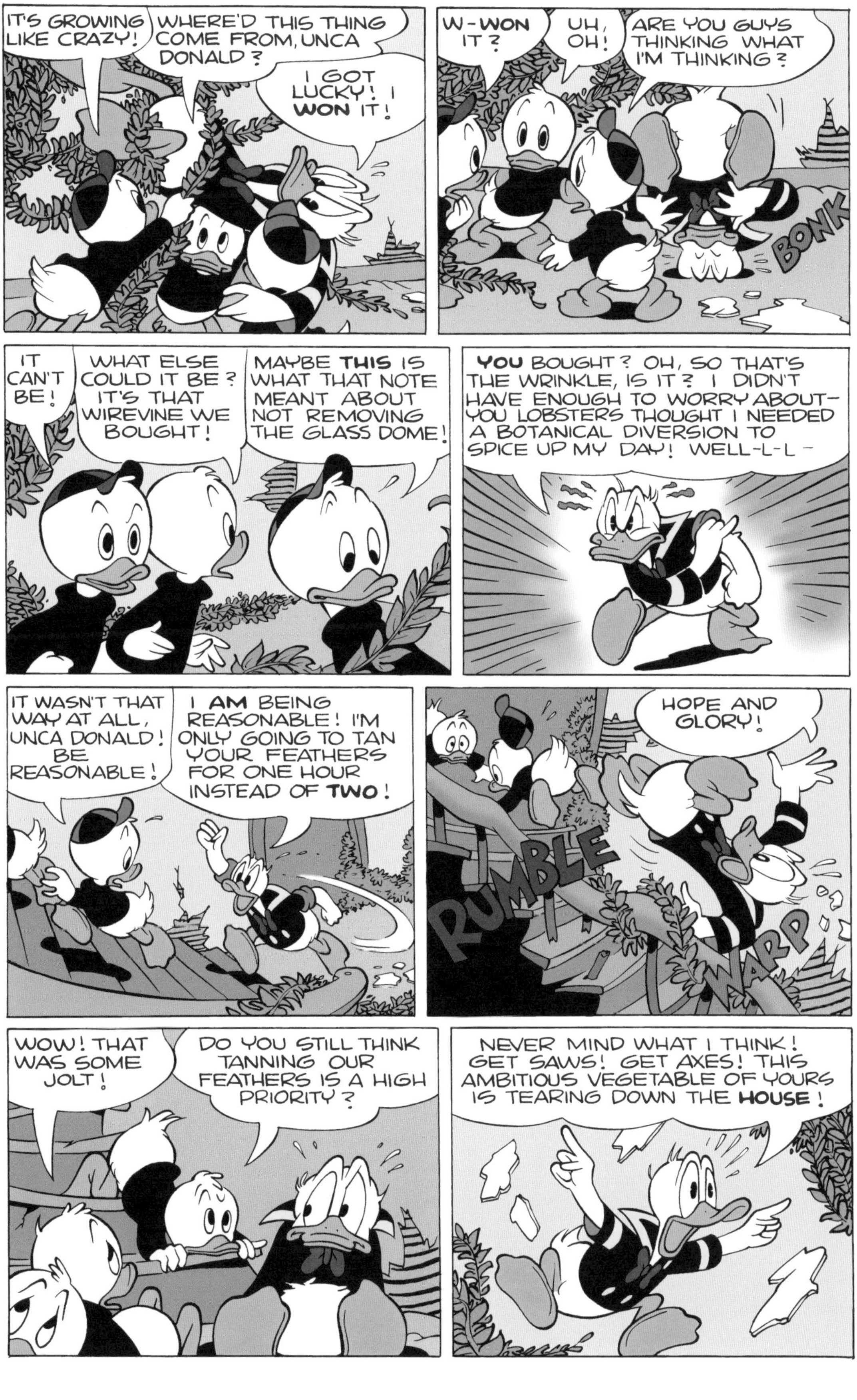
IT'S GROWING LIKE CRAZY!
WHERE'D THIS THING COME FROM, UNCA DONALD?
I GOT LUCKY! I **WON** IT!
W-**WON** IT?
UH, OH!
ARE YOU GUYS THINKING WHAT I'M THINKING?
BONK
IT CAN'T BE!
WHAT ELSE COULD IT BE? IT'S THAT WIREVINE WE BOUGHT!
MAYBE **THIS** IS WHAT THAT NOTE MEANT ABOUT NOT REMOVING THE GLASS DOME!
YOU BOUGHT? OH, SO THAT'S THE WRINKLE, IS IT? I DIDN'T HAVE ENOUGH TO WORRY ABOUT— YOU LOBSTERS THOUGHT I NEEDED A BOTANICAL DIVERSION TO SPICE UP MY DAY! WELL-L-L—
IT WASN'T THAT WAY AT ALL, UNCA DONALD! BE REASONABLE!
I **AM** BEING REASONABLE! I'M ONLY GOING TO TAN YOUR FEATHERS FOR ONE HOUR INSTEAD OF **TWO**!
HOPE AND GLORY!
RUMBLE
WARP
WOW! THAT WAS SOME JOLT!
DO YOU STILL THINK TANNING OUR FEATHERS IS A HIGH PRIORITY?
NEVER MIND WHAT I THINK! GET SAWS! GET AXES! THIS AMBITIOUS VEGETABLE OF YOURS IS TEARING DOWN THE **HOUSE**!

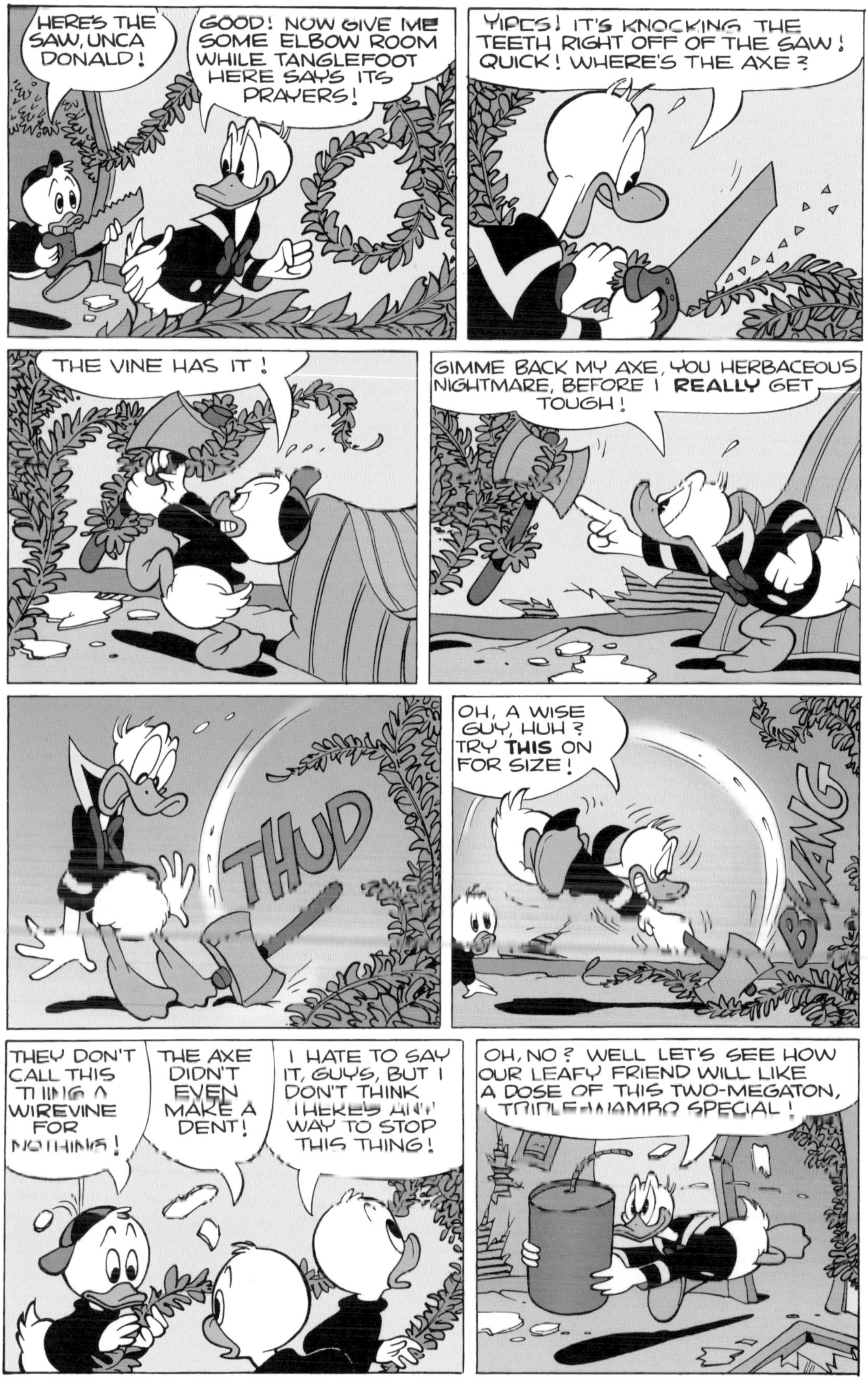
HERE'S THE SAW, UNCA DONALD!
GOOD! NOW GIVE ME SOME ELBOW ROOM WHILE TANGLEFOOT HERE SAYS ITS PRAYERS!
YIPES! IT'S KNOCKING THE TEETH RIGHT OFF OF THE SAW! QUICK! WHERE'S THE AXE?
THE VINE HAS IT!
GIMME BACK MY AXE, YOU HERBACEOUS NIGHTMARE, BEFORE I **REALLY** GET TOUGH!
THUD
OH, A WISE GUY, HUH? TRY **THIS** ON FOR SIZE!
BWANG
THEY DON'T CALL THIS THING A WIREVINE FOR NOTHING!
THE AXE DIDN'T EVEN MAKE A DENT!
I HATE TO SAY IT, GUYS, BUT I DON'T THINK THERE'S ANY WAY TO STOP THIS THING!
OH, NO? WELL LET'S SEE HOW OUR LEAFY FRIEND WILL LIKE A DOSE OF THIS TWO-MEGATON, TRIPLE-WAMBO SPECIAL!

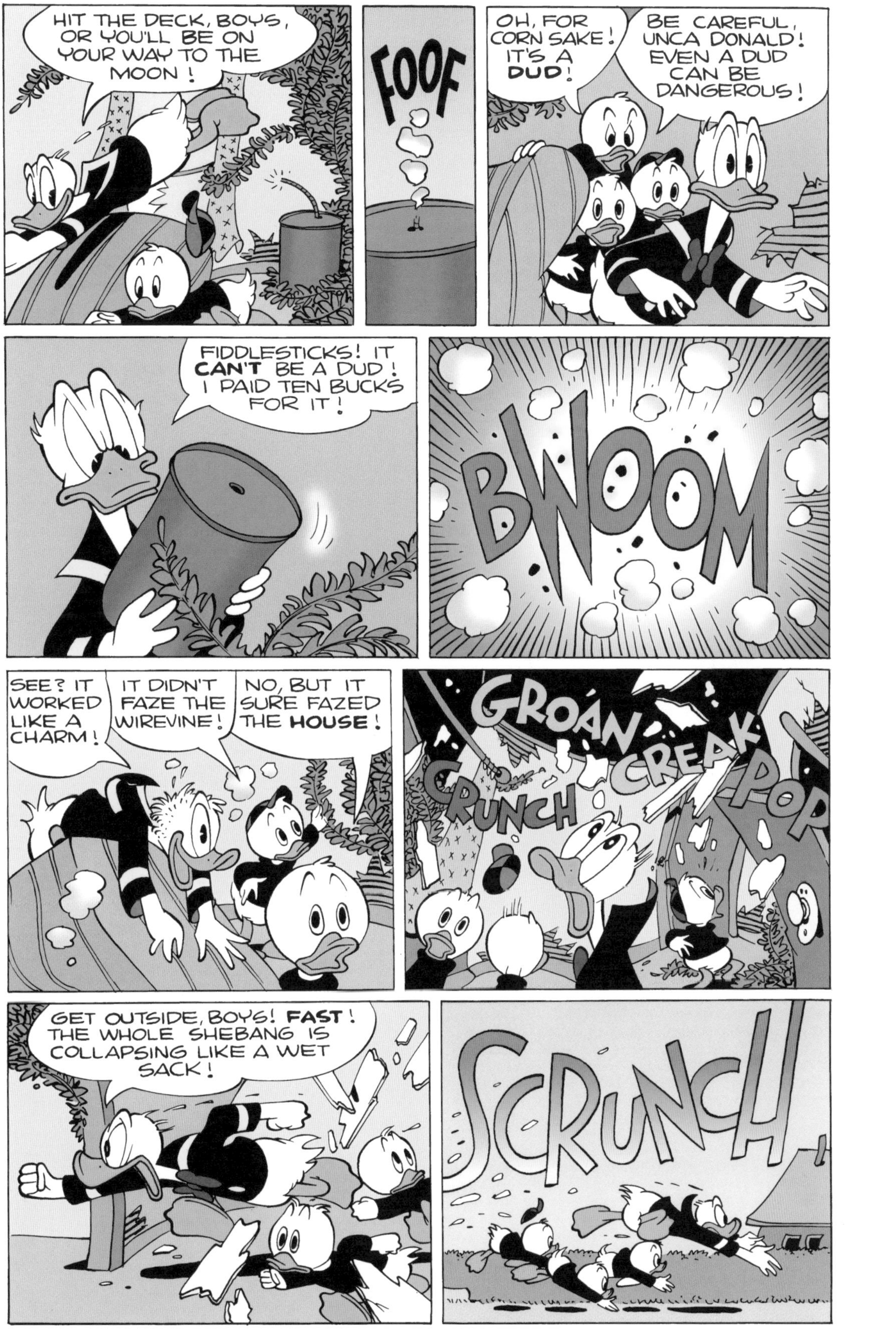
HIT THE DECK, BOYS, OR YOU'LL BE ON YOUR WAY TO THE MOON!
FOOF
OH, FOR CORN SAKE! IT'S A **DUD**!
BE CAREFUL, UNCA DONALD! EVEN A DUD CAN BE DANGEROUS!
FIDDLESTICKS! IT **CAN'T** BE A DUD! I PAID TEN BUCKS FOR IT!
BWOOM
SEE? IT WORKED LIKE A CHARM!
IT DIDN'T FAZE THE WIREVINE!
NO, BUT IT SURE FAZED THE **HOUSE**!
GROAN
CREAK
CRUNCH
POP
GET OUTSIDE, BOYS! **FAST**! THE WHOLE SHEBANG IS COLLAPSING LIKE A WET SACK!
SCRUNCH

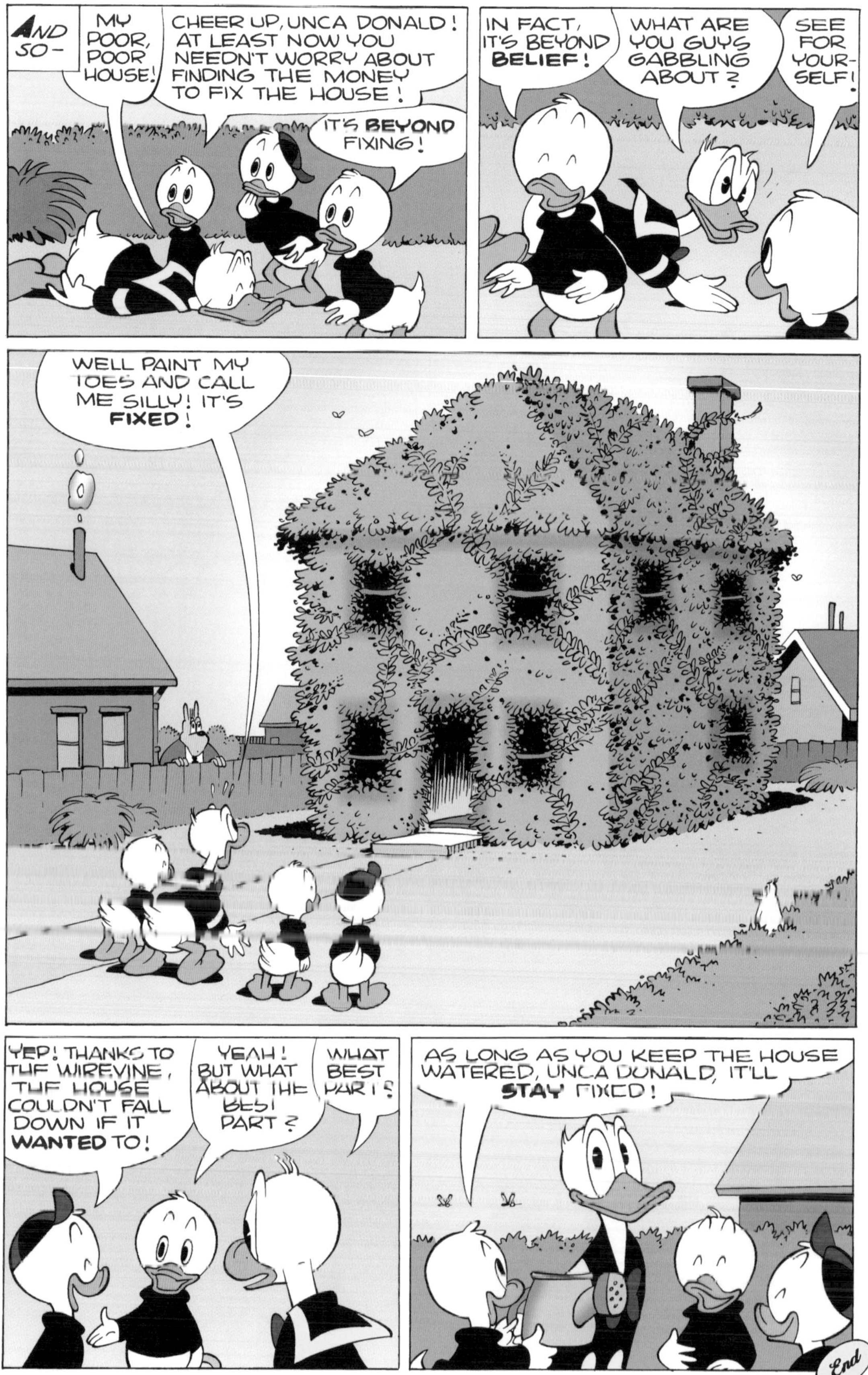

AND SO –
MY POOR, POOR HOUSE!
CHEER UP, UNCA DONALD! AT LEAST NOW YOU NEEDN'T WORRY ABOUT FINDING THE MONEY TO FIX THE HOUSE!
IT'S BEYOND FIXING!
IN FACT, IT'S BEYOND BELIEF!
WHAT ARE YOU GUYS GABBLING ABOUT?
SEE FOR YOURSELF!
WELL PAINT MY TOES AND CALL ME SILLY! IT'S FIXED!
YEP! THANKS TO THE WIREVINE, THE HOUSE COULDN'T FALL DOWN IF IT WANTED TO!
YEAH! BUT WHAT ABOUT THE BEST PART?
WHAT BEST PART?
AS LONG AS YOU KEEP THE HOUSE WATERED, UNCA DONALD, IT'LL STAY FIXED!
End

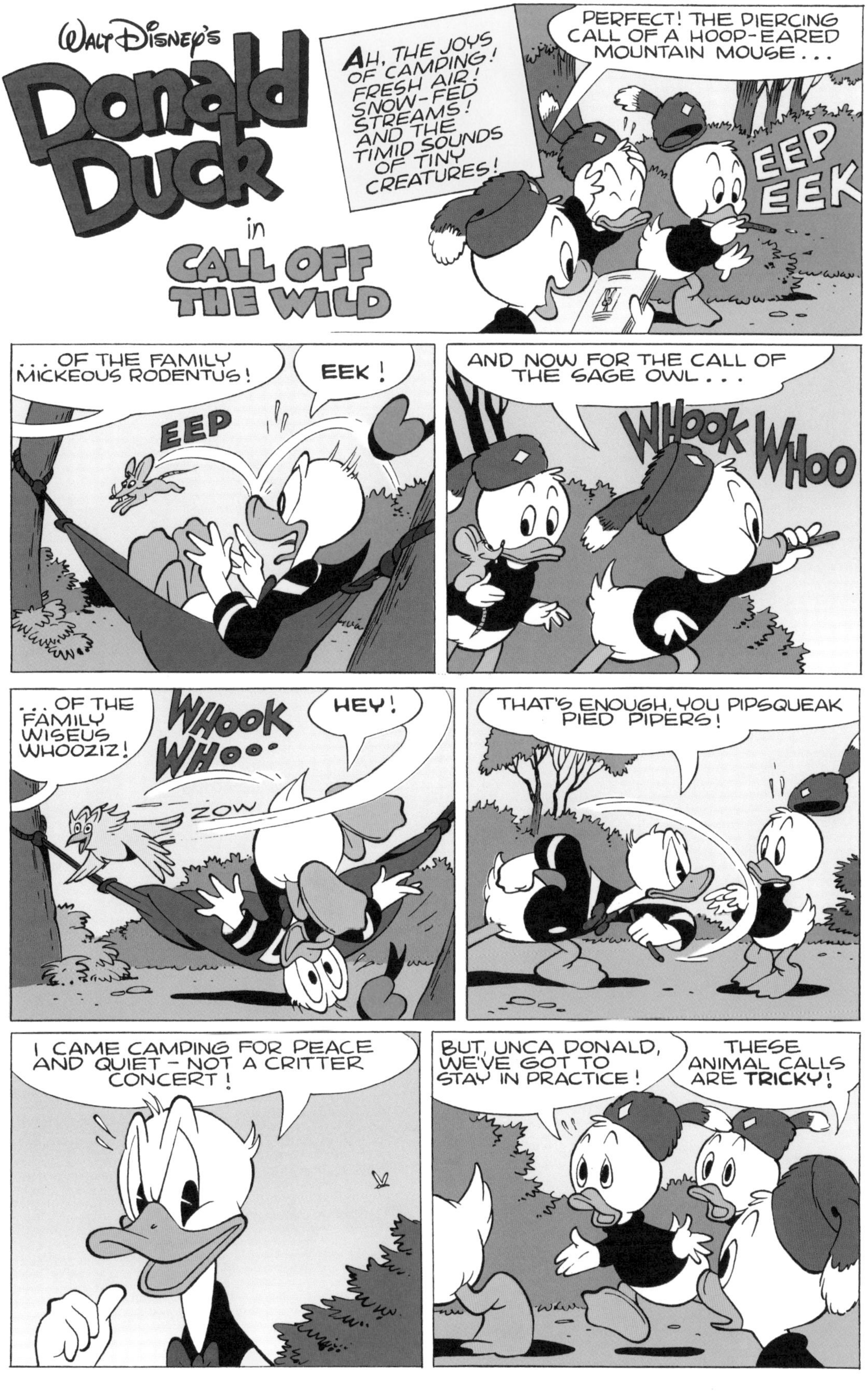
Walt Disney's
Donald Duck
in
CALL OFF THE WILD
AH, THE JOYS OF CAMPING! FRESH AIR! SNOW-FED STREAMS! AND THE TIMID SOUNDS OF TINY CREATURES!
PERFECT! THE PIERCING CALL OF A HOOP-EARED MOUNTAIN MOUSE . . .
EEP EEK
. . . OF THE FAMILY MICKEOUS RODENTUS!
EEK!
EEP
AND NOW FOR THE CALL OF THE SAGE OWL . . .
WHOOK WHOO
. . . OF THE FAMILY WISEUS WHOOZIZ!
WHOOK WHO...
HEY!
ZOW
THAT'S ENOUGH, YOU PIPSQUEAK PIED PIPERS!
I CAME CAMPING FOR PEACE AND QUIET - NOT A CRITTER CONCERT!
BUT, UNCA DONALD, WE'VE GOT TO STAY IN PRACTICE!
THESE ANIMAL CALLS ARE TRICKY!

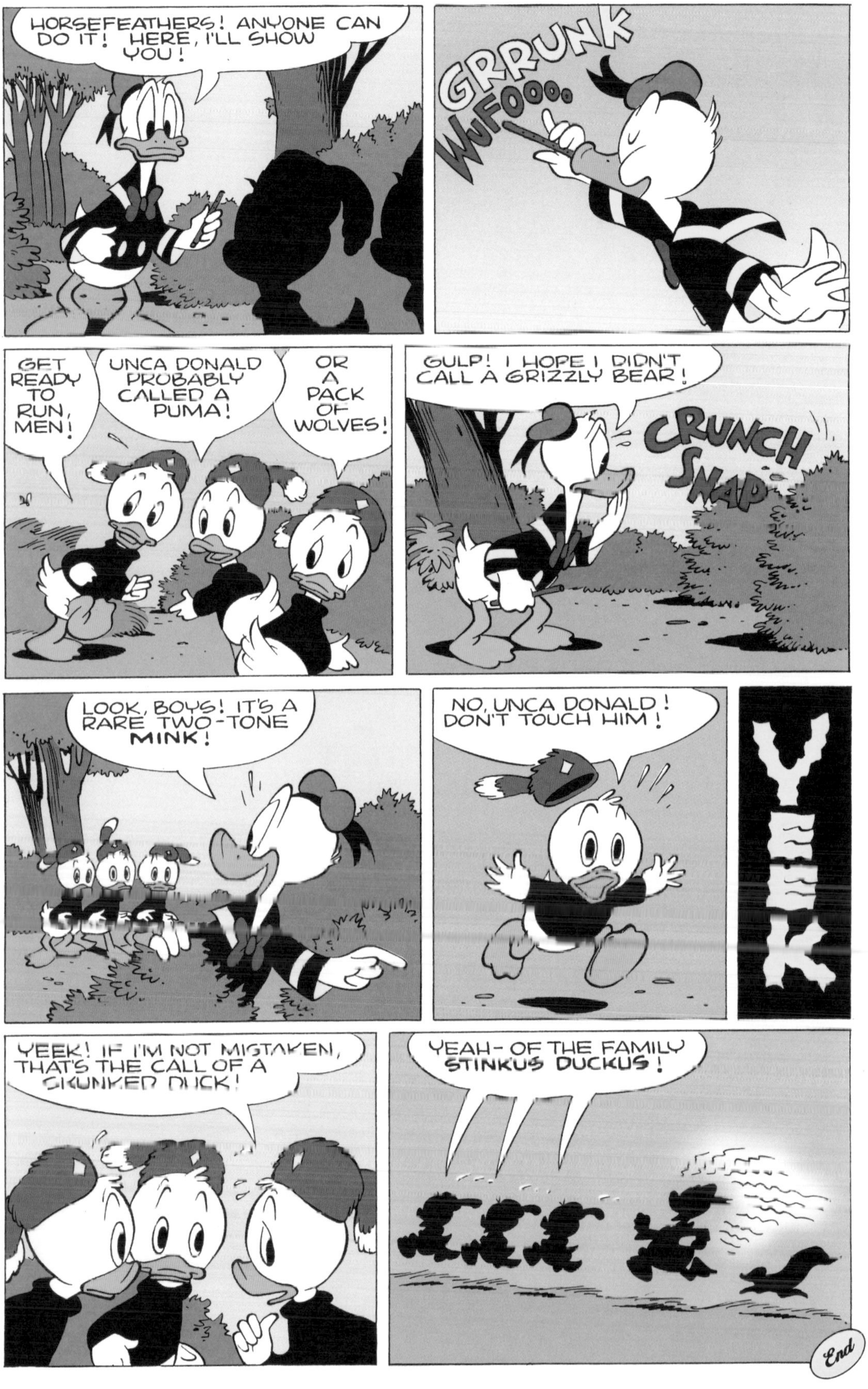
HORSEFEATHERS! ANYONE CAN DO IT! HERE, I'LL SHOW YOU!
GRRUNK
WUFOOOO
GET READY TO RUN, MEN!
UNCA DONALD PROBABLY CALLED A PUMA!
OR A PACK OF WOLVES!
GULP! I HOPE I DIDN'T CALL A GRIZZLY BEAR!
CRUNCH
SNAP
LOOK, BOYS! IT'S A RARE TWO-TONE MINK!
NO, UNCA DONALD! DON'T TOUCH HIM!
YEEK
YEEK! IF I'M NOT MISTAKEN, THAT'S THE CALL OF A SKUNKED DUCK!
YEAH– OF THE FAMILY STINKUS DUCKUS!
End

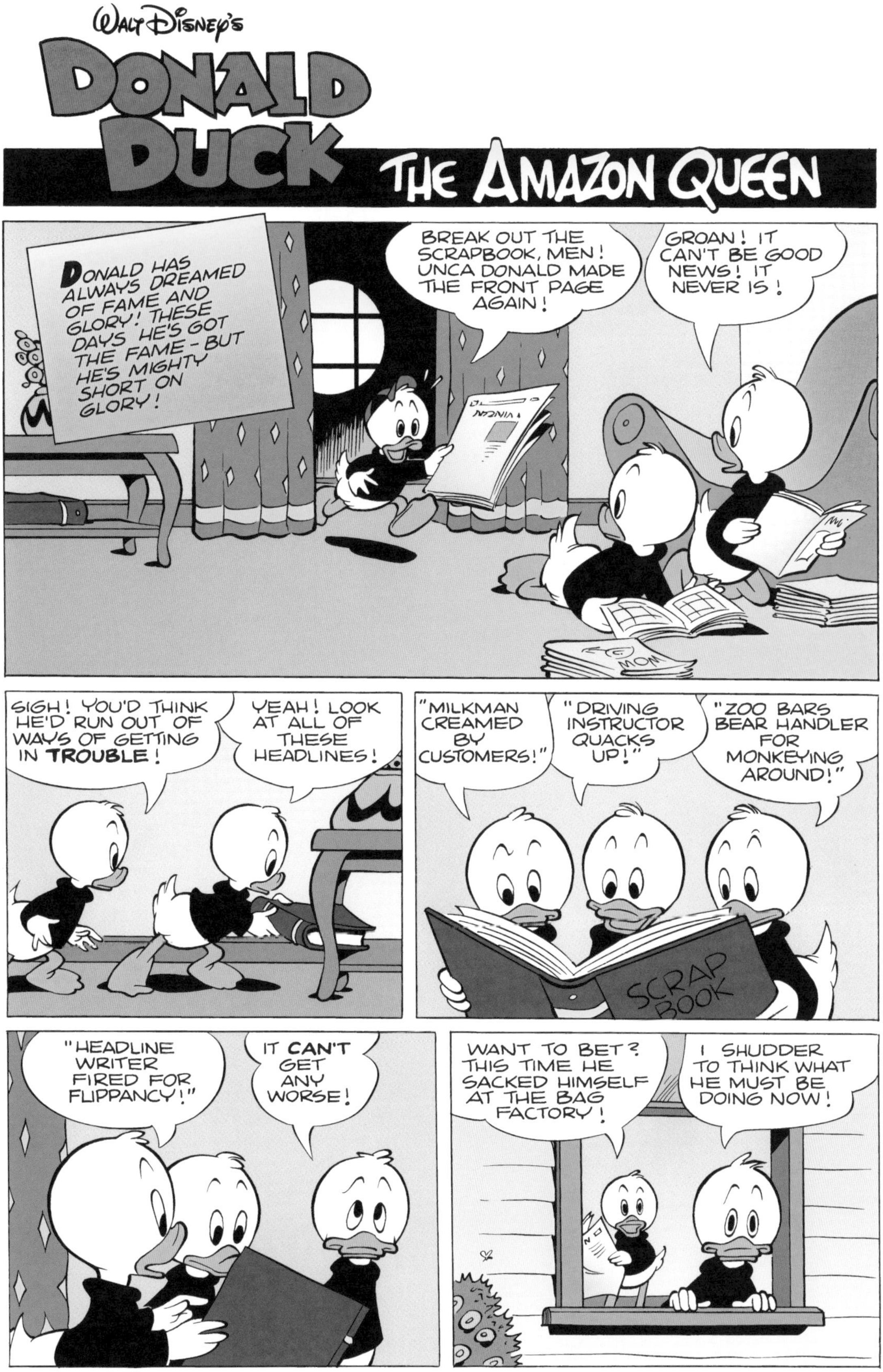
WALT DISNEY'S
DONALD DUCK
THE AMAZON QUEEN
DONALD HAS ALWAYS DREAMED OF FAME AND GLORY! THESE DAYS HE'S GOT THE FAME - BUT HE'S MIGHTY SHORT ON GLORY!
BREAK OUT THE SCRAPBOOK, MEN! UNCA DONALD MADE THE FRONT PAGE AGAIN!
GROAN! IT CAN'T BE GOOD NEWS! IT NEVER IS!
SIGH! YOU'D THINK HE'D RUN OUT OF WAYS OF GETTING IN **TROUBLE**!
YEAH! LOOK AT ALL OF THESE HEADLINES!
"MILKMAN CREAMED BY CUSTOMERS!"
"DRIVING INSTRUCTOR QUACKS UP!"
"ZOO BARS BEAR HANDLER FOR MONKEYING AROUND!"
SCRAP BOOK
"HEADLINE WRITER FIRED FOR FLIPPANCY!"
IT **CAN'T** GET ANY WORSE!
WANT TO BET? THIS TIME HE SACKED HIMSELF AT THE BAG FACTORY!
I SHUDDER TO THINK WHAT HE MUST BE DOING NOW!

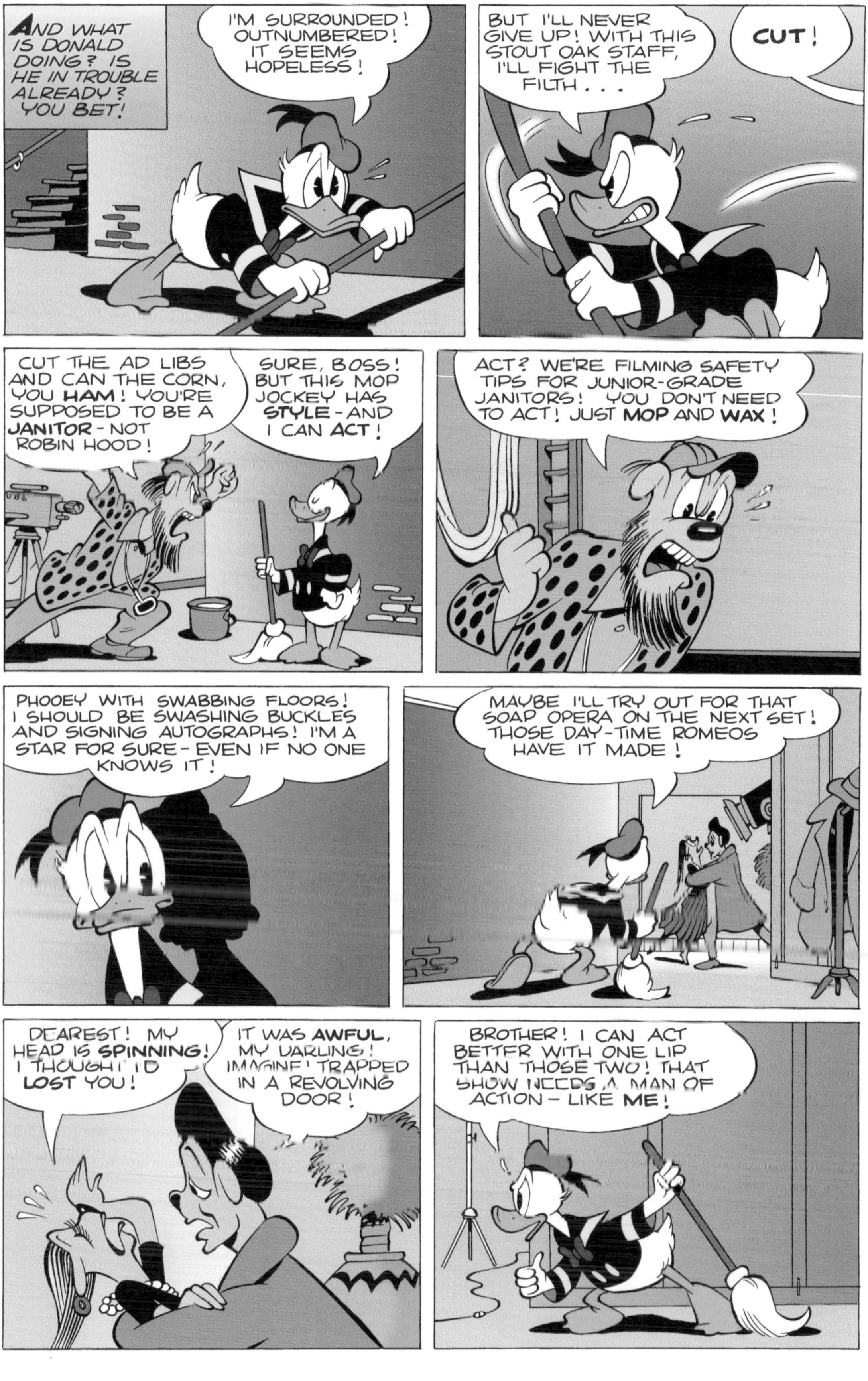
AND WHAT IS DONALD DOING? IS HE IN TROUBLE ALREADY? YOU BET!
I'M SURROUNDED! OUTNUMBERED! IT SEEMS HOPELESS!
BUT I'LL NEVER GIVE UP! WITH THIS STOUT OAK STAFF, I'LL FIGHT THE FILTH . . .
CUT!
CUT THE AD LIBS AND CAN THE CORN, YOU HAM! YOU'RE SUPPOSED TO BE A JANITOR - NOT ROBIN HOOD!
SURE, BOSS! BUT THIS MOP JOCKEY HAS STYLE - AND I CAN ACT!
ACT? WE'RE FILMING SAFETY TIPS FOR JUNIOR-GRADE JANITORS! YOU DON'T NEED TO ACT! JUST MOP AND WAX!
PHOOEY WITH SWABBING FLOORS! I SHOULD BE SWASHING BUCKLES AND SIGNING AUTOGRAPHS! I'M A STAR FOR SURE - EVEN IF NO ONE KNOWS IT!
MAYBE I'LL TRY OUT FOR THAT SOAP OPERA ON THE NEXT SET! THOSE DAY-TIME ROMEOS HAVE IT MADE!
DEAREST! MY HEAD IS SPINNING! I THOUGHT I'D LOST YOU!
IT WAS AWFUL, MY DARLING! IMAGINE! TRAPPED IN A REVOLVING DOOR!
BROTHER! I CAN ACT BETTER WITH ONE LIP THAN THOSE TWO! THAT SHOW NEEDS A MAN OF ACTION - LIKE ME!

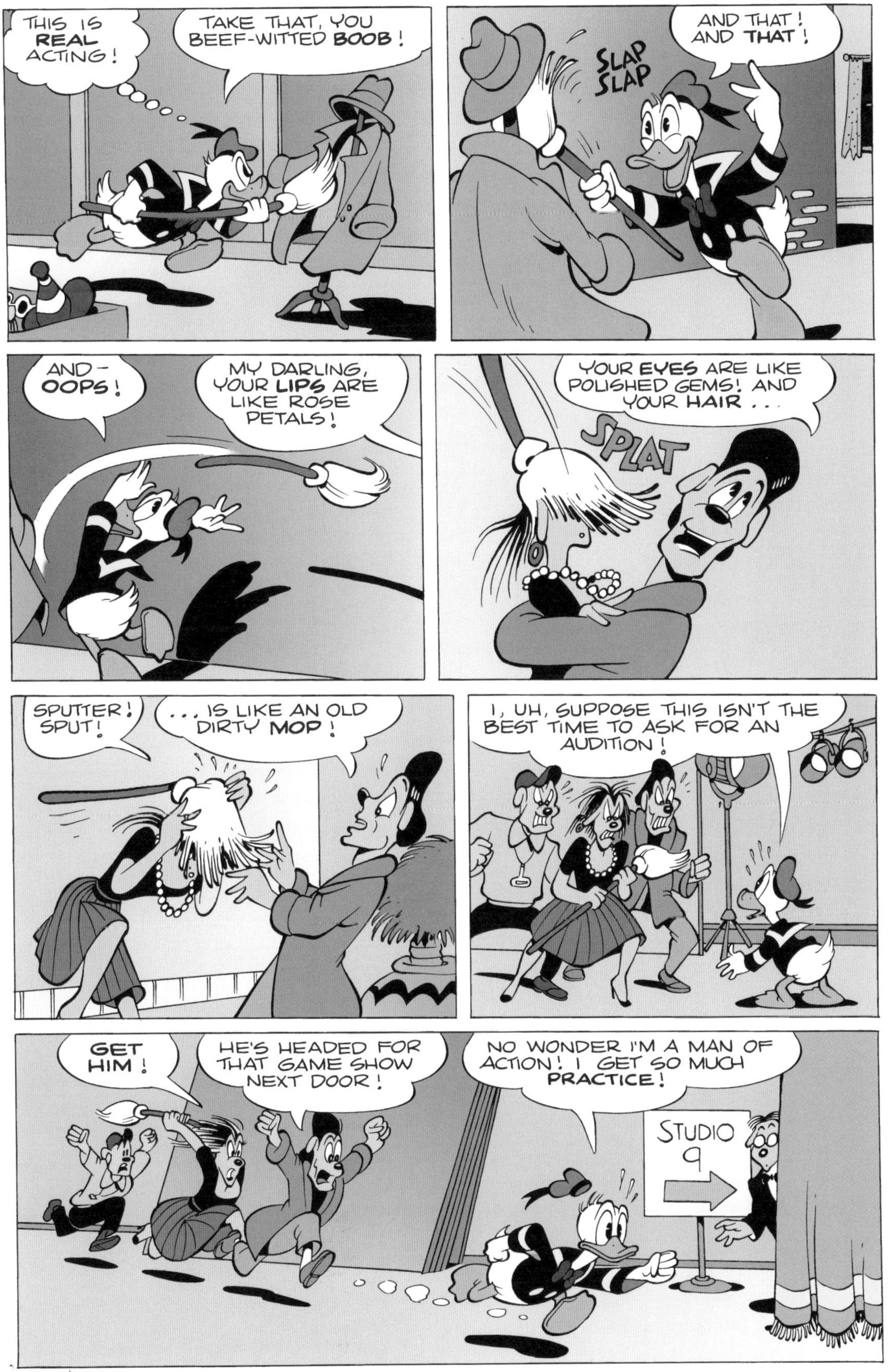

THIS IS REAL ACTING!
TAKE THAT, YOU BEEF-WITTED BOOB!
SLAP SLAP
AND THAT! AND THAT!
AND– OOPS!
MY DARLING, YOUR LIPS ARE LIKE ROSE PETALS!
YOUR EYES ARE LIKE POLISHED GEMS! AND YOUR HAIR . . .
SPLAT
SPUTTER! SPUT!
. . . IS LIKE AN OLD DIRTY MOP!
I, UH, SUPPOSE THIS ISN'T THE BEST TIME TO ASK FOR AN AUDITION!
GET HIM!
HE'S HEADED FOR THAT GAME SHOW NEXT DOOR!
NO WONDER I'M A MAN OF ACTION! I GET SO MUCH PRACTICE!
STUDIO 9

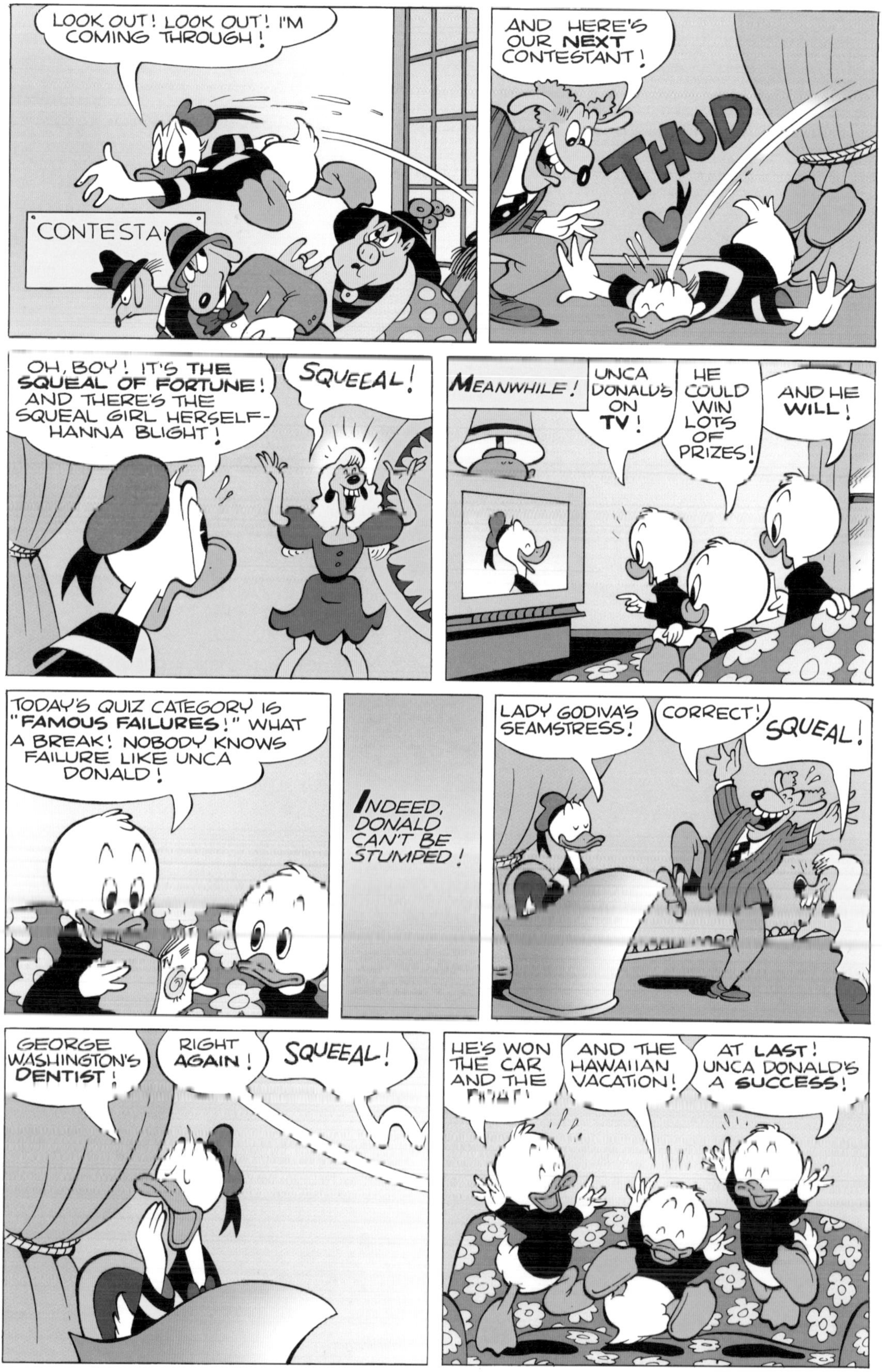
LOOK OUT! LOOK OUT! I'M COMING THROUGH!
CONTESTAN
AND HERE'S OUR NEXT CONTESTANT!
THUD
OH, BOY! IT'S THE SQUEAL OF FORTUNE! AND THERE'S THE SQUEAL GIRL HERSELF-HANNA BLIGHT!
SQUEEAL!
MEANWHILE!
UNCA DONALD'S ON TV!
HE COULD WIN LOTS OF PRIZES!
AND HE WILL!
TODAY'S QUIZ CATEGORY IS "FAMOUS FAILURES!" WHAT A BREAK! NOBODY KNOWS FAILURE LIKE UNCA DONALD!
INDEED, DONALD CAN'T BE STUMPED!
LADY GODIVA'S SEAMSTRESS!
CORRECT!
SQUEAL!
GEORGE WASHINGTON'S DENTIST!
RIGHT AGAIN!
SQUEEAL!
HE'S WON THE CAR AND THE
AND THE HAWAIIAN VACATION!
AT LAST! UNCA DONALD'S A SUCCESS!

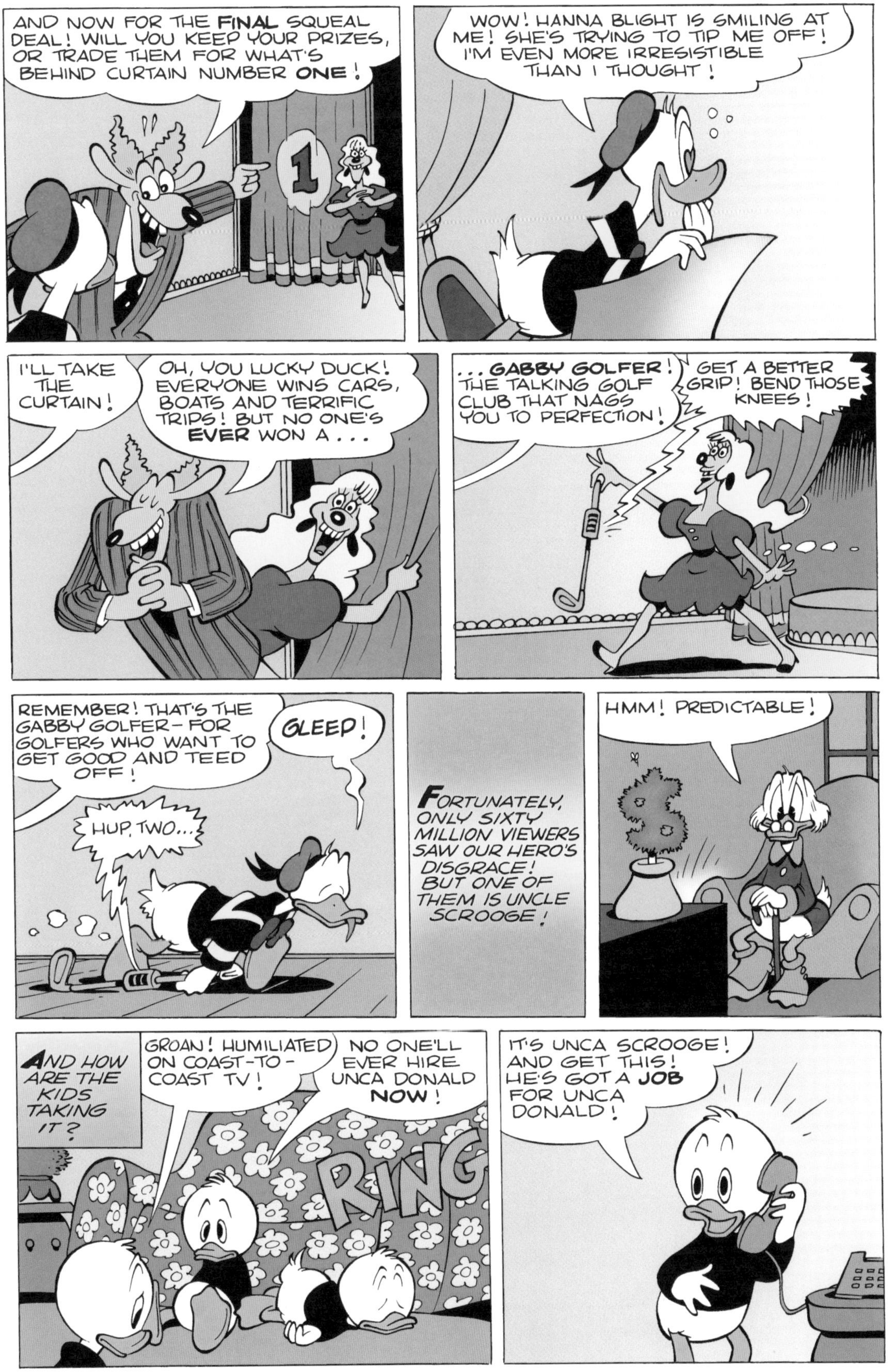
AND NOW FOR THE FINAL SQUEAL DEAL! WILL YOU KEEP YOUR PRIZES, OR TRADE THEM FOR WHAT'S BEHIND CURTAIN NUMBER ONE!
1
WOW! HANNA BLIGHT IS SMILING AT ME! SHE'S TRYING TO TIP ME OFF! I'M EVEN MORE IRRESISTIBLE THAN I THOUGHT!
I'LL TAKE THE CURTAIN!
OH, YOU LUCKY DUCK! EVERYONE WINS CARS, BOATS AND TERRIFIC TRIPS! BUT NO ONE'S EVER WON A . . .
. . . GABBY GOLFER! THE TALKING GOLF CLUB THAT NAGS YOU TO PERFECTION!
GET A BETTER GRIP! BEND THOSE KNEES!
REMEMBER! THAT'S THE GABBY GOLFER— FOR GOLFERS WHO WANT TO GET GOOD AND TEED OFF!
GLEEP!
HUP, TWO...
FORTUNATELY, ONLY SIXTY MILLION VIEWERS SAW OUR HERO'S DISGRACE! BUT ONE OF THEM IS UNCLE SCROOGE!
HMM! PREDICTABLE!
AND HOW ARE THE KIDS TAKING IT?
GROAN! HUMILIATED ON COAST-TO-COAST TV!
NO ONE'LL EVER HIRE UNCA DONALD NOW!
RING
IT'S UNCA SCROOGE! AND GET THIS! HE'S GOT A JOB FOR UNCA DONALD!

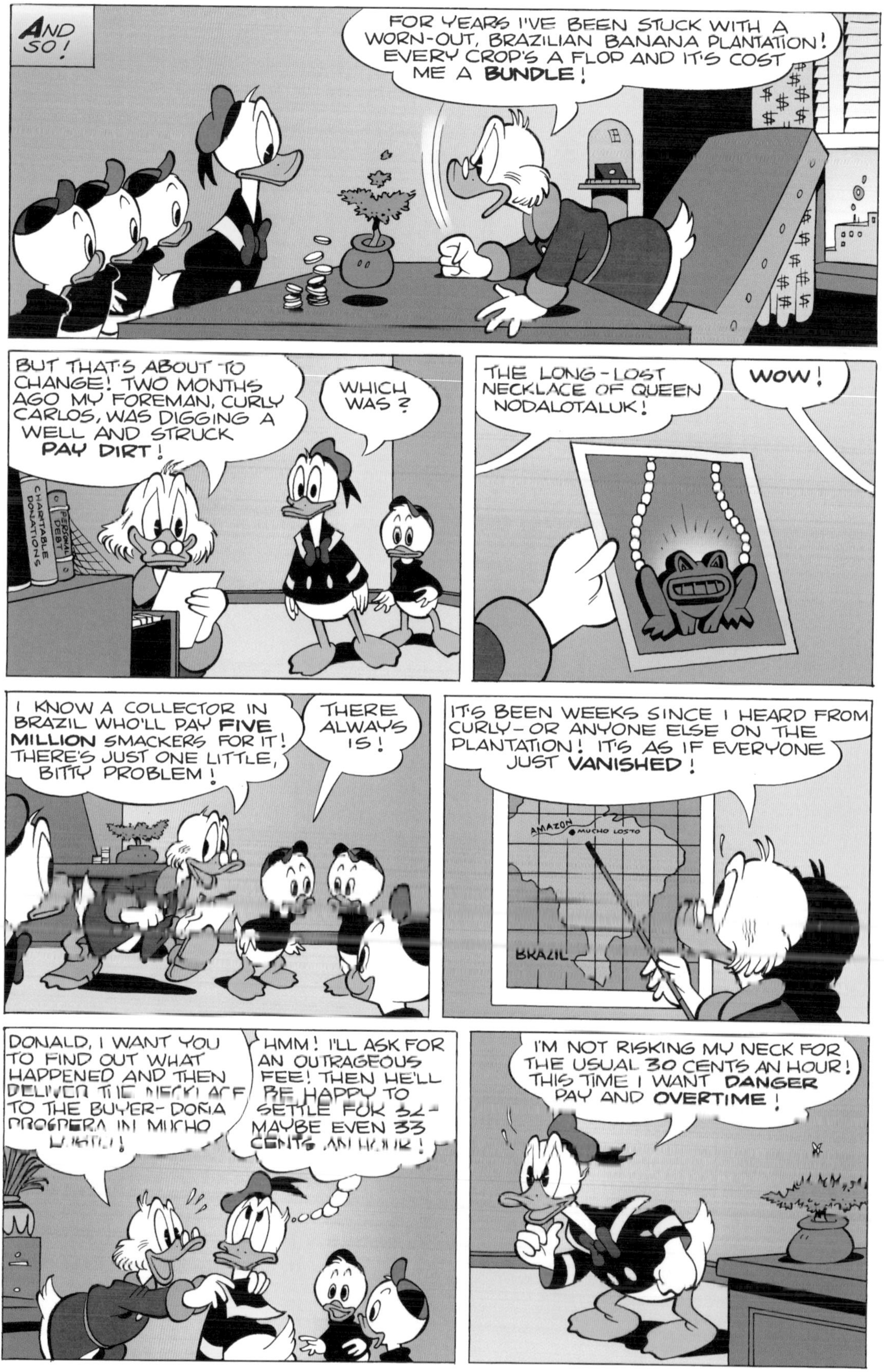
AND SO!
FOR YEARS I'VE BEEN STUCK WITH A WORN-OUT, BRAZILIAN BANANA PLANTATION! EVERY CROP'S A FLOP AND IT'S COST ME A **BUNDLE**!
BUT THAT'S ABOUT TO CHANGE! TWO MONTHS AGO MY FOREMAN, CURLY CARLOS, WAS DIGGING A WELL AND STRUCK **PAY DIRT**!
WHICH WAS?
CHARITABLE DONATIONS
PERSONAL DEBT
THE LONG-LOST NECKLACE OF QUEEN NODALOTALUK!
WOW!
I KNOW A COLLECTOR IN BRAZIL WHO'LL PAY **FIVE MILLION** SMACKERS FOR IT! THERE'S JUST ONE LITTLE, BITTY PROBLEM!
THERE ALWAYS IS!
IT'S BEEN WEEKS SINCE I HEARD FROM CURLY—OR ANYONE ELSE ON THE PLANTATION! IT'S AS IF EVERYONE JUST **VANISHED**!
AMAZON
MUCHO LOSTO
BRAZIL
DONALD, I WANT YOU TO FIND OUT WHAT HAPPENED AND THEN DELIVER THE NECKLACE TO THE BUYER—DOÑA PROSPERA IN MUCHO
HMM! I'LL ASK FOR AN OUTRAGEOUS FEE! THEN HE'LL BE HAPPY TO SETTLE FOR 32—MAYBE EVEN 33
I'M NOT RISKING MY NECK FOR THE USUAL **30 CENTS AN HOUR**! THIS TIME I WANT **DANGER** PAY AND **OVERTIME**!

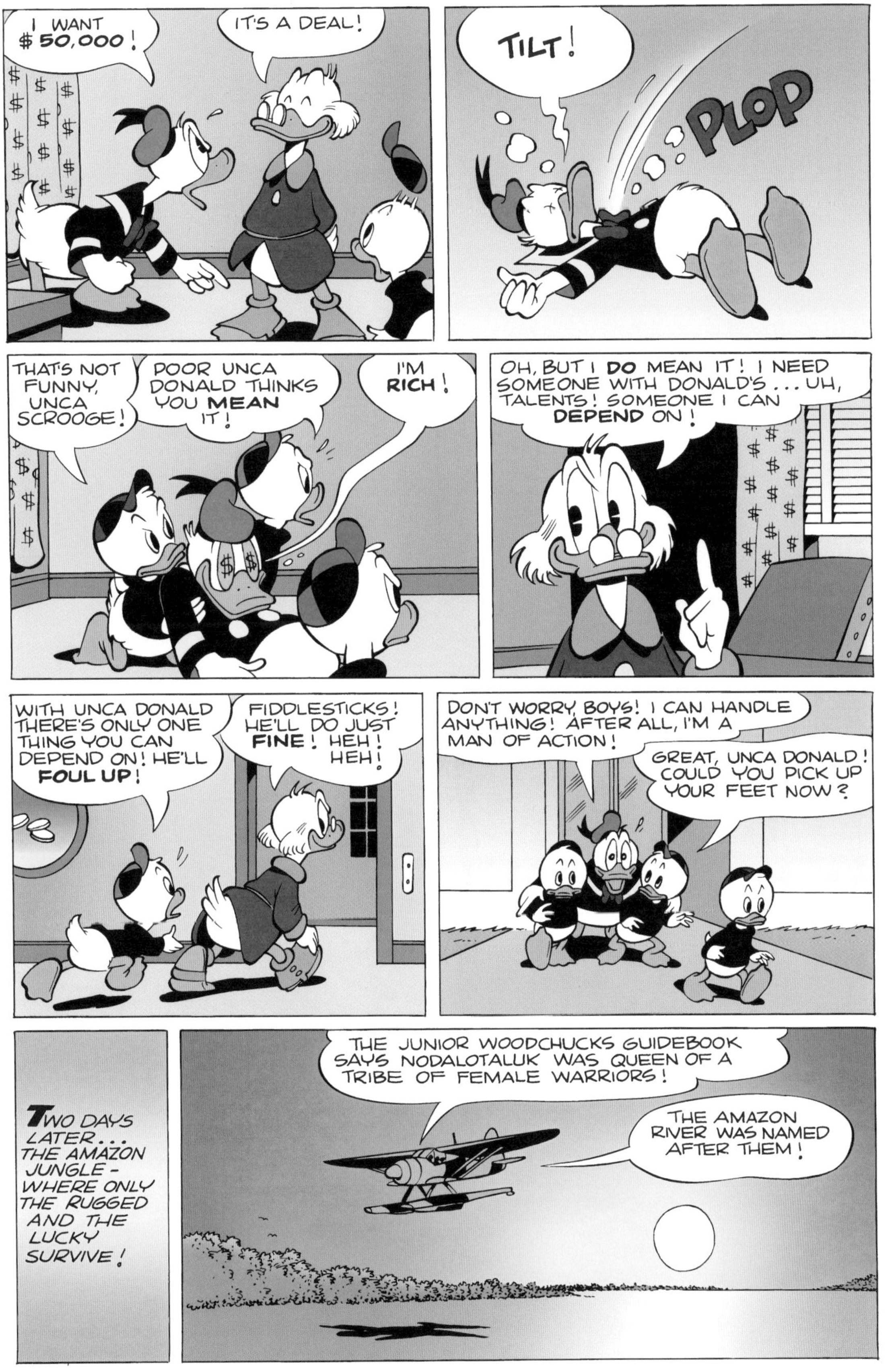
I WANT $ 50,000 !
IT'S A DEAL!
TILT !
PLOP
THAT'S NOT FUNNY, UNCA SCROOGE!
POOR UNCA DONALD THINKS YOU MEAN IT !
I'M RICH !
OH, BUT I DO MEAN IT ! I NEED SOMEONE WITH DONALD'S ... UH, TALENTS ! SOMEONE I CAN DEPEND ON !
WITH UNCA DONALD THERE'S ONLY ONE THING YOU CAN DEPEND ON ! HE'LL FOUL UP !
FIDDLESTICKS ! HE'LL DO JUST FINE ! HEH ! HEH !
DON'T WORRY, BOYS ! I CAN HANDLE ANYTHING ! AFTER ALL, I'M A MAN OF ACTION !
GREAT, UNCA DONALD ! COULD YOU PICK UP YOUR FEET NOW ?
TWO DAYS LATER... THE AMAZON JUNGLE - WHERE ONLY THE RUGGED AND THE LUCKY SURVIVE !
THE JUNIOR WOODCHUCKS GUIDEBOOK SAYS NODALOTALUK WAS QUEEN OF A TRIBE OF FEMALE WARRIORS !
THE AMAZON RIVER WAS NAMED AFTER THEM !

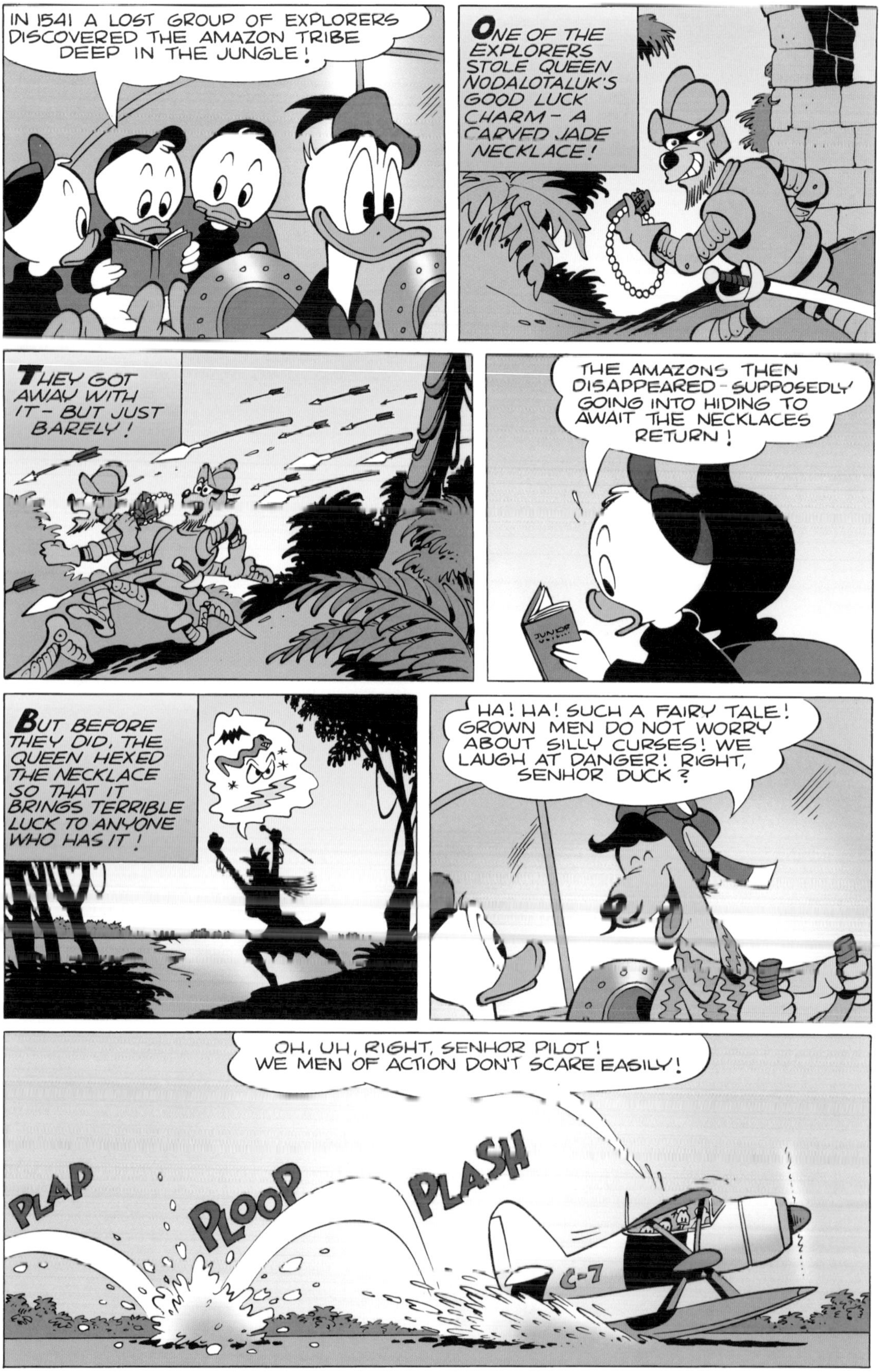
IN 1541 A LOST GROUP OF EXPLORERS DISCOVERED THE AMAZON TRIBE DEEP IN THE JUNGLE!
ONE OF THE EXPLORERS STOLE QUEEN NODALOTALUK'S GOOD LUCK CHARM – A CARVED JADE NECKLACE!
THEY GOT AWAY WITH IT – BUT JUST BARELY!
THE AMAZONS THEN DISAPPEARED – SUPPOSEDLY GOING INTO HIDING TO AWAIT THE NECKLACES RETURN!
BUT BEFORE THEY DID, THE QUEEN HEXED THE NECKLACE SO THAT IT BRINGS TERRIBLE LUCK TO ANYONE WHO HAS IT!
HA! HA! SUCH A FAIRY TALE! GROWN MEN DO NOT WORRY ABOUT SILLY CURSES! WE LAUGH AT DANGER! RIGHT, SENHOR DUCK?
OH, UH, RIGHT, SENHOR PILOT! WE MEN OF ACTION DON'T SCARE EASILY!
PLAP
PLOOP
PLASH
C-7

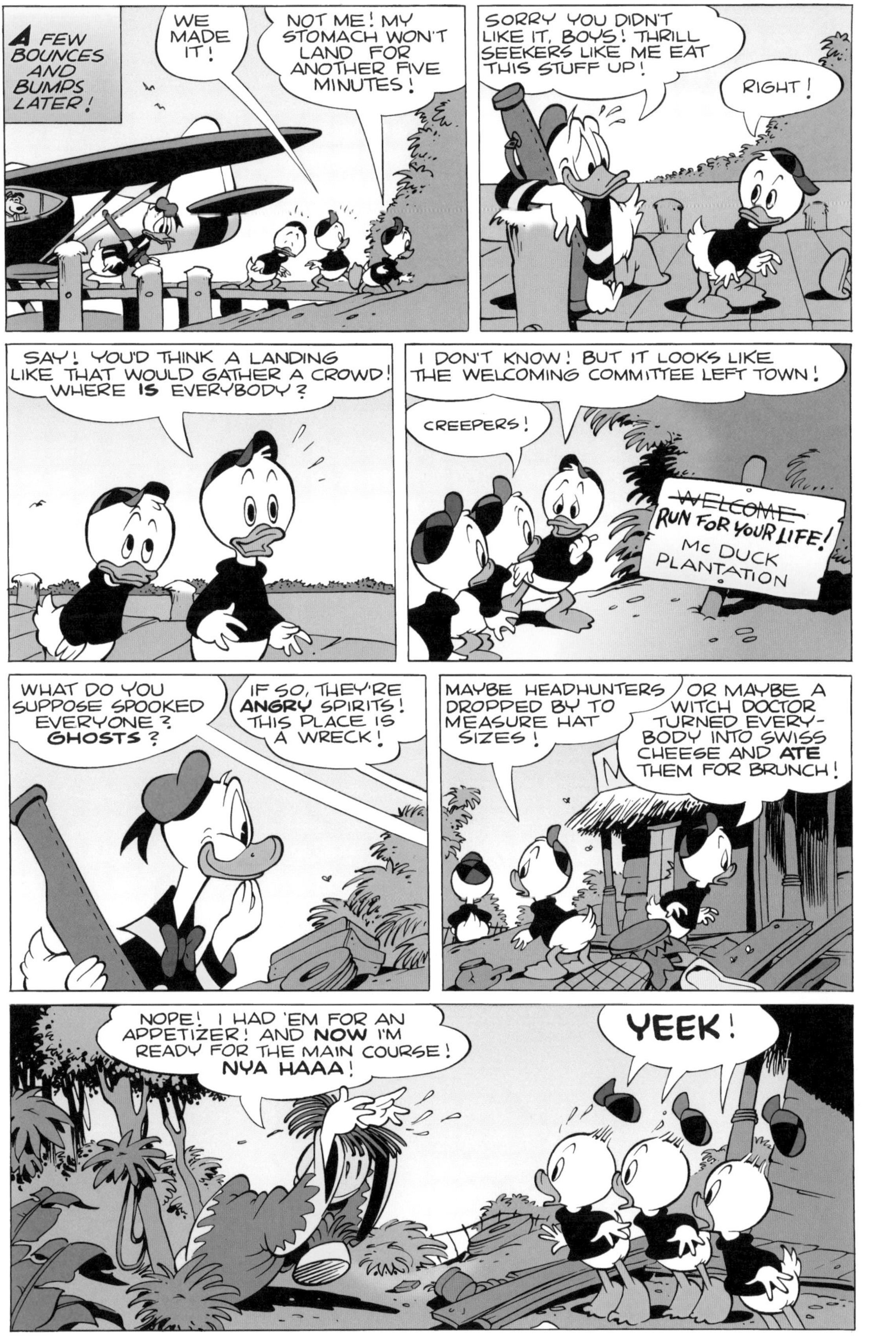
A FEW BOUNCES AND BUMPS LATER!
WE MADE IT!
NOT ME! MY STOMACH WON'T LAND FOR ANOTHER FIVE MINUTES!
SORRY YOU DIDN'T LIKE IT, BOYS! THRILL SEEKERS LIKE ME EAT THIS STUFF UP!
RIGHT!
SAY! YOU'D THINK A LANDING LIKE THAT WOULD GATHER A CROWD! WHERE IS EVERYBODY?
I DON'T KNOW! BUT IT LOOKS LIKE THE WELCOMING COMMITTEE LEFT TOWN!
CREEPERS!
WELCOME
RUN FOR YOUR LIFE!
Mc DUCK PLANTATION
WHAT DO YOU SUPPOSE SPOOKED EVERYONE? GHOSTS?
IF SO, THEY'RE ANGRY SPIRITS! THIS PLACE IS A WRECK!
MAYBE HEADHUNTERS DROPPED BY TO MEASURE HAT SIZES!
OR MAYBE A WITCH DOCTOR TURNED EVERYBODY INTO SWISS CHEESE AND ATE THEM FOR BRUNCH!
NOPE! I HAD 'EM FOR AN APPETIZER! AND NOW I'M READY FOR THE MAIN COURSE! NYA HAAA!
YEEK!

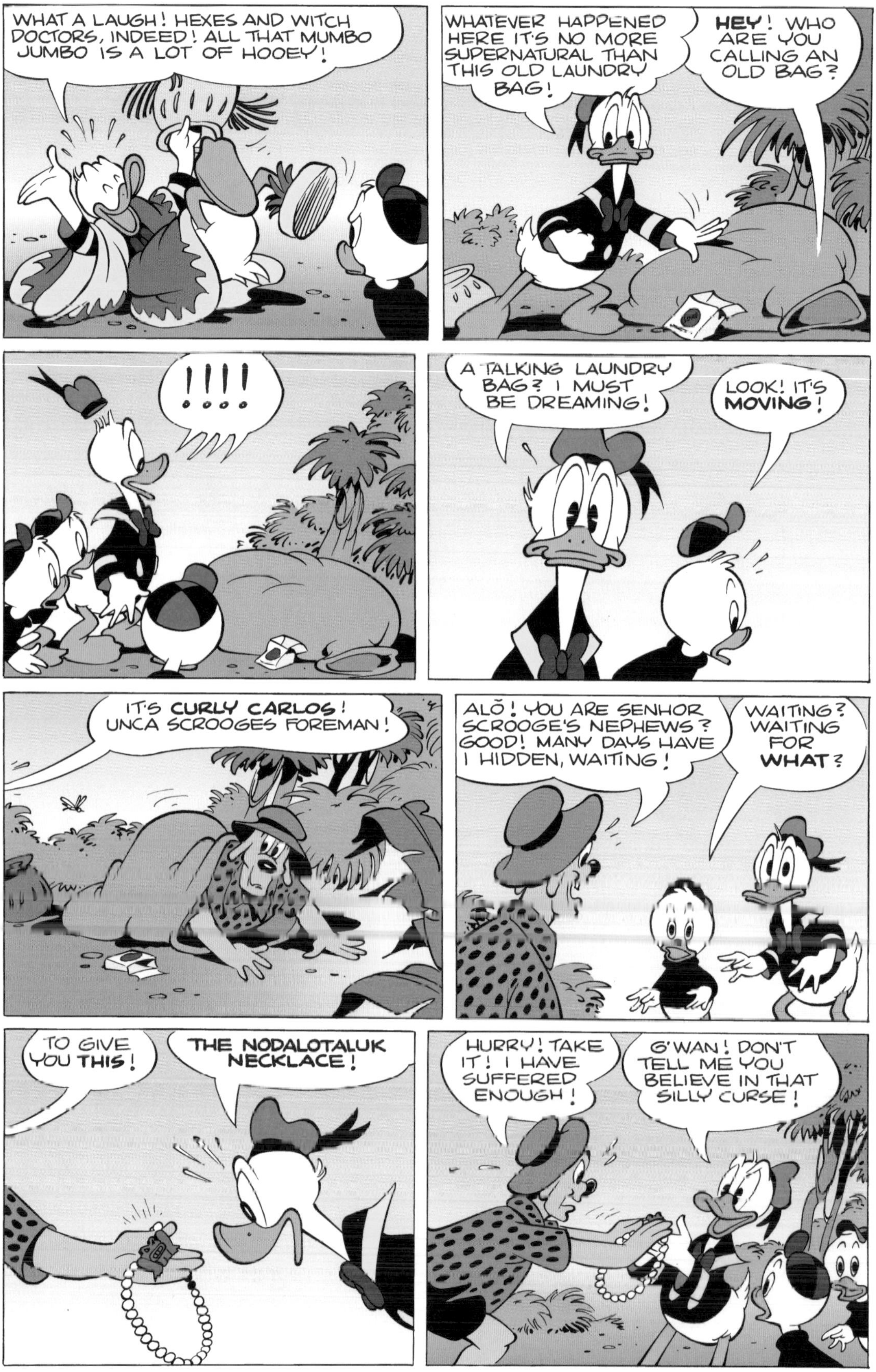
WHAT A LAUGH! HEXES AND WITCH DOCTORS, INDEED! ALL THAT MUMBO JUMBO IS A LOT OF HOOEY!
WHATEVER HAPPENED HERE IT'S NO MORE SUPERNATURAL THAN THIS OLD LAUNDRY BAG!
HEY! WHO ARE YOU CALLING AN OLD BAG?
!!!!
A TALKING LAUNDRY BAG? I MUST BE DREAMING!
LOOK! IT'S MOVING!
IT'S CURLY CARLOS! UNCA SCROOGE'S FOREMAN!
ALÔ! YOU ARE SENHOR SCROOGE'S NEPHEWS? GOOD! MANY DAYS HAVE I HIDDEN, WAITING!
WAITING? WAITING FOR WHAT?
TO GIVE YOU THIS!
THE NODALOTALUK NECKLACE!
HURRY! TAKE IT! I HAVE SUFFERED ENOUGH!
G'WAN! DON'T TELL ME YOU BELIEVE IN THAT SILLY CURSE!

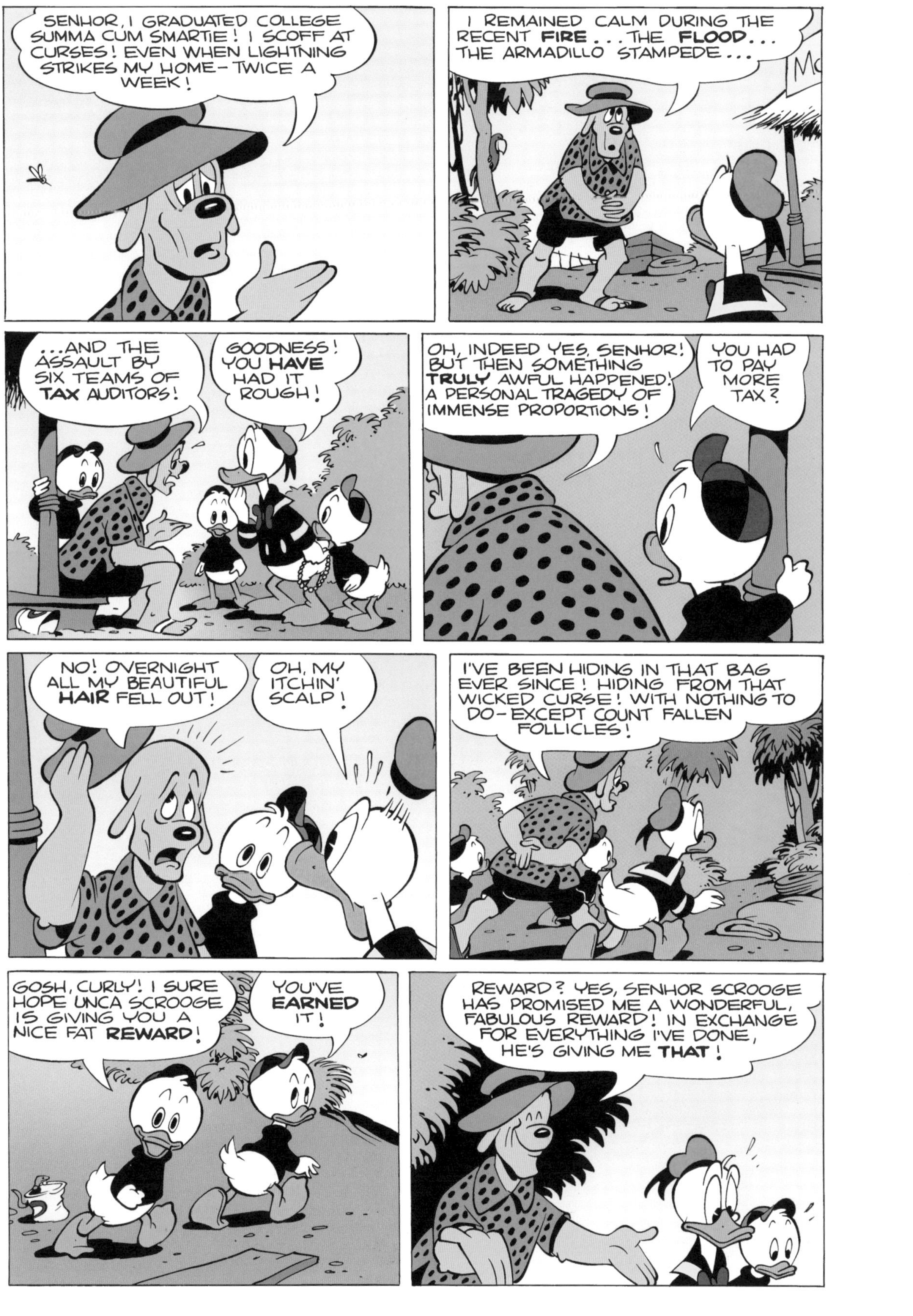
SENHOR, I GRADUATED COLLEGE SUMMA CUM SMARTIE! I SCOFF AT CURSES! EVEN WHEN LIGHTNING STRIKES MY HOME–TWICE A WEEK!
I REMAINED CALM DURING THE RECENT FIRE... THE FLOOD... THE ARMADILLO STAMPEDE...
...AND THE ASSAULT BY SIX TEAMS OF TAX AUDITORS!
GOODNESS! YOU HAVE HAD IT ROUGH!
OH, INDEED YES, SENHOR! BUT THEN SOMETHING TRULY AWFUL HAPPENED! A PERSONAL TRAGEDY OF IMMENSE PROPORTIONS!
YOU HAD TO PAY MORE TAX?
NO! OVERNIGHT ALL MY BEAUTIFUL HAIR FELL OUT!
OH, MY ITCHIN' SCALP!
I'VE BEEN HIDING IN THAT BAG EVER SINCE! HIDING FROM THAT WICKED CURSE! WITH NOTHING TO DO–EXCEPT COUNT FALLEN FOLLICLES!
GOSH, CURLY! I SURE HOPE UNCA SCROOGE IS GIVING YOU A NICE FAT REWARD!
YOU'VE EARNED IT!
REWARD? YES, SENHOR SCROOGE HAS PROMISED ME A WONDERFUL, FABULOUS REWARD! IN EXCHANGE FOR EVERYTHING I'VE DONE, HE'S GIVING ME THAT!

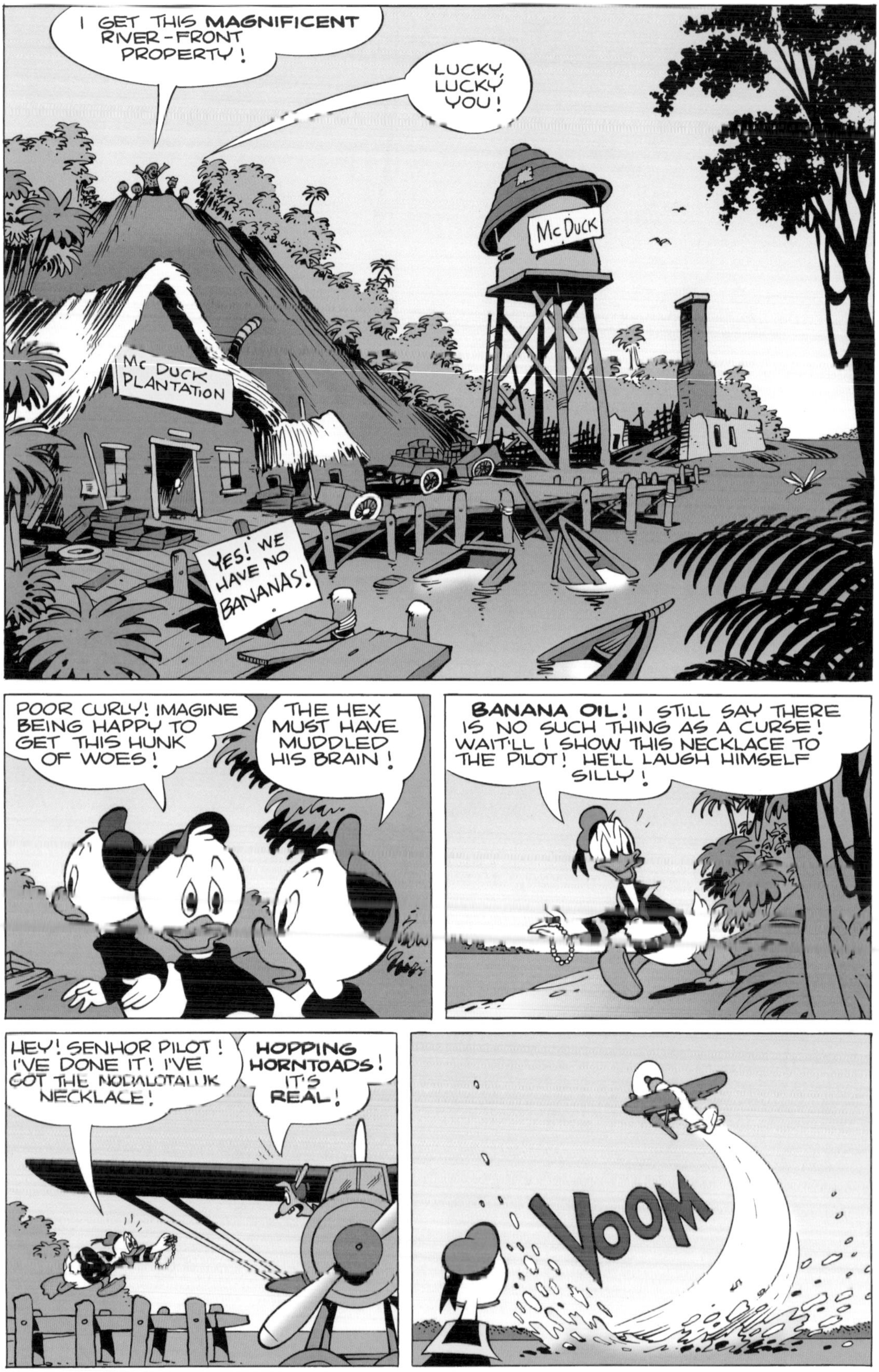
I GET THIS MAGNIFICENT RIVER-FRONT PROPERTY!
LUCKY, LUCKY YOU!
McDUCK
Mc DUCK PLANTATION
YES! WE HAVE NO BANANAS!
POOR CURLY! IMAGINE BEING HAPPY TO GET THIS HUNK OF WOES!
THE HEX MUST HAVE MUDDLED HIS BRAIN!
BANANA OIL! I STILL SAY THERE IS NO SUCH THING AS A CURSE! WAIT'LL I SHOW THIS NECKLACE TO THE PILOT! HE'LL LAUGH HIMSELF SILLY!
HEY! SENHOR PILOT! I'VE DONE IT! I'VE GOT THE NODALOTALUK NECKLACE!
HOPPING HORNTOADS! IT'S REAL!
VOOM

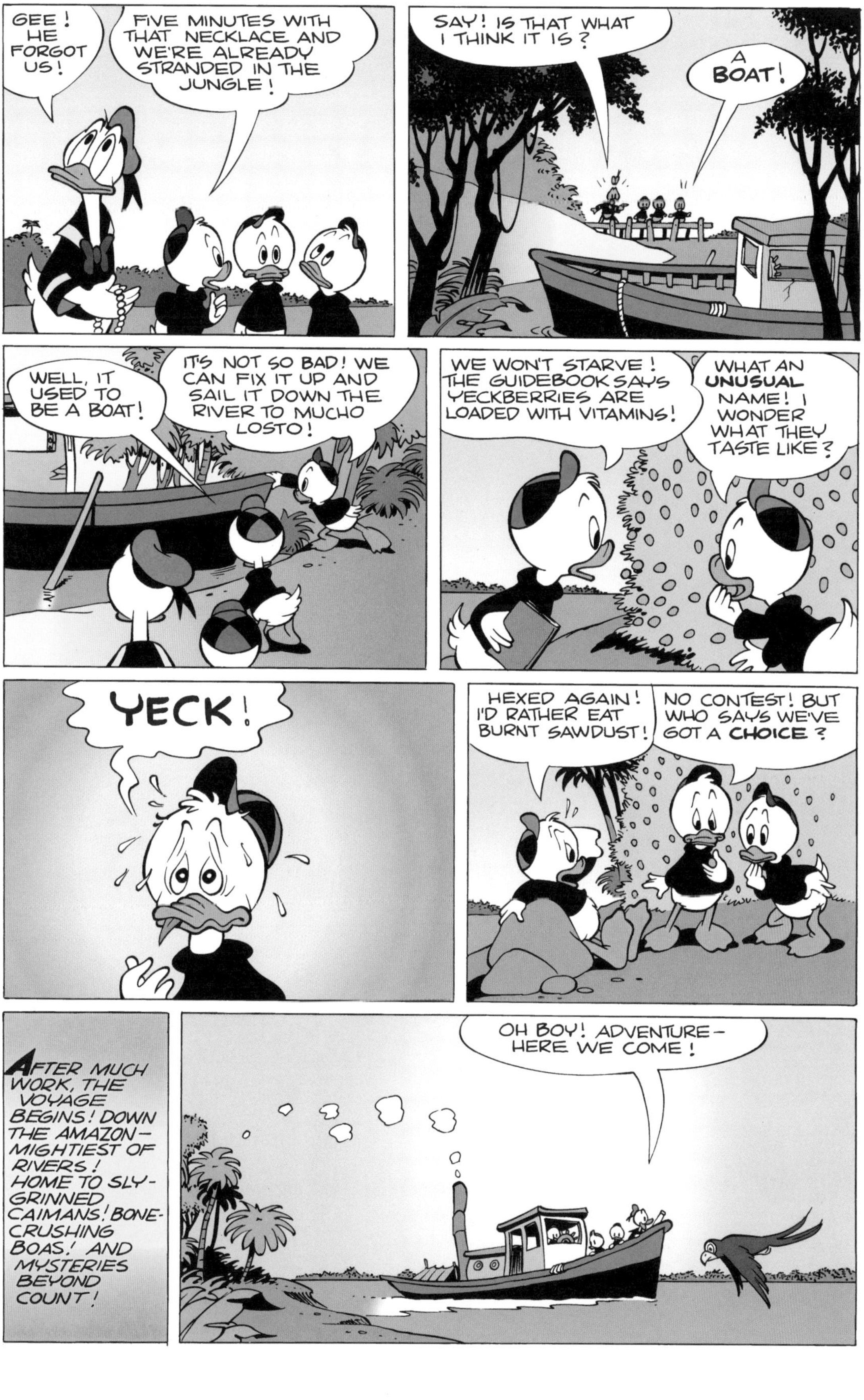

GEE! HE FORGOT US!
FIVE MINUTES WITH THAT NECKLACE AND WE'RE ALREADY STRANDED IN THE JUNGLE!
SAY! IS THAT WHAT I THINK IT IS?
A BOAT!
WELL, IT USED TO BE A BOAT!
IT'S NOT SO BAD! WE CAN FIX IT UP AND SAIL IT DOWN THE RIVER TO MUCHO LOSTO!
WE WON'T STARVE! THE GUIDEBOOK SAYS YECKBERRIES ARE LOADED WITH VITAMINS!
WHAT AN UNUSUAL NAME! I WONDER WHAT THEY TASTE LIKE?
YECK!
HEXED AGAIN! I'D RATHER EAT BURNT SAWDUST!
NO CONTEST! BUT WHO SAYS WE'VE GOT A CHOICE?
AFTER MUCH WORK, THE VOYAGE BEGINS! DOWN THE AMAZON—MIGHTIEST OF RIVERS! HOME TO SLY-GRINNED CAIMANS! BONE-CRUSHING BOAS! AND MYSTERIES BEYOND COUNT!
OH BOY! ADVENTURE—HERE WE COME!

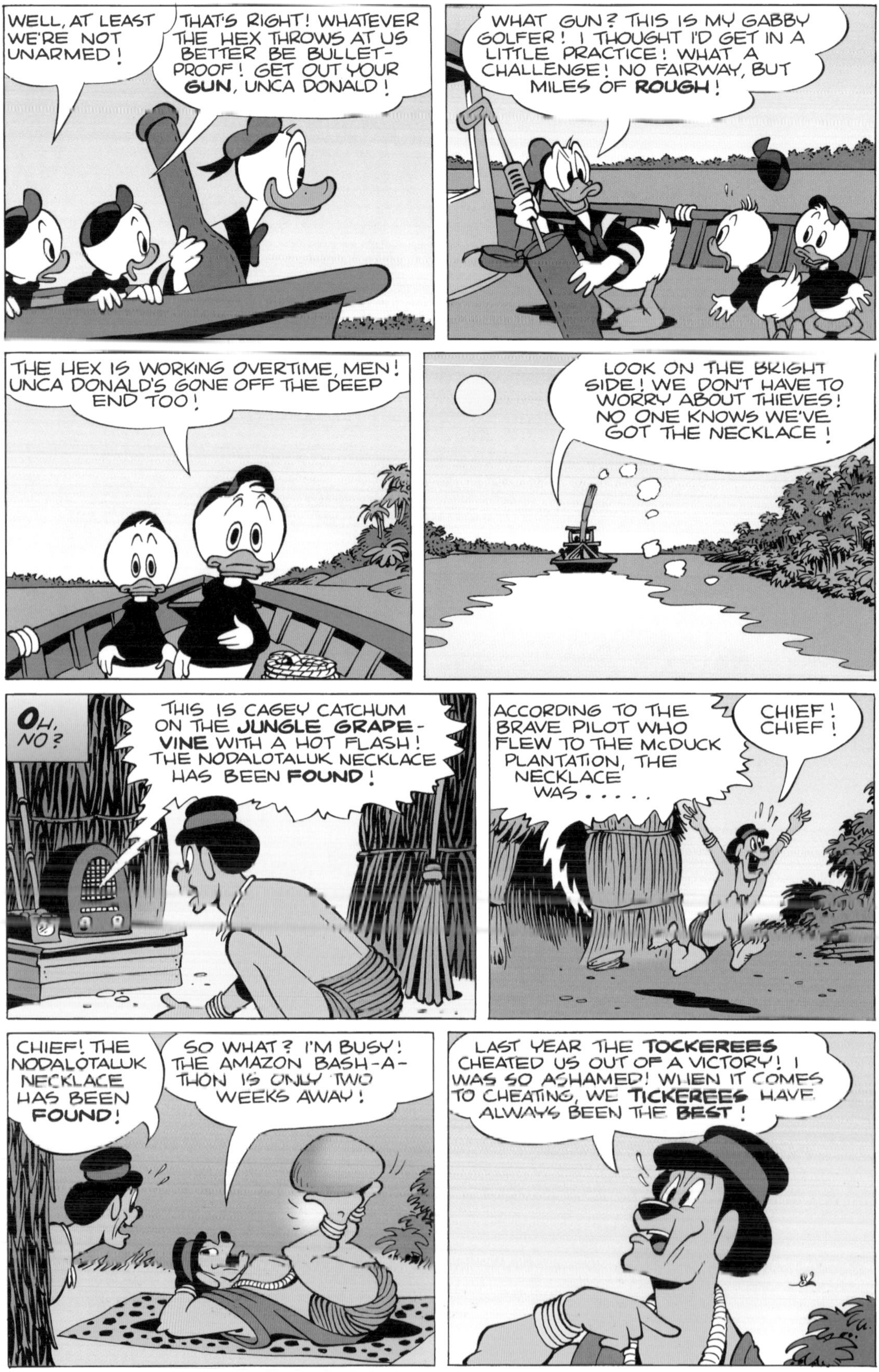
WELL, AT LEAST WE'RE NOT UNARMED!
THAT'S RIGHT! WHATEVER THE HEX THROWS AT US BETTER BE BULLET-PROOF! GET OUT YOUR GUN, UNCA DONALD!
WHAT GUN? THIS IS MY GABBY GOLFER! I THOUGHT I'D GET IN A LITTLE PRACTICE! WHAT A CHALLENGE! NO FAIRWAY, BUT MILES OF ROUGH!
THE HEX IS WORKING OVERTIME, MEN! UNCA DONALD'S GONE OFF THE DEEP END TOO!
LOOK ON THE BRIGHT SIDE! WE DON'T HAVE TO WORRY ABOUT THIEVES! NO ONE KNOWS WE'VE GOT THE NECKLACE!
OH, NO?
THIS IS CAGEY CATCHUM ON THE JUNGLE GRAPE-VINE WITH A HOT FLASH! THE NODALOTALUK NECKLACE HAS BEEN FOUND!
ACCORDING TO THE BRAVE PILOT WHO FLEW TO THE McDUCK PLANTATION, THE NECKLACE WAS....
CHIEF! CHIEF!
CHIEF! THE NODALOTALUK NECKLACE HAS BEEN FOUND!
SO WHAT? I'M BUSY! THE AMAZON BASH-A-THON IS ONLY TWO WEEKS AWAY!
LAST YEAR THE TOCKEREES CHEATED US OUT OF A VICTORY! I WAS SO ASHAMED! WHEN IT COMES TO CHEATING, WE TICKEREES HAVE ALWAYS BEEN THE BEST!

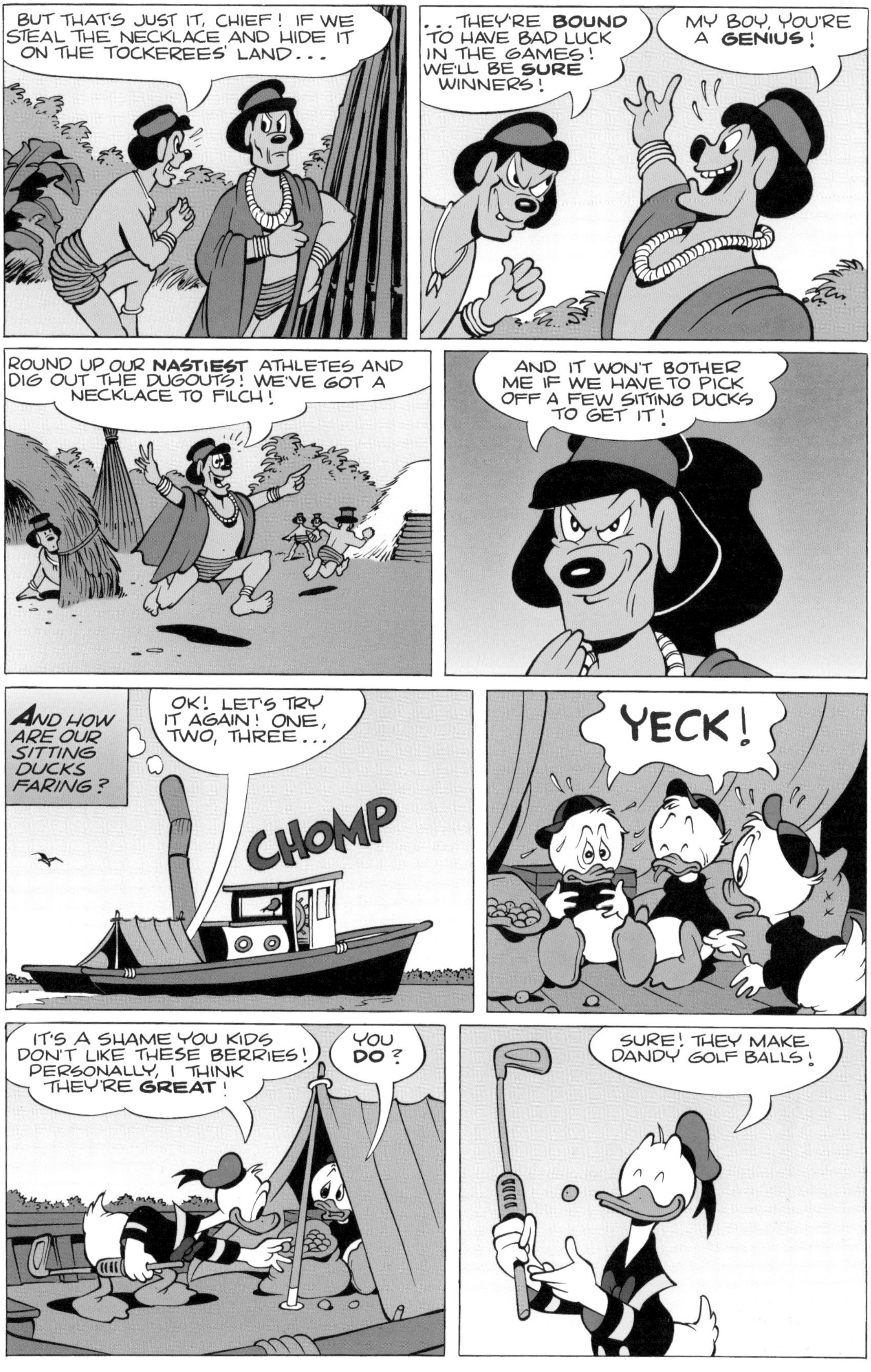
BUT THAT'S JUST IT, CHIEF! IF WE STEAL THE NECKLACE AND HIDE IT ON THE TOCKEREES' LAND...
...THEY'RE **BOUND** TO HAVE BAD LUCK IN THE GAMES! WE'LL BE **SURE** WINNERS!
MY BOY, YOU'RE A **GENIUS**!
ROUND UP OUR **NASTIEST** ATHLETES AND DIG OUT THE DUGOUTS! WE'VE GOT A NECKLACE TO FILCH!
AND IT WON'T BOTHER ME IF WE HAVE TO PICK OFF A FEW SITTING DUCKS TO GET IT!
AND HOW ARE OUR SITTING DUCKS FARING?
OK! LET'S TRY IT AGAIN! ONE, TWO, THREE...
CHOMP
YECK!
IT'S A SHAME YOU KIDS DON'T LIKE THESE BERRIES! PERSONALLY, I THINK THEY'RE **GREAT**!
YOU **DO**?
SURE! THEY MAKE DANDY GOLF BALLS!

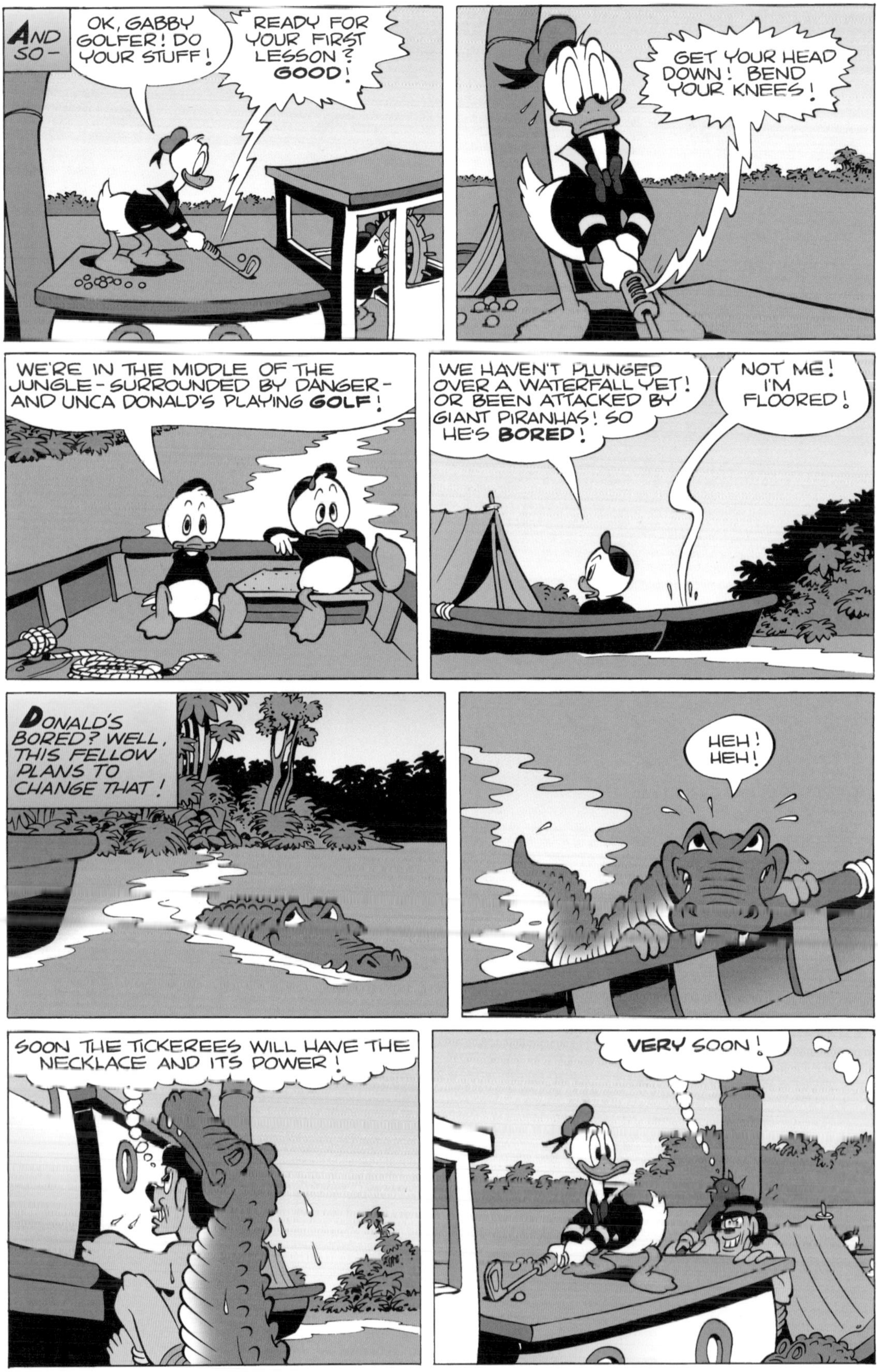
AND SO—
OK, GABBY GOLFER! DO YOUR STUFF!
READY FOR YOUR FIRST LESSON? GOOD!
GET YOUR HEAD DOWN! BEND YOUR KNEES!
WE'RE IN THE MIDDLE OF THE JUNGLE—SURROUNDED BY DANGER—AND UNCA DONALD'S PLAYING GOLF!
WE HAVEN'T PLUNGED OVER A WATERFALL YET! OR BEEN ATTACKED BY GIANT PIRANHAS! SO HE'S BORED!
NOT ME! I'M FLOORED!
DONALD'S BORED? WELL, THIS FELLOW PLANS TO CHANGE THAT!
HEH! HEH!
SOON THE TICKEREES WILL HAVE THE NECKLACE AND ITS POWER!
VERY SOON!

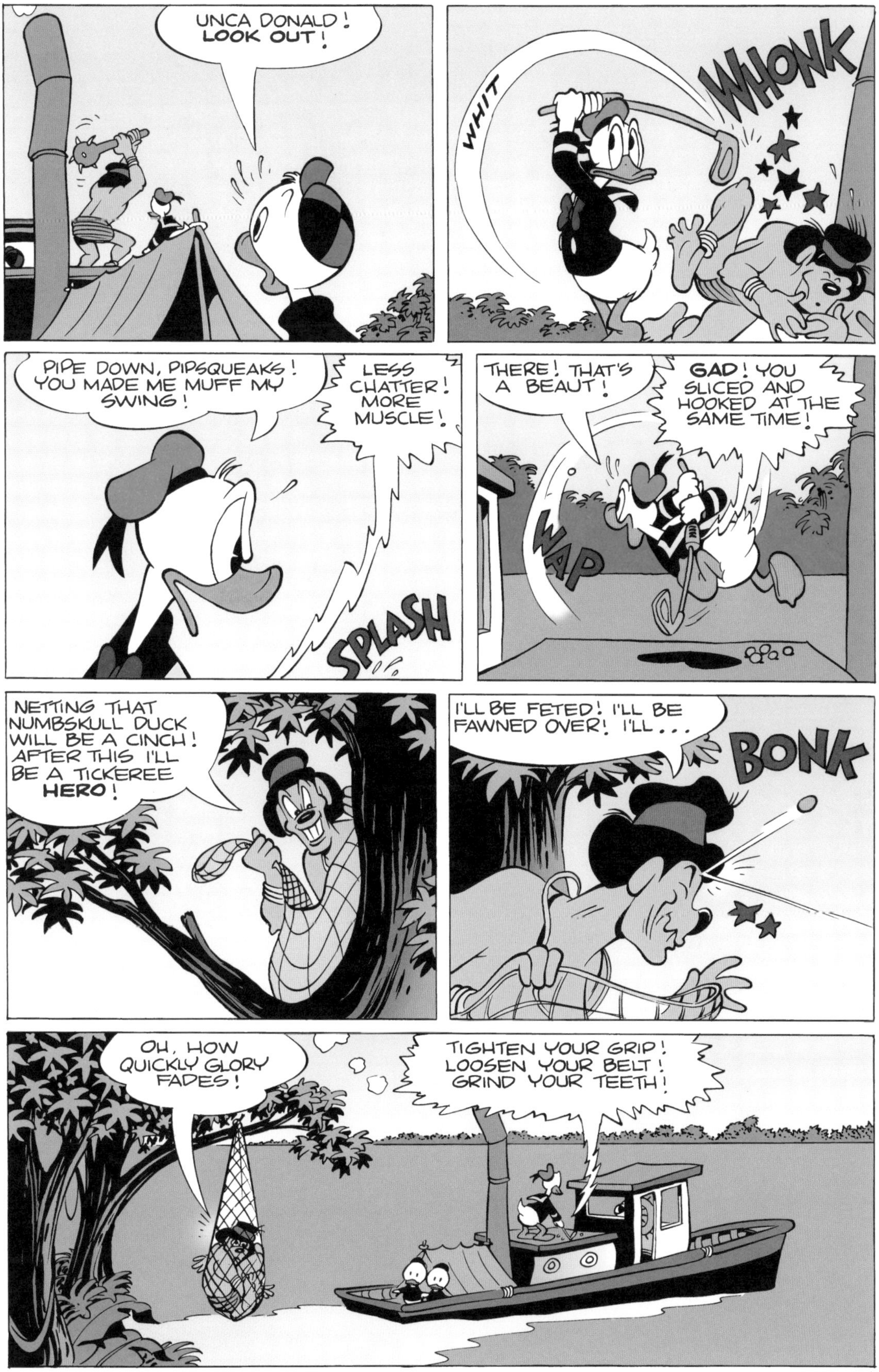

UNCA DONALD! LOOK OUT!
WHIT
WHONK
PIPE DOWN, PIPSQUEAKS! YOU MADE ME MUFF MY SWING!
LESS CHATTER! MORE MUSCLE!
SPLASH
THERE! THAT'S A BEAUT!
GAD! YOU SLICED AND HOOKED AT THE SAME TIME!
WAP
NETTING THAT NUMBSKULL DUCK WILL BE A CINCH! AFTER THIS I'LL BE A TICKEREE HERO!
I'LL BE FETED! I'LL BE FAWNED OVER! I'LL...
BONK
OH, HOW QUICKLY GLORY FADES!
TIGHTEN YOUR GRIP! LOOSEN YOUR BELT! GRIND YOUR TEETH!

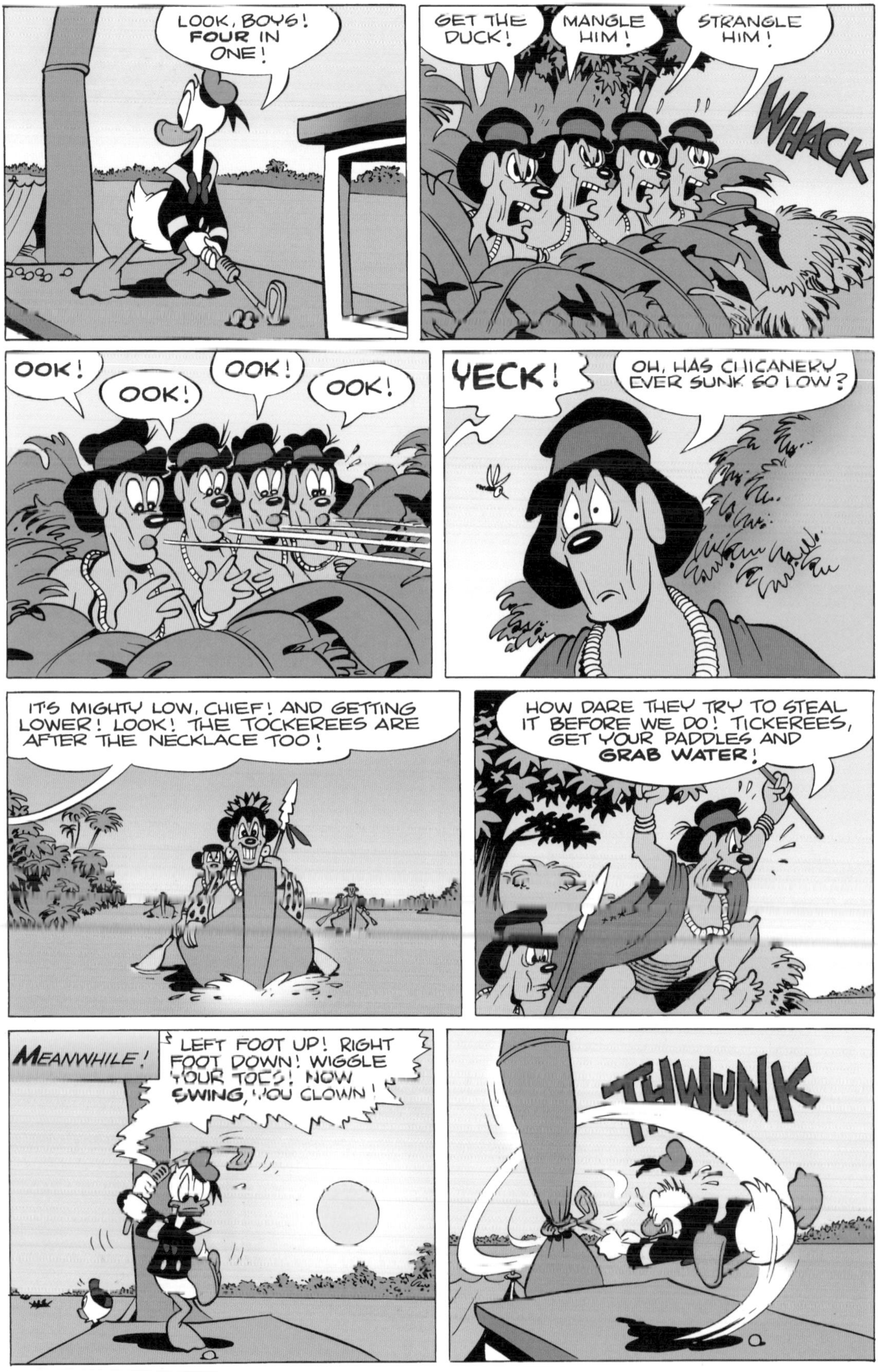
LOOK, BOYS! FOUR IN ONE!
GET THE DUCK!
MANGLE HIM!
STRANGLE HIM!
WHACK
OOK!
OOK!
OOK!
OOK!
YECK!
OH, HAS CHICANERY EVER SUNK SO LOW?
IT'S MIGHTY LOW, CHIEF! AND GETTING LOWER! LOOK! THE TOCKEREES ARE AFTER THE NECKLACE TOO!
HOW DARE THEY TRY TO STEAL IT BEFORE WE DO! TICKEREES, GET YOUR PADDLES AND GRAB WATER!
MEANWHILE!
LEFT FOOT UP! RIGHT FOOT DOWN! WIGGLE YOUR TOES! NOW SWING, YOU CLOWN!
THWUNK

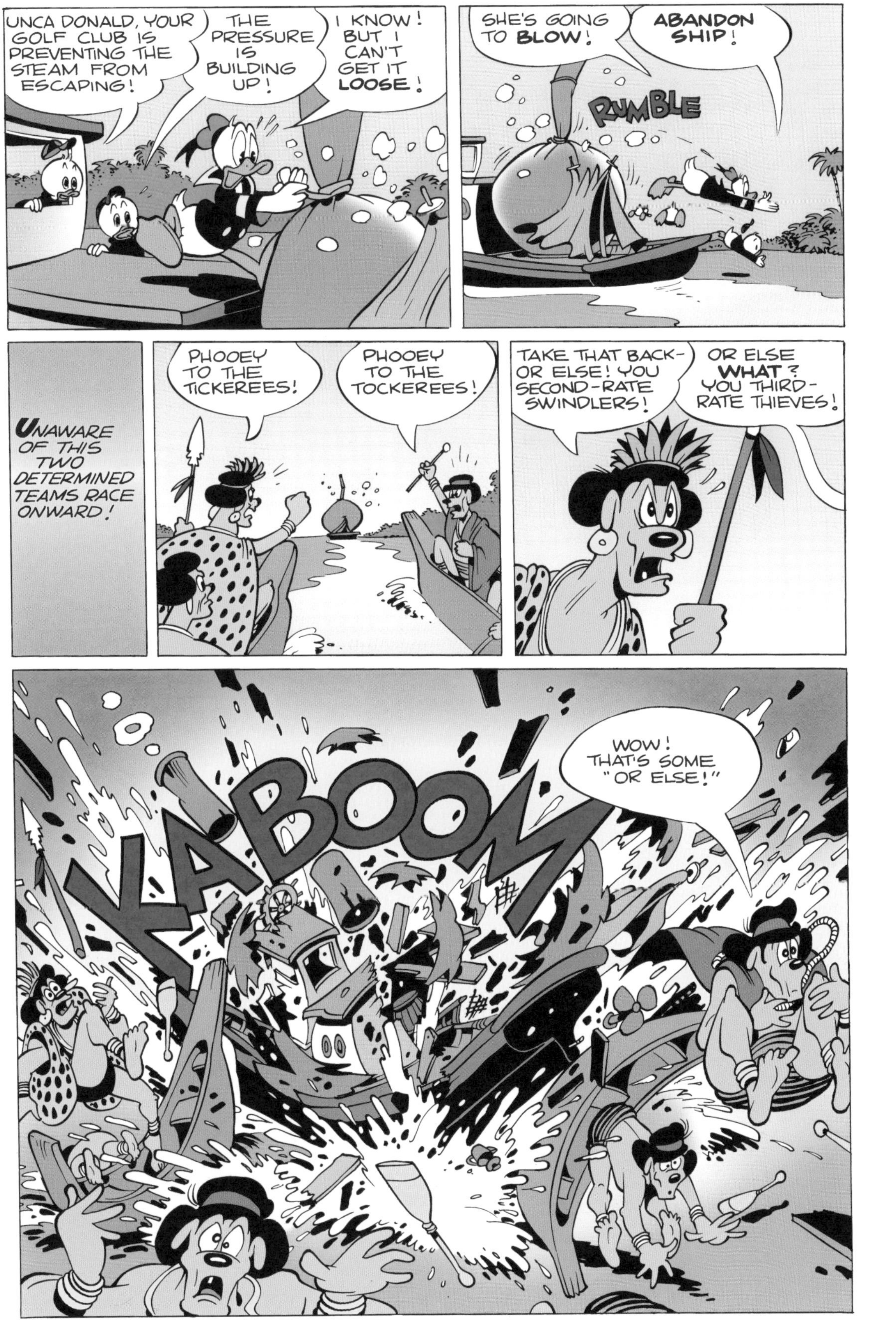
UNCA DONALD, YOUR GOLF CLUB IS PREVENTING THE STEAM FROM ESCAPING!
THE PRESSURE IS BUILDING UP!
I KNOW! BUT I CAN'T GET IT LOOSE!
SHE'S GOING TO BLOW!
ABANDON SHIP!
RUMBLE
UNAWARE OF THIS TWO DETERMINED TEAMS RACE ONWARD!
PHOOEY TO THE TICKEREES!
PHOOEY TO THE TOCKEREES!
TAKE THAT BACK-OR ELSE! YOU SECOND-RATE SWINDLERS!
OR ELSE WHAT? YOU THIRD-RATE THIEVES!
KABOOM
WOW! THAT'S SOME "OR ELSE!"

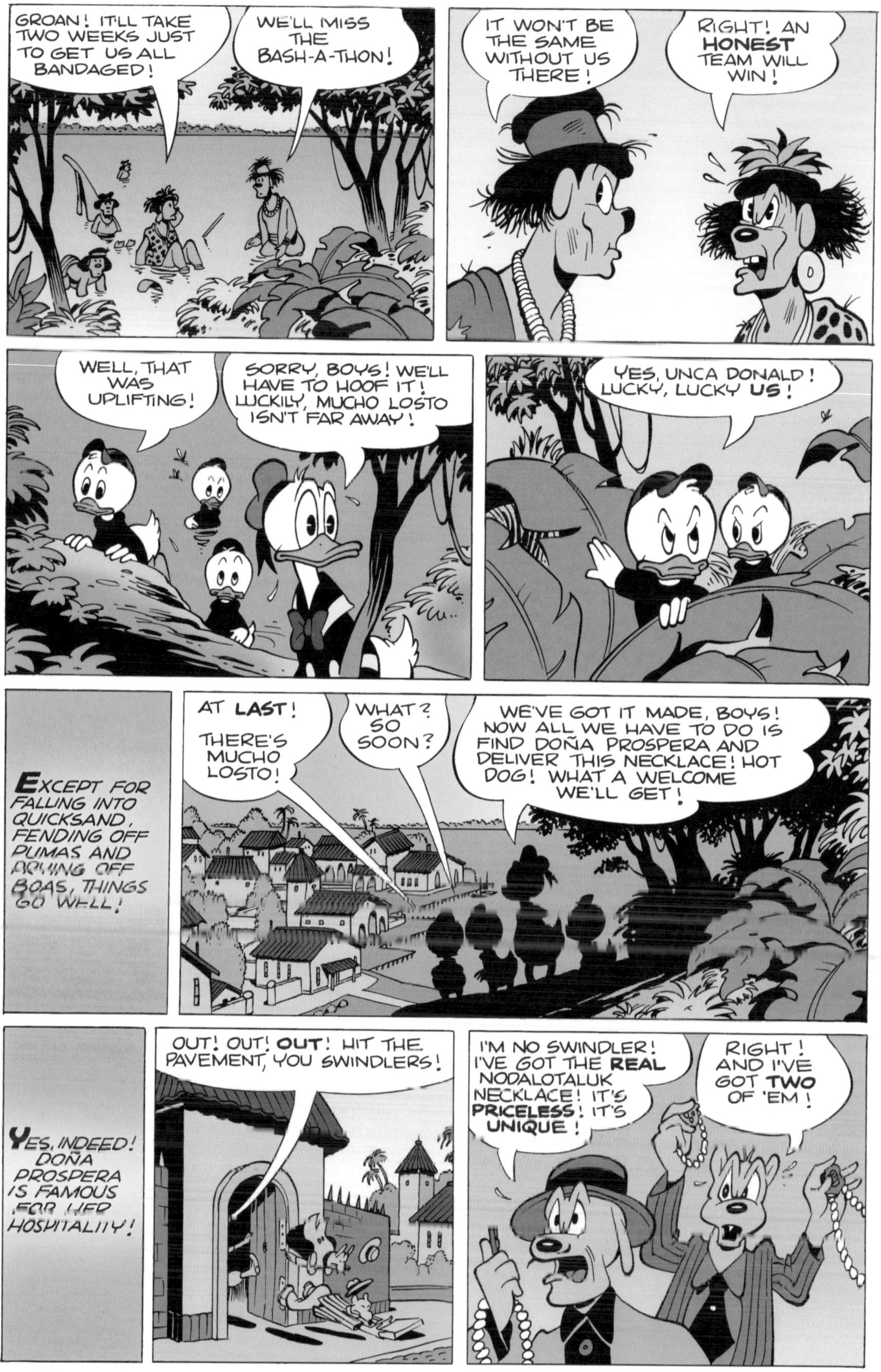
GROAN! IT'LL TAKE TWO WEEKS JUST TO GET US ALL BANDAGED!
WE'LL MISS THE BASH-A-THON!
IT WON'T BE THE SAME WITHOUT US THERE!
RIGHT! AN HONEST TEAM WILL WIN!
WELL, THAT WAS UPLIFTING!
SORRY, BOYS! WE'LL HAVE TO HOOF IT! LUCKILY, MUCHO LOSTO ISN'T FAR AWAY!
YES, UNCA DONALD! LUCKY, LUCKY US!
EXCEPT FOR FALLING INTO QUICKSAND, FENDING OFF PUMAS AND DRIVING OFF BOAS, THINGS GO WELL!
AT LAST!
THERE'S MUCHO LOSTO!
WHAT? SO SOON?
WE'VE GOT IT MADE, BOYS! NOW ALL WE HAVE TO DO IS FIND DOÑA PROSPERA AND DELIVER THIS NECKLACE! HOT DOG! WHAT A WELCOME WE'LL GET!
YES, INDEED! DOÑA PROSPERA IS FAMOUS FOR HER HOSPITALITY!
OUT! OUT! OUT! HIT THE PAVEMENT, YOU SWINDLERS!
I'M NO SWINDLER! I'VE GOT THE REAL NODALOTALUK NECKLACE! IT'S PRICELESS! IT'S UNIQUE!
RIGHT! AND I'VE GOT TWO OF 'EM!

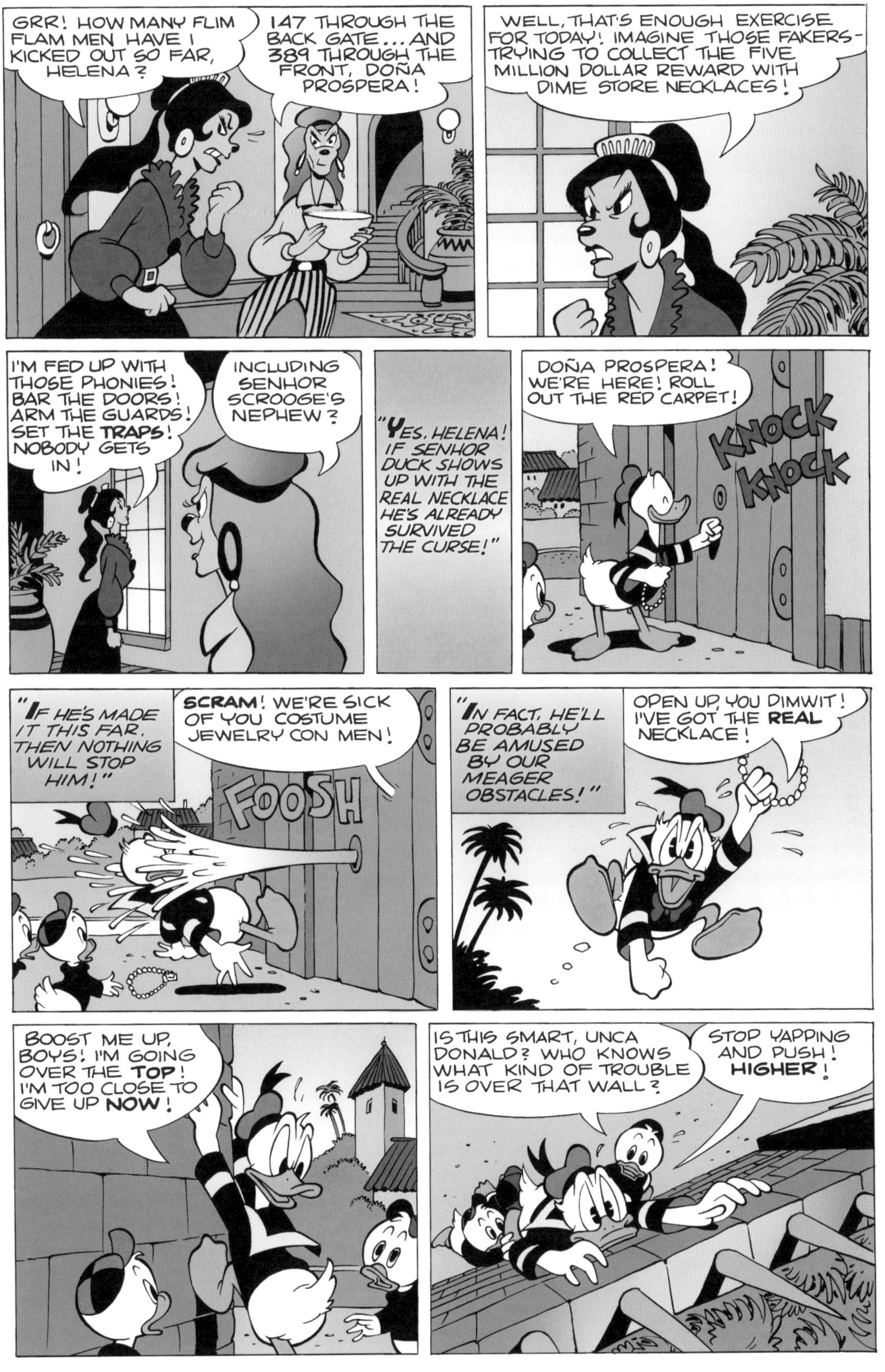

GRR! HOW MANY FLIM FLAM MEN HAVE I KICKED OUT SO FAR, HELENA?
147 THROUGH THE BACK GATE... AND 389 THROUGH THE FRONT, DOÑA PROSPERA!
WELL, THAT'S ENOUGH EXERCISE FOR TODAY! IMAGINE THOSE FAKERS-TRYING TO COLLECT THE FIVE MILLION DOLLAR REWARD WITH DIME STORE NECKLACES!
I'M FED UP WITH THOSE PHONIES! BAR THE DOORS! ARM THE GUARDS! SET THE **TRAPS**! NOBODY GETS IN!
INCLUDING SENHOR SCROOGE'S NEPHEW?
"YES, HELENA! IF SENHOR DUCK SHOWS UP WITH THE REAL NECKLACE HE'S ALREADY SURVIVED THE CURSE!"
DOÑA PROSPERA! WE'RE HERE! ROLL OUT THE RED CARPET!
KNOCK KNOCK
"IF HE'S MADE IT THIS FAR, THEN NOTHING WILL STOP HIM!"
SCRAM! WE'RE SICK OF YOU COSTUME JEWELRY CON MEN!
FOOSH
"IN FACT, HE'LL PROBABLY BE AMUSED BY OUR MEAGER OBSTACLES!"
OPEN UP, YOU DIMWIT! I'VE GOT THE **REAL** NECKLACE!
BOOST ME UP, BOYS! I'M GOING OVER THE **TOP**! I'M TOO CLOSE TO GIVE UP **NOW**!
IS THIS SMART, UNCA DONALD? WHO KNOWS WHAT KIND OF TROUBLE IS OVER THAT WALL?
STOP YAPPING AND PUSH! **HIGHER**!

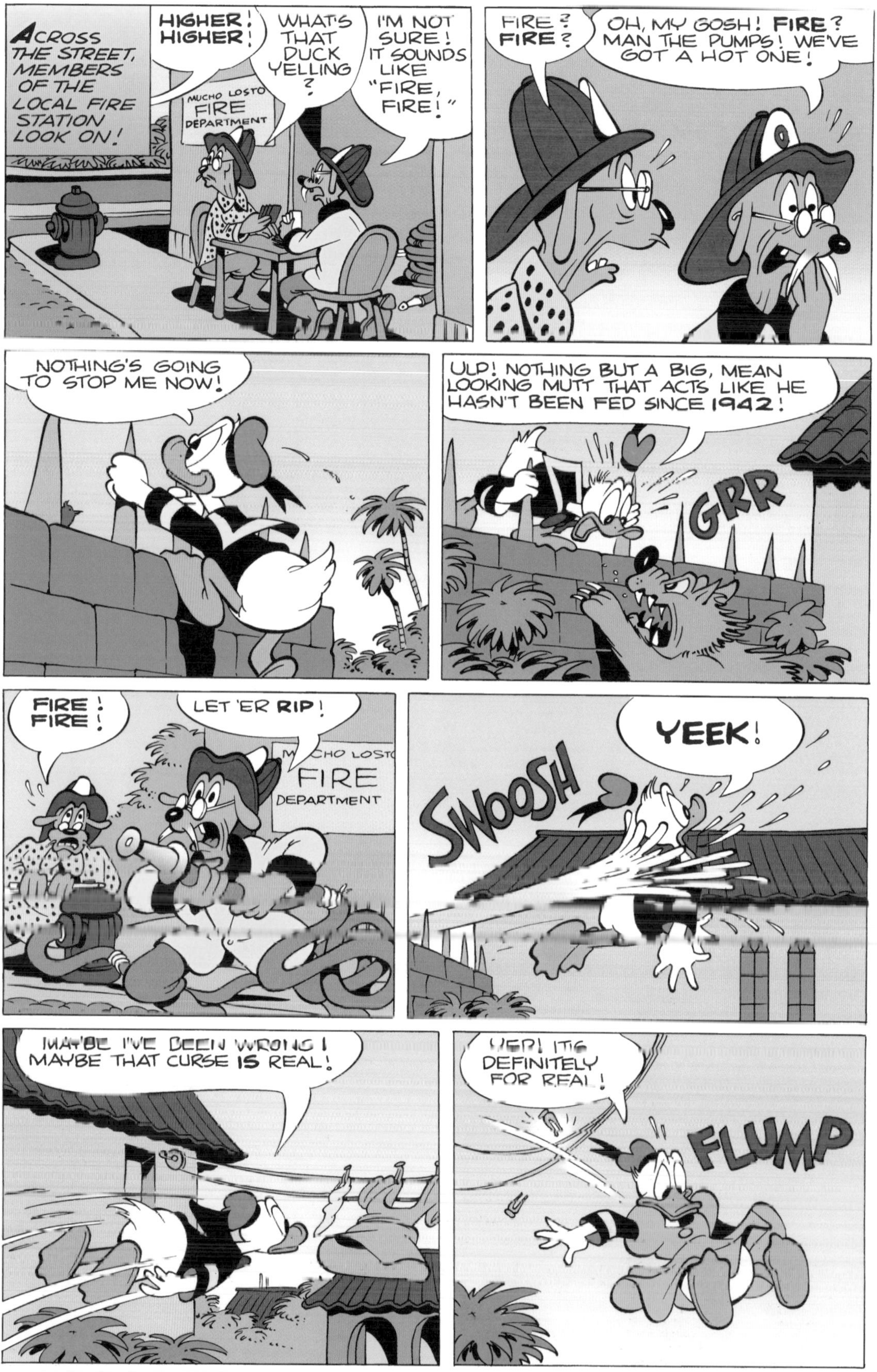
ACROSS THE STREET, MEMBERS OF THE LOCAL FIRE STATION LOOK ON!
HIGHER! HIGHER!
MUCHO LOSTO FIRE DEPARTMENT
WHAT'S THAT DUCK YELLING?
I'M NOT SURE! IT SOUNDS LIKE "FIRE, FIRE!"
FIRE? FIRE?
OH, MY GOSH! FIRE? MAN THE PUMPS! WE'VE GOT A HOT ONE!
NOTHING'S GOING TO STOP ME NOW!
ULP! NOTHING BUT A BIG, MEAN LOOKING MUTT THAT ACTS LIKE HE HASN'T BEEN FED SINCE 1942!
GRR
FIRE! FIRE!
LET 'ER RIP!
FIRE DEPARTMENT
YEEK!
SWOOSH
MAYBE I'VE BEEN WRONG! MAYBE THAT CURSE IS REAL!
YEP! IT'S DEFINITELY FOR REAL!
FLUMP

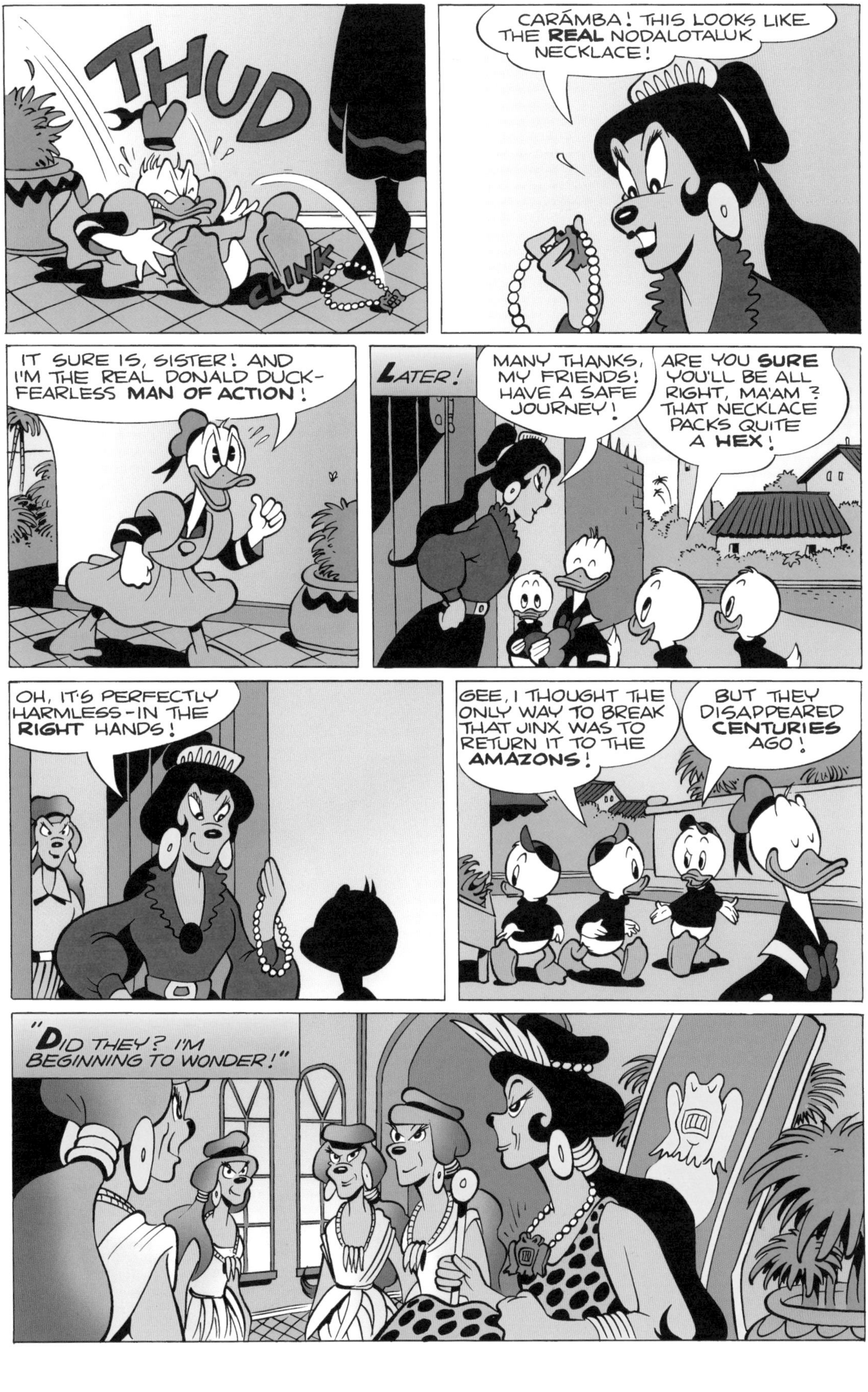
THUD
CLINK
CARÁMBA! THIS LOOKS LIKE THE REAL NODALOTALUK NECKLACE!
IT SURE IS, SISTER! AND I'M THE REAL DONALD DUCK-FEARLESS MAN OF ACTION!
LATER!
MANY THANKS, MY FRIENDS! HAVE A SAFE JOURNEY!
ARE YOU SURE YOU'LL BE ALL RIGHT, MA'AM? THAT NECKLACE PACKS QUITE A HEX!
OH, IT'S PERFECTLY HARMLESS-IN THE RIGHT HANDS!
GEE, I THOUGHT THE ONLY WAY TO BREAK THAT JINX WAS TO RETURN IT TO THE AMAZONS!
BUT THEY DISAPPEARED CENTURIES AGO!
"DID THEY? I'M BEGINNING TO WONDER!"

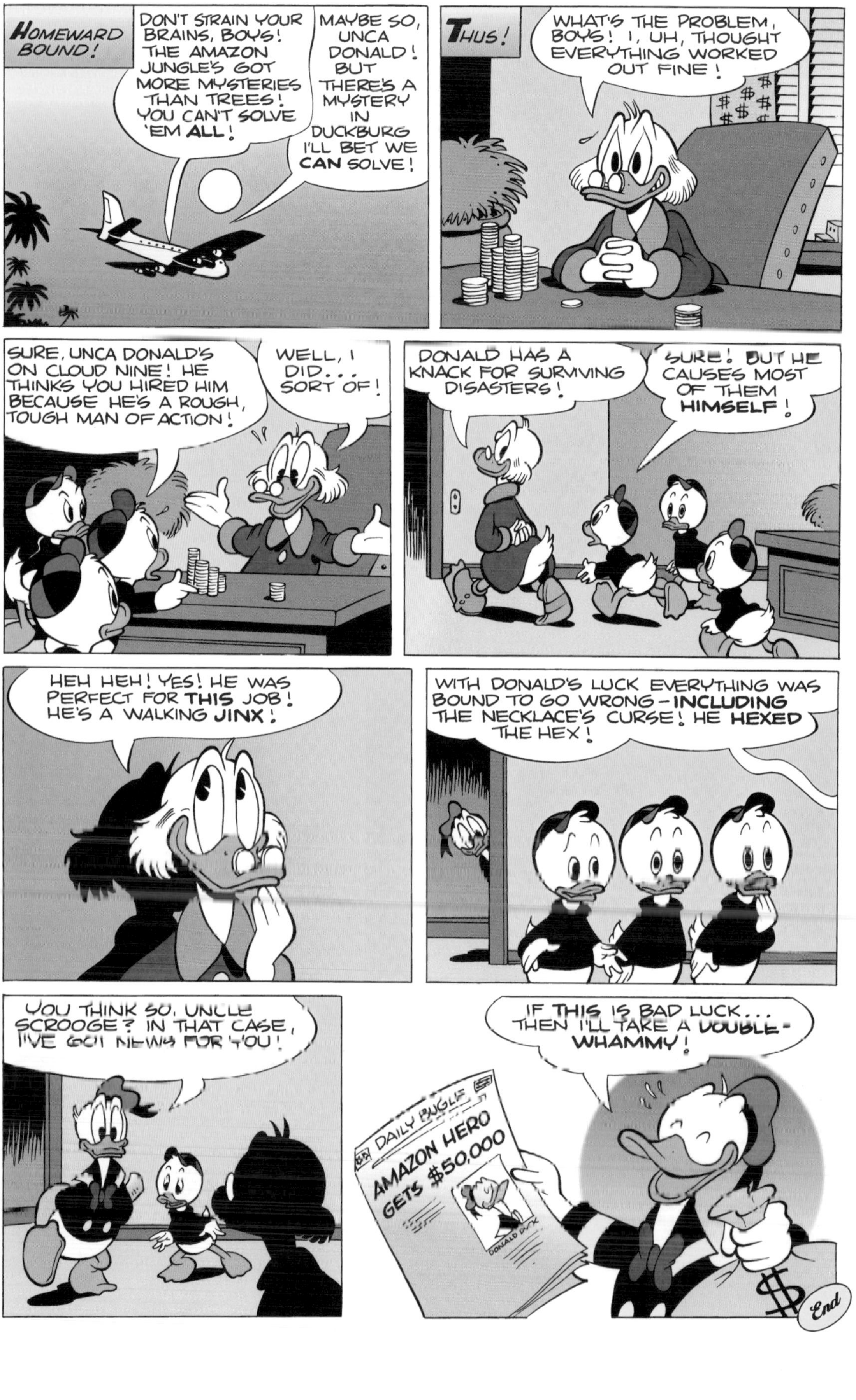
HOMEWARD BOUND!
DON'T STRAIN YOUR BRAINS, BOYS! THE AMAZON JUNGLE'S GOT MORE MYSTERIES THAN TREES! YOU CAN'T SOLVE 'EM ALL!
MAYBE SO, UNCA DONALD! BUT THERE'S A MYSTERY IN DUCKBURG I'LL BET WE CAN SOLVE!
THUS!
WHAT'S THE PROBLEM, BOYS! I, UH, THOUGHT EVERYTHING WORKED OUT FINE!
SURE, UNCA DONALD'S ON CLOUD NINE! HE THINKS YOU HIRED HIM BECAUSE HE'S A ROUGH, TOUGH MAN OF ACTION!
WELL, I DID... SORT OF!
DONALD HAS A KNACK FOR SURVIVING DISASTERS!
SURE! BUT HE CAUSES MOST OF THEM HIMSELF!
HEH HEH! YES! HE WAS PERFECT FOR THIS JOB! HE'S A WALKING JINX!
WITH DONALD'S LUCK EVERYTHING WAS BOUND TO GO WRONG–INCLUDING THE NECKLACE'S CURSE! HE HEXED THE HEX!
YOU THINK SO, UNCLE SCROOGE? IN THAT CASE, I'VE GOT NEWS FOR YOU!
IF THIS IS BAD LUCK... THEN I'LL TAKE A DOUBLE-WHAMMY!
DAILY BUGLE
AMAZON HERO GETS $50,000
End

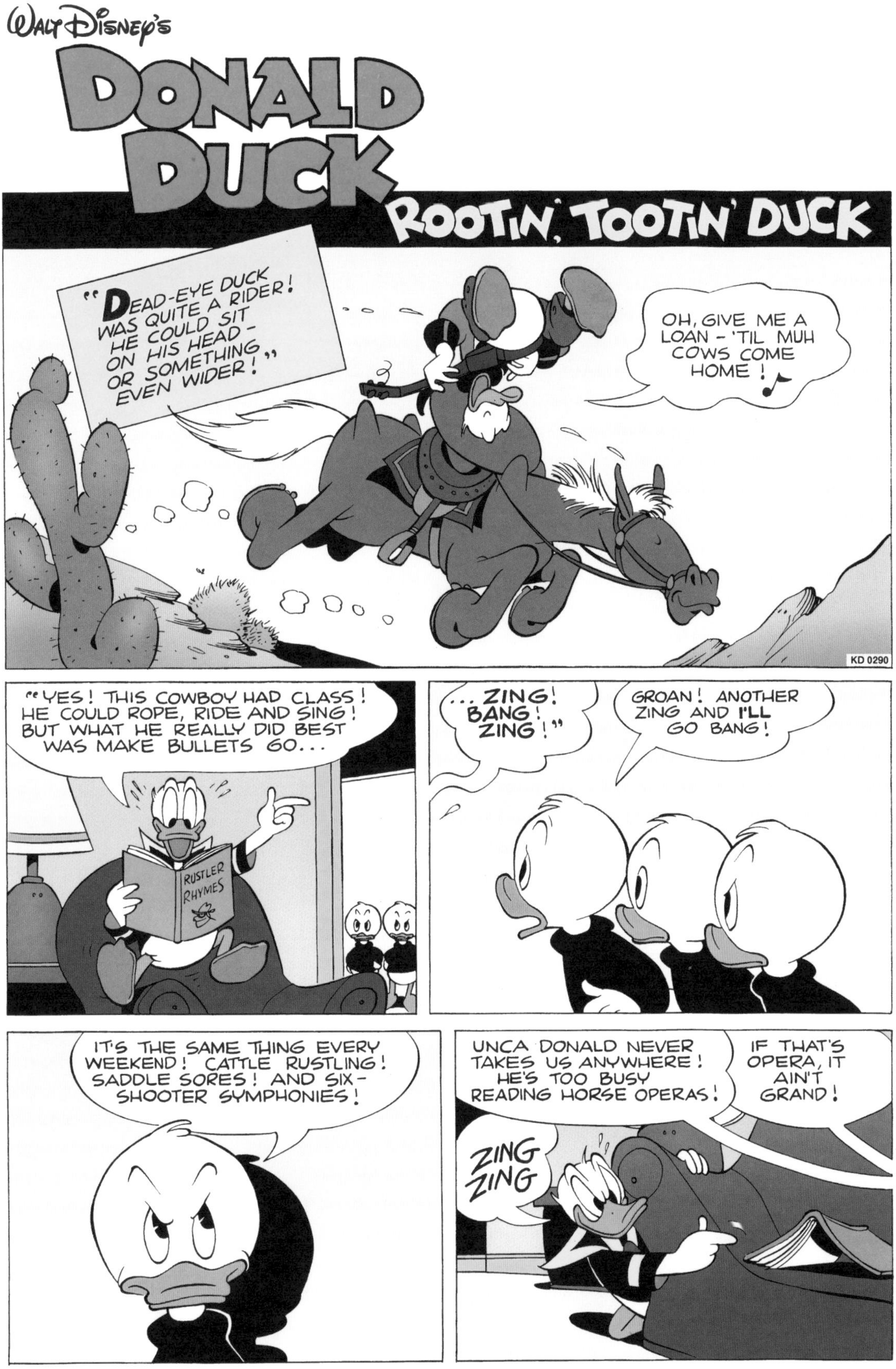
Walt Disney's
DONALD DUCK
ROOTIN', TOOTIN' DUCK
"DEAD-EYE DUCK WAS QUITE A RIDER! HE COULD SIT ON HIS HEAD - OR SOMETHING EVEN WIDER!"
OH, GIVE ME A LOAN - 'TIL MUH COWS COME HOME!
KD 0290
"YES! THIS COWBOY HAD CLASS! HE COULD ROPE, RIDE AND SING! BUT WHAT HE REALLY DID BEST WAS MAKE BULLETS GO...
RUSTLER RHYMES
... ZING! BANG! ZING!"
GROAN! ANOTHER ZING AND I'LL GO BANG!
IT'S THE SAME THING EVERY WEEKEND! CATTLE RUSTLING! SADDLE SORES! AND SIX-SHOOTER SYMPHONIES!
UNCA DONALD NEVER TAKES US ANYWHERE! HE'S TOO BUSY READING HORSE OPERAS!
IF THAT'S OPERA, IT AIN'T GRAND!
ZING ZING

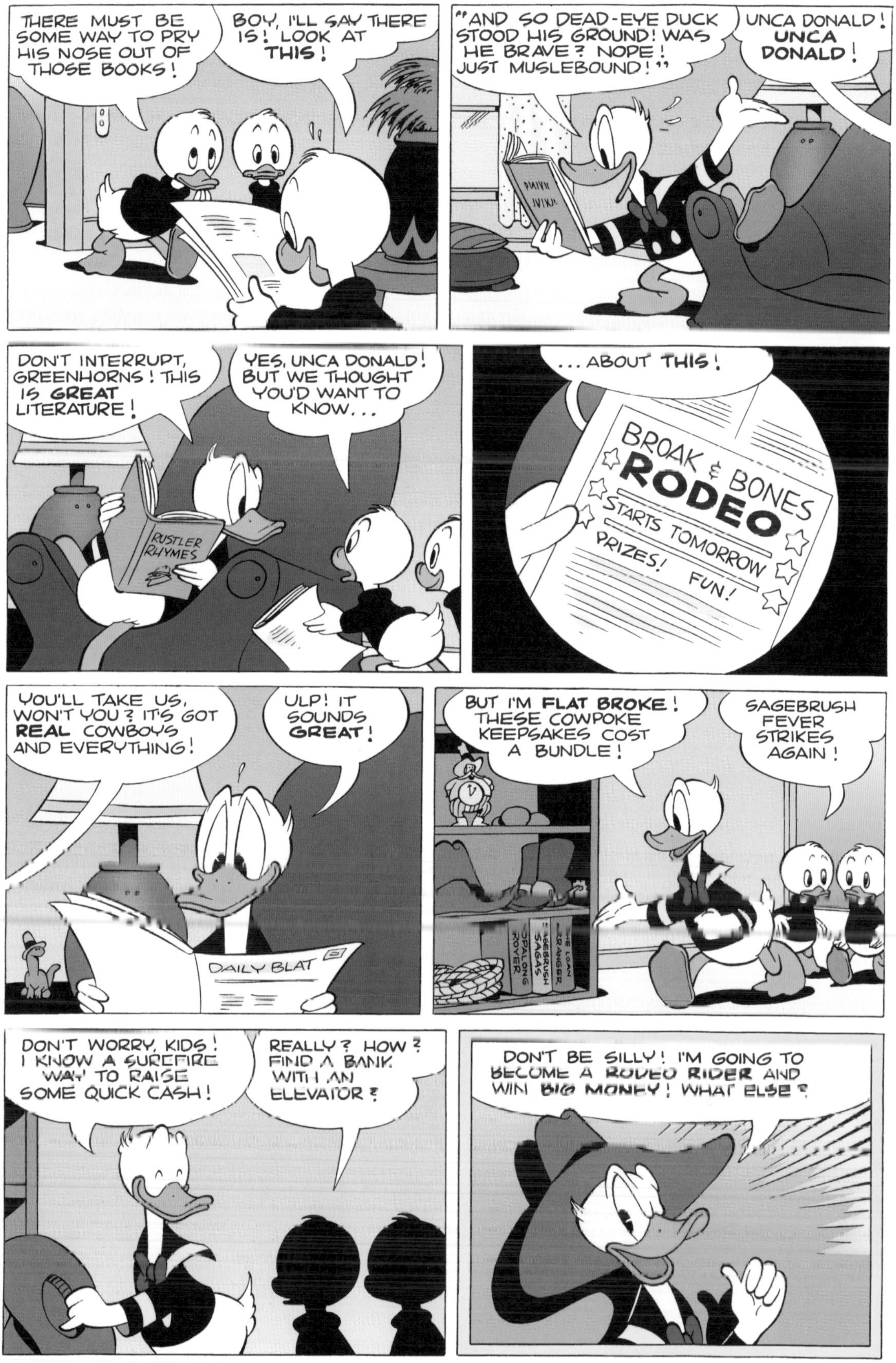
THERE MUST BE SOME WAY TO PRY HIS NOSE OUT OF THOSE BOOKS!
BOY, I'LL SAY THERE IS! LOOK AT THIS!
"AND SO DEAD-EYE DUCK STOOD HIS GROUND! WAS HE BRAVE? NOPE! JUST MUSLEBOUND!"
UNCA DONALD! UNCA DONALD!
DON'T INTERRUPT, GREENHORNS! THIS IS GREAT LITERATURE!
RUSTLER RHYMES
YES, UNCA DONALD! BUT WE THOUGHT YOU'D WANT TO KNOW...
...ABOUT THIS!
BROAK & BONES RODEO STARTS TOMORROW PRIZES! FUN!
YOU'LL TAKE US, WON'T YOU? IT'S GOT REAL COWBOYS AND EVERYTHING!
ULP! IT SOUNDS GREAT!
DAILY BLAT
BUT I'M FLAT BROKE! THESE COWPOKE KEEPSAKES COST A BUNDLE!
SAGEBRUSH FEVER STRIKES AGAIN!
HOPALONG ROYER
SAGEBRUSH SAGAS
THE LOAN ARRANGER
DON'T WORRY, KIDS! I KNOW A SUREFIRE WAY TO RAISE SOME QUICK CASH!
REALLY? HOW? FIND A BANK WITH AN ELEVATOR?
DON'T BE SILLY! I'M GOING TO BECOME A RODEO RIDER AND WIN BIG MONEY! WHAT ELSE?

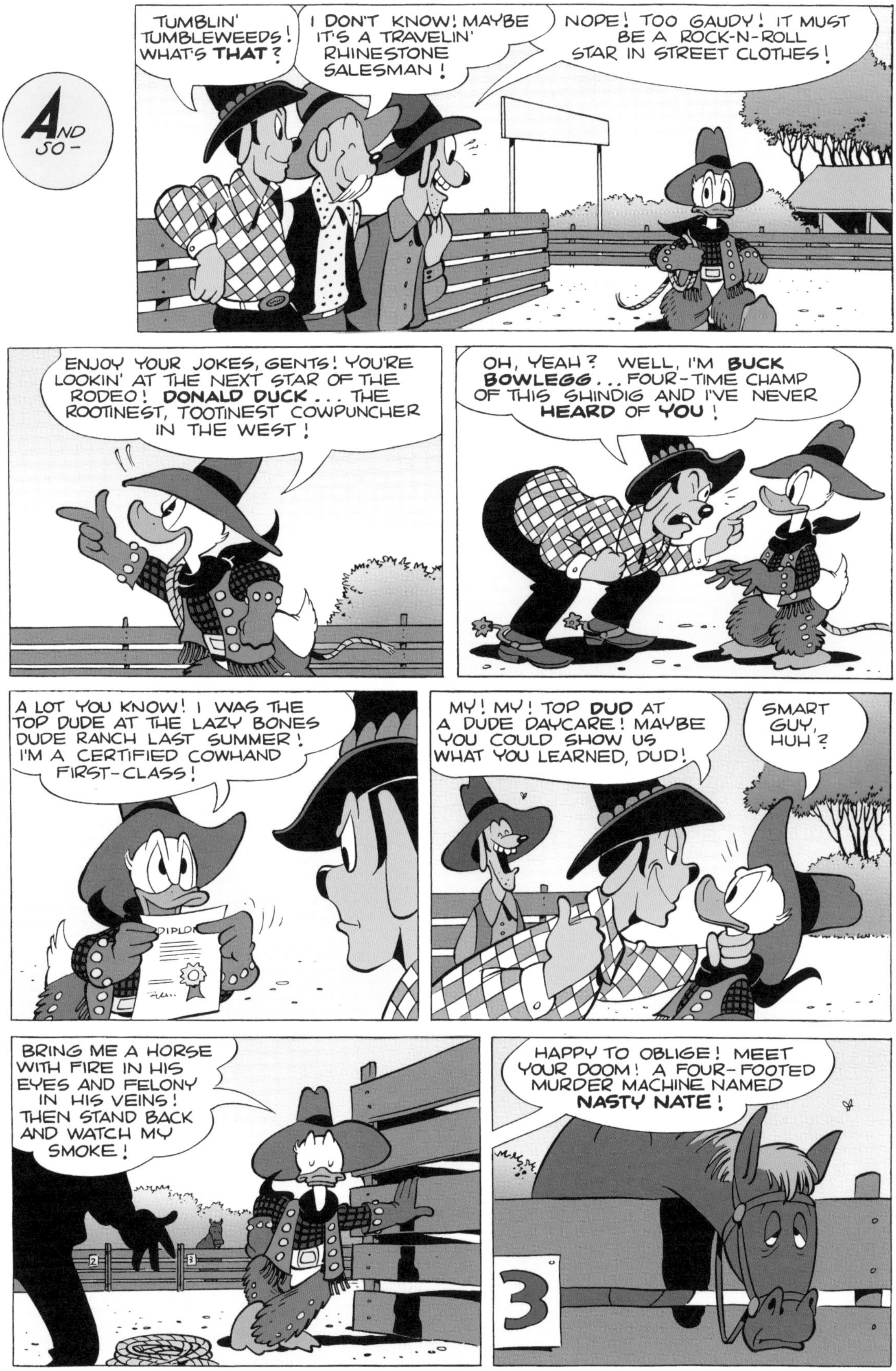
AND SO -
TUMBLIN' TUMBLEWEEDS! WHAT'S **THAT**?
I DON'T KNOW! MAYBE IT'S A TRAVELIN' RHINESTONE SALESMAN!
NOPE! TOO GAUDY! IT MUST BE A ROCK-N-ROLL STAR IN STREET CLOTHES!
ENJOY YOUR JOKES, GENTS! YOU'RE LOOKIN' AT THE NEXT STAR OF THE RODEO! **DONALD DUCK**... THE ROOTINEST, TOOTINEST COWPUNCHER IN THE WEST!
OH, YEAH? WELL, I'M **BUCK BOWLEGG**... FOUR-TIME CHAMP OF THIS SHINDIG AND I'VE NEVER **HEARD** OF **YOU**!
A LOT YOU KNOW! I WAS THE TOP DUDE AT THE LAZY BONES DUDE RANCH LAST SUMMER! I'M A CERTIFIED COWHAND FIRST-CLASS!
MY! MY! TOP **DUD** AT A DUDE DAYCARE! MAYBE YOU COULD SHOW US WHAT YOU LEARNED, DUD!
SMART GUY, HUH?
BRING ME A HORSE WITH FIRE IN HIS EYES AND FELONY IN HIS VEINS! THEN STAND BACK AND WATCH MY SMOKE!
HAPPY TO OBLIGE! MEET YOUR DOOM! A FOUR-FOOTED MURDER MACHINE NAMED **NASTY NATE**!
3

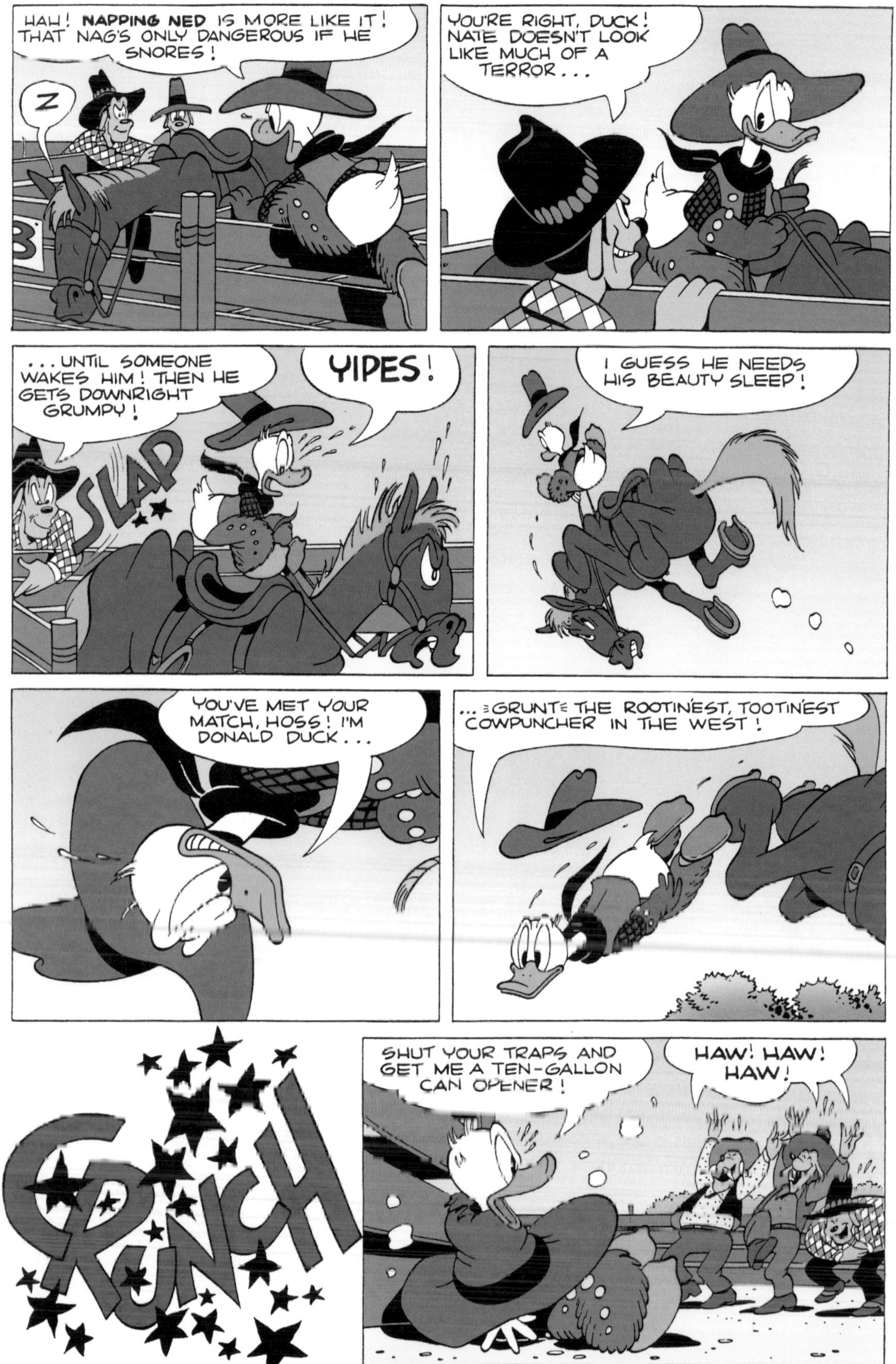
HAH! NAPPING NED IS MORE LIKE IT! THAT NAG'S ONLY DANGEROUS IF HE SNORES!
Z
YOU'RE RIGHT, DUCK! NATE DOESN'T LOOK LIKE MUCH OF A TERROR...
...UNTIL SOMEONE WAKES HIM! THEN HE GETS DOWNRIGHT GRUMPY!
YIPES!
SLAP
I GUESS HE NEEDS HIS BEAUTY SLEEP!
YOU'VE MET YOUR MATCH, HOSS! I'M DONALD DUCK...
...GRUNT THE ROOTIN'EST, TOOTIN'EST COWPUNCHER IN THE WEST!
CRUNCH
SHUT YOUR TRAPS AND GET ME A TEN-GALLON CAN OPENER!
HAW! HAW! HAW!

NEXT, DONALD TRIES STEER WRESTLING!

TWO FALLS OUT OF THREE?

HA! HA!

THEN IT'S CALF ROPING!

JUST MY LUCK! A COW WHO CAN GIFT WRAP!

HEE! HEE!

MEANWHILE, BACK AT THE OLD HOMESTEAD!

THE FURNITURE IS NAILED DOWN!

THE WINDOWS ARE BOARDED UP!

AND THE GOLDFISH BOWL IS IN THE SAFE!

OK! WE'RE READY FOR UNCA DONALD!

I HOPE SO! HE ALWAYS HAS A GRADE-A TEMPER TANTRUM WHEN ONE OF HIS SCHEMES FAILS!

SAY! MAYBE WE'RE BEING SILLY! MAYBE UNCA DONALD WILL DO **GREAT** AT THE RODEO! MAYBE HE'LL COME HOME SMILING!

OR MAYBE NOT!

SNARL!

CRASH

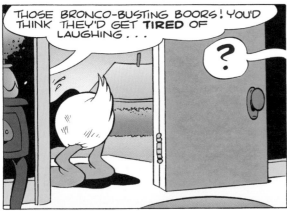

THOSE BRONCO-BUSTING BOORS! YOU'D THINK THEY'D GET **TIRED** OF LAUGHING...

?

...AFTER MY FIRST FORTY OR FIFTY FALLS!

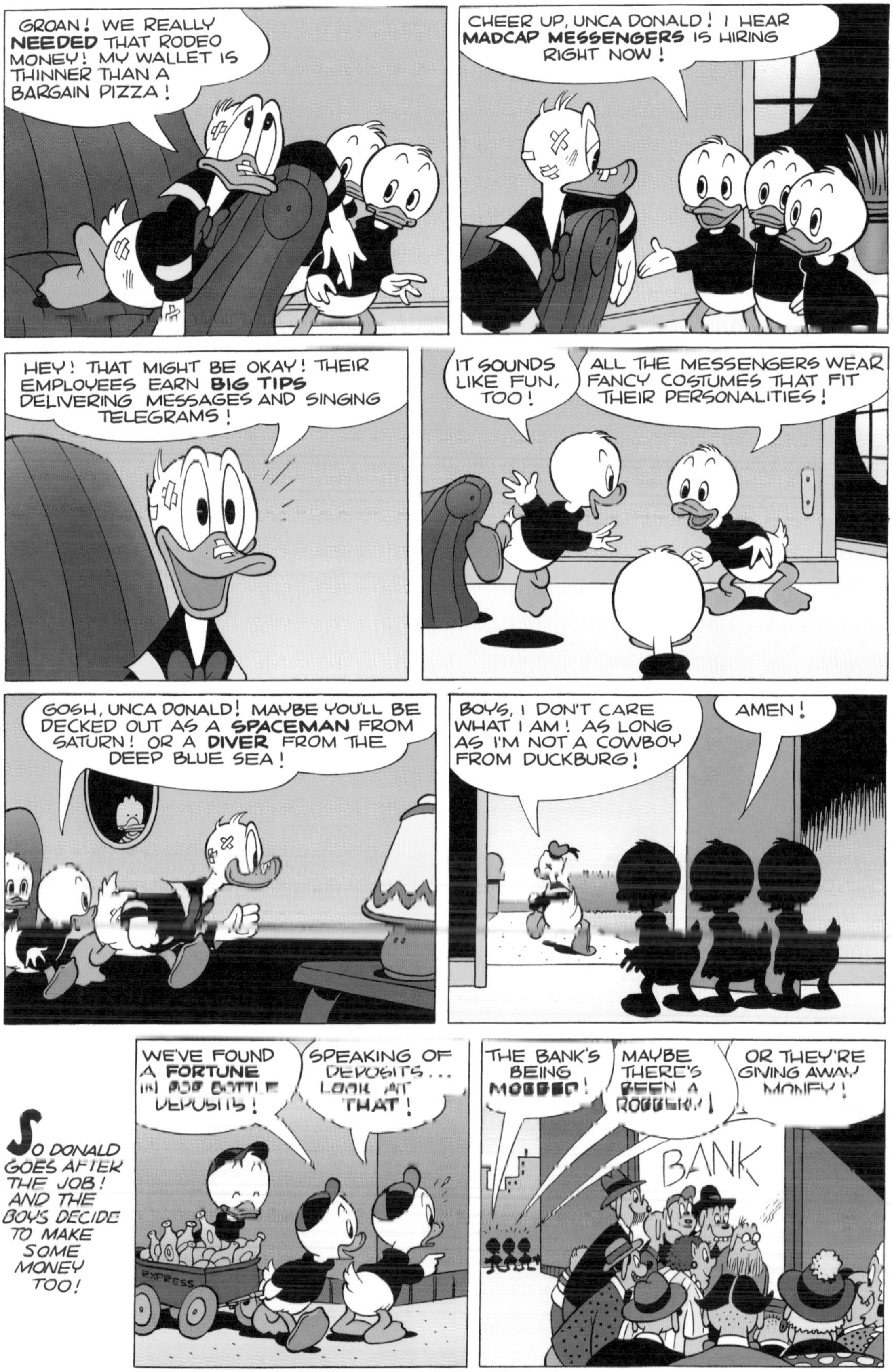
GROAN! WE REALLY **NEEDED** THAT RODEO MONEY! MY WALLET IS THINNER THAN A BARGAIN PIZZA!
CHEER UP, UNCA DONALD! I HEAR **MADCAP MESSENGERS** IS HIRING RIGHT NOW!
HEY! THAT MIGHT BE OKAY! THEIR EMPLOYEES EARN **BIG TIPS** DELIVERING MESSAGES AND SINGING TELEGRAMS!
IT SOUNDS LIKE FUN, TOO!
ALL THE MESSENGERS WEAR FANCY COSTUMES THAT FIT THEIR PERSONALITIES!
GOSH, UNCA DONALD! MAYBE YOU'LL BE DECKED OUT AS A **SPACEMAN** FROM SATURN! OR A **DIVER** FROM THE DEEP BLUE SEA!
BOYS, I DON'T CARE WHAT I AM! AS LONG AS I'M NOT A COWBOY FROM DUCKBURG!
AMEN!
SO DONALD GOES AFTER THE JOB! AND THE BOYS DECIDE TO MAKE SOME MONEY TOO!
WE'VE FOUND A **FORTUNE** IN POP BOTTLE DEPOSITS!
SPEAKING OF DEPOSITS... LOOK AT **THAT**!
THE BANK'S BEING **MOBBED**!
MAYBE THERE'S BEEN A ROBBERY!
OR THEY'RE GIVING AWAY MONEY!
BANK
EXPRESS

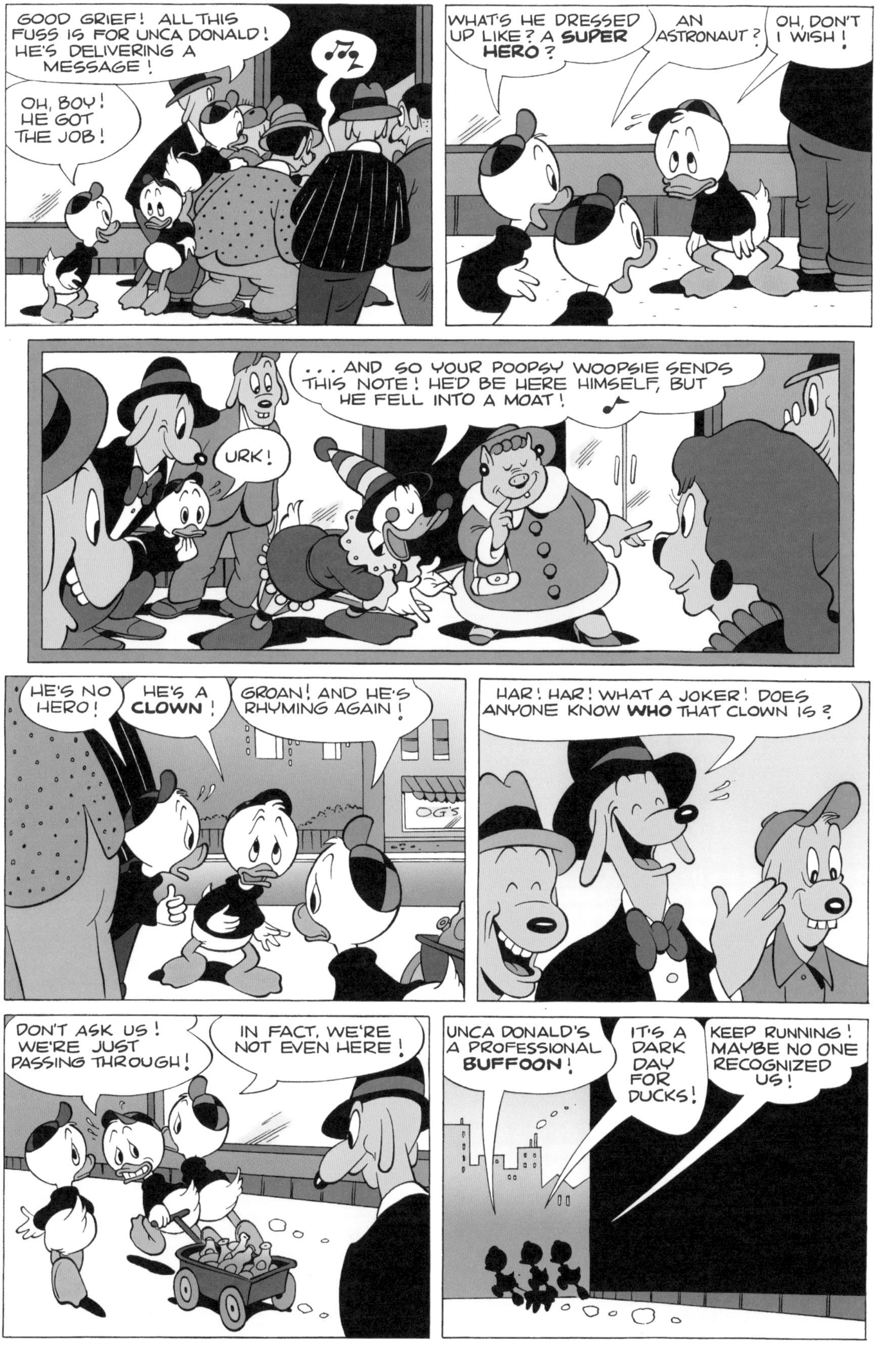
GOOD GRIEF! ALL THIS FUSS IS FOR UNCA DONALD! HE'S DELIVERING A MESSAGE!
OH, BOY! HE GOT THE JOB!
WHAT'S HE DRESSED UP LIKE? A **SUPER HERO**?
AN ASTRONAUT?
OH, DON'T I WISH!
. . . AND SO YOUR POOPSY WOOPSIE SENDS THIS NOTE! HE'D BE HERE HIMSELF, BUT HE FELL INTO A MOAT!
URK!
HE'S NO HERO!
HE'S A **CLOWN**!
GROAN! AND HE'S RHYMING AGAIN!
OG'S
HAR! HAR! WHAT A JOKER! DOES ANYONE KNOW **WHO** THAT CLOWN IS?
DON'T ASK US! WE'RE JUST PASSING THROUGH!
IN FACT, WE'RE NOT EVEN HERE!
UNCA DONALD'S A PROFESSIONAL **BUFFOON**!
IT'S A DARK DAY FOR DUCKS!
KEEP RUNNING! MAYBE NO ONE RECOGNIZED US!

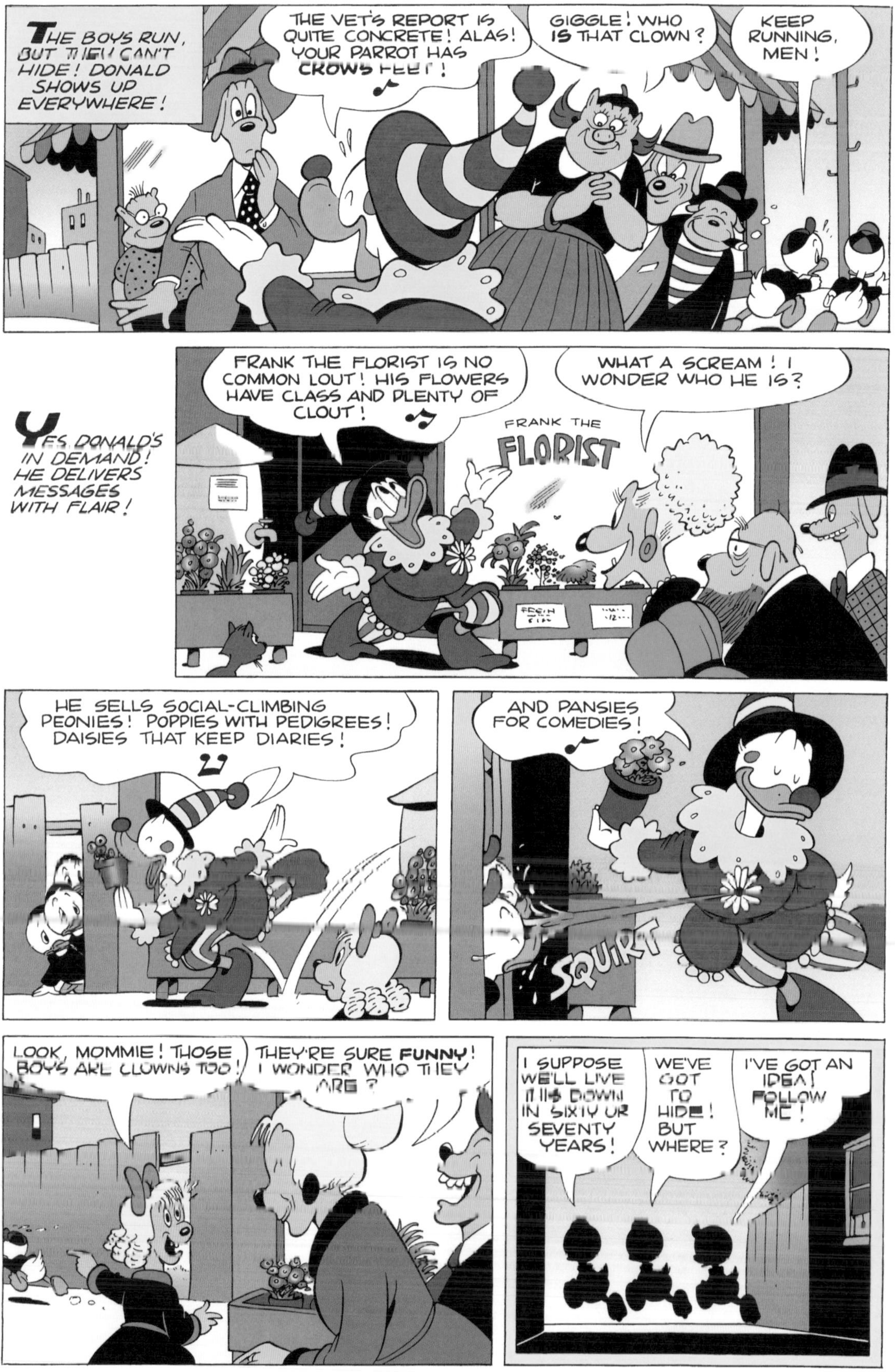
THE BOYS RUN, BUT THEY CAN'T HIDE! DONALD SHOWS UP EVERYWHERE!
THE VET'S REPORT IS QUITE CONCRETE! ALAS! YOUR PARROT HAS CROWS FEET!
GIGGLE! WHO IS THAT CLOWN?
KEEP RUNNING, MEN!
YES DONALD'S IN DEMAND! HE DELIVERS MESSAGES WITH FLAIR!
FRANK THE FLORIST IS NO COMMON LOUT! HIS FLOWERS HAVE CLASS AND PLENTY OF CLOUT!
WHAT A SCREAM! I WONDER WHO HE IS?
FRANK THE FLORIST
HE SELLS SOCIAL-CLIMBING PEONIES! POPPIES WITH PEDIGREES! DAISIES THAT KEEP DIARIES!
AND PANSIES FOR COMEDIES!
SQUIRT
LOOK, MOMMIE! THOSE BOYS ARE CLOWNS TOO!
THEY'RE SURE FUNNY! I WONDER WHO THEY ARE?
I SUPPOSE WE'LL LIVE THIS DOWN IN SIXTY OR SEVENTY YEARS!
WE'VE GOT TO HIDE! BUT WHERE?
I'VE GOT AN IDEA! FOLLOW ME!

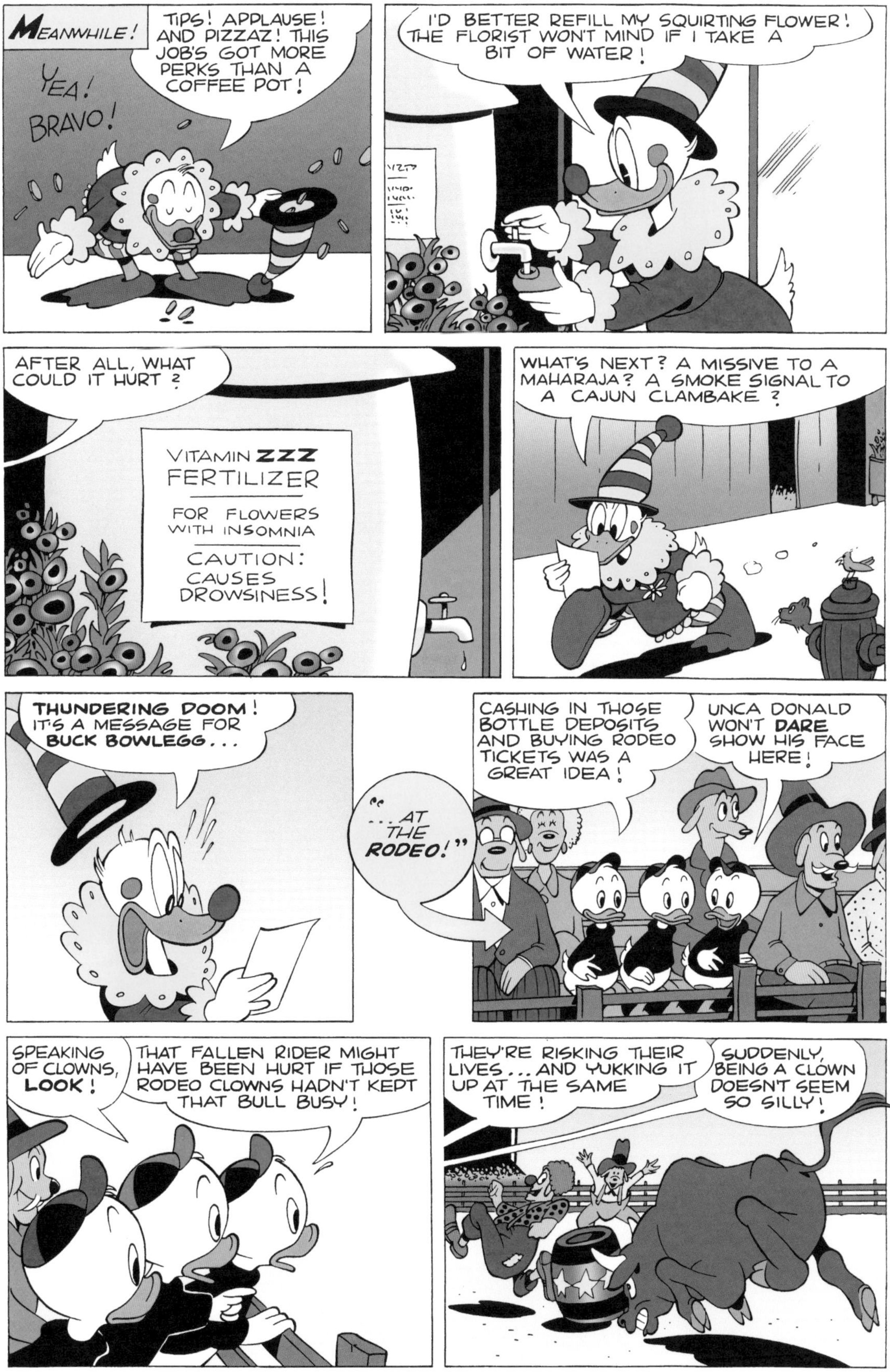
MEANWHILE!
TIPS! APPLAUSE! AND PIZZAZ! THIS JOB'S GOT MORE PERKS THAN A COFFEE POT!
YEA!
BRAVO!
I'D BETTER REFILL MY SQUIRTING FLOWER! THE FLORIST WON'T MIND IF I TAKE A BIT OF WATER!
AFTER ALL, WHAT COULD IT HURT?
VITAMIN ZZZ FERTILIZER
FOR FLOWERS WITH INSOMNIA
CAUTION: CAUSES DROWSINESS!
WHAT'S NEXT? A MISSIVE TO A MAHARAJA? A SMOKE SIGNAL TO A CAJUN CLAMBAKE?
THUNDERING DOOM! IT'S A MESSAGE FOR BUCK BOWLEGG...
"...AT THE RODEO!"
CASHING IN THOSE BOTTLE DEPOSITS AND BUYING RODEO TICKETS WAS A GREAT IDEA!
UNCA DONALD WON'T DARE SHOW HIS FACE HERE!
SPEAKING OF CLOWNS, LOOK!
THAT FALLEN RIDER MIGHT HAVE BEEN HURT IF THOSE RODEO CLOWNS HADN'T KEPT THAT BULL BUSY!
THEY'RE RISKING THEIR LIVES... AND YUKKING IT UP AT THE SAME TIME!
SUDDENLY, BEING A CLOWN DOESN'T SEEM SO SILLY!

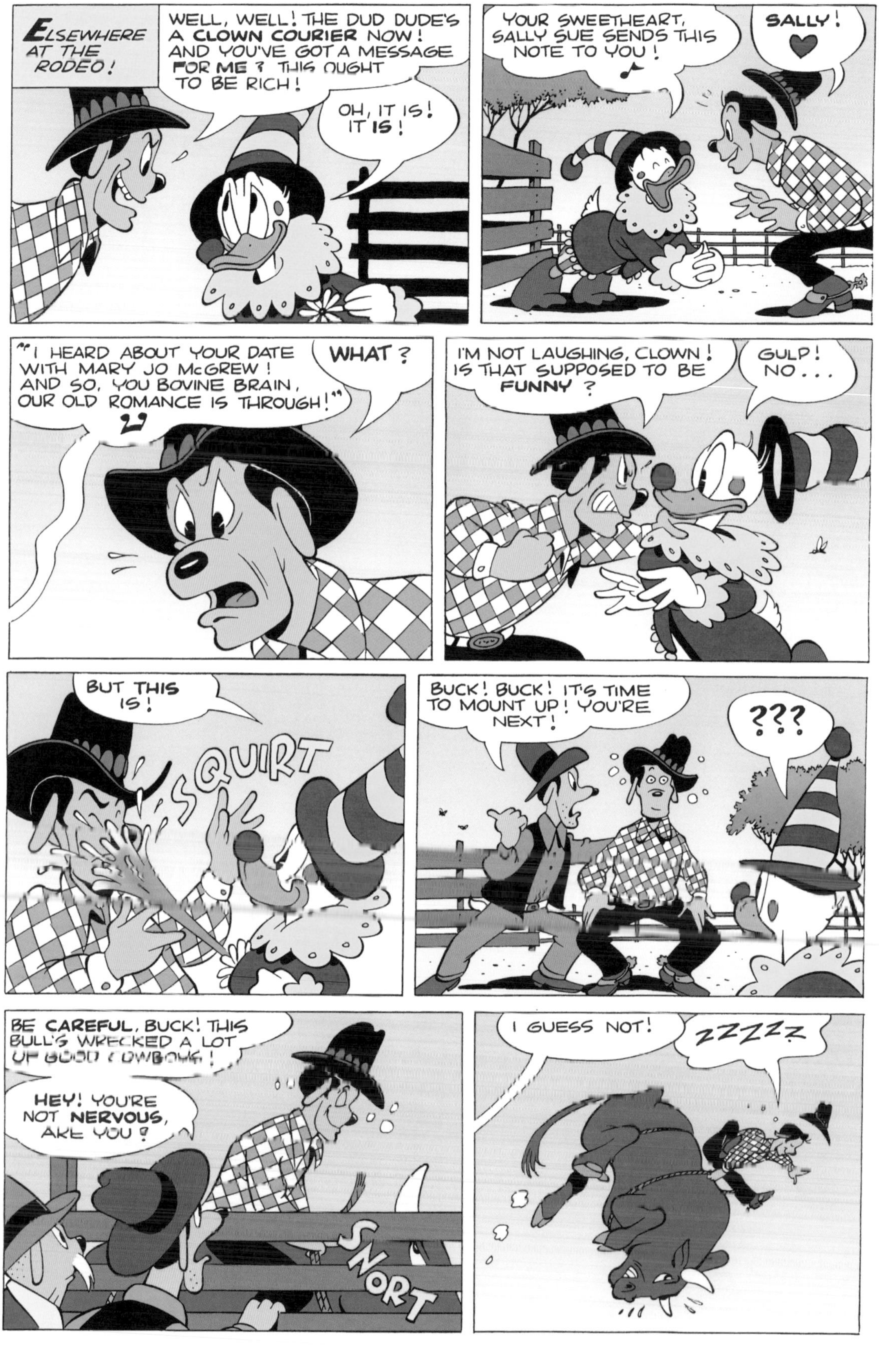
ELSEWHERE AT THE RODEO!
WELL, WELL! THE DUD DUDE'S A CLOWN COURIER NOW! AND YOU'VE GOT A MESSAGE FOR ME? THIS OUGHT TO BE RICH!
OH, IT IS! IT IS!
YOUR SWEETHEART, SALLY SUE SENDS THIS NOTE TO YOU!
SALLY!
"I HEARD ABOUT YOUR DATE WITH MARY JO McGREW! AND SO, YOU BOVINE BRAIN, OUR OLD ROMANCE IS THROUGH!"
WHAT?
I'M NOT LAUGHING, CLOWN! IS THAT SUPPOSED TO BE FUNNY?
GULP! NO...
BUT THIS IS!
SQUIRT
BUCK! BUCK! IT'S TIME TO MOUNT UP! YOU'RE NEXT!
???
BE CAREFUL, BUCK! THIS BULL'S WRECKED A LOT OF GOOD COWBOYS!
HEY! YOU'RE NOT NERVOUS, ARE YOU?
SNORT
I GUESS NOT!
ZZZZZ

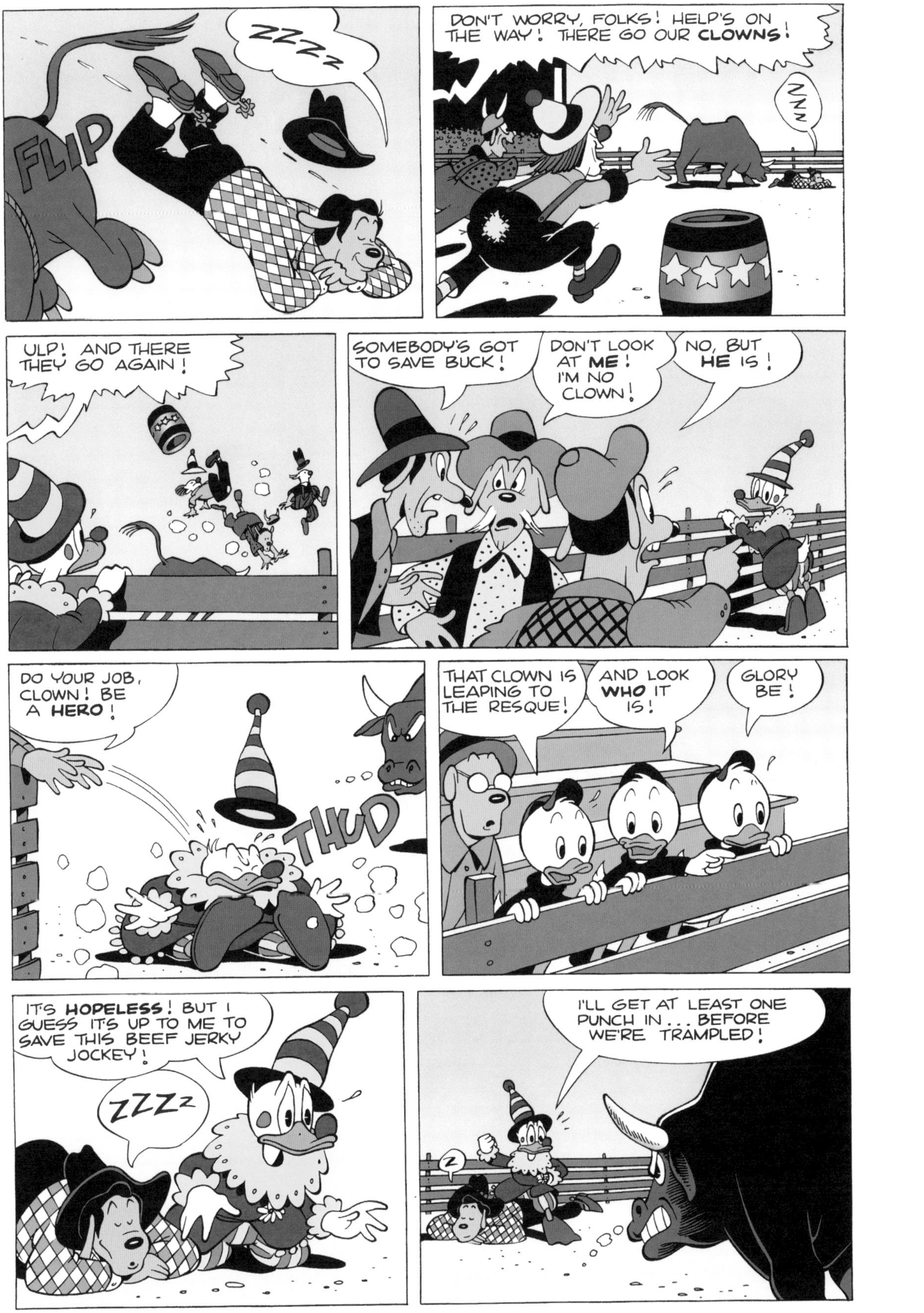
FLIP
ZZZz
DON'T WORRY, FOLKS! HELP'S ON THE WAY! THERE GO OUR CLOWNS!
ZZZ
ULP! AND THERE THEY GO AGAIN!
SOMEBODY'S GOT TO SAVE BUCK!
DON'T LOOK AT ME! I'M NO CLOWN!
NO, BUT HE IS!
DO YOUR JOB, CLOWN! BE A HERO!
THUD
THAT CLOWN IS LEAPING TO THE RESQUE!
AND LOOK WHO IT IS!
GLORY BE!
IT'S HOPELESS! BUT I GUESS IT'S UP TO ME TO SAVE THIS BEEF JERKY JOCKEY!
ZZZz
I'LL GET AT LEAST ONE PUNCH IN... BEFORE WE'RE TRAMPLED!
Z

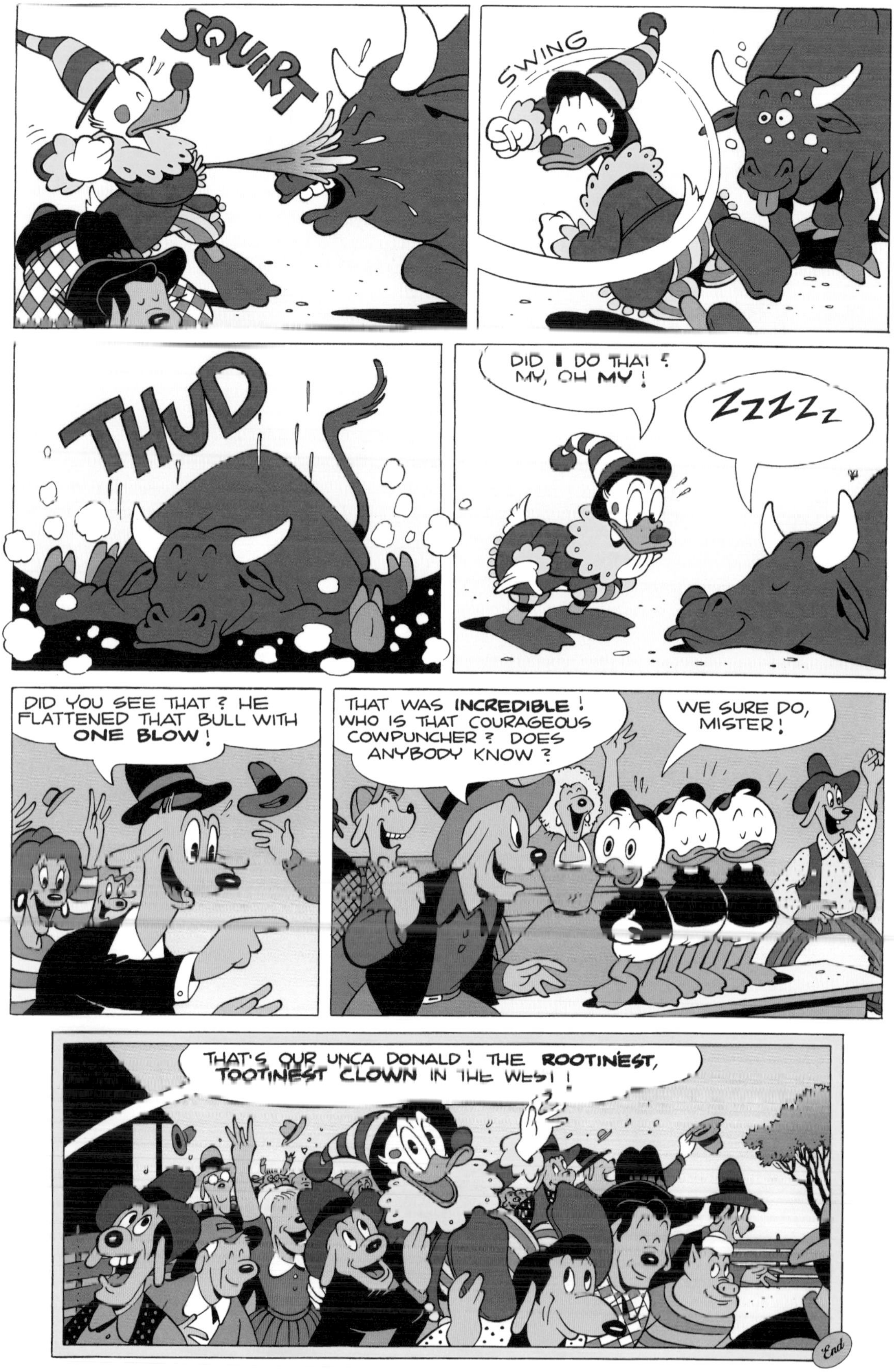
SQUIRT
SWING
THUD
DID I DO THAT? MY, OH MY!
ZZZZz
DID YOU SEE THAT? HE FLATTENED THAT BULL WITH ONE BLOW!
THAT WAS INCREDIBLE! WHO IS THAT COURAGEOUS COWPUNCHER? DOES ANYBODY KNOW?
WE SURE DO, MISTER!
THAT'S OUR UNCA DONALD! THE ROOTINEST, TOOTINEST CLOWN IN THE WEST!
End

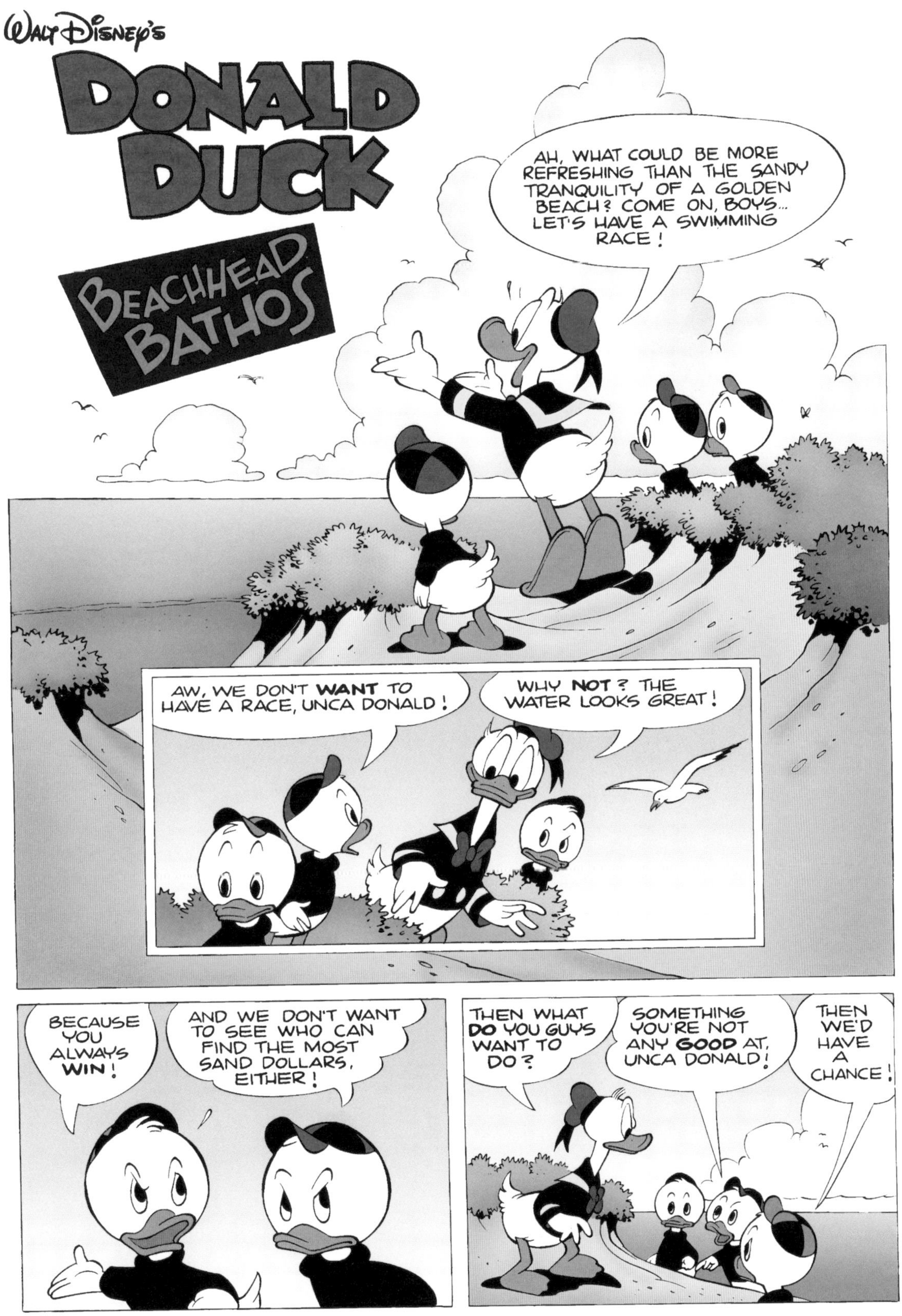

WALT DISNEY'S
DONALD DUCK
BEACHHEAD BATHOS
AH, WHAT COULD BE MORE REFRESHING THAN THE SANDY TRANQUILITY OF A GOLDEN BEACH? COME ON, BOYS... LET'S HAVE A SWIMMING RACE!
AW, WE DON'T **WANT** TO HAVE A RACE, UNCA DONALD!
WHY **NOT**? THE WATER LOOKS GREAT!
BECAUSE YOU ALWAYS **WIN**!
AND WE DON'T WANT TO SEE WHO CAN FIND THE MOST SAND DOLLARS, EITHER!
THEN WHAT **DO** YOU GUYS WANT TO DO?
SOMETHING YOU'RE NOT ANY **GOOD** AT, UNCA DONALD!
THEN WE'D HAVE A CHANCE!

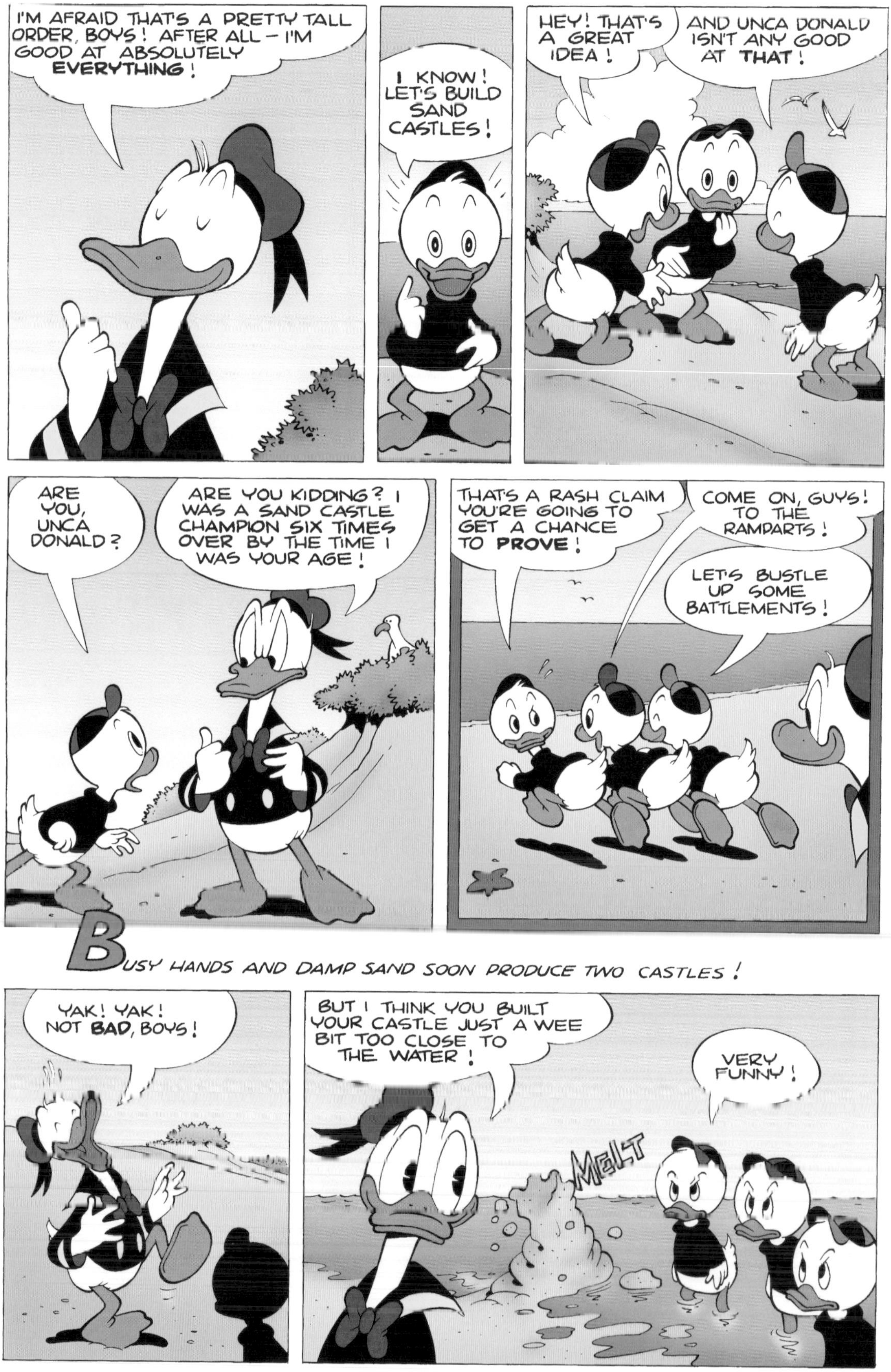

I'M AFRAID THAT'S A PRETTY TALL ORDER, BOYS! AFTER ALL – I'M GOOD AT ABSOLUTELY **EVERYTHING**!
I KNOW! LET'S BUILD SAND CASTLES!
HEY! THAT'S A GREAT IDEA!
AND UNCA DONALD ISN'T ANY GOOD AT **THAT**!
ARE YOU, UNCA DONALD?
ARE YOU KIDDING? I WAS A SAND CASTLE CHAMPION SIX TIMES OVER BY THE TIME I WAS YOUR AGE!
THAT'S A RASH CLAIM YOU'RE GOING TO GET A CHANCE TO **PROVE**!
COME ON, GUYS! TO THE RAMPARTS!
LET'S BUSTLE UP SOME BATTLEMENTS!
BUSY HANDS AND DAMP SAND SOON PRODUCE TWO CASTLES!
YAK! YAK! NOT **BAD**, BOYS!
BUT I THINK YOU BUILT YOUR CASTLE JUST A WEE BIT TOO CLOSE TO THE WATER!
VERY FUNNY!
MELT

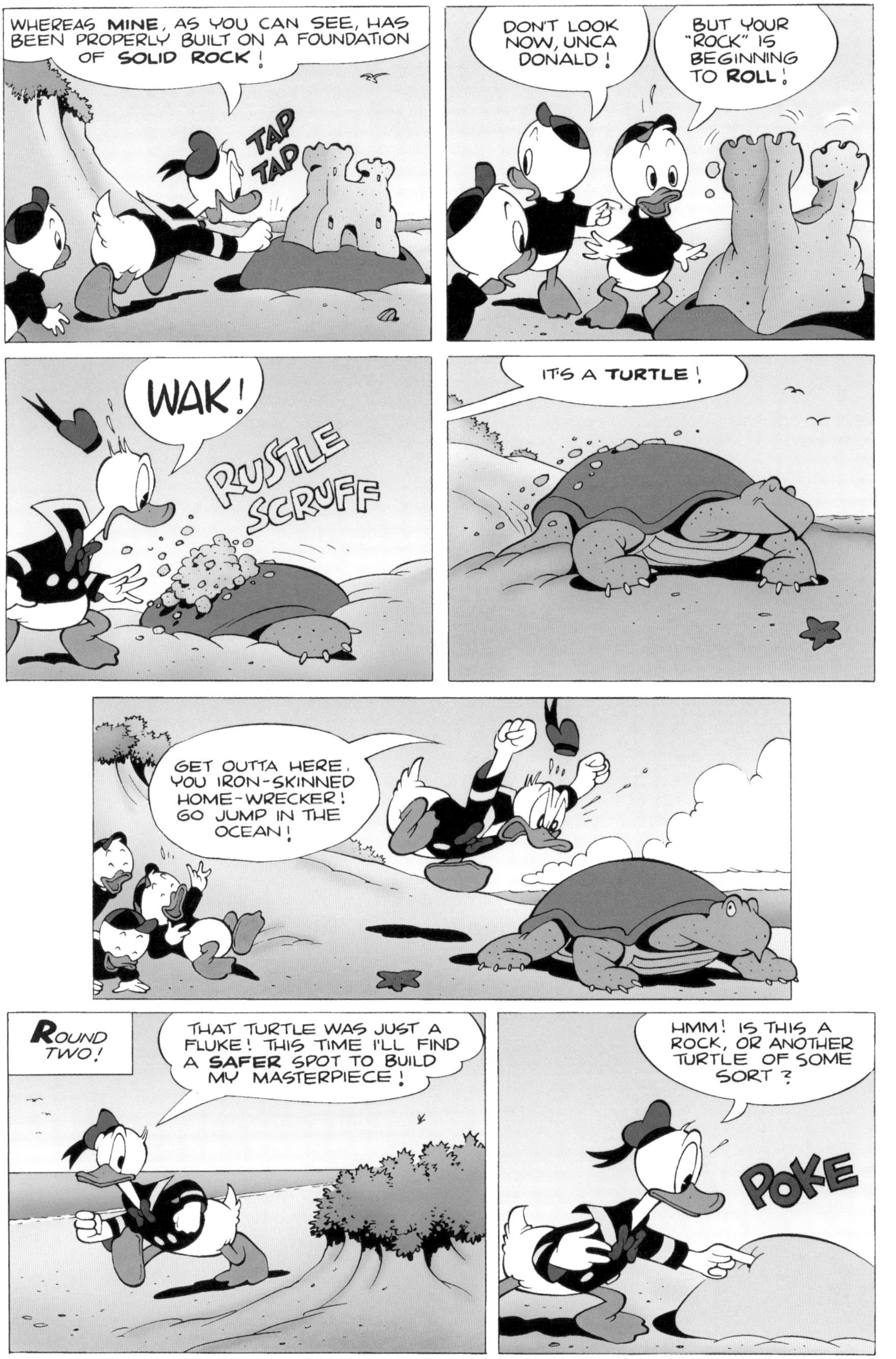

WHEREAS **MINE**, AS YOU CAN SEE, HAS BEEN PROPERLY BUILT ON A FOUNDATION OF **SOLID ROCK**!
TAP TAP
DON'T LOOK NOW, UNCA DONALD!
BUT YOUR "ROCK" IS BEGINNING TO **ROLL**!
WAK!
RUSTLE SCRUFF
IT'S A **TURTLE**!
GET OUTTA HERE, YOU IRON-SKINNED HOME-WRECKER! GO JUMP IN THE OCEAN!
ROUND TWO!
THAT TURTLE WAS JUST A FLUKE! THIS TIME I'LL FIND A **SAFER** SPOT TO BUILD MY MASTERPIECE!
HMM! IS THIS A ROCK, OR ANOTHER TURTLE OF SOME SORT?
POKE

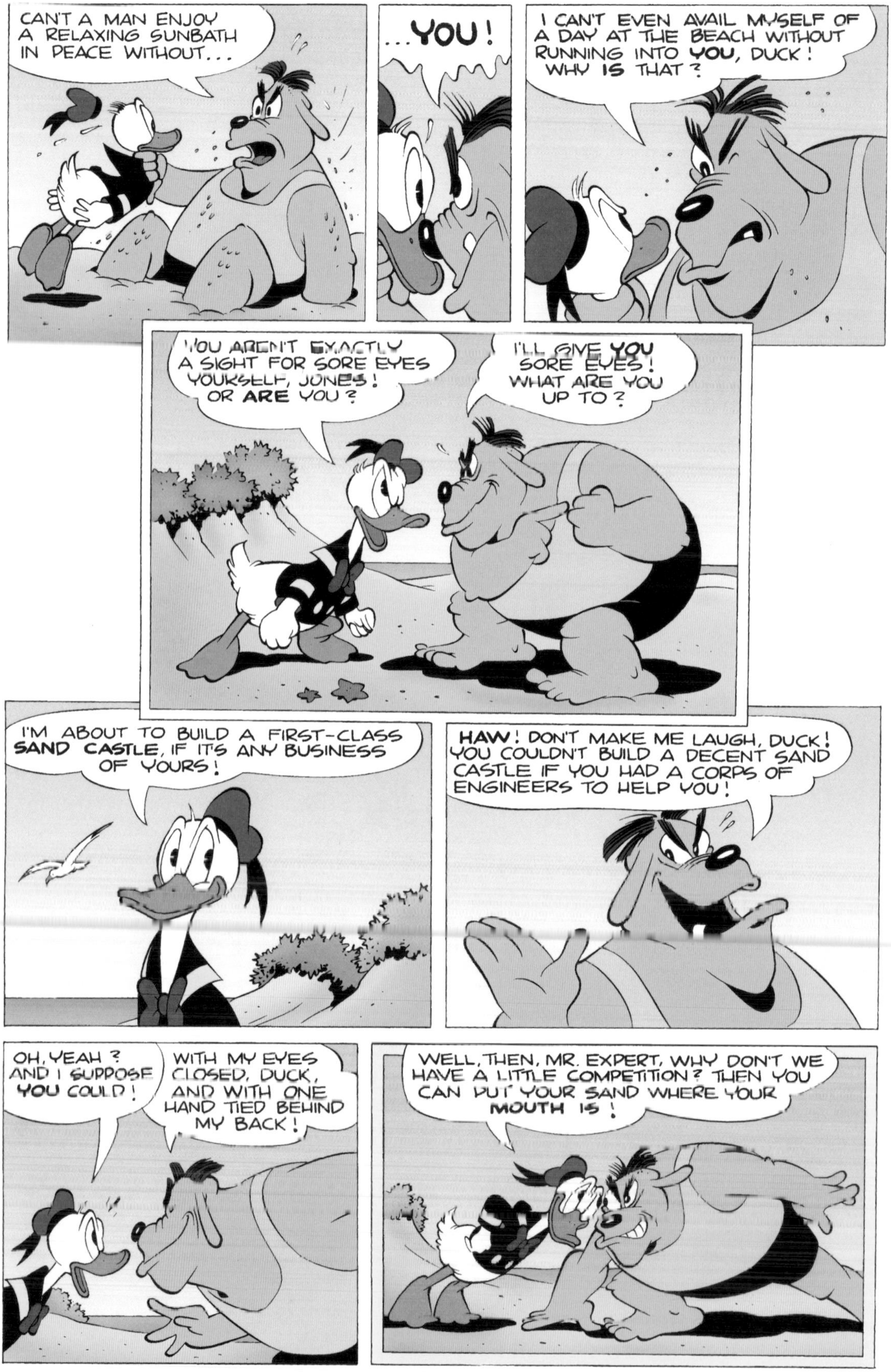

CAN'T A MAN ENJOY A RELAXING SUNBATH IN PEACE WITHOUT...
...YOU!
I CAN'T EVEN AVAIL MYSELF OF A DAY AT THE BEACH WITHOUT RUNNING INTO YOU, DUCK! WHY IS THAT?
YOU AREN'T EXACTLY A SIGHT FOR SORE EYES YOURSELF, JONES! OR ARE YOU?
I'LL GIVE YOU SORE EYES! WHAT ARE YOU UP TO?
I'M ABOUT TO BUILD A FIRST-CLASS SAND CASTLE, IF IT'S ANY BUSINESS OF YOURS!
HAW! DON'T MAKE ME LAUGH, DUCK! YOU COULDN'T BUILD A DECENT SAND CASTLE IF YOU HAD A CORPS OF ENGINEERS TO HELP YOU!
OH, YEAH? AND I SUPPOSE YOU COULD!
WITH MY EYES CLOSED, DUCK, AND WITH ONE HAND TIED BEHIND MY BACK!
WELL, THEN, MR. EXPERT, WHY DON'T WE HAVE A LITTLE COMPETITION? THEN YOU CAN PUT YOUR SAND WHERE YOUR MOUTH IS!

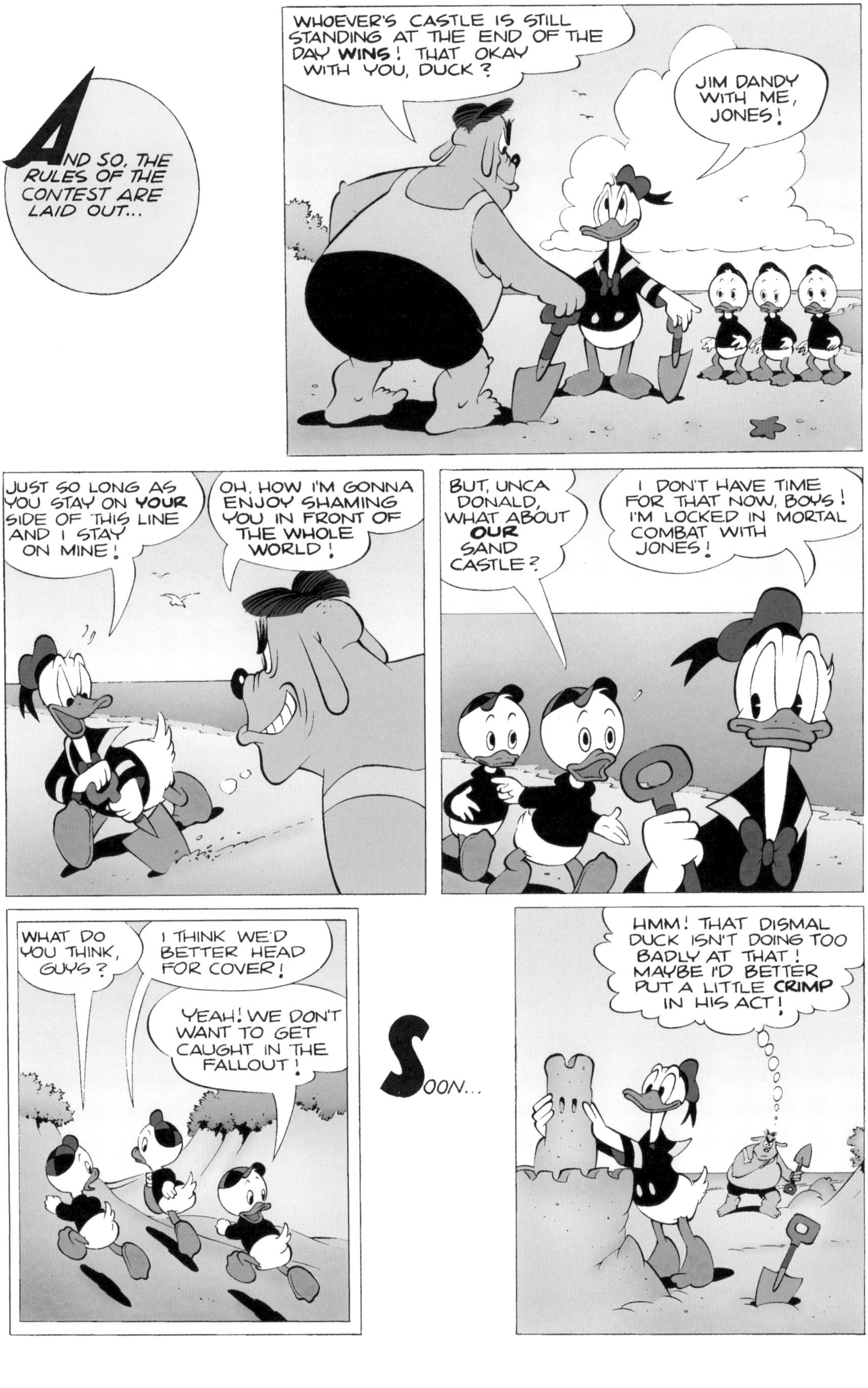
AND SO, THE RULES OF THE CONTEST ARE LAID OUT...
WHOEVER'S CASTLE IS STILL STANDING AT THE END OF THE DAY WINS! THAT OKAY WITH YOU, DUCK?
JIM DANDY WITH ME, JONES!
JUST SO LONG AS YOU STAY ON YOUR SIDE OF THIS LINE AND I STAY ON MINE!
OH, HOW I'M GONNA ENJOY SHAMING YOU IN FRONT OF THE WHOLE WORLD!
BUT, UNCA DONALD, WHAT ABOUT OUR SAND CASTLE?
I DON'T HAVE TIME FOR THAT NOW, BOYS! I'M LOCKED IN MORTAL COMBAT WITH JONES!
WHAT DO YOU THINK, GUYS?
I THINK WE'D BETTER HEAD FOR COVER!
YEAH! WE DON'T WANT TO GET CAUGHT IN THE FALLOUT!
SOON...
HMM! THAT DISMAL DUCK ISN'T DOING TOO BADLY AT THAT! MAYBE I'D BETTER PUT A LITTLE CRIMP IN HIS ACT!

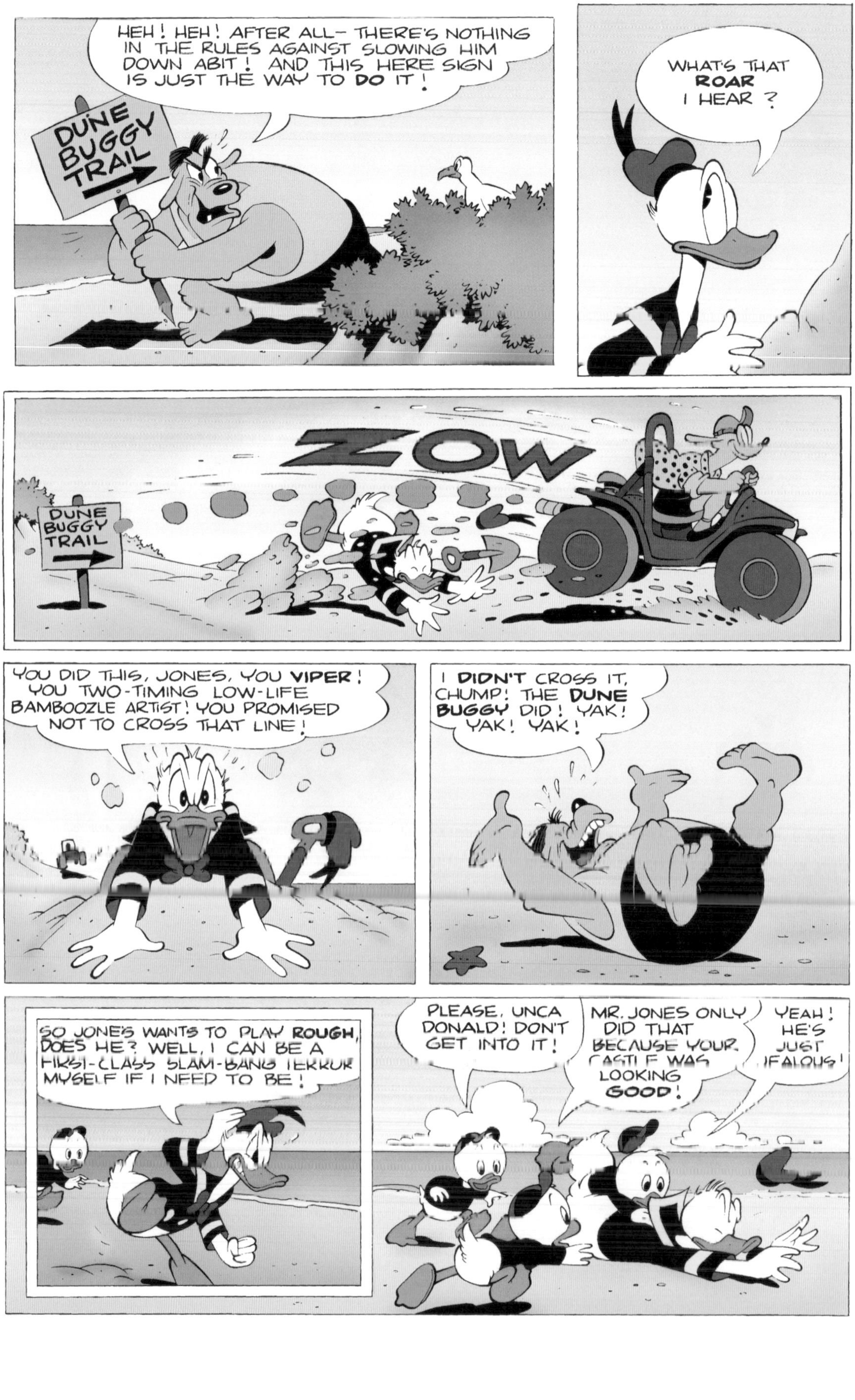
HEH! HEH! AFTER ALL— THERE'S NOTHING IN THE RULES AGAINST SLOWING HIM DOWN ABIT! AND THIS HERE SIGN IS JUST THE WAY TO **DO** IT!
DUNE BUGGY TRAIL
WHAT'S THAT **ROAR** I HEAR?
ZOW
DUNE BUGGY TRAIL
YOU DID THIS, JONES, YOU **VIPER**! YOU TWO-TIMING LOW-LIFE BAMBOOZLE ARTIST! YOU PROMISED NOT TO CROSS THAT LINE!
I **DIDN'T** CROSS IT, CHUMP! THE **DUNE BUGGY** DID! YAK! YAK! YAK!
SO JONES WANTS TO PLAY **ROUGH**, DOES HE? WELL, I CAN BE A FIRST-CLASS SLAM-BANG TERROR MYSELF IF I NEED TO BE!
PLEASE, UNCA DONALD! DON'T GET INTO IT!
MR. JONES ONLY DID THAT BECAUSE YOUR CASTLE WAS LOOKING **GOOD**!
YEAH! HE'S JUST JEALOUS!

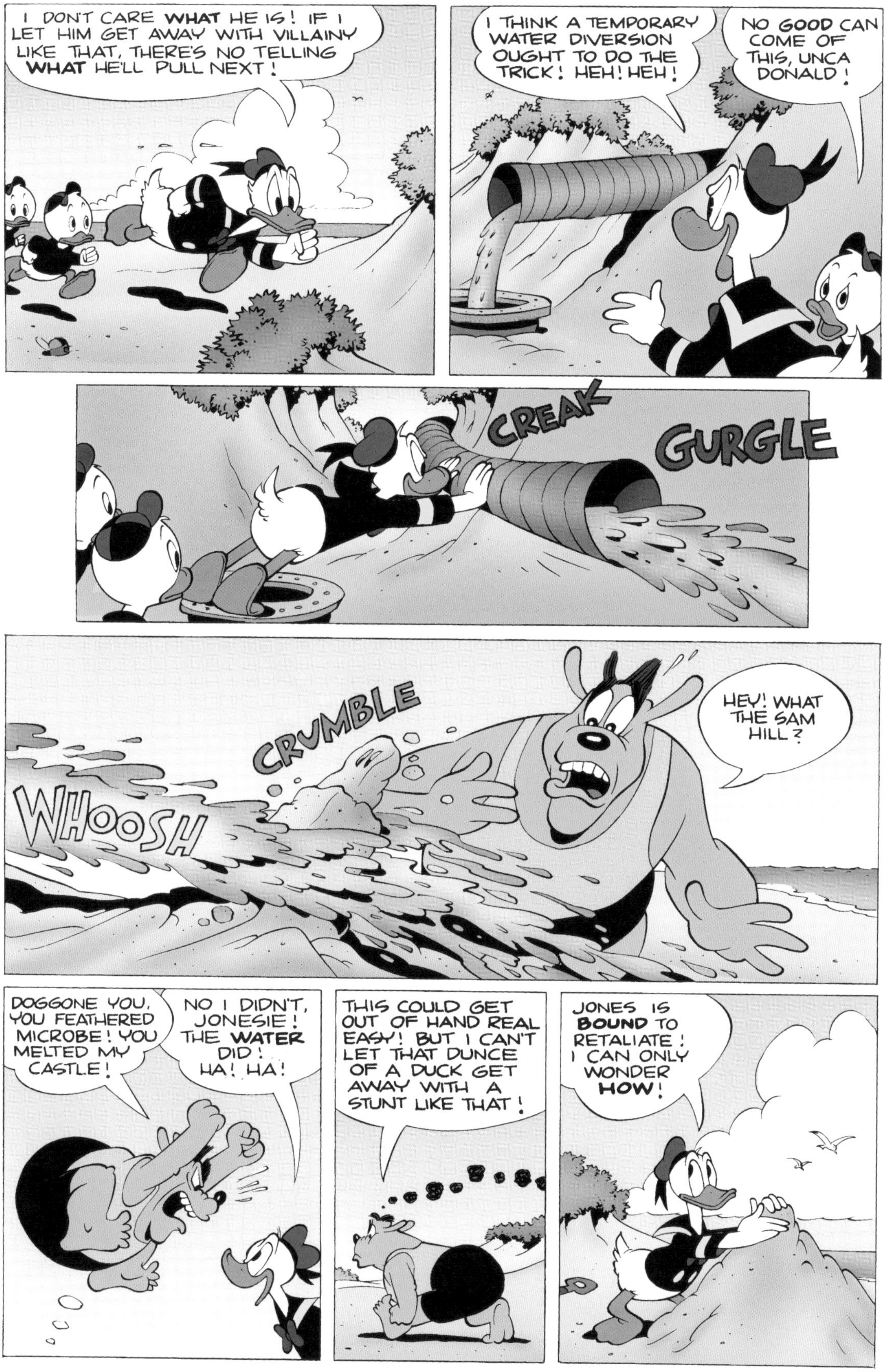

I DON'T CARE WHAT HE IS! IF I LET HIM GET AWAY WITH VILLAINY LIKE THAT, THERE'S NO TELLING WHAT HE'LL PULL NEXT!
I THINK A TEMPORARY WATER DIVERSION OUGHT TO DO THE TRICK! HEH! HEH!
NO GOOD CAN COME OF THIS, UNCA DONALD!
CREAK
GURGLE
CRUMBLE
WHOOSH
HEY! WHAT THE SAM HILL?
DOGGONE YOU, YOU FEATHERED MICROBE! YOU MELTED MY CASTLE!
NO I DIDN'T, JONESIE! THE WATER DID! HA! HA!
THIS COULD GET OUT OF HAND REAL EASY! BUT I CAN'T LET THAT DUNCE OF A DUCK GET AWAY WITH A STUNT LIKE THAT!
JONES IS BOUND TO RETALIATE! I CAN ONLY WONDER HOW!

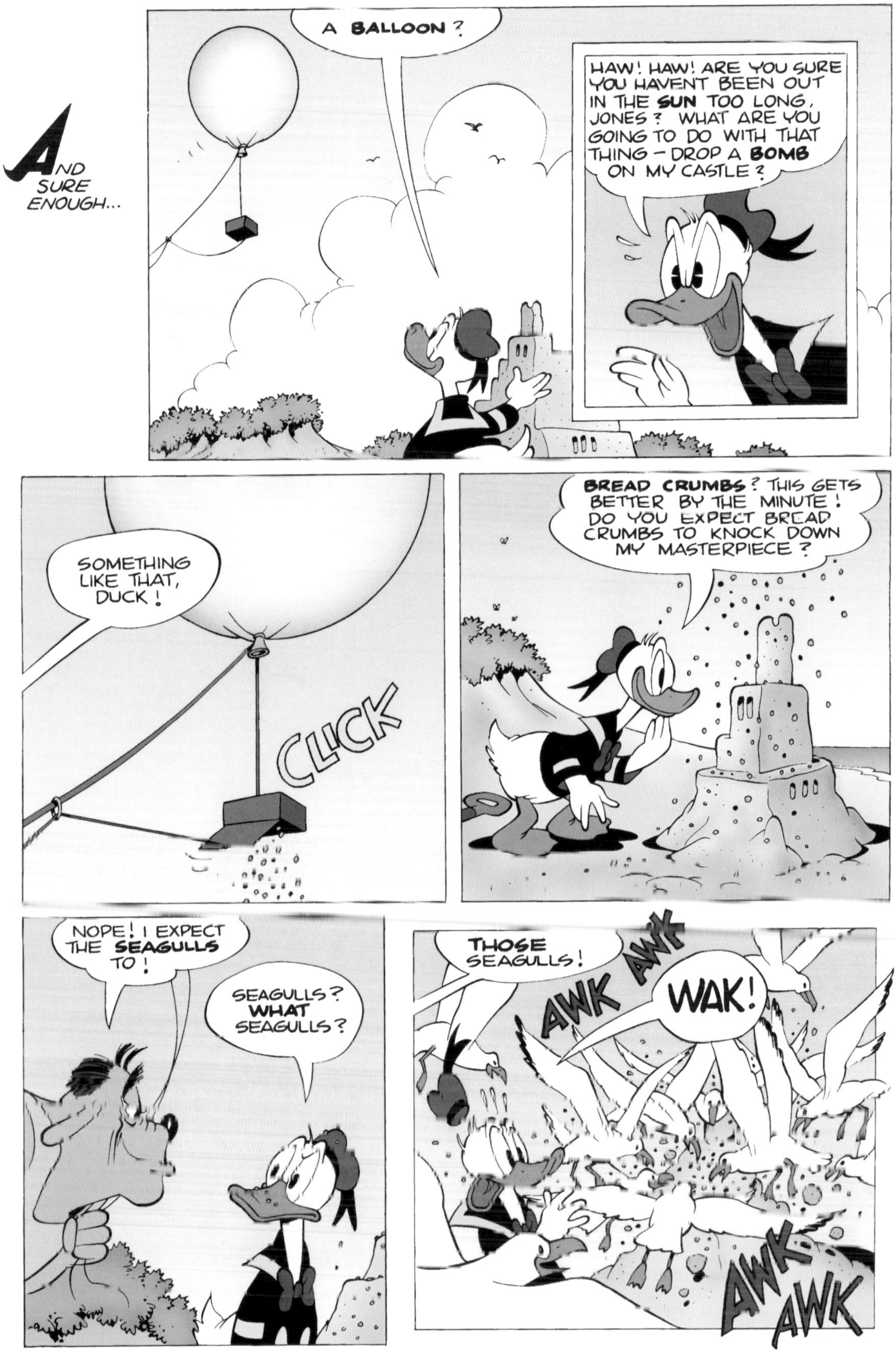
AND SURE ENOUGH...
A BALLOON?
HAW! HAW! ARE YOU SURE YOU HAVEN'T BEEN OUT IN THE SUN TOO LONG, JONES? WHAT ARE YOU GOING TO DO WITH THAT THING – DROP A BOMB ON MY CASTLE?
SOMETHING LIKE THAT, DUCK!
CLICK
BREAD CRUMBS? THIS GETS BETTER BY THE MINUTE! DO YOU EXPECT BREAD CRUMBS TO KNOCK DOWN MY MASTERPIECE?
NOPE! I EXPECT THE SEAGULLS TO!
SEAGULLS? WHAT SEAGULLS?
THOSE SEAGULLS!
AWK AWK
AWK
WAK!
AWK AWK

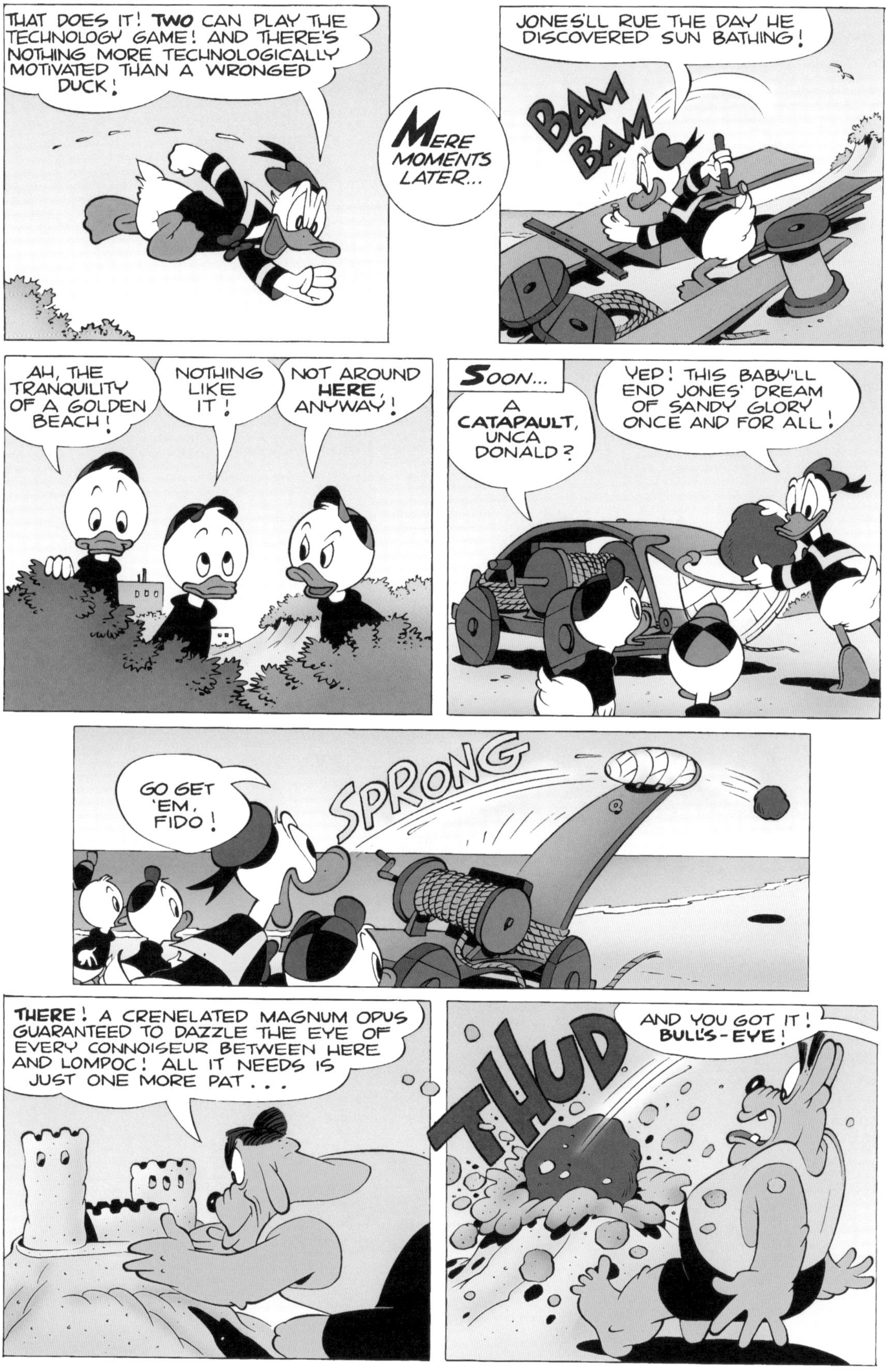
THAT DOES IT! TWO CAN PLAY THE TECHNOLOGY GAME! AND THERE'S NOTHING MORE TECHNOLOGICALLY MOTIVATED THAN A WRONGED DUCK!
MERE MOMENTS LATER...
JONES'LL RUE THE DAY HE DISCOVERED SUN BATHING!
BAM BAM
AH, THE TRANQUILITY OF A GOLDEN BEACH!
NOTHING LIKE IT!
NOT AROUND HERE, ANYWAY!
SOON...
A CATAPAULT, UNCA DONALD?
YEP! THIS BABY'LL END JONES' DREAM OF SANDY GLORY ONCE AND FOR ALL!
GO GET 'EM, FIDO!
SPRONG
THERE! A CRENELATED MAGNUM OPUS GUARANTEED TO DAZZLE THE EYE OF EVERY CONNOISEUR BETWEEN HERE AND LOMPOC! ALL IT NEEDS IS JUST ONE MORE PAT . . .
THUD
AND YOU GOT IT! BULL'S-EYE!

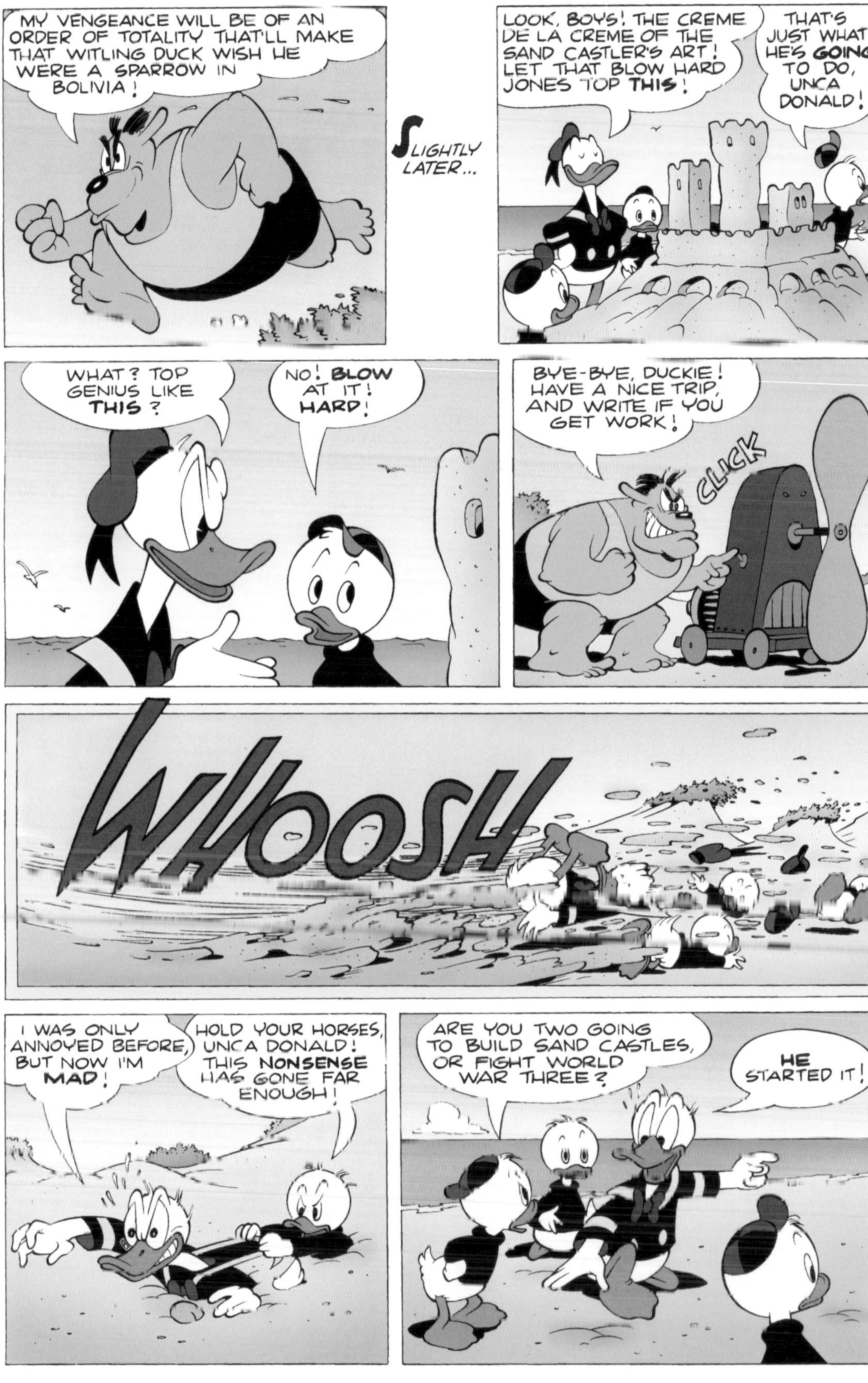
MY VENGEANCE WILL BE OF AN ORDER OF TOTALITY THAT'LL MAKE THAT WITLING DUCK WISH HE WERE A SPARROW IN BOLIVIA!
SLIGHTLY LATER...
LOOK, BOYS! THE CREME DE LA CREME OF THE SAND CASTLER'S ART! LET THAT BLOW HARD JONES TOP THIS!
THAT'S JUST WHAT HE'S GOING TO DO, UNCA DONALD!
WHAT? TOP GENIUS LIKE THIS?
NO! BLOW AT IT! HARD!
BYE-BYE, DUCKIE! HAVE A NICE TRIP, AND WRITE IF YOU GET WORK!
CLICK
WHOOSH
I WAS ONLY ANNOYED BEFORE, BUT NOW I'M MAD!
HOLD YOUR HORSES, UNCA DONALD! THIS NONSENSE HAS GONE FAR ENOUGH!
ARE YOU TWO GOING TO BUILD SAND CASTLES, OR FIGHT WORLD WAR THREE?
HE STARTED IT!

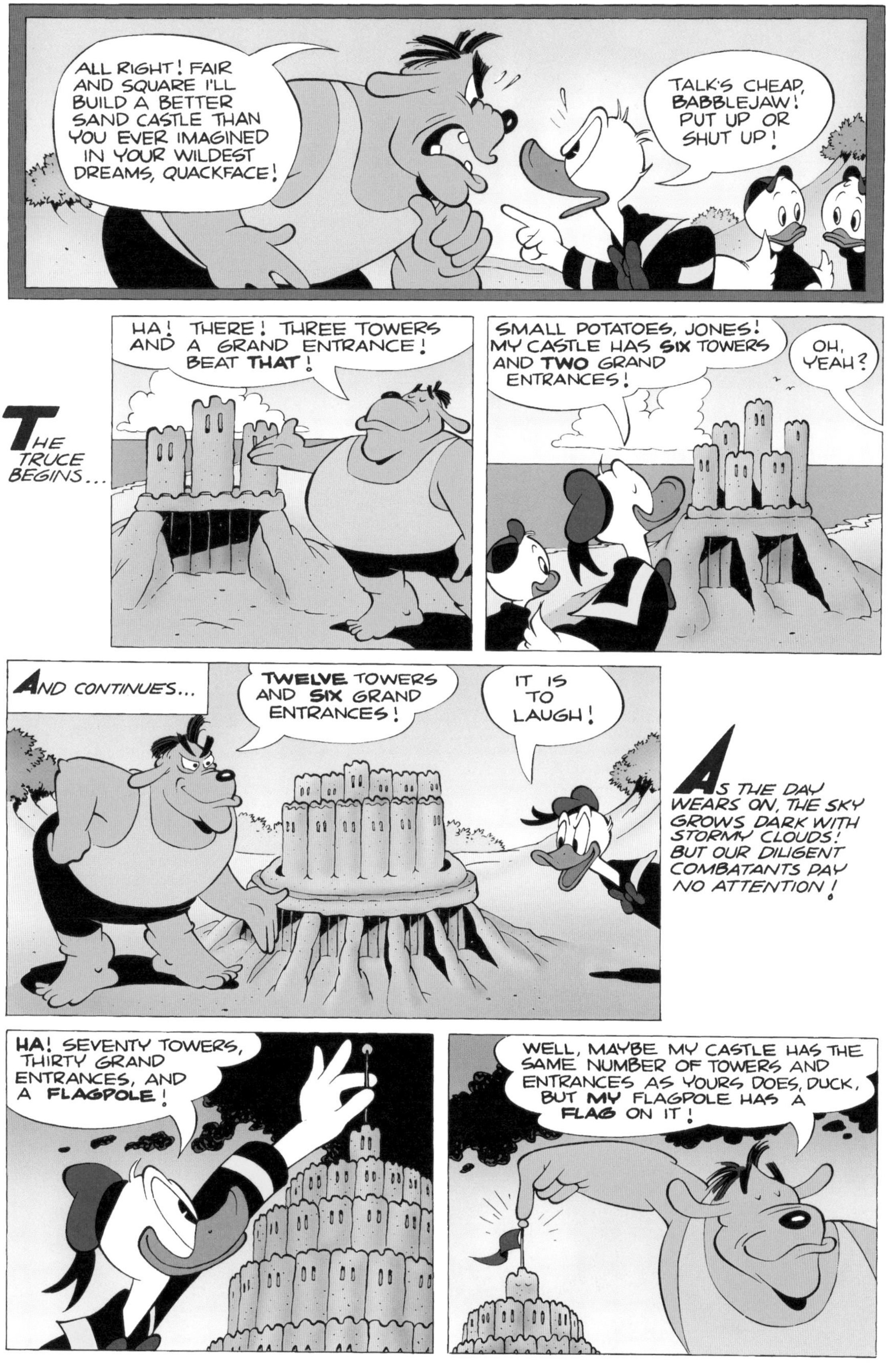
ALL RIGHT! FAIR AND SQUARE I'LL BUILD A BETTER SAND CASTLE THAN YOU EVER IMAGINED IN YOUR WILDEST DREAMS, QUACKFACE!
TALK'S CHEAP, BABBLEJAW! PUT UP OR SHUT UP!
THE TRUCE BEGINS...
HA! THERE! THREE TOWERS AND A GRAND ENTRANCE! BEAT THAT!
SMALL POTATOES, JONES! MY CASTLE HAS SIX TOWERS AND TWO GRAND ENTRANCES!
OH, YEAH?
AND CONTINUES...
TWELVE TOWERS AND SIX GRAND ENTRANCES!
IT IS TO LAUGH!
AS THE DAY WEARS ON, THE SKY GROWS DARK WITH STORMY CLOUDS! BUT OUR DILIGENT COMBATANTS PAY NO ATTENTION!
HA! SEVENTY TOWERS, THIRTY GRAND ENTRANCES, AND A FLAGPOLE!
WELL, MAYBE MY CASTLE HAS THE SAME NUMBER OF TOWERS AND ENTRANCES AS YOURS DOES, DUCK, BUT MY FLAGPOLE HAS A FLAG ON IT!

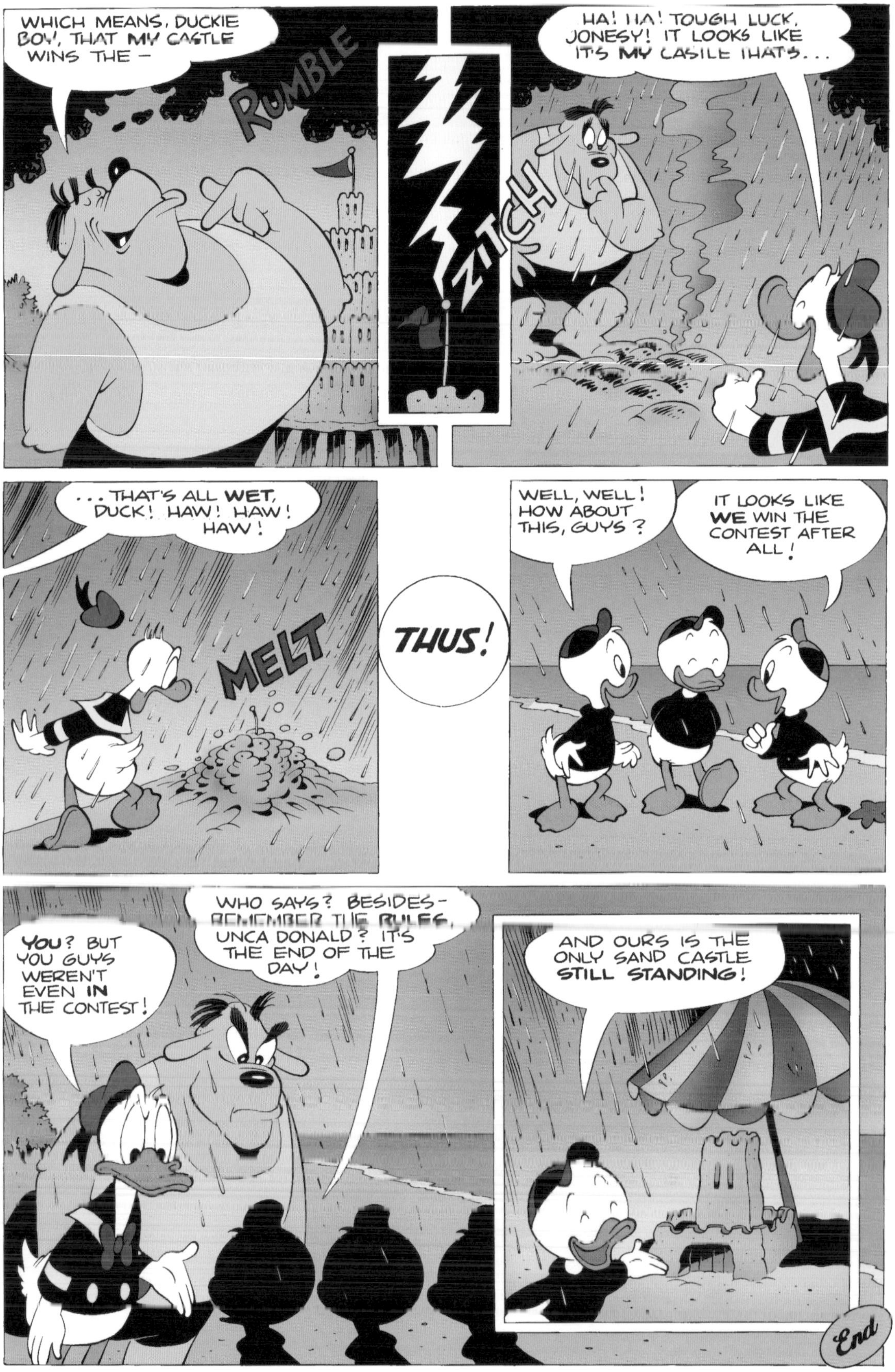
WHICH MEANS, DUCKIE BOY, THAT MY CASTLE WINS THE –
RUMBLE
ZITCH
HA! HA! TOUGH LUCK, JONESY! IT LOOKS LIKE IT'S MY CASTLE THAT'S...
... THAT'S ALL WET, DUCK! HAW! HAW! HAW!
MELT
THUS!
WELL, WELL! HOW ABOUT THIS, GUYS?
IT LOOKS LIKE WE WIN THE CONTEST AFTER ALL!
YOU? BUT YOU GUYS WEREN'T EVEN IN THE CONTEST!
WHO SAYS? BESIDES– REMEMBER THE RULES, UNCA DONALD? IT'S THE END OF THE DAY!
AND OURS IS THE ONLY SAND CASTLE STILL STANDING!
End

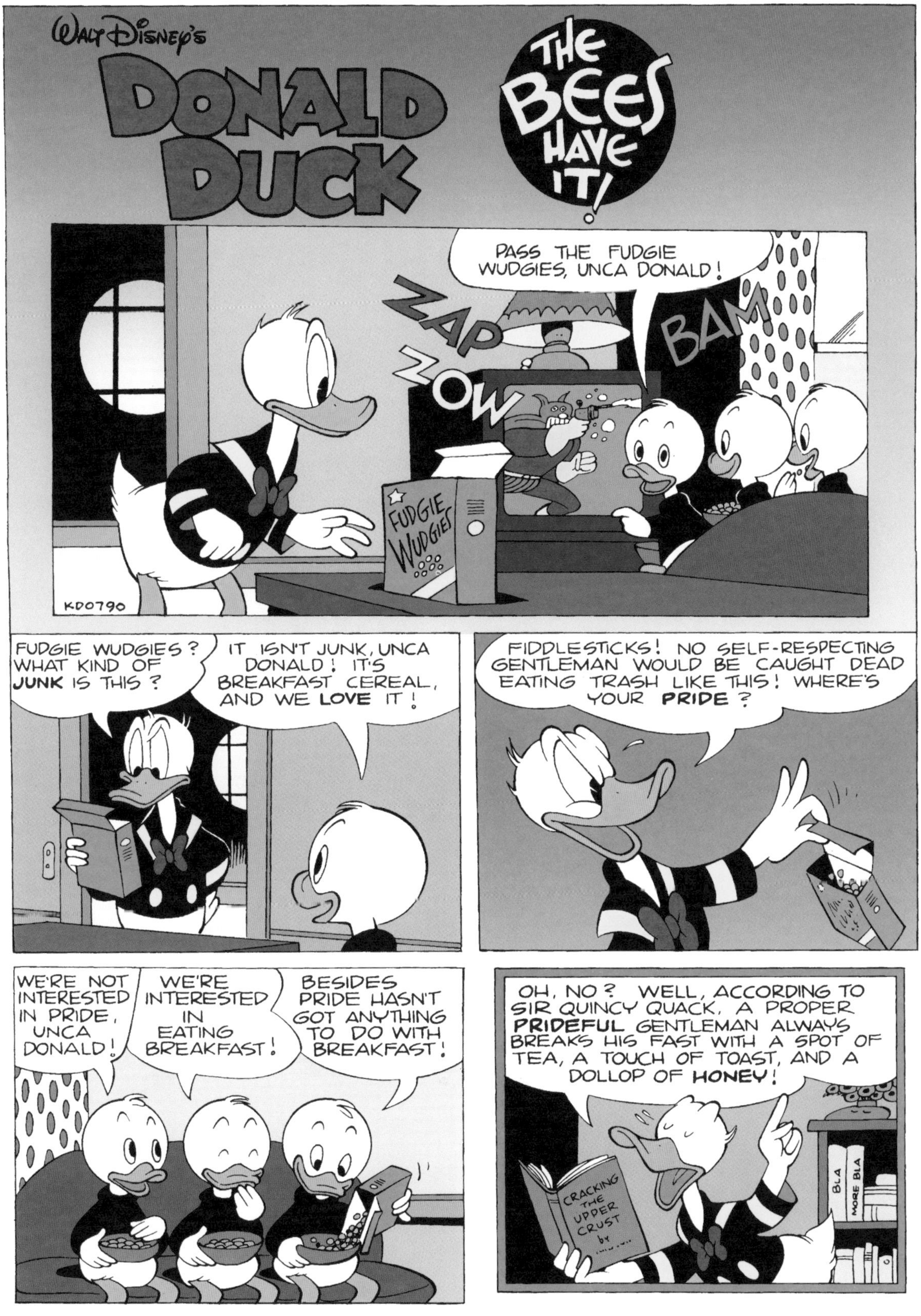
WALT DISNEY'S
DONALD DUCK
THE BEES HAVE IT!
PASS THE FUDGIE WUDGIES, UNCA DONALD!
ZAP
ZOW
BAM
FUDGIE WUDGIES
KDO790
FUDGIE WUDGIES? WHAT KIND OF **JUNK** IS THIS?
IT ISN'T JUNK, UNCA DONALD! IT'S BREAKFAST CEREAL, AND WE **LOVE** IT!
FIDDLESTICKS! NO SELF-RESPECTING GENTLEMAN WOULD BE CAUGHT DEAD EATING TRASH LIKE THIS! WHERE'S YOUR **PRIDE**?
WE'RE NOT INTERESTED IN PRIDE, UNCA DONALD!
WE'RE INTERESTED IN EATING BREAKFAST!
BESIDES PRIDE HASN'T GOT ANYTHING TO DO WITH BREAKFAST!
OH, NO? WELL, ACCORDING TO SIR QUINCY QUACK, A PROPER **PRIDEFUL** GENTLEMAN ALWAYS BREAKS HIS FAST WITH A SPOT OF TEA, A TOUCH OF TOAST, AND A DOLLOP OF **HONEY**!
CRACKING THE UPPER CRUST by
BLA
MORE BLA

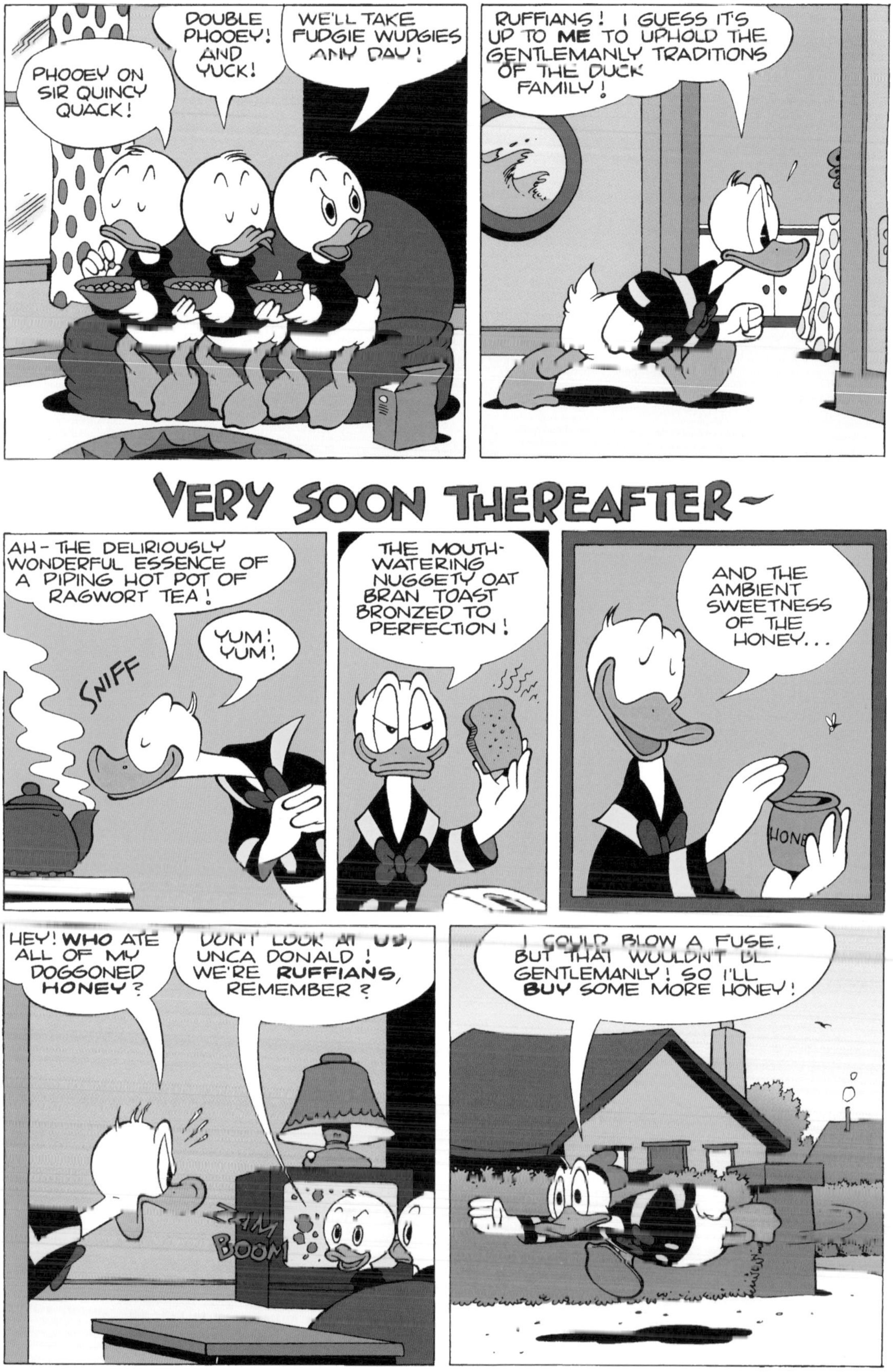
PHOOEY ON SIR QUINCY QUACK!
DOUBLE PHOOEY! AND YUCK!
WE'LL TAKE FUDGIE WUDGIES ANY DAY!
RUFFIANS! I GUESS IT'S UP TO ME TO UPHOLD THE GENTLEMANLY TRADITIONS OF THE DUCK FAMILY!
VERY SOON THEREAFTER—
AH—THE DELIRIOUSLY WONDERFUL ESSENCE OF A PIPING HOT POT OF RAGWORT TEA!
YUM! YUM!
SNIFF
THE MOUTH-WATERING NUGGETY OAT BRAN TOAST BRONZED TO PERFECTION!
AND THE AMBIENT SWEETNESS OF THE HONEY...
HONE
HEY! WHO ATE ALL OF MY DOGGONED HONEY?
DON'T LOOK AT US, UNCA DONALD! WE'RE RUFFIANS, REMEMBER?
BOOM
I COULD BLOW A FUSE, BUT THAT WOULDN'T BE GENTLEMANLY! SO I'LL BUY SOME MORE HONEY!

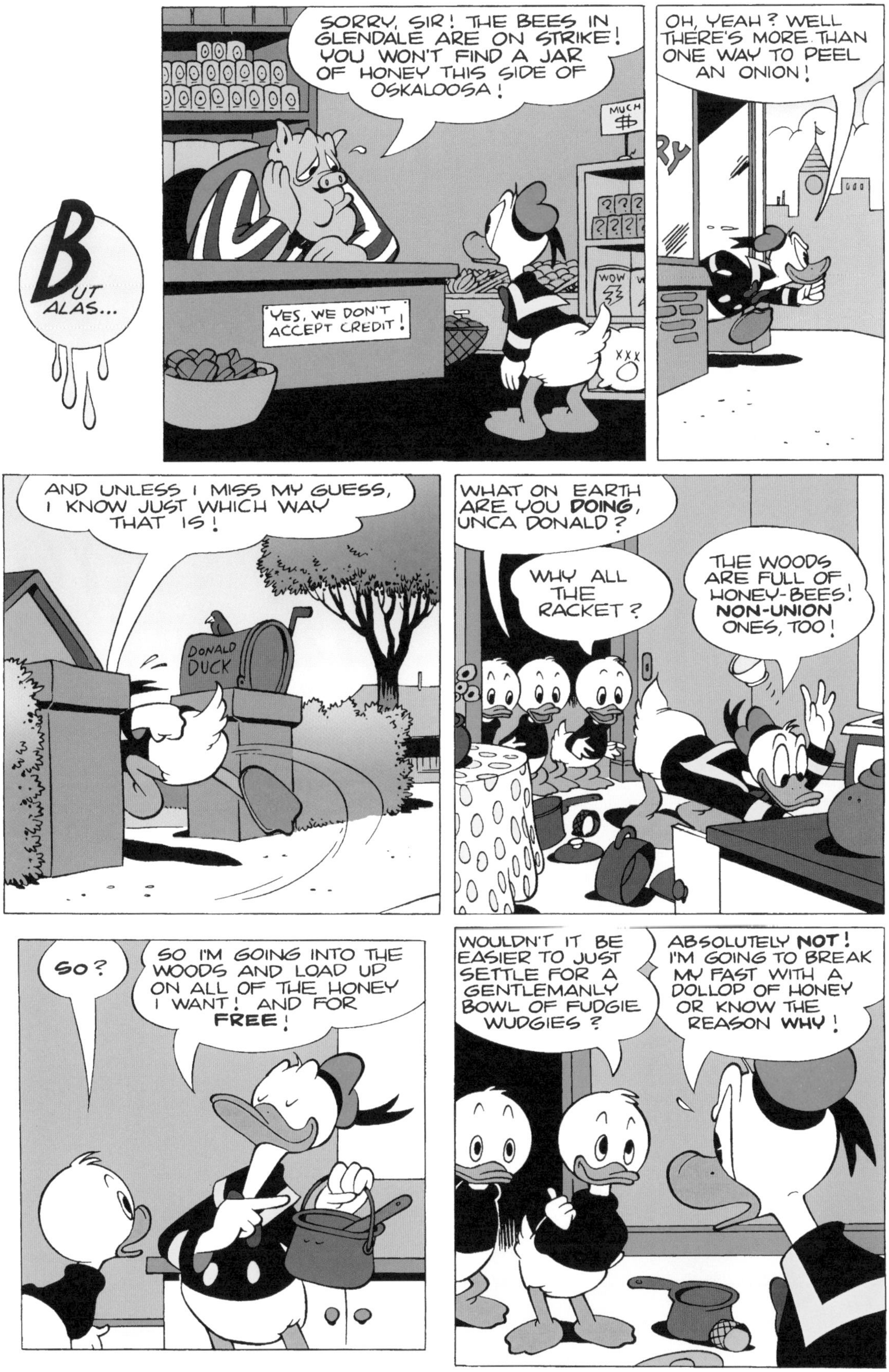
BUT ALAS...
SORRY, SIR! THE BEES IN GLENDALE ARE ON STRIKE! YOU WON'T FIND A JAR OF HONEY THIS SIDE OF OSKALOOSA!
YES, WE DON'T ACCEPT CREDIT!
MUCH $
OH, YEAH? WELL THERE'S MORE THAN ONE WAY TO PEEL AN ONION!
AND UNLESS I MISS MY GUESS, I KNOW JUST WHICH WAY THAT IS!
DONALD DUCK
WHAT ON EARTH ARE YOU **DOING**, UNCA DONALD?
WHY ALL THE RACKET?
THE WOODS ARE FULL OF HONEY-BEES! **NON-UNION** ONES, TOO!
SO?
SO I'M GOING INTO THE WOODS AND LOAD UP ON ALL OF THE HONEY I WANT! AND FOR **FREE**!
WOULDN'T IT BE EASIER TO JUST SETTLE FOR A GENTLEMANLY BOWL OF FUDGIE WUDGIES?
ABSOLUTELY **NOT**! I'M GOING TO BREAK MY FAST WITH A DOLLOP OF HONEY OR KNOW THE REASON **WHY**!

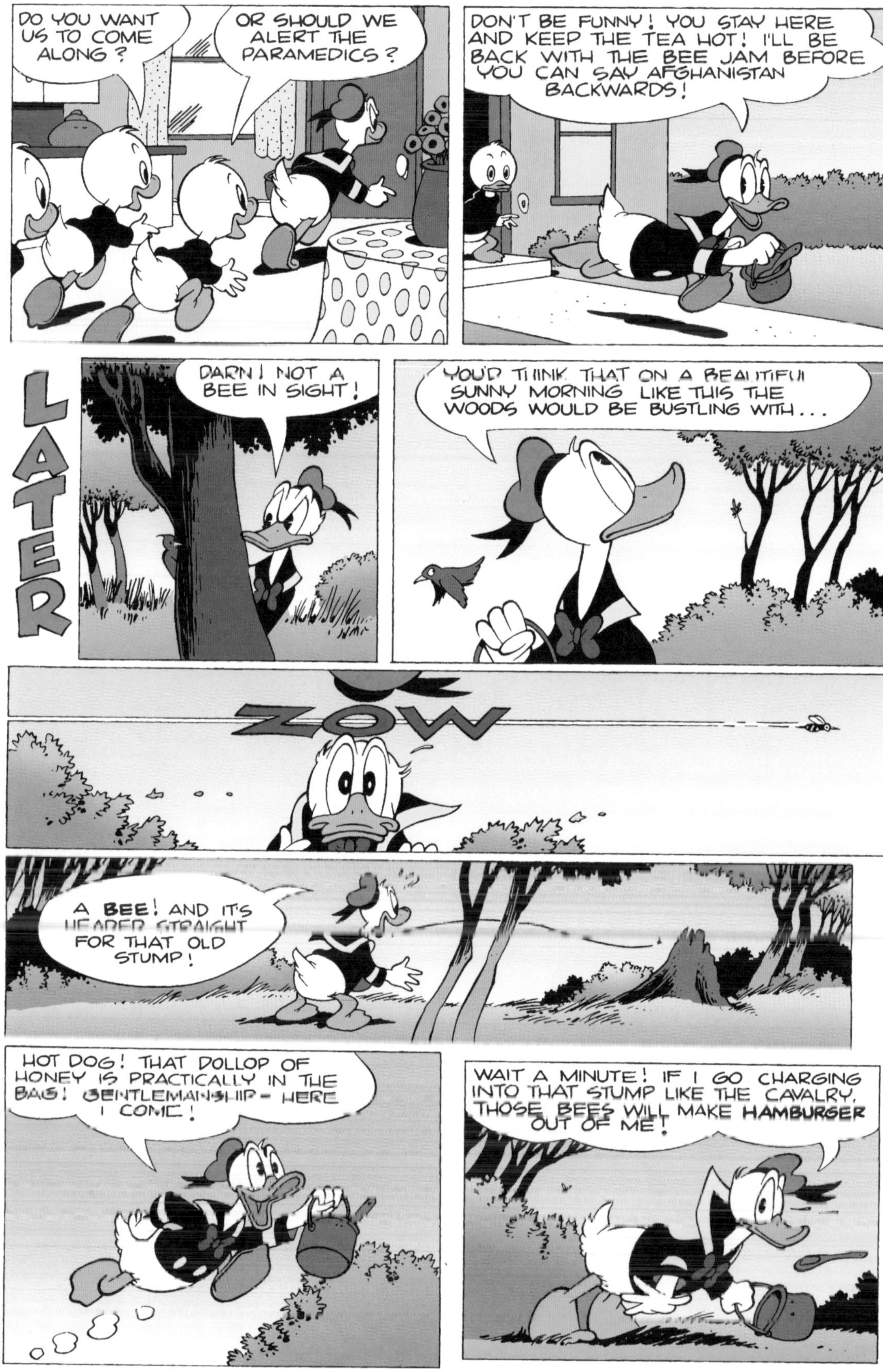
DO YOU WANT US TO COME ALONG?
OR SHOULD WE ALERT THE PARAMEDICS?
DON'T BE FUNNY! YOU STAY HERE AND KEEP THE TEA HOT! I'LL BE BACK WITH THE BEE JAM BEFORE YOU CAN SAY AFGHANISTAN BACKWARDS!
LATER
DARN! NOT A BEE IN SIGHT!
YOU'D THINK THAT ON A BEAUTIFUL SUNNY MORNING LIKE THIS THE WOODS WOULD BE BUSTLING WITH...
ZOW
A BEE! AND IT'S HEADED STRAIGHT FOR THAT OLD STUMP!
HOT DOG! THAT DOLLOP OF HONEY IS PRACTICALLY IN THE BAG! GENTLEMANSHIP- HERE I COME!
WAIT A MINUTE! IF I GO CHARGING INTO THAT STUMP LIKE THE CAVALRY, THOSE BEES WILL MAKE HAMBURGER OUT OF ME!

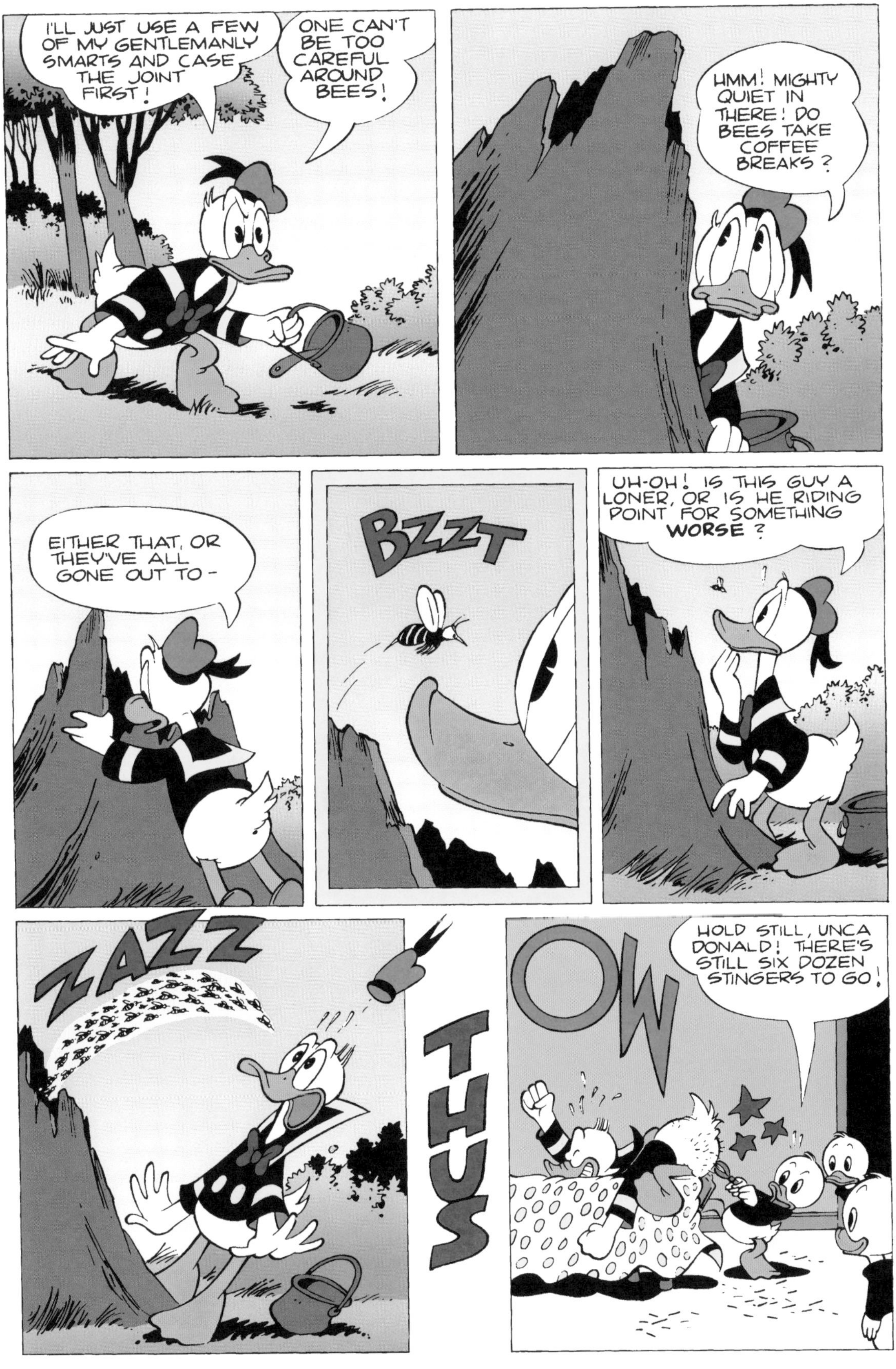
I'LL JUST USE A FEW OF MY GENTLEMANLY SMARTS AND CASE THE JOINT FIRST!
ONE CAN'T BE TOO CAREFUL AROUND BEES!
HMM! MIGHTY QUIET IN THERE! DO BEES TAKE COFFEE BREAKS?
EITHER THAT, OR THEY'VE ALL GONE OUT TO-
BZZT
UH-OH! IS THIS GUY A LONER, OR IS HE RIDING POINT FOR SOMETHING **WORSE**?
ZAZZ
THUS
OW
HOLD STILL, UNCA DONALD! THERE'S STILL SIX DOZEN STINGERS TO GO!

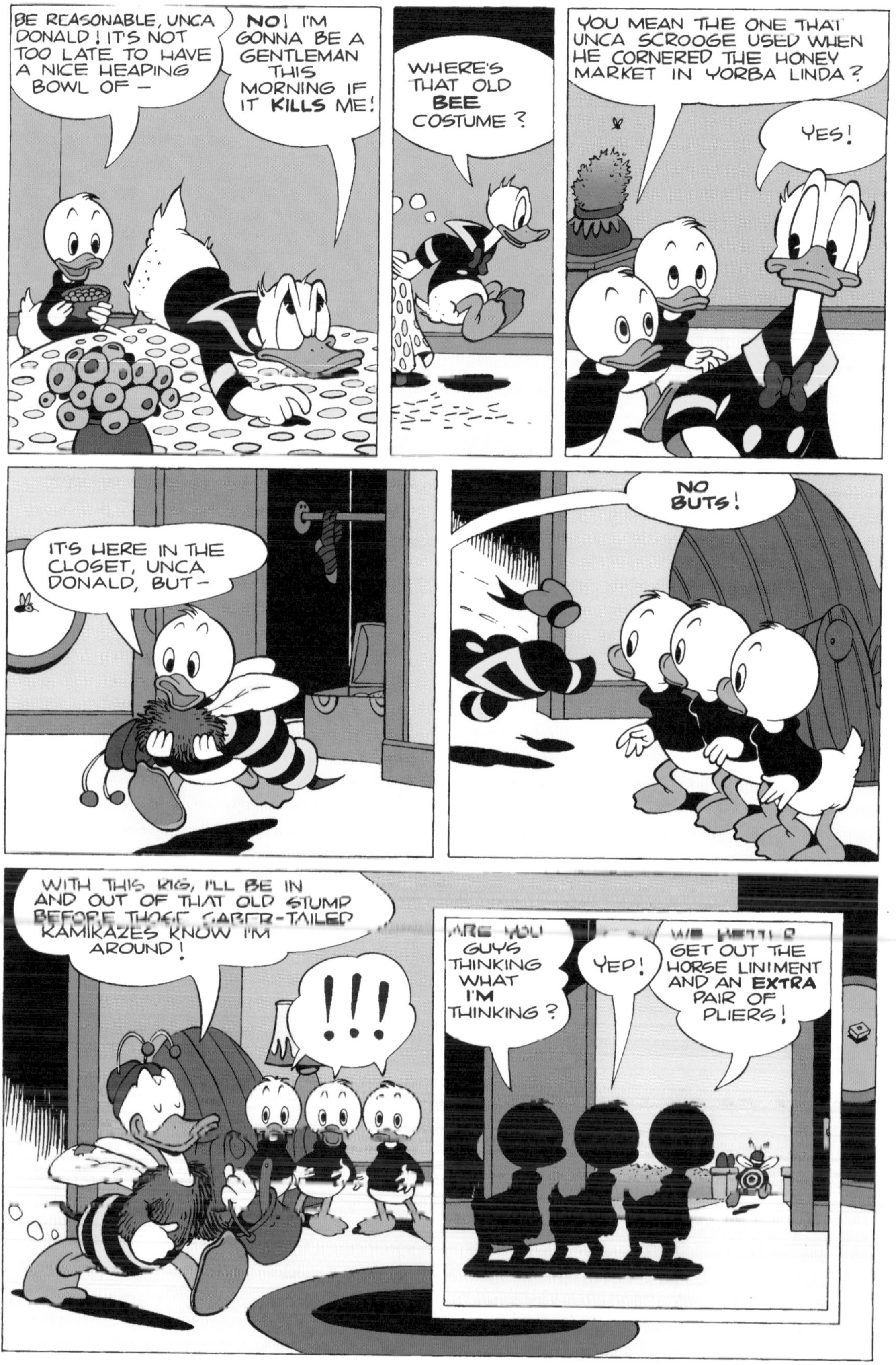
BE REASONABLE, UNCA DONALD! IT'S NOT TOO LATE TO HAVE A NICE HEAPING BOWL OF –
NO! I'M GONNA BE A GENTLEMAN THIS MORNING IF IT KILLS ME!
WHERE'S THAT OLD BEE COSTUME?
YOU MEAN THE ONE THAT UNCA SCROOGE USED WHEN HE CORNERED THE HONEY MARKET IN YORBA LINDA?
YES!
IT'S HERE IN THE CLOSET, UNCA DONALD, BUT–
NO BUTS!
WITH THIS RIG, I'LL BE IN AND OUT OF THAT OLD STUMP BEFORE THOSE SABER-TAILED KAMIKAZES KNOW I'M AROUND!
!!!
ARE YOU GUYS THINKING WHAT I'M THINKING?
YEP!
WE BETTER GET OUT THE HORSE LINIMENT AND AN EXTRA PAIR OF PLIERS!

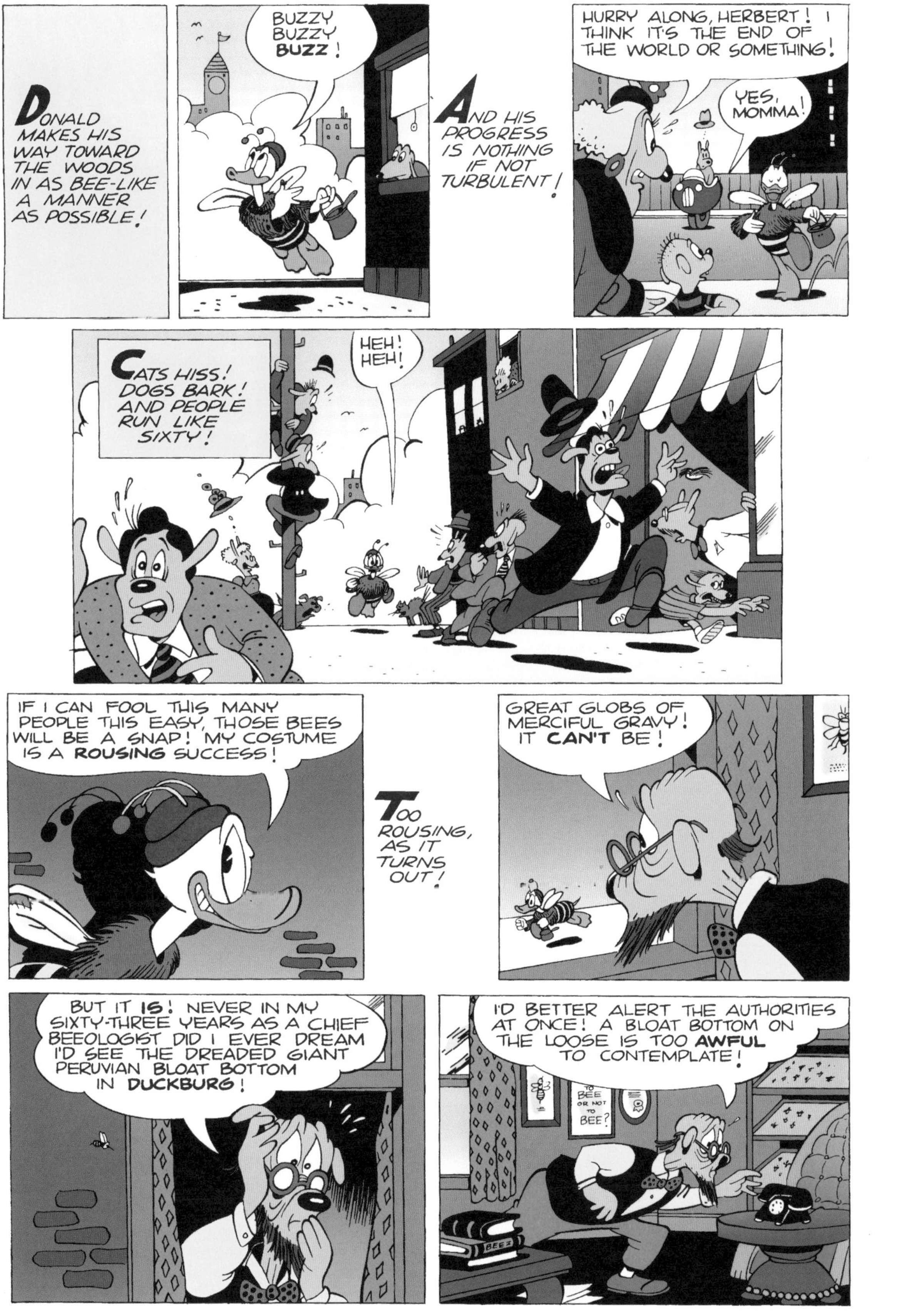
DONALD MAKES HIS WAY TOWARD THE WOODS IN AS BEE-LIKE A MANNER AS POSSIBLE!
BUZZY BUZZY BUZZ!
AND HIS PROGRESS IS NOTHING IF NOT TURBULENT!
HURRY ALONG, HERBERT! I THINK IT'S THE END OF THE WORLD OR SOMETHING!
YES, MOMMA!
CATS HISS! DOGS BARK! AND PEOPLE RUN LIKE SIXTY!
HEH! HEH!
IF I CAN FOOL THIS MANY PEOPLE THIS EASY, THOSE BEES WILL BE A SNAP! MY COSTUME IS A ROUSING SUCCESS!
TOO ROUSING, AS IT TURNS OUT!
GREAT GLOBS OF MERCIFUL GRAVY! IT CAN'T BE!
BUT IT IS! NEVER IN MY SIXTY-THREE YEARS AS A CHIEF BEEOLOGIST DID I EVER DREAM I'D SEE THE DREADED GIANT PERUVIAN BLOAT BOTTOM IN DUCKBURG!
I'D BETTER ALERT THE AUTHORITIES AT ONCE! A BLOAT BOTTOM ON THE LOOSE IS TOO AWFUL TO CONTEMPLATE!
TO BEE OR NOT TO BEE?
BEEZ

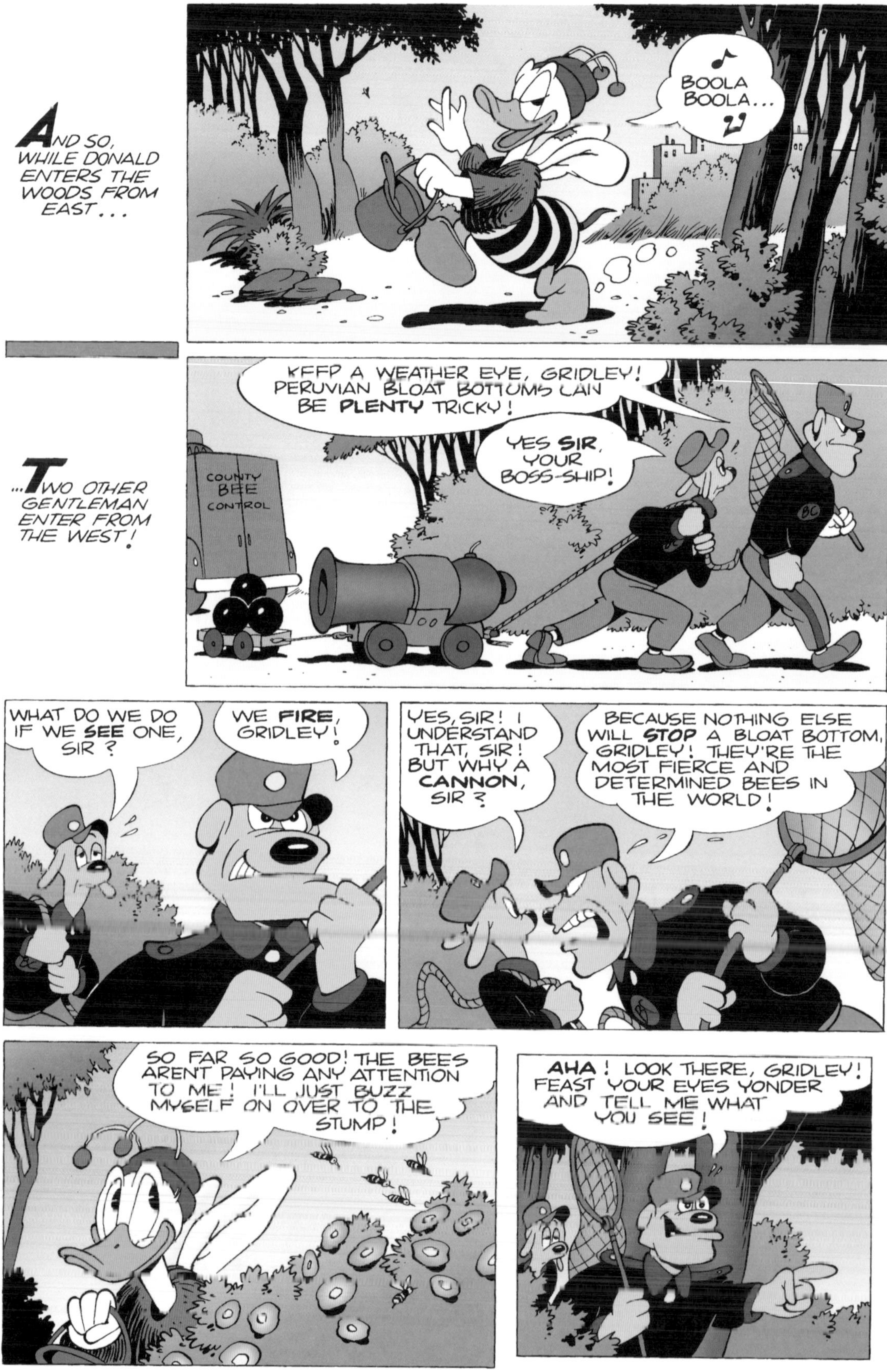
AND SO, WHILE DONALD ENTERS THE WOODS FROM EAST...
BOOLA BOOLA...
...TWO OTHER GENTLEMAN ENTER FROM THE WEST!
KEEP A WEATHER EYE, GRIDLEY! PERUVIAN BLOAT BOTTOMS CAN BE PLENTY TRICKY!
YES SIR, YOUR BOSS-SHIP!
COUNTY BEE CONTROL
WHAT DO WE DO IF WE SEE ONE, SIR?
WE FIRE, GRIDLEY!
YES, SIR! I UNDERSTAND THAT, SIR! BUT WHY A CANNON, SIR?
BECAUSE NOTHING ELSE WILL STOP A BLOAT BOTTOM, GRIDLEY! THEY'RE THE MOST FIERCE AND DETERMINED BEES IN THE WORLD!
SO FAR SO GOOD! THE BEES ARENT PAYING ANY ATTENTION TO ME! I'LL JUST BUZZ MYSELF ON OVER TO THE STUMP!
AHA! LOOK THERE, GRIDLEY! FEAST YOUR EYES YONDER AND TELL ME WHAT YOU SEE!

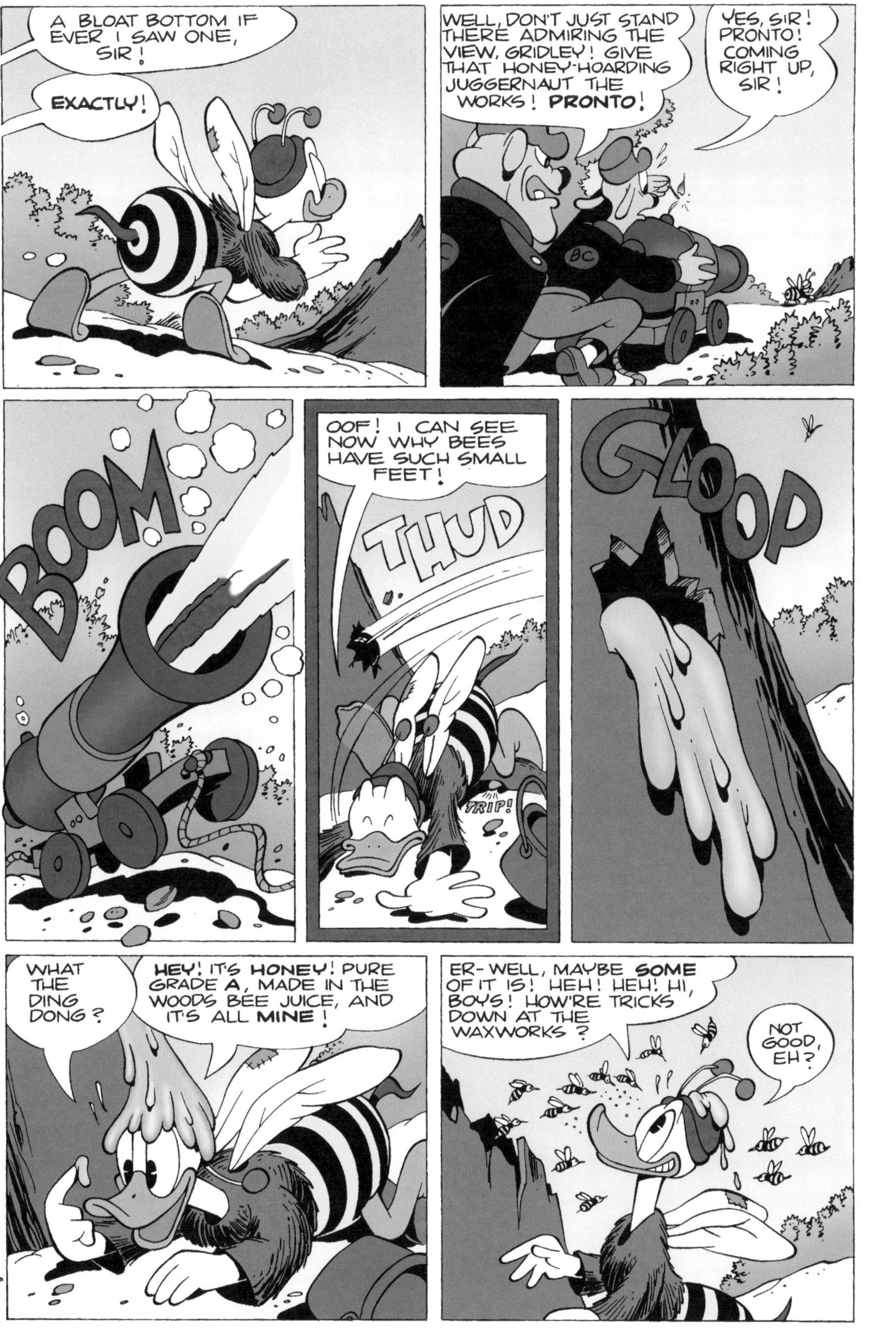
A BLOAT BOTTOM IF EVER I SAW ONE, SIR!
EXACTLY!
WELL, DON'T JUST STAND THERE ADMIRING THE VIEW, GRIDLEY! GIVE THAT HONEY-HOARDING JUGGERNAUT THE WORKS! PRONTO!
YES, SIR! PRONTO! COMING RIGHT UP, SIR!
BC
BOOM
OOF! I CAN SEE NOW WHY BEES HAVE SUCH SMALL FEET!
THUD
TRIP!
GLOOP
WHAT THE DING DONG?
HEY! IT'S HONEY! PURE GRADE A, MADE IN THE WOODS BEE JUICE, AND IT'S ALL MINE!
ER-WELL, MAYBE SOME OF IT IS! HEH! HEH! HI, BOYS! HOW'RE TRICKS DOWN AT THE WAXWORKS?
NOT GOOD, EH?

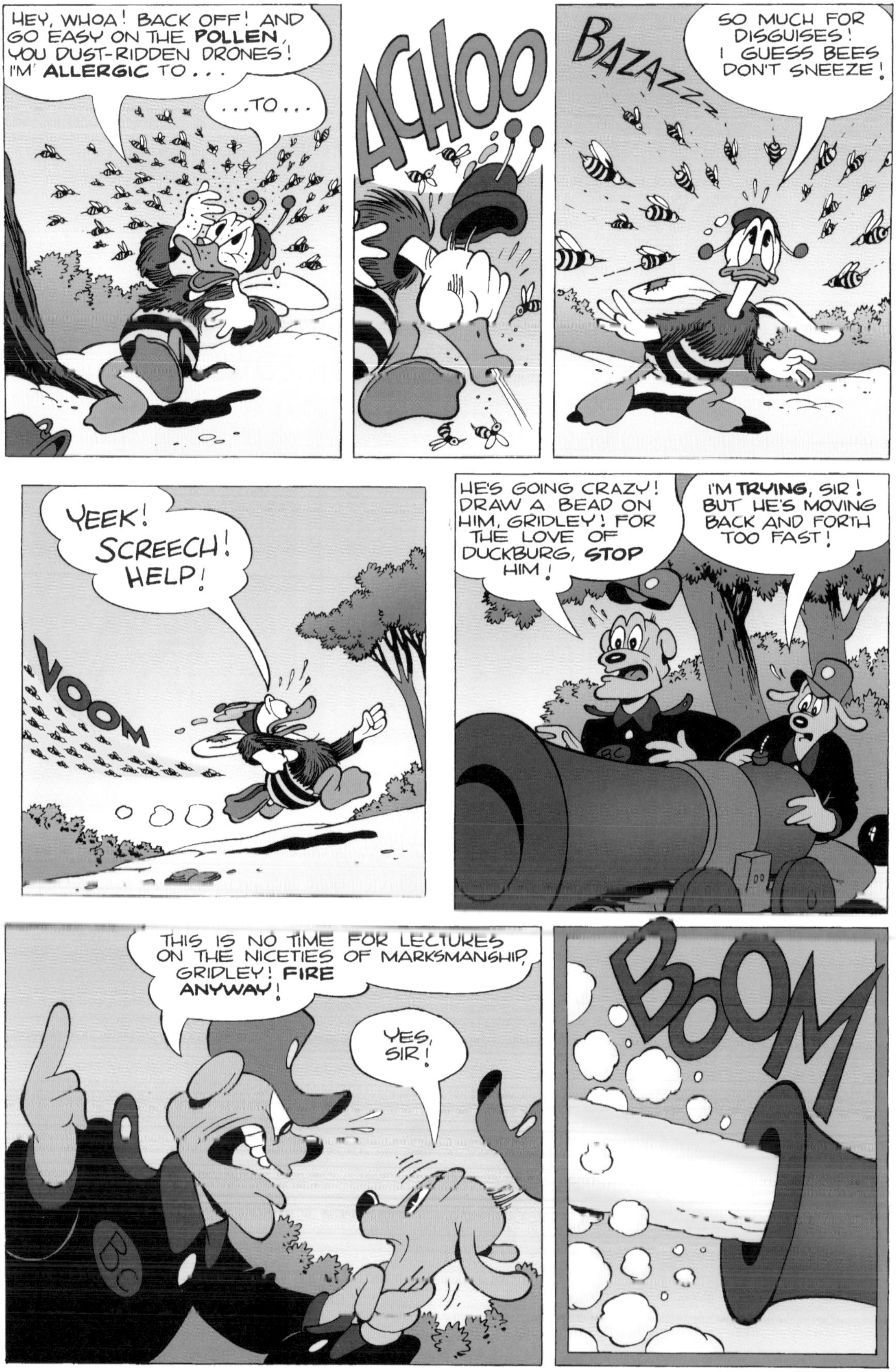
HEY, WHOA! BACK OFF! AND GO EASY ON THE POLLEN, YOU DUST-RIDDEN DRONES! I'M ALLERGIC TO . . .
. . .TO. . .
ACHOO
BAZAZZzz
SO MUCH FOR DISGUISES! I GUESS BEES DON'T SNEEZE!
YEEK! SCREECH! HELP!
VOOM
HE'S GOING CRAZY! DRAW A BEAD ON HIM, GRIDLEY! FOR THE LOVE OF DUCKBURG, STOP HIM!
I'M TRYING, SIR! BUT HE'S MOVING BACK AND FORTH TOO FAST!
THIS IS NO TIME FOR LECTURES ON THE NICETIES OF MARKSMANSHIP, GRIDLEY! FIRE ANYWAY!
YES, SIR!
BOOM

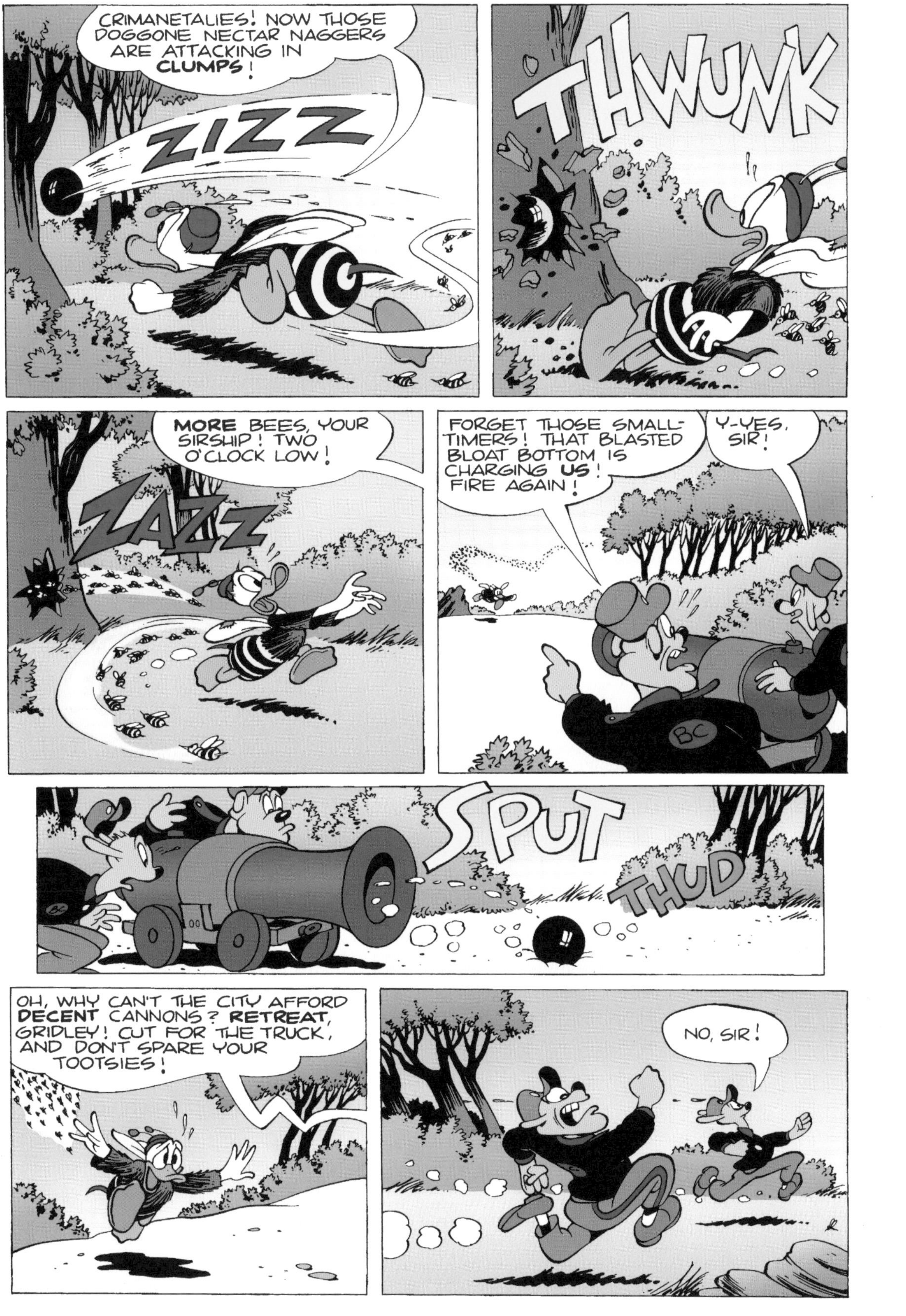

CRIMANETALIES! NOW THOSE DOGGONE NECTAR NAGGERS ARE ATTACKING IN **CLUMPS**!
ZIZZ
THWUNK
MORE BEES, YOUR SIRSHIP! TWO O'CLOCK LOW!
ZAZZ
FORGET THOSE SMALL-TIMERS! THAT BLASTED BLOAT BOTTOM IS CHARGING **US**! FIRE AGAIN!
Y-YES, SIR!
BC
SPUT
THUD
OH, WHY CAN'T THE CITY AFFORD **DECENT** CANNONS? **RETREAT**, GRIDLEY! CUT FOR THE TRUCK, AND DON'T SPARE YOUR TOOTSIES!
NO, SIR!

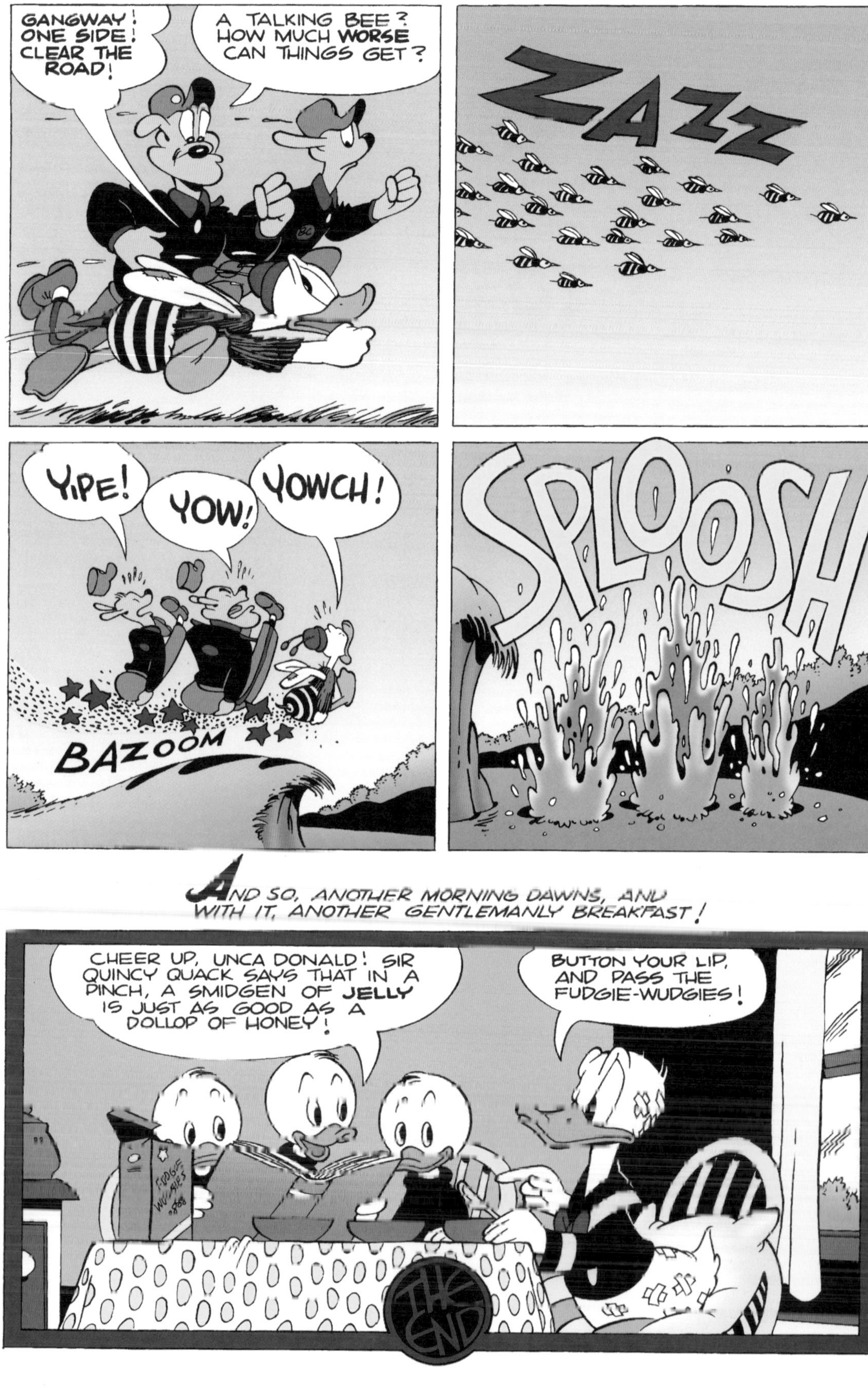
GANGWAY! ONE SIDE! CLEAR THE ROAD!
A TALKING BEE? HOW MUCH WORSE CAN THINGS GET?
ZAZZ
YIPE!
YOW!
YOWCH!
BAZOOM
SPLOOSH
AND SO, ANOTHER MORNING DAWNS, AND WITH IT, ANOTHER GENTLEMANLY BREAKFAST!
CHEER UP, UNCA DONALD! SIR QUINCY QUACK SAYS THAT IN A PINCH, A SMIDGEN OF JELLY IS JUST AS GOOD AS A DOLLOP OF HONEY!
BUTTON YOUR LIP, AND PASS THE FUDGIE-WUDGIES!
FUDGIE WUDGIES
THE END

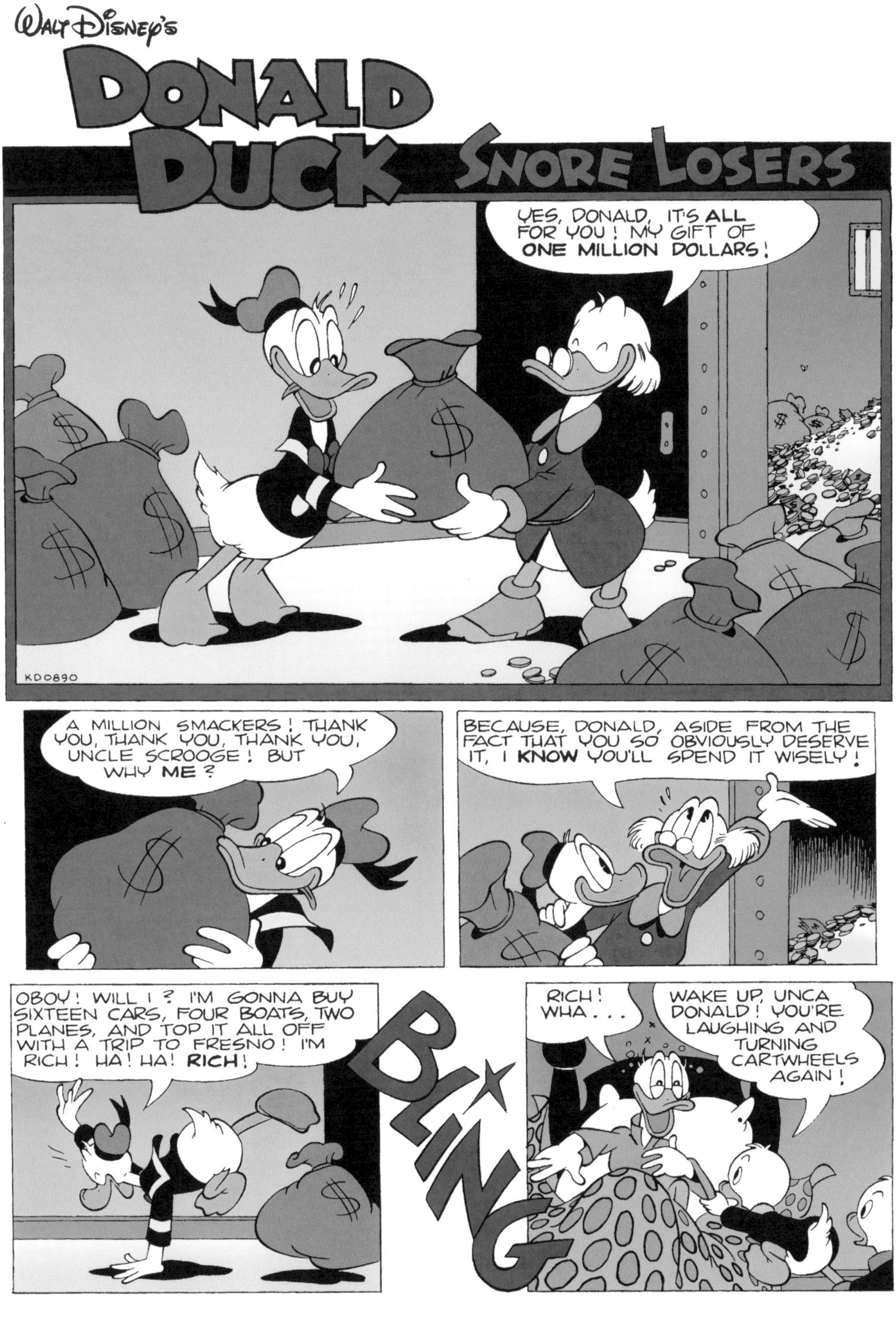
WALT DISNEY'S
DONALD DUCK
SNORE LOSERS
YES, DONALD, IT'S ALL FOR YOU! MY GIFT OF ONE MILLION DOLLARS!
KD0890
A MILLION SMACKERS! THANK YOU, THANK YOU, THANK YOU, UNCLE SCROOGE! BUT WHY ME?
BECAUSE, DONALD, ASIDE FROM THE FACT THAT YOU SO OBVIOUSLY DESERVE IT, I KNOW YOU'LL SPEND IT WISELY!
OBOY! WILL I? I'M GONNA BUY SIXTEEN CARS, FOUR BOATS, TWO PLANES, AND TOP IT ALL OFF WITH A TRIP TO FRESNO! I'M RICH! HA! HA! RICH!
BLING
RICH! WHA...
WAKE UP, UNCA DONALD! YOU'RE LAUGHING AND TURNING CARTWHEELS AGAIN!

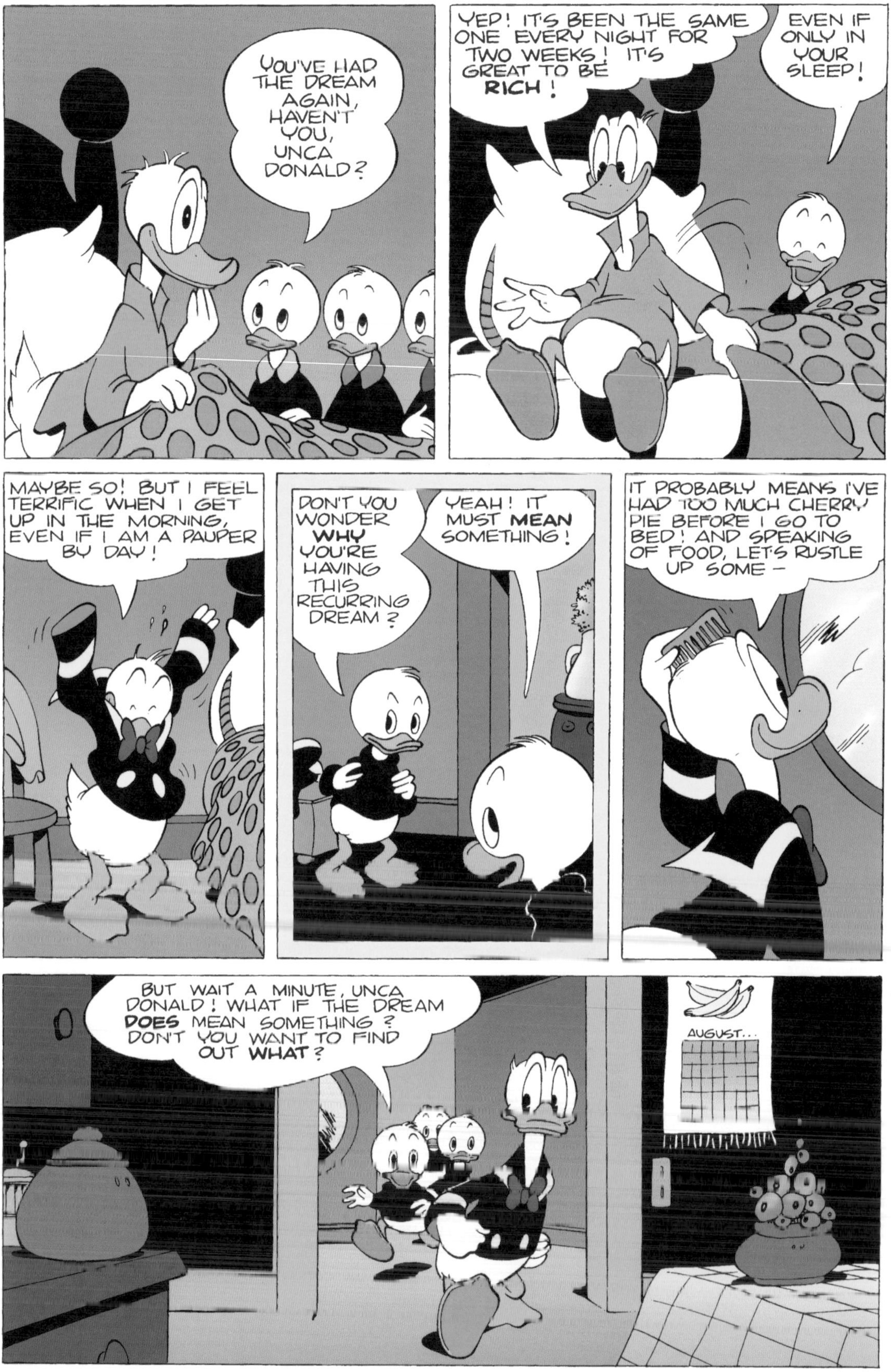
YOU'VE HAD THE DREAM AGAIN, HAVEN'T YOU, UNCA DONALD?
YEP! IT'S BEEN THE SAME ONE EVERY NIGHT FOR TWO WEEKS! IT'S GREAT TO BE RICH!
EVEN IF ONLY IN YOUR SLEEP!
MAYBE SO! BUT I FEEL TERRIFIC WHEN I GET UP IN THE MORNING, EVEN IF I AM A PAUPER BY DAY!
DON'T YOU WONDER WHY YOU'RE HAVING THIS RECURRING DREAM?
YEAH! IT MUST MEAN SOMETHING!
IT PROBABLY MEANS I'VE HAD TOO MUCH CHERRY PIE BEFORE I GO TO BED! AND SPEAKING OF FOOD, LET'S RUSTLE UP SOME –
BUT WAIT A MINUTE, UNCA DONALD! WHAT IF THE DREAM DOES MEAN SOMETHING? DON'T YOU WANT TO FIND OUT WHAT?
AUGUST...

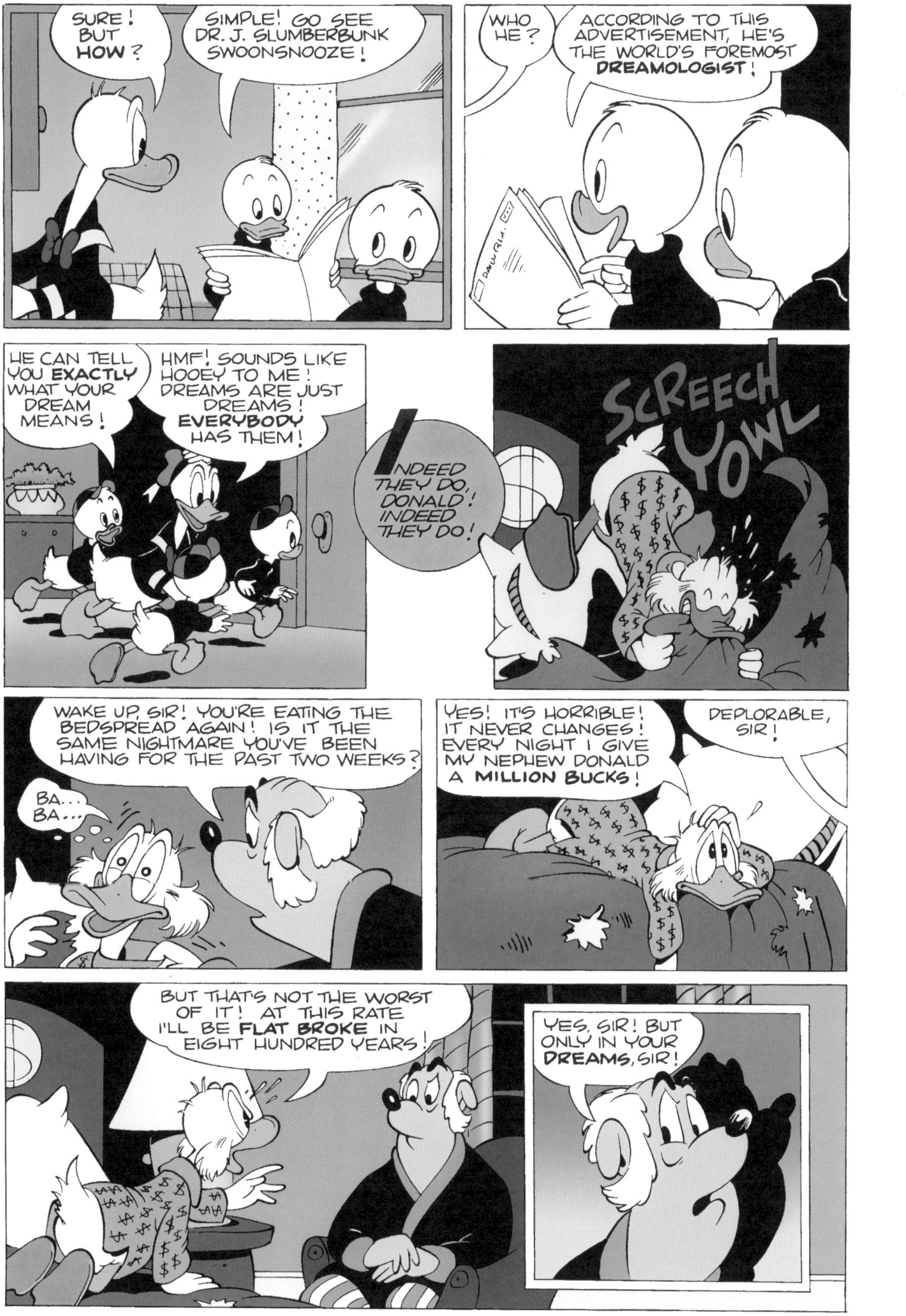
SURE! BUT HOW?
SIMPLE! GO SEE DR. J. SLUMBERBUNK SWOONSNOOZE!
WHO HE?
ACCORDING TO THIS ADVERTISEMENT, HE'S THE WORLD'S FOREMOST DREAMOLOGIST!
HE CAN TELL YOU EXACTLY WHAT YOUR DREAM MEANS!
HMF! SOUNDS LIKE HOOEY TO ME! DREAMS ARE JUST DREAMS! EVERYBODY HAS THEM!
INDEED THEY DO, DONALD! INDEED THEY DO!
SCREECH
YOWL
WAKE UP, SIR! YOU'RE EATING THE BEDSPREAD AGAIN! IS IT THE SAME NIGHTMARE YOU'VE BEEN HAVING FOR THE PAST TWO WEEKS?
BA... BA...
YES! IT'S HORRIBLE! IT NEVER CHANGES! EVERY NIGHT I GIVE MY NEPHEW DONALD A MILLION BUCKS!
DEPLORABLE, SIR!
BUT THAT'S NOT THE WORST OF IT! AT THIS RATE I'LL BE FLAT BROKE IN EIGHT HUNDRED YEARS!
YES, SIR! BUT ONLY IN YOUR DREAMS, SIR!

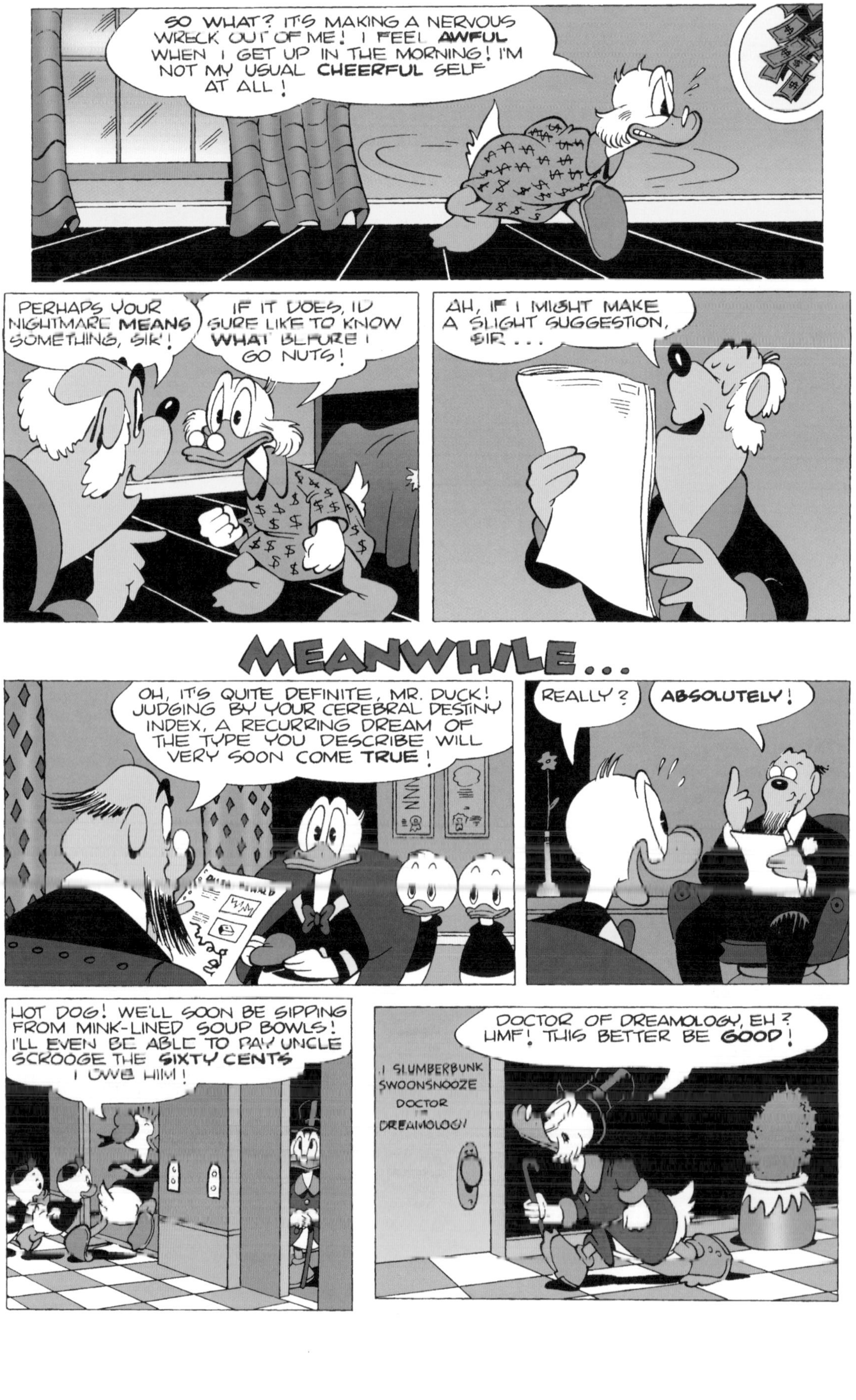

SO WHAT? IT'S MAKING A NERVOUS WRECK OUT OF ME! I FEEL AWFUL WHEN I GET UP IN THE MORNING! I'M NOT MY USUAL CHEERFUL SELF AT ALL!
PERHAPS YOUR NIGHTMARE MEANS SOMETHING, SIR!
IF IT DOES, I'D SURE LIKE TO KNOW WHAT BEFORE I GO NUTS!
AH, IF I MIGHT MAKE A SLIGHT SUGGESTION, SIR . . .
MEANWHILE . . .
OH, IT'S QUITE DEFINITE, MR. DUCK! JUDGING BY YOUR CEREBRAL DESTINY INDEX, A RECURRING DREAM OF THE TYPE YOU DESCRIBE WILL VERY SOON COME TRUE!
REALLY?
ABSOLUTELY!
HOT DOG! WE'LL SOON BE SIPPING FROM MINK-LINED SOUP BOWLS! I'LL EVEN BE ABLE TO PAY UNCLE SCROOGE THE SIXTY CENTS I OWE HIM!
DOCTOR OF DREAMOLOGY, EH? HMF! THIS BETTER BE GOOD!
SLUMBERBUNK
SWOONSNOOZE
DOCTOR
DREAMOLOGY

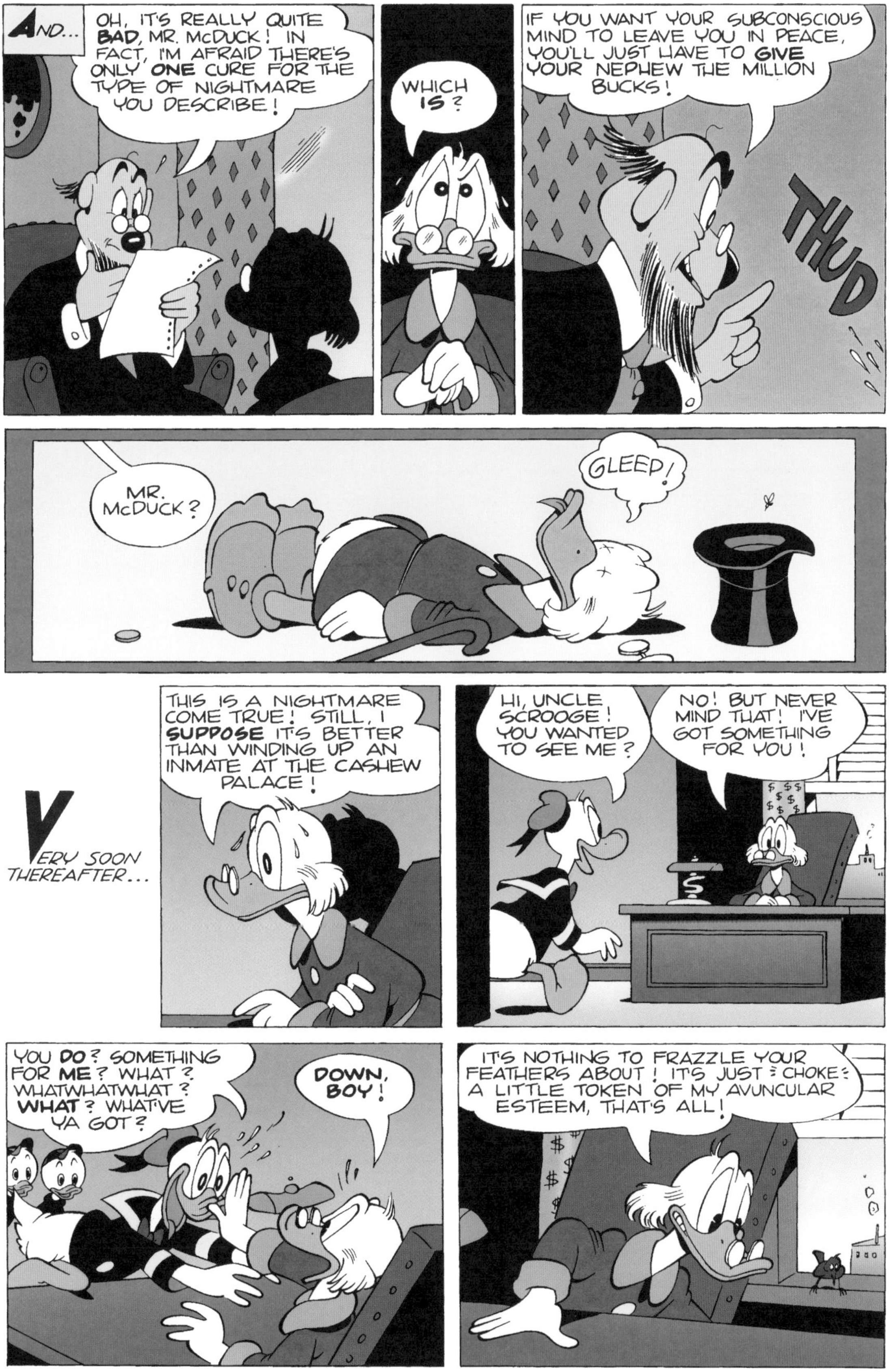
AND...
OH, IT'S REALLY QUITE BAD, MR. McDUCK! IN FACT, I'M AFRAID THERE'S ONLY ONE CURE FOR THE TYPE OF NIGHTMARE YOU DESCRIBE!
WHICH IS?
IF YOU WANT YOUR SUBCONSCIOUS MIND TO LEAVE YOU IN PEACE, YOU'LL JUST HAVE TO GIVE YOUR NEPHEW THE MILLION BUCKS!
THUD
MR. McDUCK?
GLEEP!
VERY SOON THEREAFTER...
THIS IS A NIGHTMARE COME TRUE! STILL, I SUPPOSE IT'S BETTER THAN WINDING UP AN INMATE AT THE CASHEW PALACE!
HI, UNCLE SCROOGE! YOU WANTED TO SEE ME?
NO! BUT NEVER MIND THAT! I'VE GOT SOMETHING FOR YOU!
YOU DO? SOMETHING FOR ME? WHAT? WHATWHATWHAT? WHAT? WHAT'VE YA GOT?
DOWN, BOY!
IT'S NOTHING TO FRAZZLE YOUR FEATHERS ABOUT! IT'S JUST CHOKE A LITTLE TOKEN OF MY AVUNCULAR ESTEEM, THAT'S ALL!

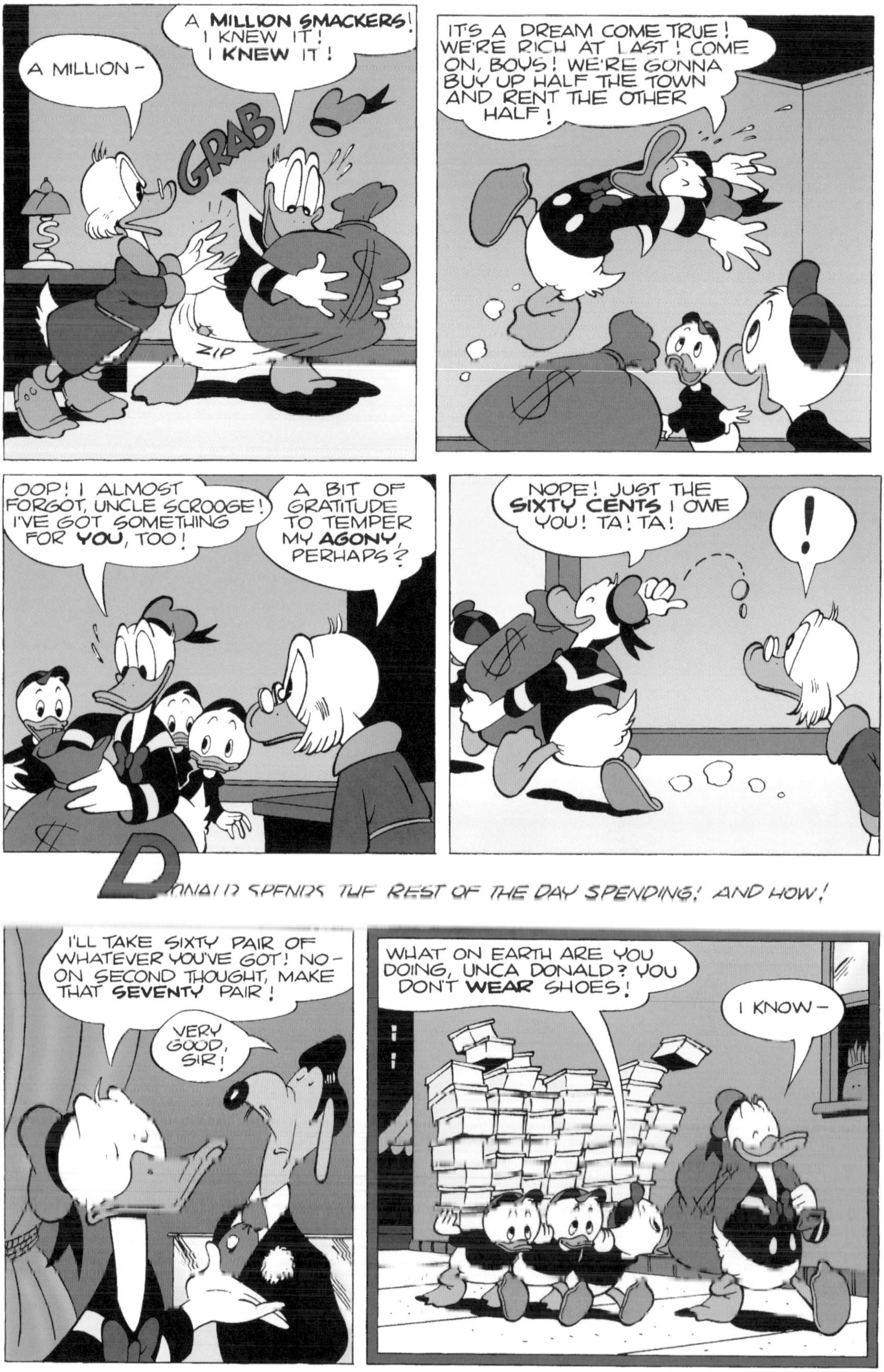
A MILLION -
A MILLION SMACKERS! I KNEW IT! I KNEW IT!
GRAB
ZIP
IT'S A DREAM COME TRUE! WE'RE RICH AT LAST! COME ON, BOYS! WE'RE GONNA BUY UP HALF THE TOWN AND RENT THE OTHER HALF!
OOP! I ALMOST FORGOT, UNCLE SCROOGE! I'VE GOT SOMETHING FOR YOU, TOO!
A BIT OF GRATITUDE TO TEMPER MY AGONY, PERHAPS?
NOPE! JUST THE SIXTY CENTS I OWE YOU! TA! TA!
!
DONALD SPENDS THE REST OF THE DAY SPENDING! AND HOW!
I'LL TAKE SIXTY PAIR OF WHATEVER YOU'VE GOT! NO- ON SECOND THOUGHT, MAKE THAT SEVENTY PAIR!
VERY GOOD, SIR!
WHAT ON EARTH ARE YOU DOING, UNCA DONALD? YOU DON'T WEAR SHOES!
I KNOW -

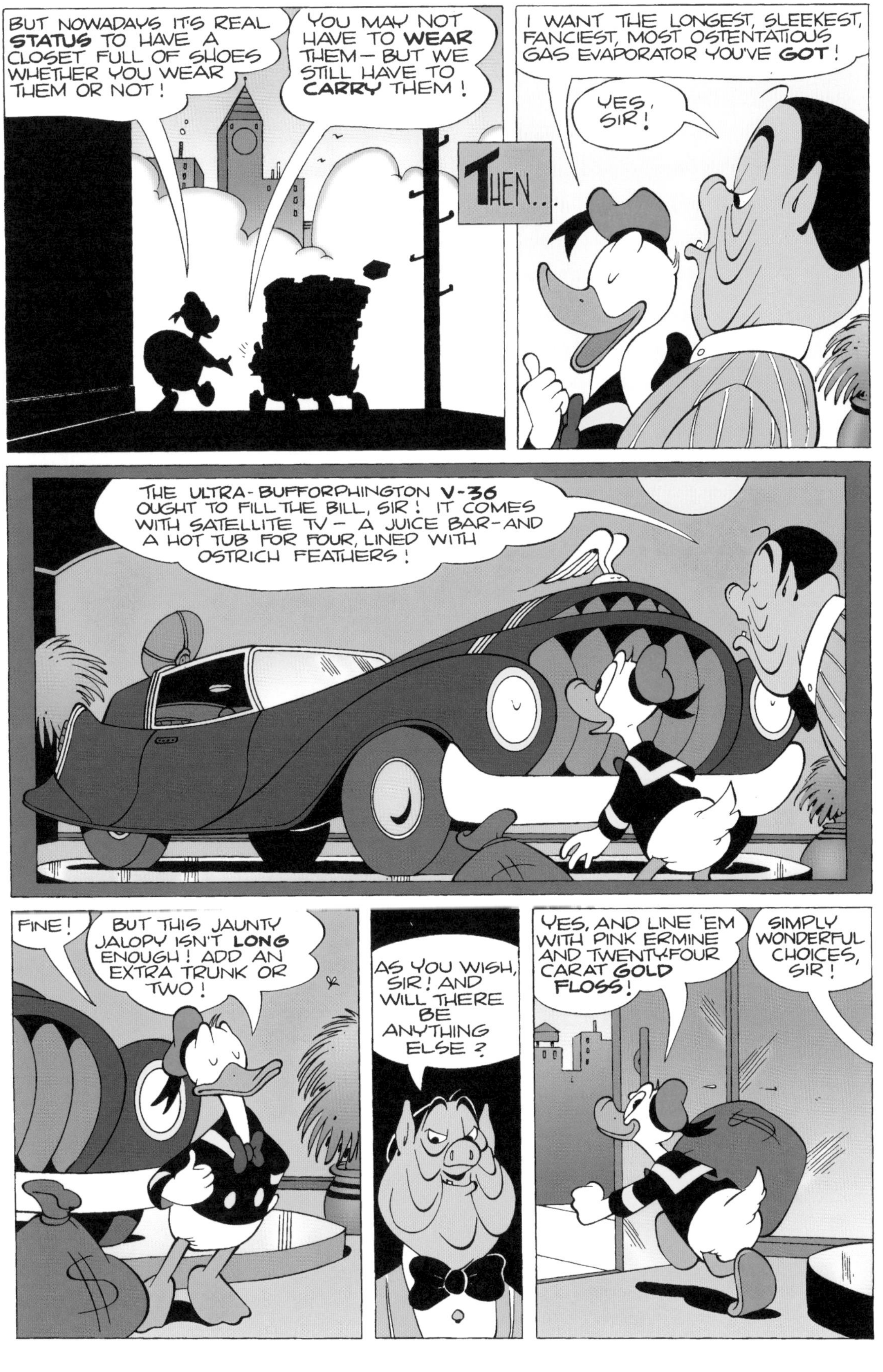

BUT NOWADAYS IT'S REAL **STATUS** TO HAVE A CLOSET FULL OF SHOES WHETHER YOU WEAR THEM OR NOT!
YOU MAY NOT HAVE TO **WEAR** THEM— BUT WE STILL HAVE TO **CARRY** THEM!
THEN...
I WANT THE LONGEST, SLEEKEST, FANCIEST, MOST OSTENTATIOUS GAS EVAPORATOR YOU'VE **GOT**!
YES, SIR!
THE ULTRA-BUFFORPHINGTON **V-36** OUGHT TO FILL THE BILL, SIR! IT COMES WITH SATELLITE TV— A JUICE BAR— AND A HOT TUB FOR FOUR, LINED WITH OSTRICH FEATHERS!
FINE!
BUT THIS JAUNTY JALOPY ISN'T **LONG** ENOUGH! ADD AN EXTRA TRUNK OR TWO!
AS YOU WISH, SIR! AND WILL THERE BE ANYTHING ELSE?
YES, AND LINE 'EM WITH PINK ERMINE AND TWENTY-FOUR CARAT **GOLD FLOSS**!
SIMPLY WONDERFUL CHOICES, SIR!

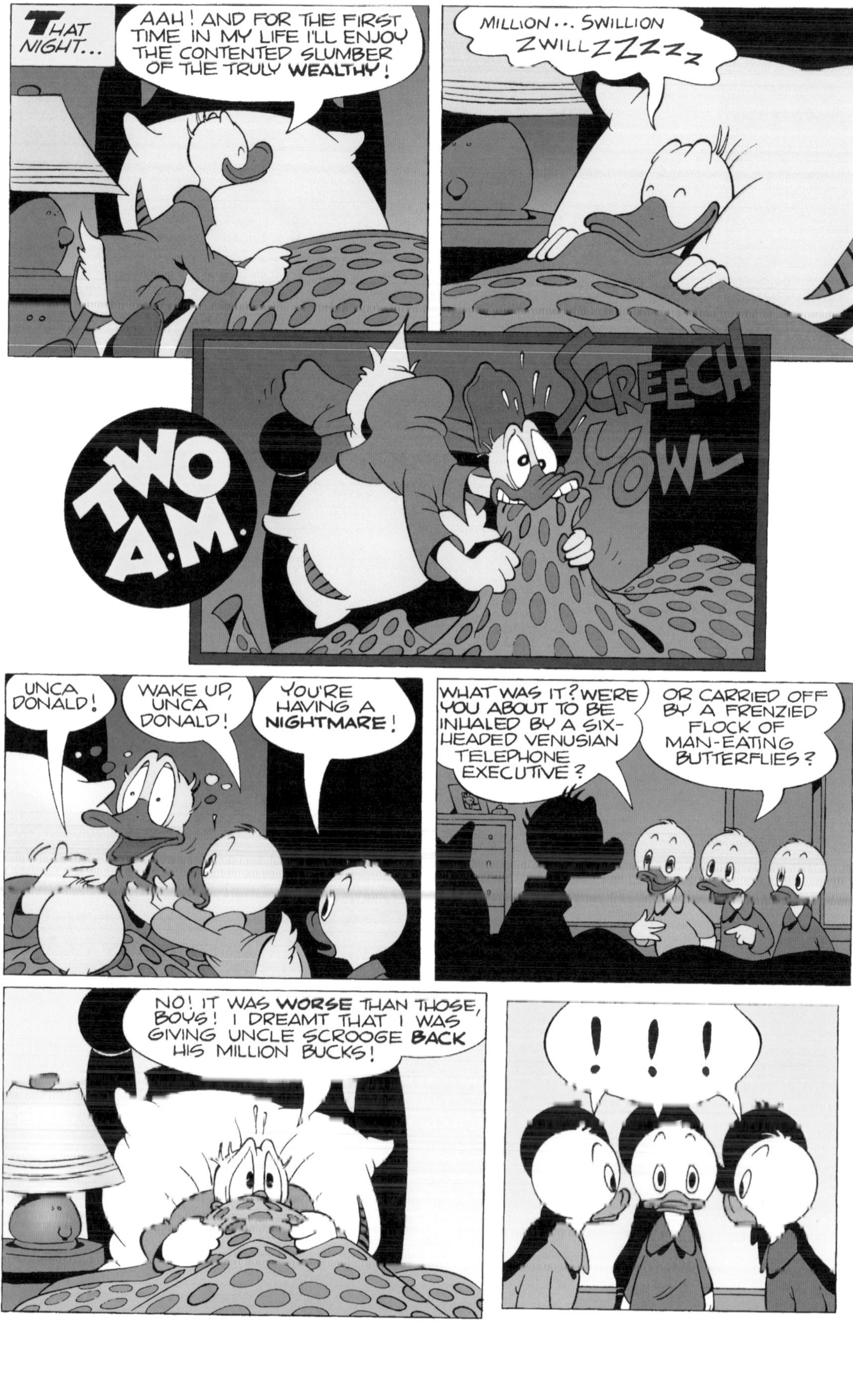
THAT NIGHT...
AAH! AND FOR THE FIRST TIME IN MY LIFE I'LL ENJOY THE CONTENTED SLUMBER OF THE TRULY **WEALTHY**!
MILLION... SWILLION ZWILLZZZZZ
TWO A.M.
SCREECH
YOWL
UNCA DONALD!
WAKE UP, UNCA DONALD!
YOU'RE HAVING A **NIGHTMARE**!
WHAT WAS IT? WERE YOU ABOUT TO BE INHALED BY A SIX-HEADED VENUSIAN TELEPHONE EXECUTIVE?
OR CARRIED OFF BY A FRENZIED FLOCK OF MAN-EATING BUTTERFLIES?
NO! IT WAS **WORSE** THAN THOSE, BOYS! I DREAMT THAT I WAS GIVING UNCLE SCROOGE **BACK** HIS MILLION BUCKS!
! ! !

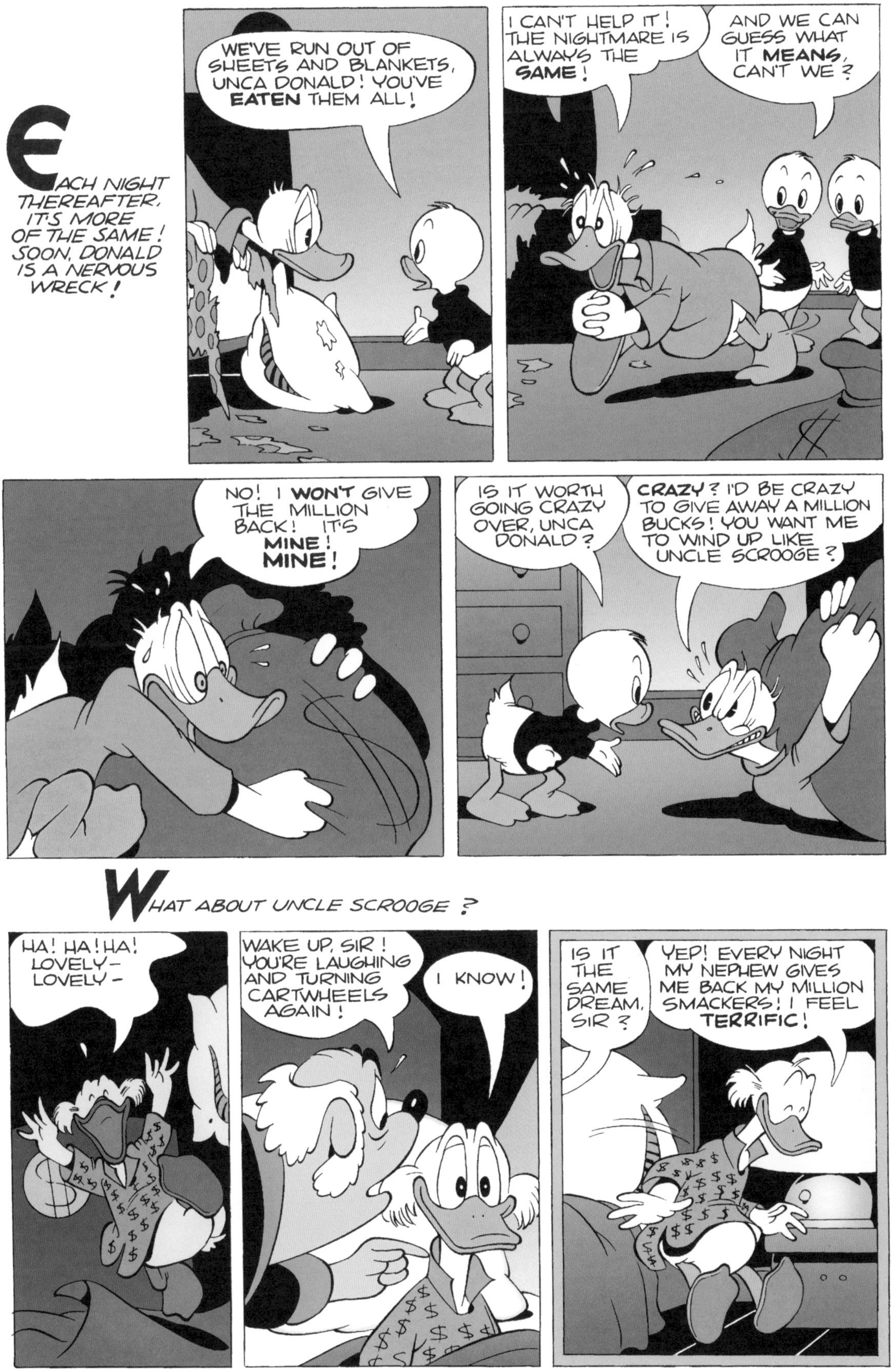
EACH NIGHT THEREAFTER, IT'S MORE OF THE SAME! SOON, DONALD IS A NERVOUS WRECK!
WE'VE RUN OUT OF SHEETS AND BLANKETS, UNCA DONALD! YOU'VE EATEN THEM ALL!
I CAN'T HELP IT! THE NIGHTMARE IS ALWAYS THE SAME!
AND WE CAN GUESS WHAT IT MEANS, CAN'T WE?
NO! I WON'T GIVE THE MILLION BACK! IT'S MINE! MINE!
IS IT WORTH GOING CRAZY OVER, UNCA DONALD?
CRAZY? I'D BE CRAZY TO GIVE AWAY A MILLION BUCKS! YOU WANT ME TO WIND UP LIKE UNCLE SCROOGE?
WHAT ABOUT UNCLE SCROOGE?
HA! HA! HA! LOVELY– LOVELY–
WAKE UP, SIR! YOU'RE LAUGHING AND TURNING CARTWHEELS AGAIN!
I KNOW!
IS IT THE SAME DREAM, SIR?
YEP! EVERY NIGHT MY NEPHEW GIVES ME BACK MY MILLION SMACKERS! I FEEL TERRIFIC!

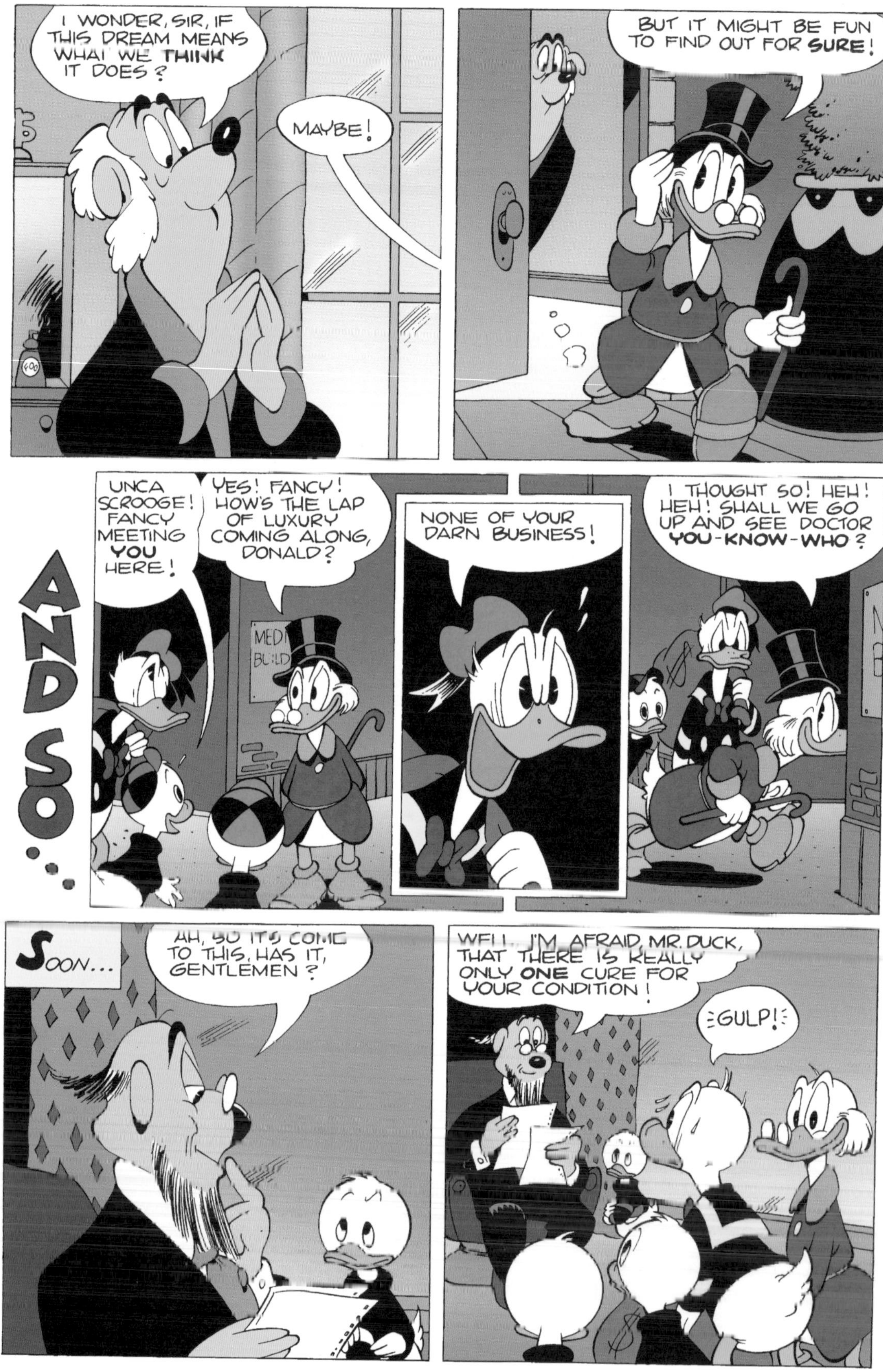

I WONDER, SIR, IF THIS DREAM MEANS WHAT WE THINK IT DOES?
MAYBE!
BUT IT MIGHT BE FUN TO FIND OUT FOR SURE!
AND SO...
UNCA SCROOGE! FANCY MEETING YOU HERE!
YES! FANCY! HOW'S THE LAP OF LUXURY COMING ALONG, DONALD?
MED BUILD
NONE OF YOUR DARN BUSINESS!
I THOUGHT SO! HEH! HEH! SHALL WE GO UP AND SEE DOCTOR YOU-KNOW-WHO?
SOON...
AH, SO IT'S COME TO THIS, HAS IT, GENTLEMEN?
WELL, I'M AFRAID, MR. DUCK, THAT THERE IS REALLY ONLY ONE CURE FOR YOUR CONDITION!
GULP!

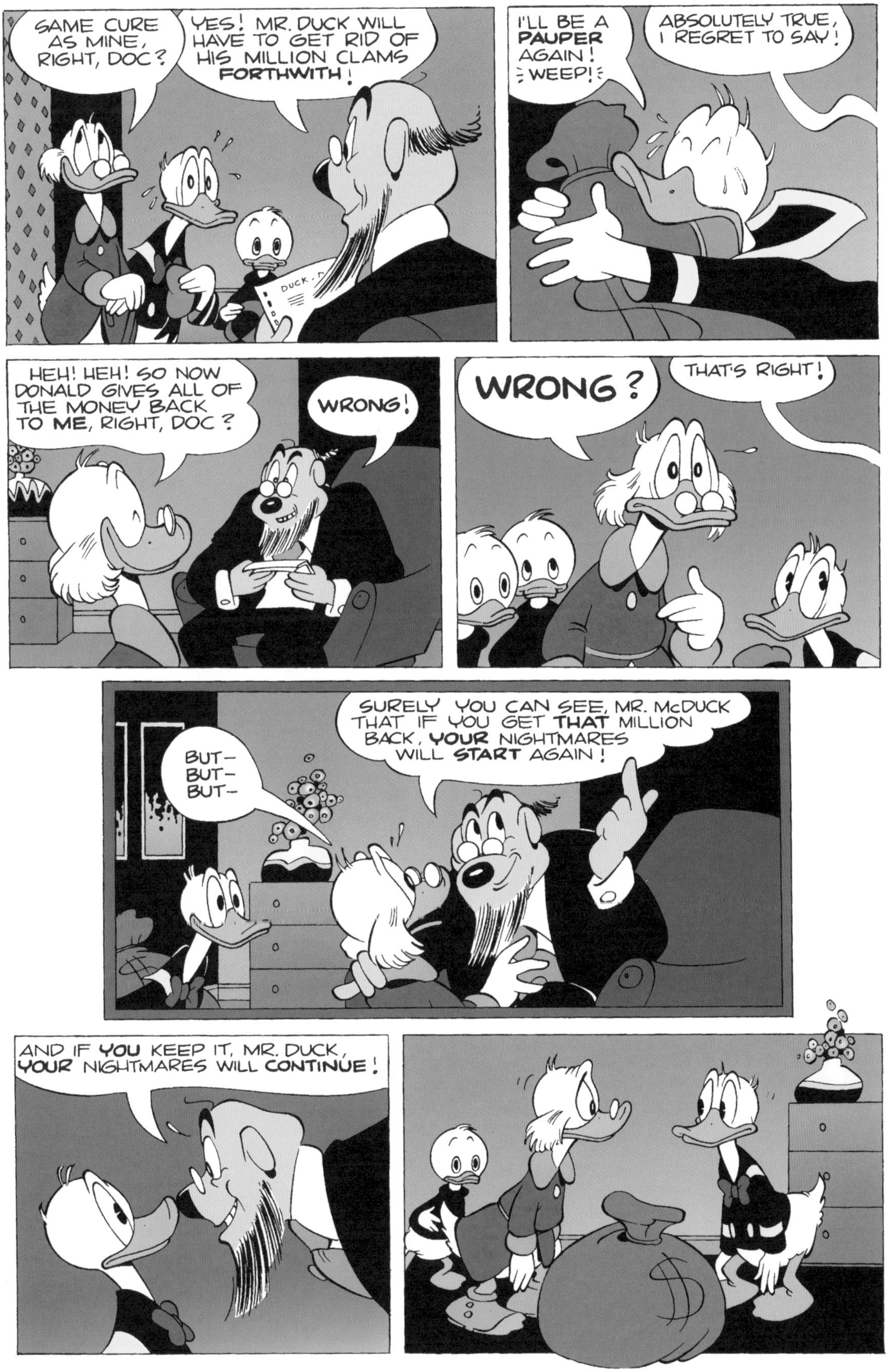

SAME CURE AS MINE, RIGHT, DOC?
YES! MR. DUCK WILL HAVE TO GET RID OF HIS MILLION CLAMS FORTHWITH!
DUCK, D
I'LL BE A PAUPER AGAIN! WEEP!
ABSOLUTELY TRUE, I REGRET TO SAY!
HEH! HEH! SO NOW DONALD GIVES ALL OF THE MONEY BACK TO ME, RIGHT, DOC?
WRONG!
WRONG?
THAT'S RIGHT!
SURELY YOU CAN SEE, MR. McDUCK THAT IF YOU GET THAT MILLION BACK, YOUR NIGHTMARES WILL START AGAIN!
BUT- BUT- BUT-
AND IF YOU KEEP IT, MR. DUCK, YOUR NIGHTMARES WILL CONTINUE!

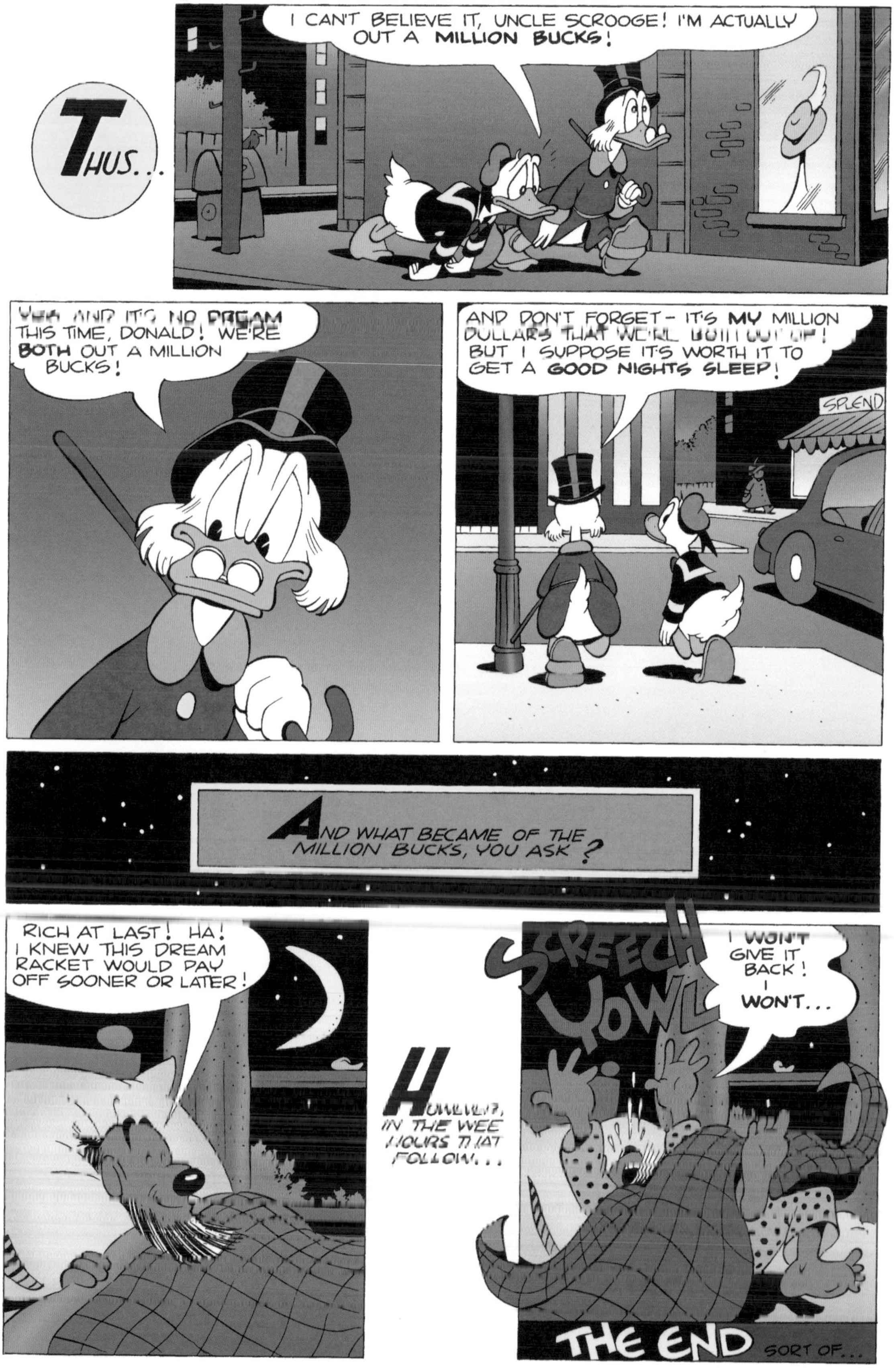
THUS...
I CAN'T BELIEVE IT, UNCLE SCROOGE! I'M ACTUALLY OUT A MILLION BUCKS!
AND IT'S NO DREAM THIS TIME, DONALD! WE'RE BOTH OUT A MILLION BUCKS!
AND DON'T FORGET – IT'S MY MILLION DOLLARS THAT WE'RE OUT OF! BUT I SUPPOSE IT'S WORTH IT TO GET A GOOD NIGHTS SLEEP!
SPLEND
AND WHAT BECAME OF THE MILLION BUCKS, YOU ASK?
RICH AT LAST! HA! I KNEW THIS DREAM RACKET WOULD PAY OFF SOONER OR LATER!
IN THE WEE HOURS THAT FOLLOW...
SCREECH
YOWL
I WON'T GIVE IT BACK! I WON'T...
THE END SORT OF...

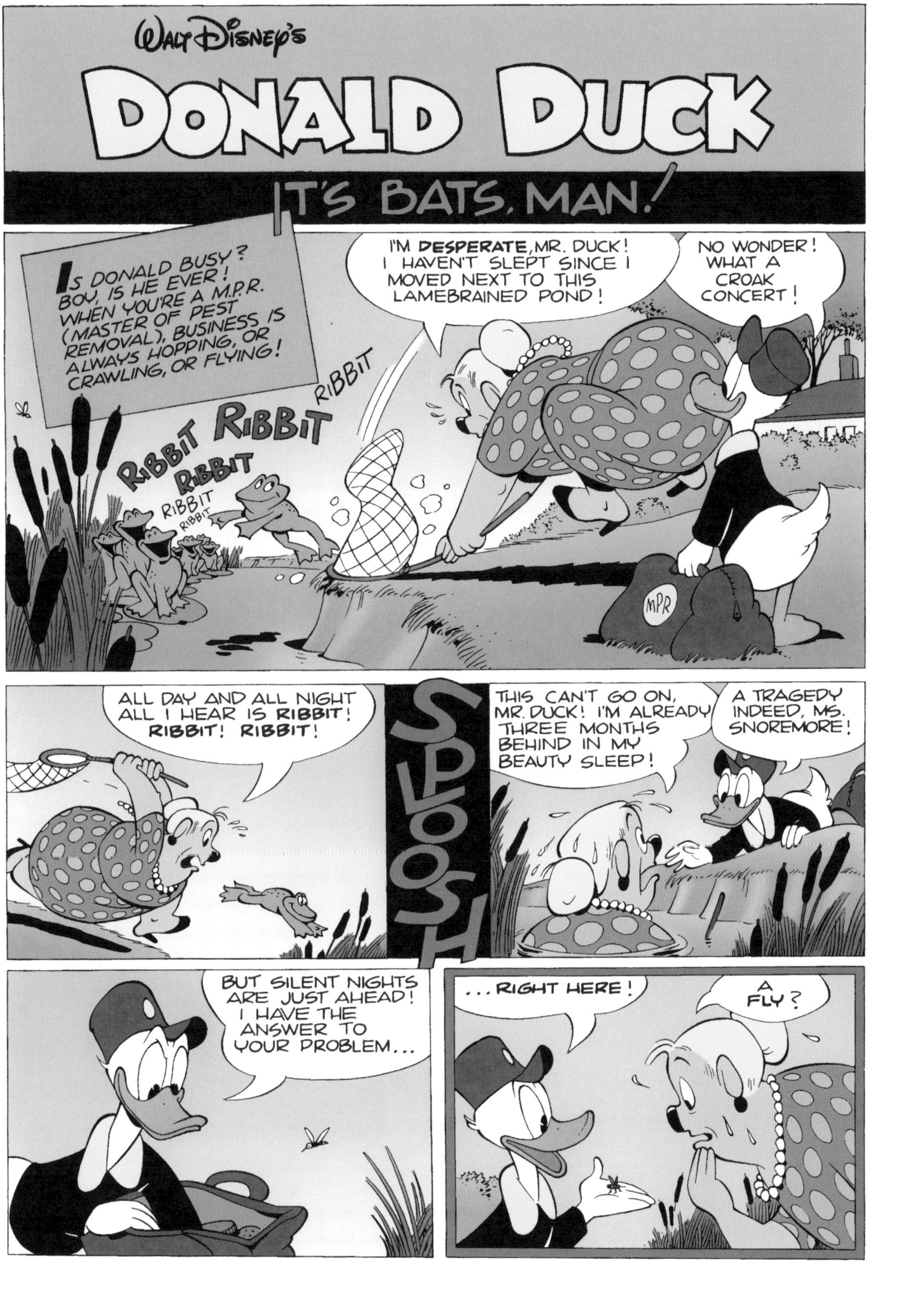

WALT DISNEY'S
DONALD DUCK
IT'S BATS, MAN!
IS DONALD BUSY? BOY, IS HE EVER! WHEN YOU'RE A M.P.R. (MASTER OF PEST REMOVAL), BUSINESS IS ALWAYS HOPPING, OR CRAWLING, OR FLYING!
I'M DESPERATE, MR. DUCK! I HAVEN'T SLEPT SINCE I MOVED NEXT TO THIS LAMEBRAINED POND!
NO WONDER! WHAT A CROAK CONCERT!
RIBBIT RIBBIT RIBBIT RIBBIT RIBBIT RIBBIT RIBBIT
MPR
ALL DAY AND ALL NIGHT ALL I HEAR IS RIBBIT! RIBBIT! RIBBIT!
SPLOOSH
THIS CAN'T GO ON, MR. DUCK! I'M ALREADY THREE MONTHS BEHIND IN MY BEAUTY SLEEP!
A TRAGEDY INDEED, MS. SNOREMORE!
BUT SILENT NIGHTS ARE JUST AHEAD! I HAVE THE ANSWER TO YOUR PROBLEM...
...RIGHT HERE!
A FLY?

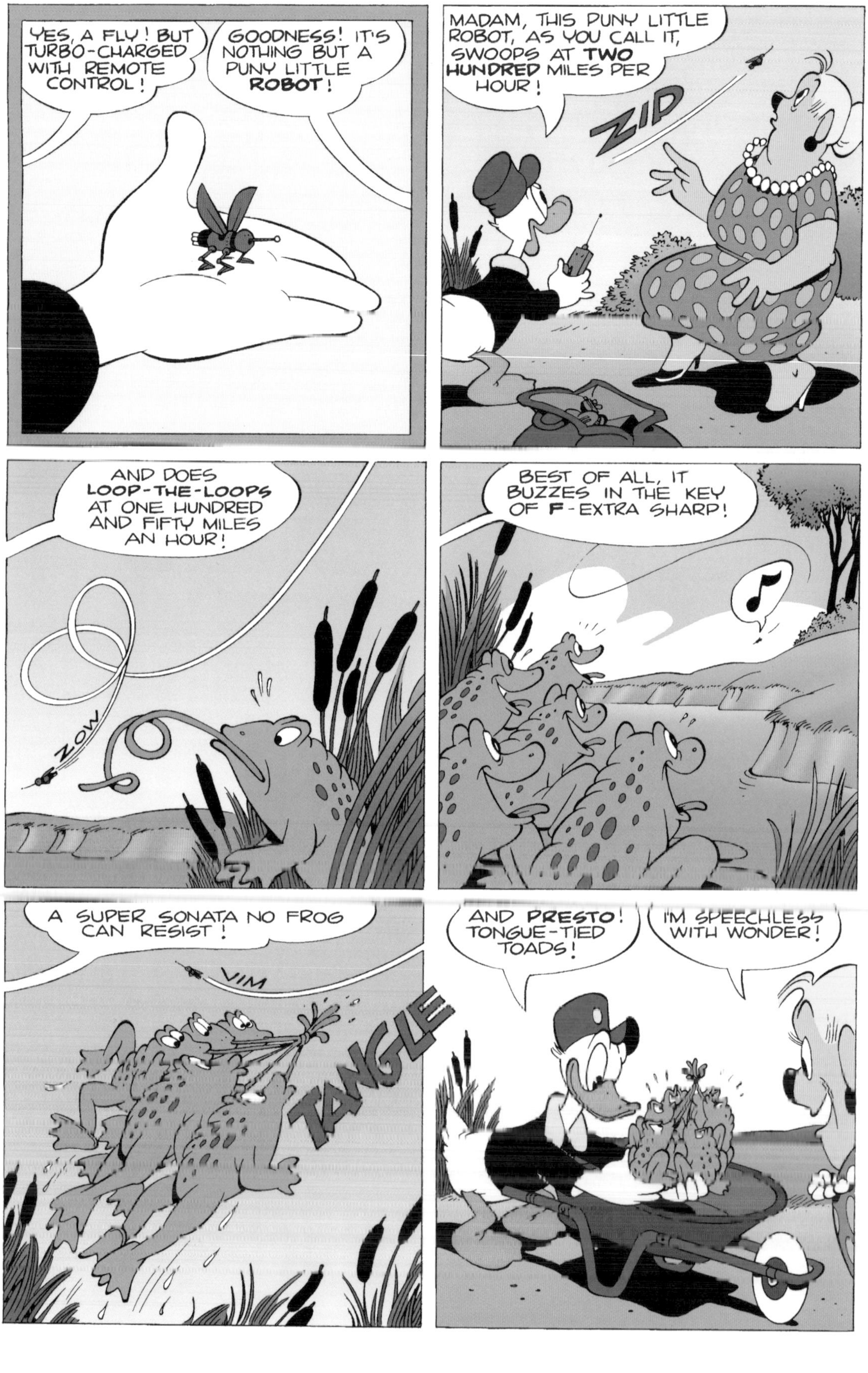
YES, A FLY! BUT TURBO-CHARGED WITH REMOTE CONTROL!
GOODNESS! IT'S NOTHING BUT A PUNY LITTLE ROBOT!
MADAM, THIS PUNY LITTLE ROBOT, AS YOU CALL IT, SWOOPS AT TWO HUNDRED MILES PER HOUR!
ZID
AND DOES LOOP-THE-LOOPS AT ONE HUNDRED AND FIFTY MILES AN HOUR!
ZOW
BEST OF ALL, IT BUZZES IN THE KEY OF F-EXTRA SHARP!
A SUPER SONATA NO FROG CAN RESIST!
VIM
TANGLE
AND PRESTO! TONGUE-TIED TOADS!
I'M SPEECHLESS WITH WONDER!

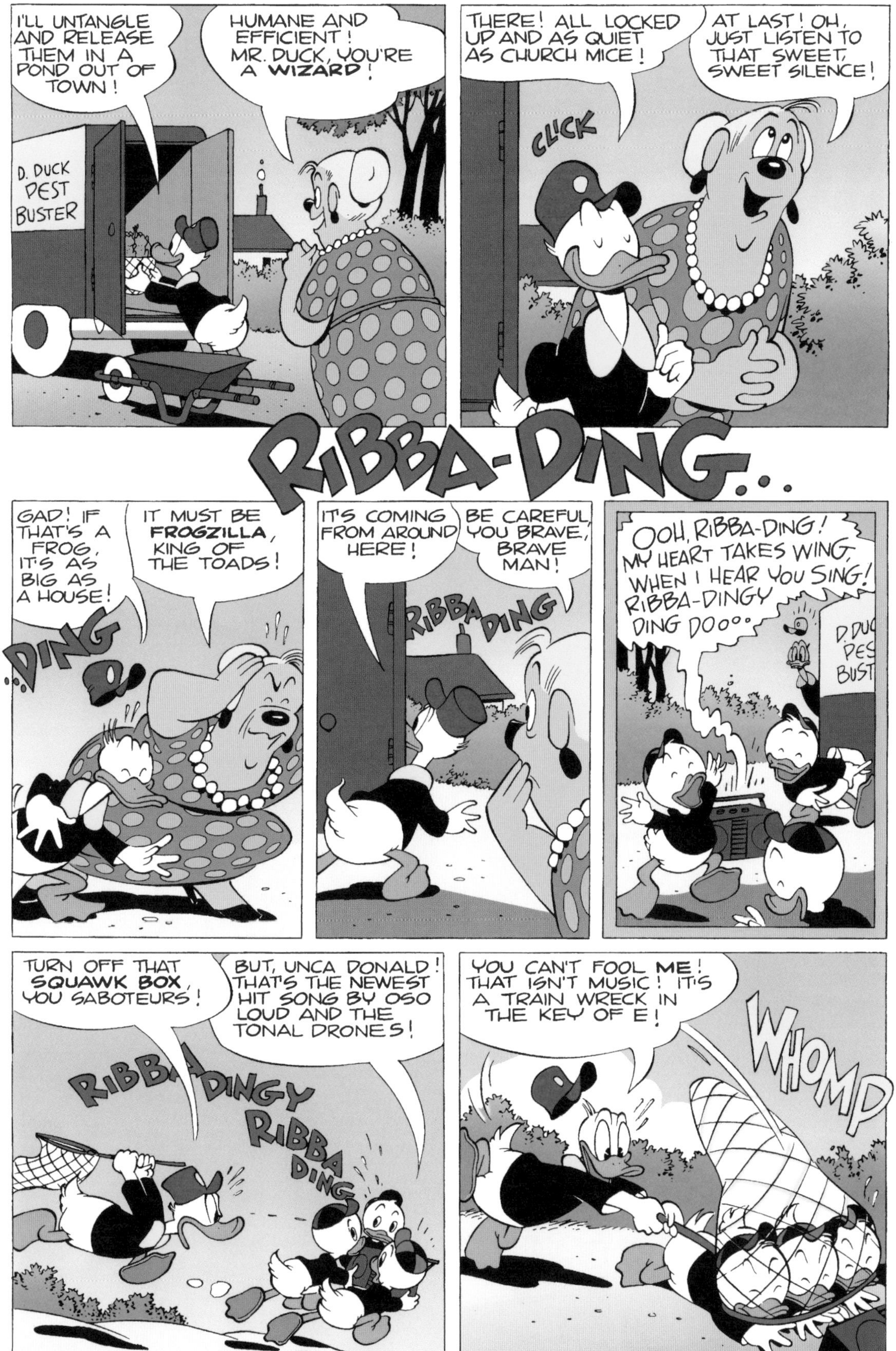
I'LL UNTANGLE AND RELEASE THEM IN A POND OUT OF TOWN!
HUMANE AND EFFICIENT! MR. DUCK, YOU'RE A **WIZARD**!
D. DUCK PEST BUSTER
THERE! ALL LOCKED UP AND AS QUIET AS CHURCH MICE!
AT LAST! OH, JUST LISTEN TO THAT SWEET, SWEET SILENCE!
CLICK
RIBBA-DING...
GAD! IF THAT'S A FROG, IT'S AS BIG AS A HOUSE!
IT MUST BE **FROGZILLA**, KING OF THE TOADS!
DING
IT'S COMING FROM AROUND HERE!
BE CAREFUL, YOU BRAVE, BRAVE MAN!
RIBBA DING
OOH, RIBBA-DING! MY HEART TAKES WING, WHEN I HEAR YOU SING! RIBBA-DINGY DING DOooo
TURN OFF THAT **SQUAWK BOX**, YOU SABOTEURS!
BUT, UNCA DONALD! THAT'S THE NEWEST HIT SONG BY OSO LOUD AND THE TONAL DRONES!
RIBBA DINGY RIBBA DING
YOU CAN'T FOOL **ME**! THAT ISN'T MUSIC! IT'S A TRAIN WRECK IN THE KEY OF E!
WHOMP

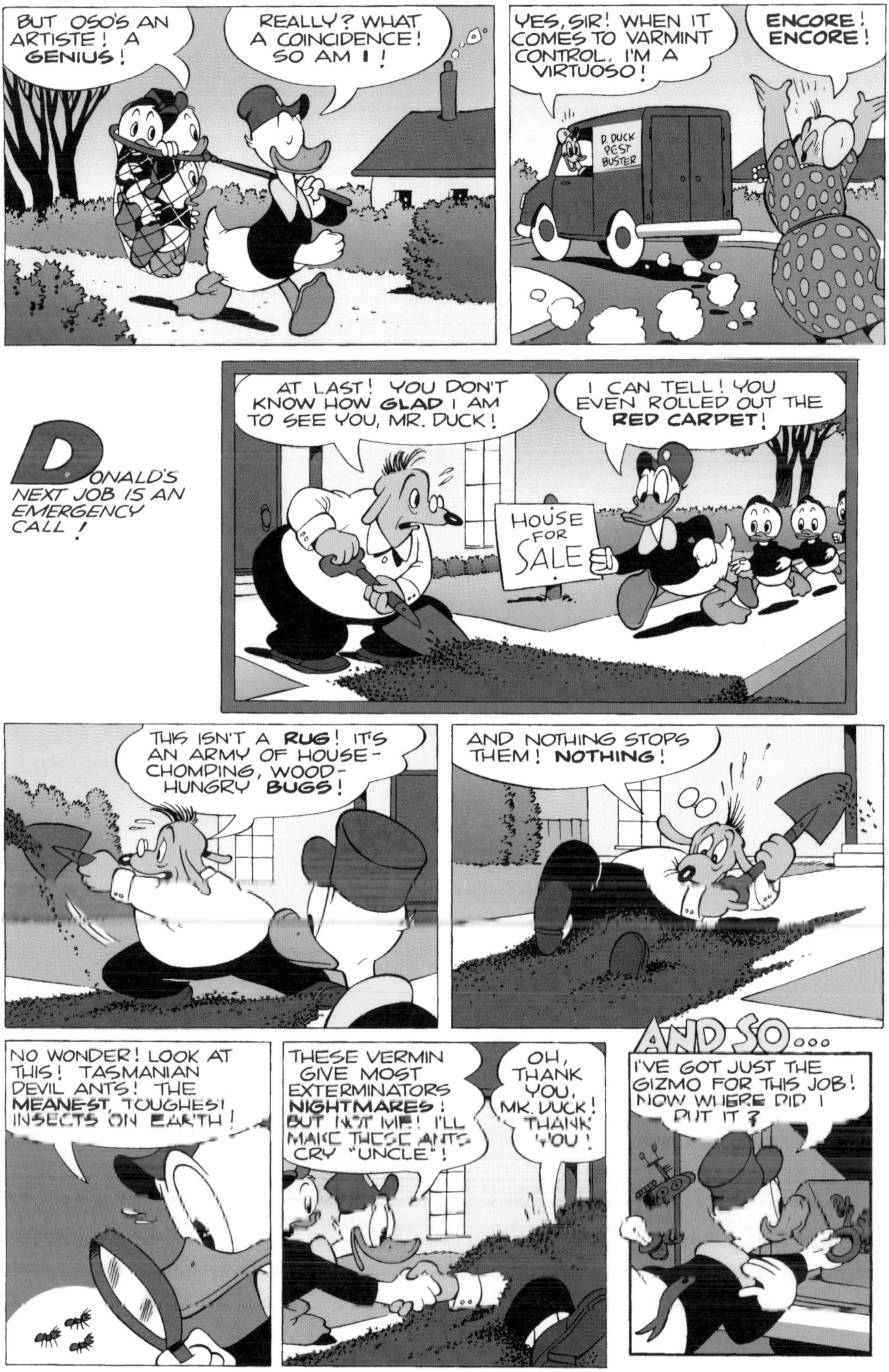

BUT OSO'S AN ARTISTE! A GENIUS!
REALLY? WHAT A COINCIDENCE! SO AM I!
YES, SIR! WHEN IT COMES TO VARMINT CONTROL, I'M A VIRTUOSO!
D. DUCK PEST BUSTER
ENCORE! ENCORE!
DONALD'S NEXT JOB IS AN EMERGENCY CALL!
AT LAST! YOU DON'T KNOW HOW GLAD I AM TO SEE YOU, MR. DUCK!
I CAN TELL! YOU EVEN ROLLED OUT THE RED CARPET!
HOUSE FOR SALE
THIS ISN'T A RUG! IT'S AN ARMY OF HOUSE-CHOMPING, WOOD-HUNGRY BUGS!
AND NOTHING STOPS THEM! NOTHING!
NO WONDER! LOOK AT THIS! TASMANIAN DEVIL ANTS! THE MEANEST, TOUGHEST INSECTS ON EARTH!
THESE VERMIN GIVE MOST EXTERMINATORS NIGHTMARES! BUT NOT ME! I'LL MAKE THESE ANTS CRY "UNCLE"!
OH, THANK YOU, MR. DUCK! THANK YOU!
AND SO...
I'VE GOT JUST THE GIZMO FOR THIS JOB! NOW WHERE DID I PUT IT?

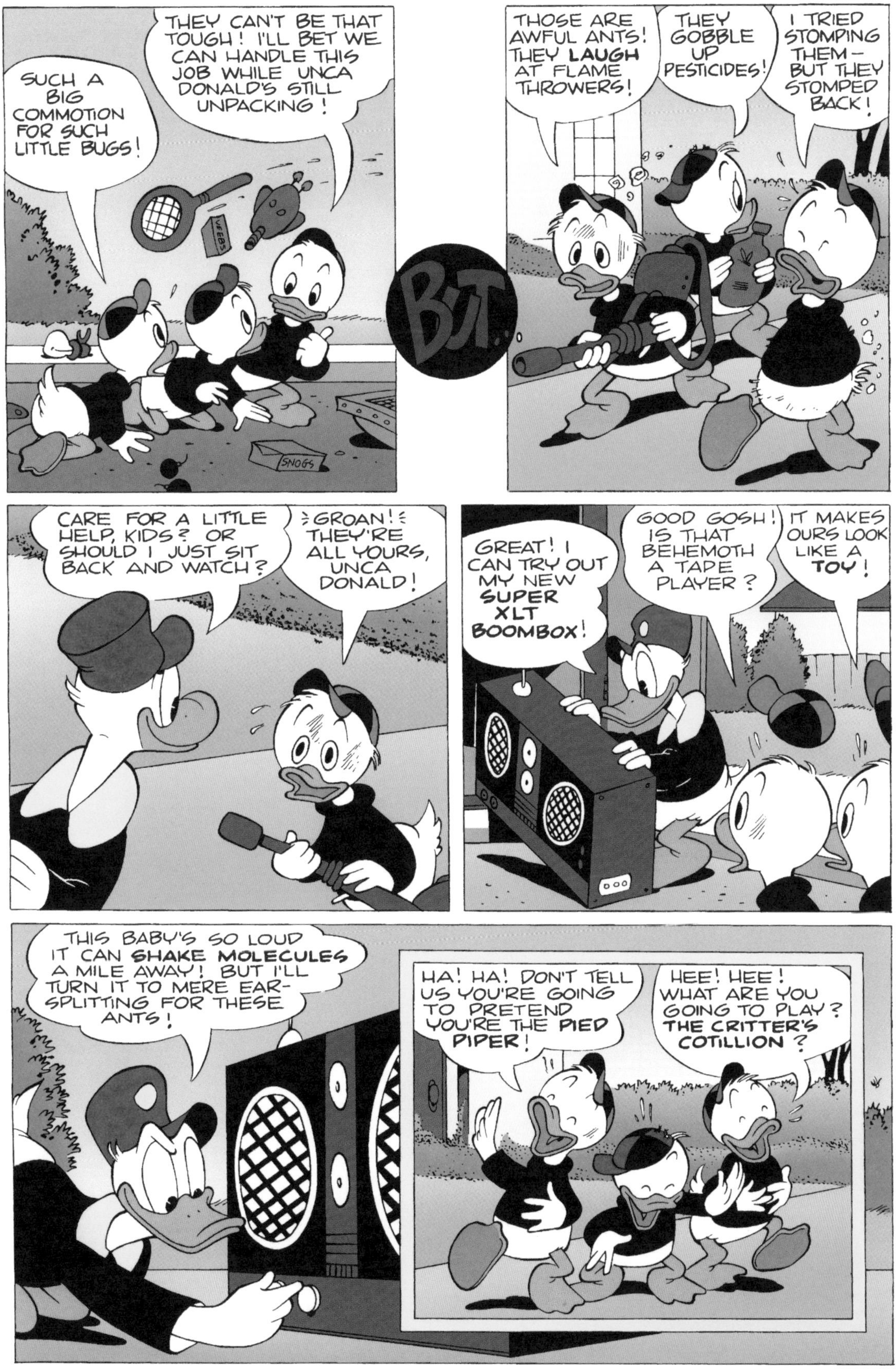
SUCH A BIG COMMOTION FOR SUCH LITTLE BUGS!
THEY CAN'T BE THAT TOUGH! I'LL BET WE CAN HANDLE THIS JOB WHILE UNCA DONALD'S STILL UNPACKING!
VEEBS
SNOGS
BUT.
THOSE ARE AWFUL ANTS! THEY LAUGH AT FLAME THROWERS!
THEY GOBBLE UP PESTICIDES!
I TRIED STOMPING THEM— BUT THEY STOMPED BACK!
CARE FOR A LITTLE HELP, KIDS? OR SHOULD I JUST SIT BACK AND WATCH?
GROAN! THEY'RE ALL YOURS, UNCA DONALD!
GREAT! I CAN TRY OUT MY NEW SUPER XLT BOOMBOX!
GOOD GOSH! IS THAT BEHEMOTH A TAPE PLAYER?
IT MAKES OURS LOOK LIKE A TOY!
THIS BABY'S SO LOUD IT CAN SHAKE MOLECULES A MILE AWAY! BUT I'LL TURN IT TO MERE EAR-SPLITTING FOR THESE ANTS!
HA! HA! DON'T TELL US YOU'RE GOING TO PRETEND YOU'RE THE PIED PIPER!
HEE! HEE! WHAT ARE YOU GOING TO PLAY? THE CRITTER'S COTILLION?

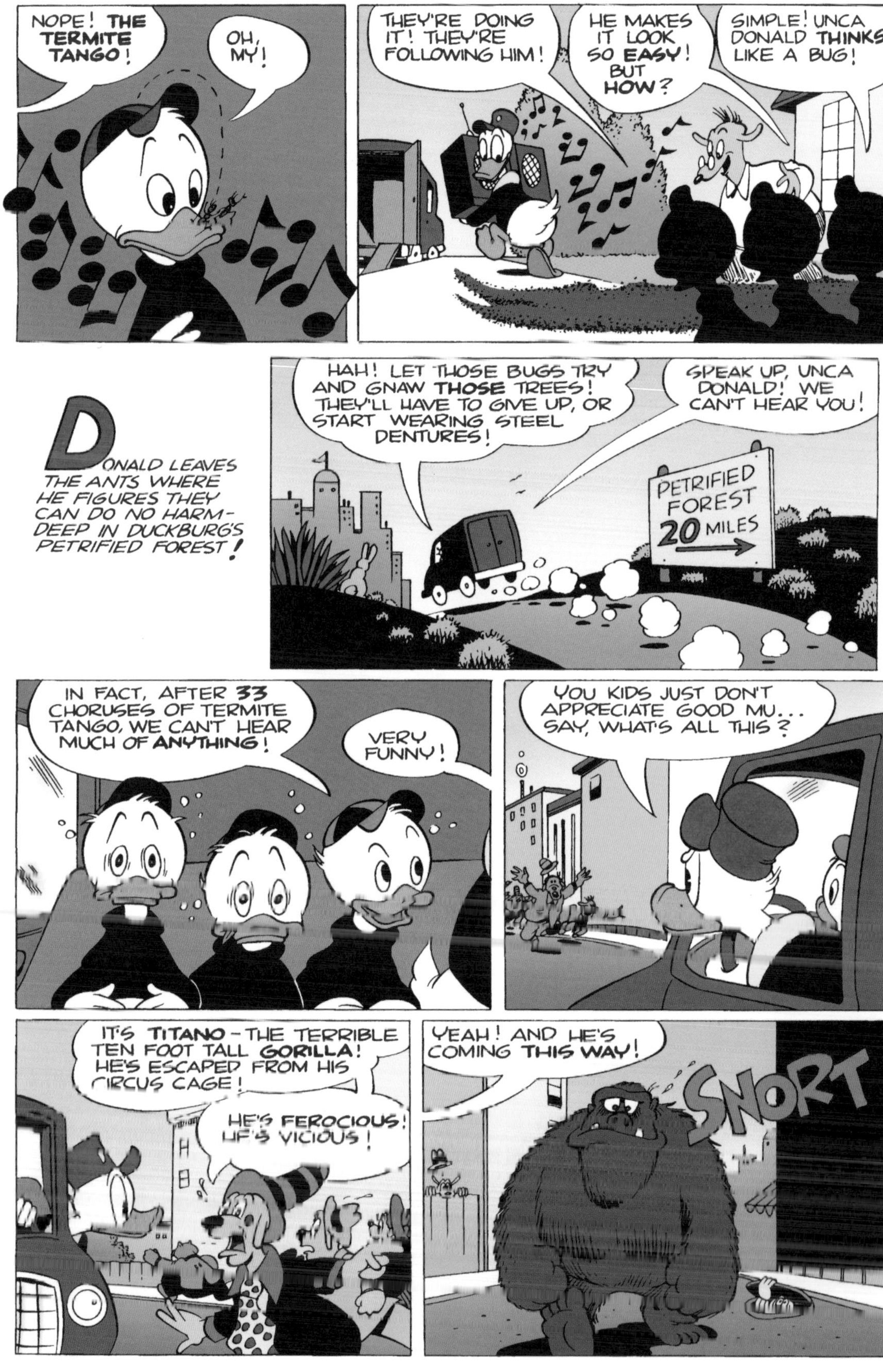
NOPE! THE TERMITE TANGO!
OH, MY!
THEY'RE DOING IT! THEY'RE FOLLOWING HIM!
HE MAKES IT LOOK SO EASY! BUT HOW?
SIMPLE! UNCA DONALD THINKS LIKE A BUG!
DONALD LEAVES THE ANTS WHERE HE FIGURES THEY CAN DO NO HARM-DEEP IN DUCKBURG'S PETRIFIED FOREST!
HAH! LET THOSE BUGS TRY AND GNAW THOSE TREES! THEY'LL HAVE TO GIVE UP, OR START WEARING STEEL DENTURES!
SPEAK UP, UNCA DONALD! WE CAN'T HEAR YOU!
PETRIFIED FOREST 20 MILES
IN FACT, AFTER 33 CHORUSES OF TERMITE TANGO, WE CAN'T HEAR MUCH OF ANYTHING!
VERY FUNNY!
YOU KIDS JUST DON'T APPRECIATE GOOD MU... SAY, WHAT'S ALL THIS?
IT'S TITANO-THE TERRIBLE TEN FOOT TALL GORILLA! HE'S ESCAPED FROM HIS CIRCUS CAGE!
HE'S FEROCIOUS! HE'S VICIOUS!
YEAH! AND HE'S COMING THIS WAY!
SNORT

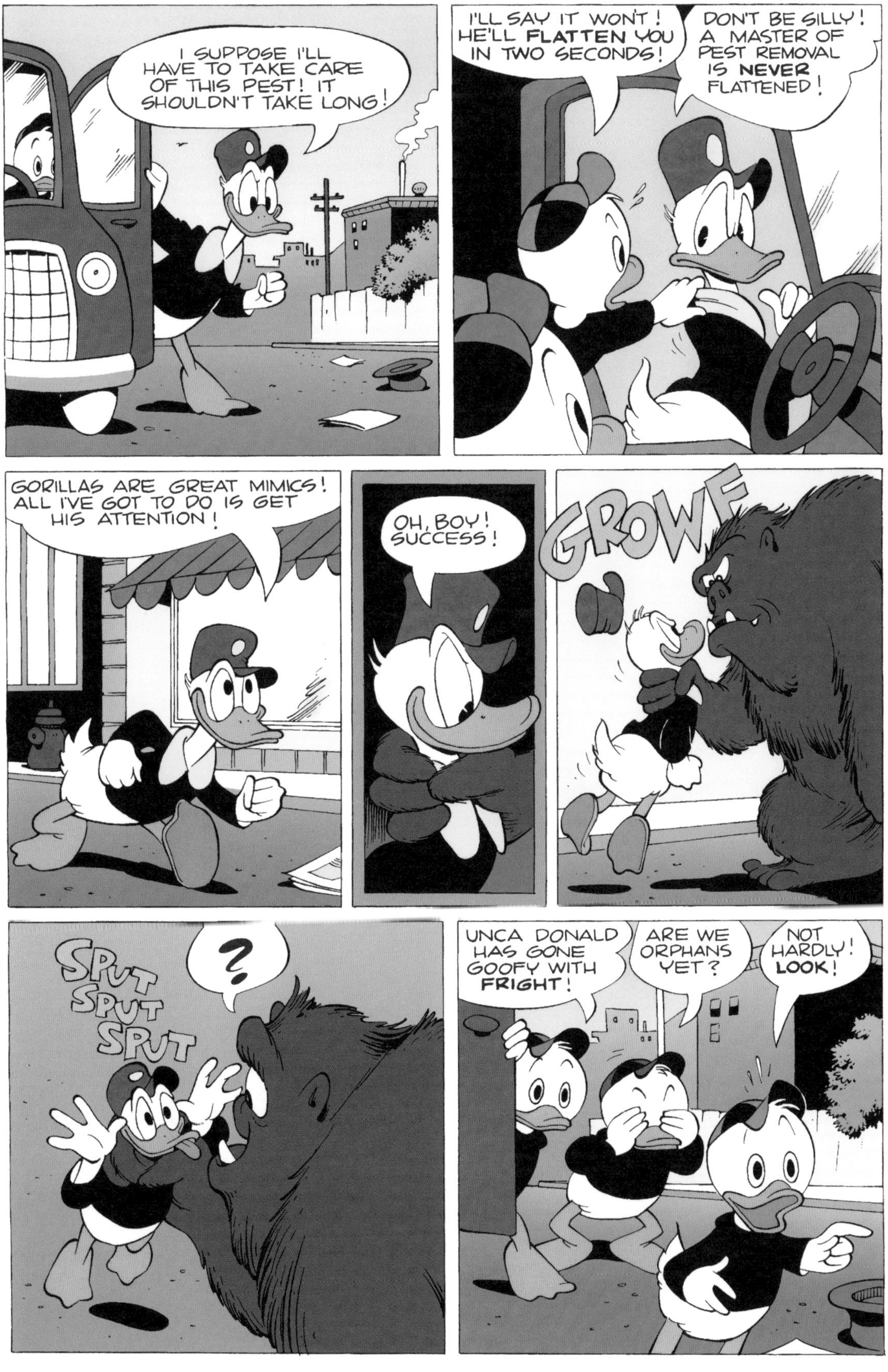
I SUPPOSE I'LL HAVE TO TAKE CARE OF THIS PEST! IT SHOULDN'T TAKE LONG!
I'LL SAY IT WON'T! HE'LL **FLATTEN** YOU IN TWO SECONDS!
DON'T BE SILLY! A MASTER OF PEST REMOVAL IS **NEVER** FLATTENED!
GORILLAS ARE GREAT MIMICS! ALL I'VE GOT TO DO IS GET HIS ATTENTION!
OH, BOY! SUCCESS!
GROWF
SPUT SPUT SPUT
?
UNCA DONALD HAS GONE GOOFY WITH **FRIGHT**!
ARE WE ORPHANS YET?
NOT HARDLY! **LOOK**!

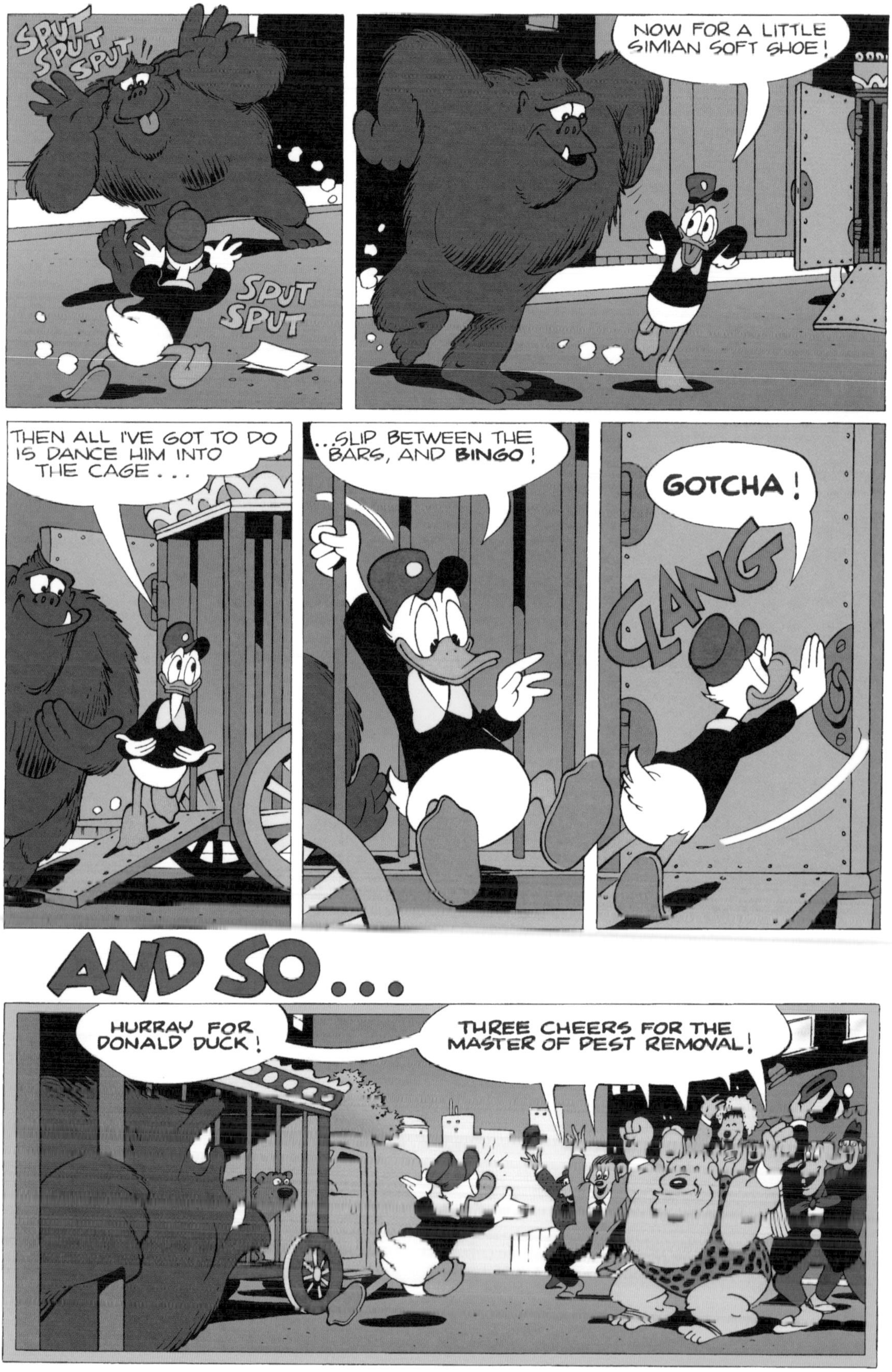
SPUT SPUT SPUT
SPUT SPUT
NOW FOR A LITTLE SIMIAN SOFT SHOE!
THEN ALL I'VE GOT TO DO IS DANCE HIM INTO THE CAGE . . .
. . .SLIP BETWEEN THE BARS, AND BINGO!
GOTCHA!
CLANG
AND SO . . .
HURRAY FOR DONALD DUCK!
THREE CHEERS FOR THE MASTER OF PEST REMOVAL!

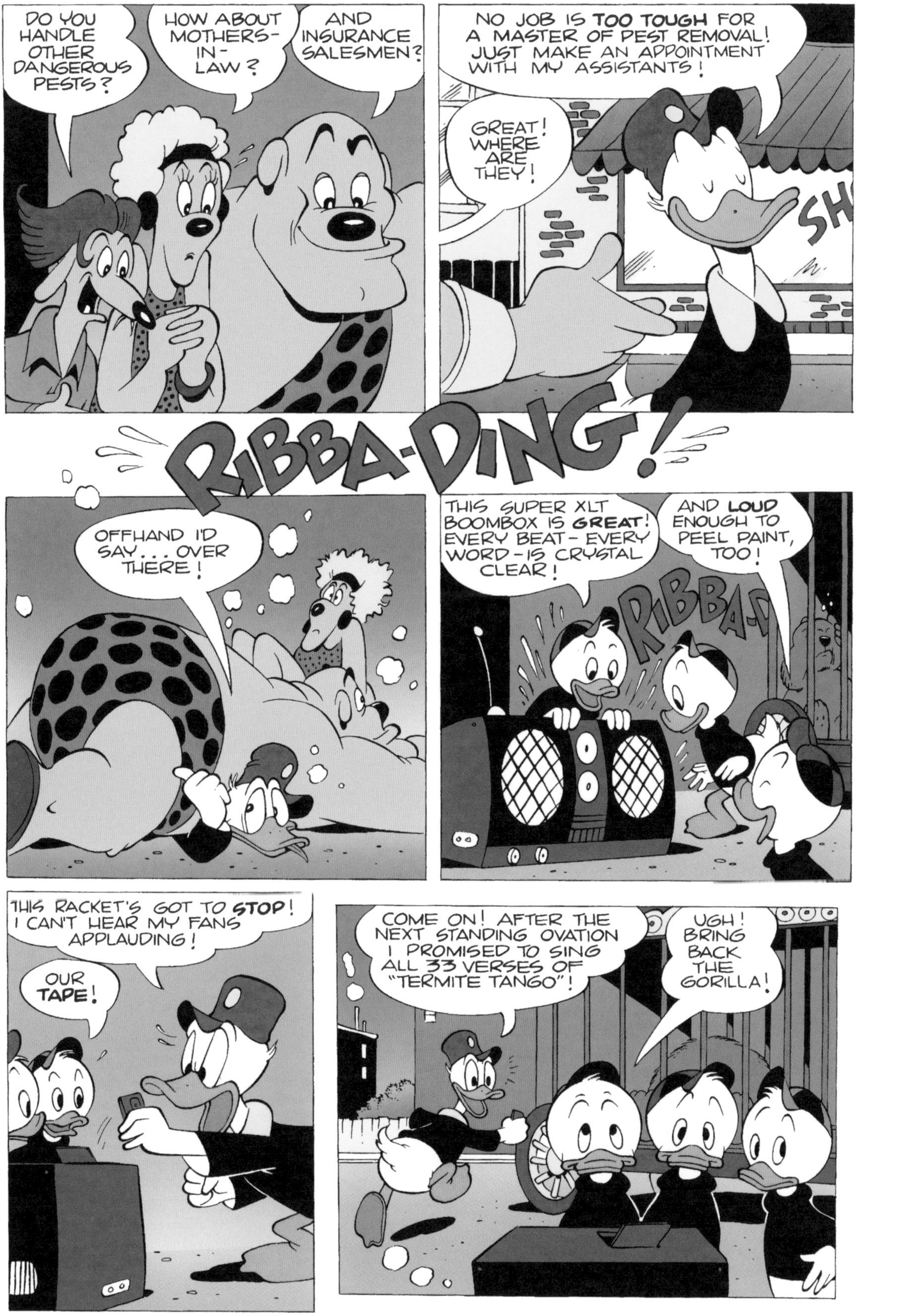

DO YOU HANDLE OTHER DANGEROUS PESTS?
HOW ABOUT MOTHERS-IN-LAW?
AND INSURANCE SALESMEN?
NO JOB IS TOO TOUGH FOR A MASTER OF PEST REMOVAL! JUST MAKE AN APPOINTMENT WITH MY ASSISTANTS!
GREAT! WHERE ARE THEY!
SH
RIBBA-DING!
OFFHAND I'D SAY... OVER THERE!
THIS SUPER XLT BOOMBOX IS GREAT! EVERY BEAT- EVERY WORD- IS CRYSTAL CLEAR!
AND LOUD ENOUGH TO PEEL PAINT, TOO!
RIBBA-D
THIS RACKET'S GOT TO STOP! I CAN'T HEAR MY FANS APPLAUDING!
OUR TAPE!
COME ON! AFTER THE NEXT STANDING OVATION I PROMISED TO SING ALL 33 VERSES OF "TERMITE TANGO"!
UGH! BRING BACK THE GORILLA!

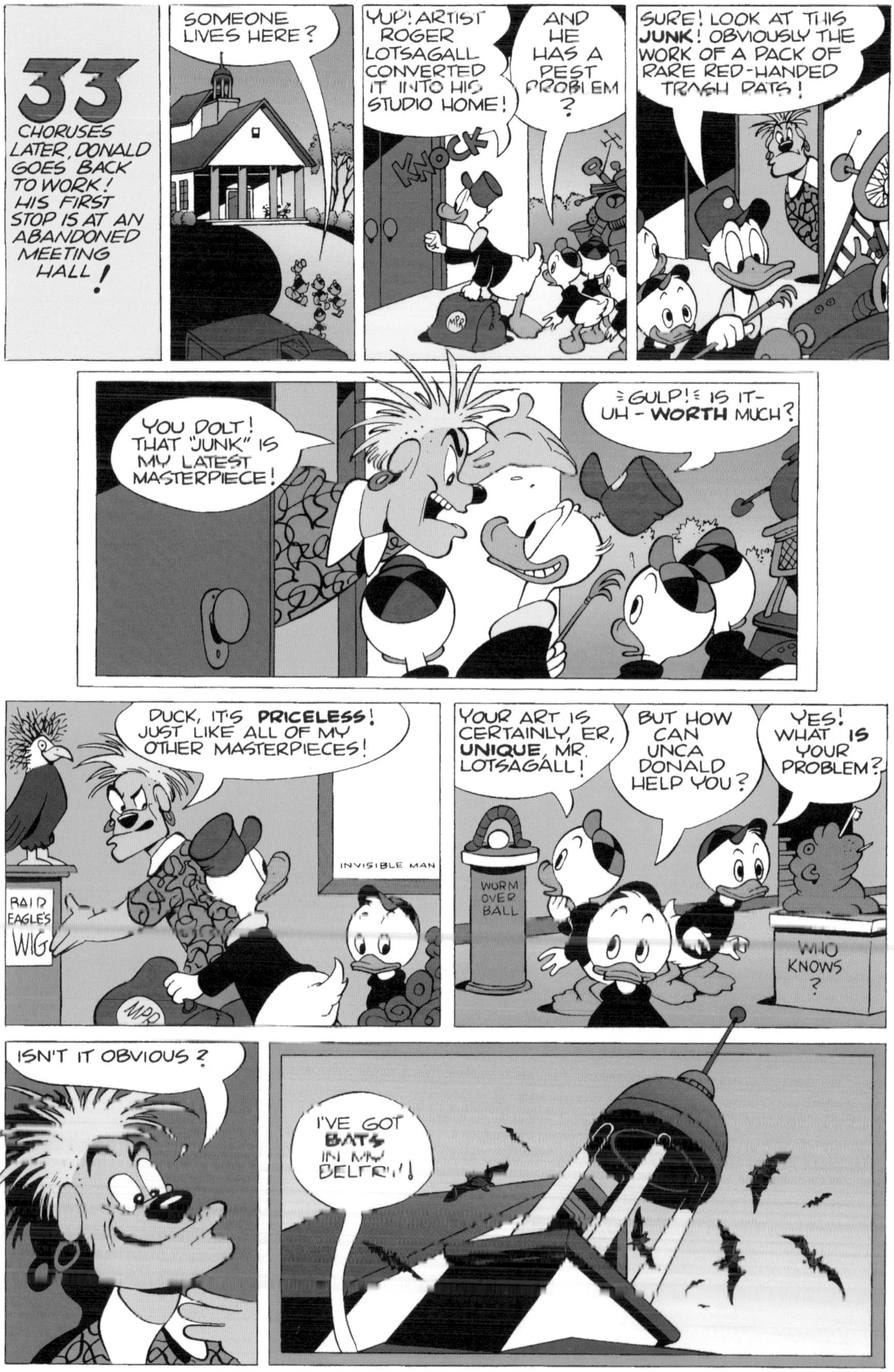
33 CHORUSES LATER, DONALD GOES BACK TO WORK! HIS FIRST STOP IS AT AN ABANDONED MEETING HALL!
SOMEONE LIVES HERE?
YUP! ARTIST ROGER LOTSAGALL CONVERTED IT INTO HIS STUDIO HOME!
AND HE HAS A PEST PROBLEM?
KNOCK
SURE! LOOK AT THIS JUNK! OBVIOUSLY THE WORK OF A PACK OF RARE RED-HANDED TRASH RATS!
YOU DOLT! THAT "JUNK" IS MY LATEST MASTERPIECE!
GULP! IS IT—UH—WORTH MUCH?
DUCK, IT'S PRICELESS! JUST LIKE ALL OF MY OTHER MASTERPIECES!
BALD EAGLE'S WIG
INVISIBLE MAN
YOUR ART IS CERTAINLY, ER, UNIQUE, MR. LOTSAGALL!
BUT HOW CAN UNCA DONALD HELP YOU?
YES! WHAT IS YOUR PROBLEM?
WORM OVER BALL
WHO KNOWS?
ISN'T IT OBVIOUS?
I'VE GOT BATS IN MY BELFRY!

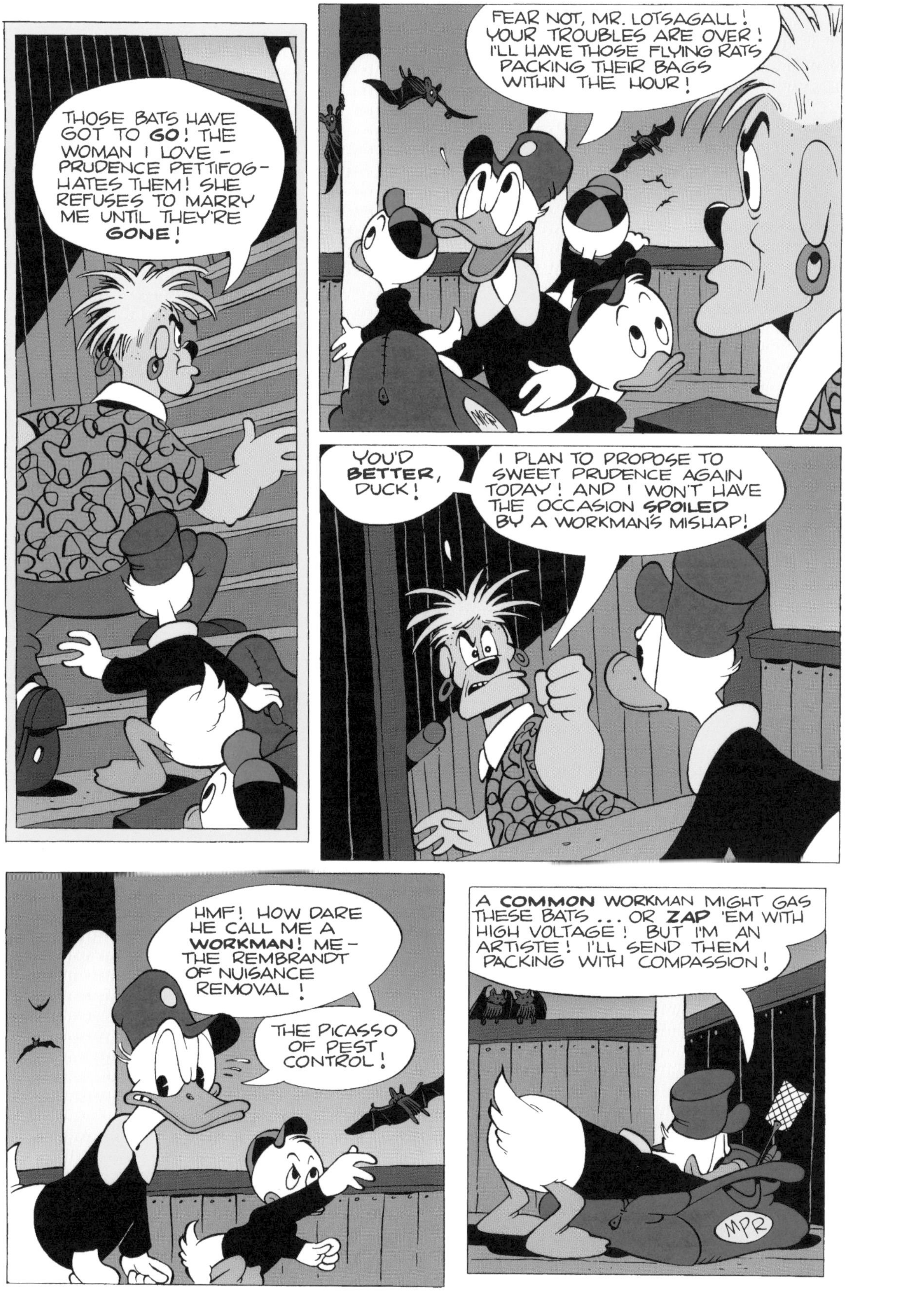
THOSE BATS HAVE GOT TO **GO**! THE WOMAN I LOVE – PRUDENCE PETTIFOG – HATES THEM! SHE REFUSES TO MARRY ME UNTIL THEY'RE **GONE**!
FEAR NOT, MR. LOTSAGALL! YOUR TROUBLES ARE OVER! I'LL HAVE THOSE FLYING RATS PACKING THEIR BAGS WITHIN THE HOUR!
MPR
YOU'D **BETTER**, DUCK!
I PLAN TO PROPOSE TO SWEET PRUDENCE AGAIN TODAY! AND I WON'T HAVE THE OCCASION **SPOILED** BY A WORKMAN'S MISHAP!
HMF! HOW DARE HE CALL ME A **WORKMAN**! ME – THE REMBRANDT OF NUISANCE REMOVAL!
THE PICASSO OF PEST CONTROL!
A **COMMON** WORKMAN MIGHT GAS THESE BATS ... OR **ZAP** 'EM WITH HIGH VOLTAGE! BUT I'M AN ARTISTE! I'LL SEND THEM PACKING WITH COMPASSION!
MPR

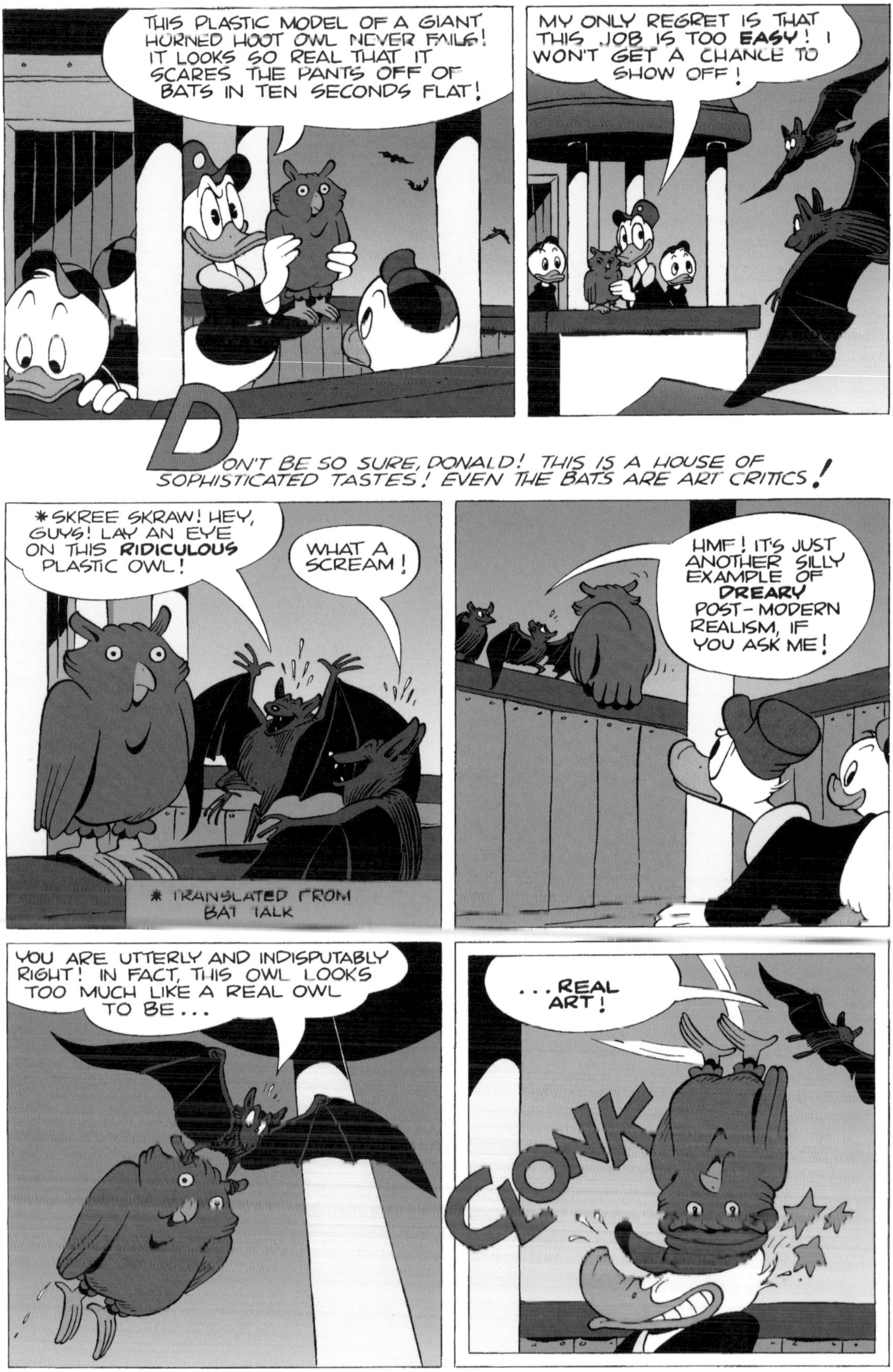

THIS PLASTIC MODEL OF A GIANT HORNED HOOT OWL NEVER FAILS! IT LOOKS SO REAL THAT IT SCARES THE PANTS OFF OF BATS IN TEN SECONDS FLAT!
MY ONLY REGRET IS THAT THIS JOB IS TOO EASY! I WON'T GET A CHANCE TO SHOW OFF!
DON'T BE SO SURE, DONALD! THIS IS A HOUSE OF SOPHISTICATED TASTES! EVEN THE BATS ARE ART CRITICS!
*SKREE SKRAW! HEY, GUYS! LAY AN EYE ON THIS RIDICULOUS PLASTIC OWL!
WHAT A SCREAM!
* TRANSLATED FROM BAT TALK
HMF! IT'S JUST ANOTHER SILLY EXAMPLE OF DREARY POST-MODERN REALISM, IF YOU ASK ME!
YOU ARE UTTERLY AND INDISPUTABLY RIGHT! IN FACT, THIS OWL LOOKS TOO MUCH LIKE A REAL OWL TO BE...
...REAL ART!
CLONK

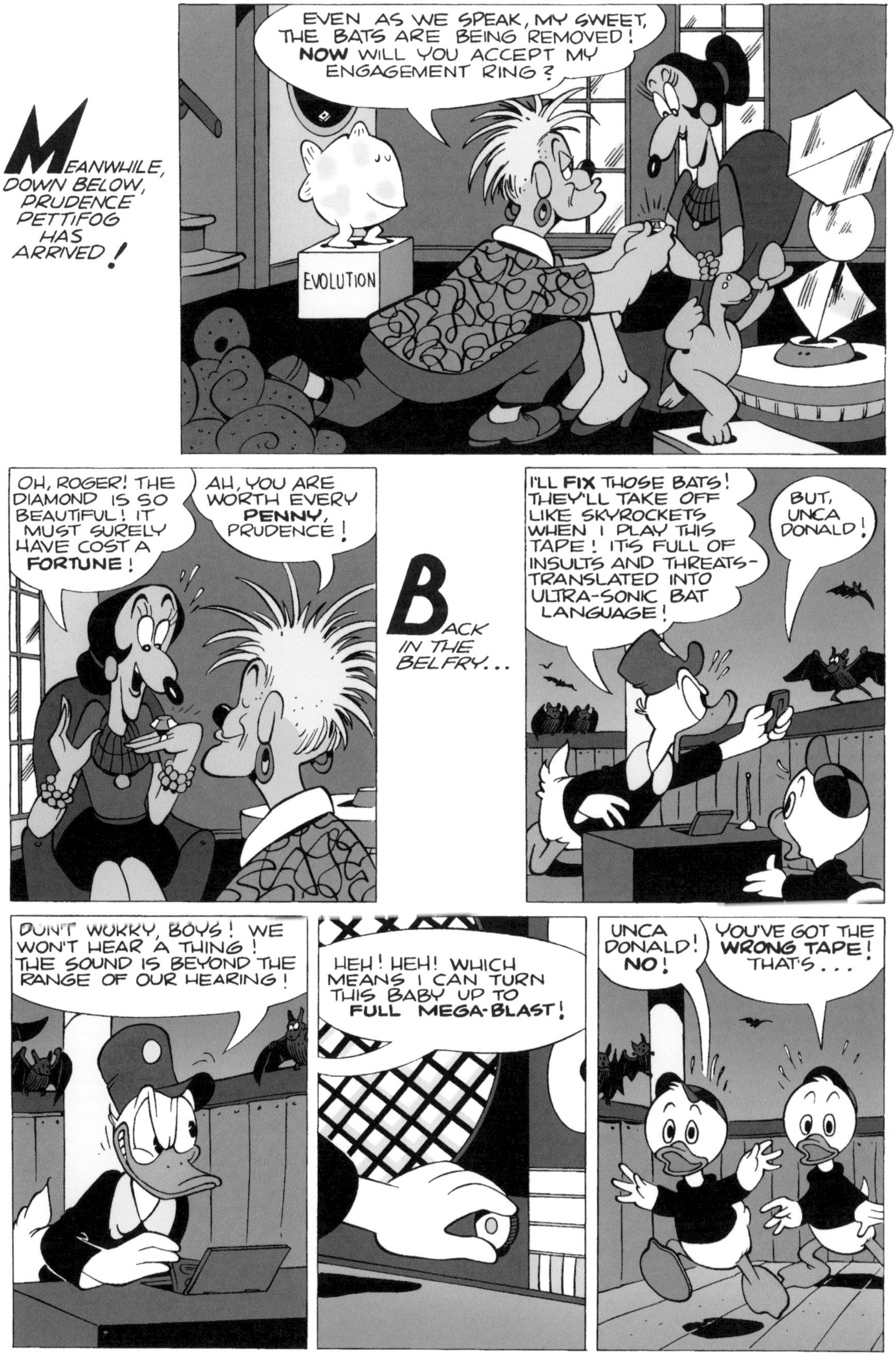
MEANWHILE, DOWN BELOW, PRUDENCE PETTIFOG HAS ARRIVED!
EVEN AS WE SPEAK, MY SWEET, THE BATS ARE BEING REMOVED! NOW WILL YOU ACCEPT MY ENGAGEMENT RING?
EVOLUTION
OH, ROGER! THE DIAMOND IS SO BEAUTIFUL! IT MUST SURELY HAVE COST A FORTUNE!
AH, YOU ARE WORTH EVERY PENNY, PRUDENCE!
BACK IN THE BELFRY...
I'LL FIX THOSE BATS! THEY'LL TAKE OFF LIKE SKYROCKETS WHEN I PLAY THIS TAPE! IT'S FULL OF INSULTS AND THREATS-TRANSLATED INTO ULTRA-SONIC BAT LANGUAGE!
BUT, UNCA DONALD!
DON'T WORRY, BOYS! WE WON'T HEAR A THING! THE SOUND IS BEYOND THE RANGE OF OUR HEARING!
HEH! HEH! WHICH MEANS I CAN TURN THIS BABY UP TO FULL MEGA-BLAST!
UNCA DONALD! NO!
YOU'VE GOT THE WRONG TAPE! THAT'S...

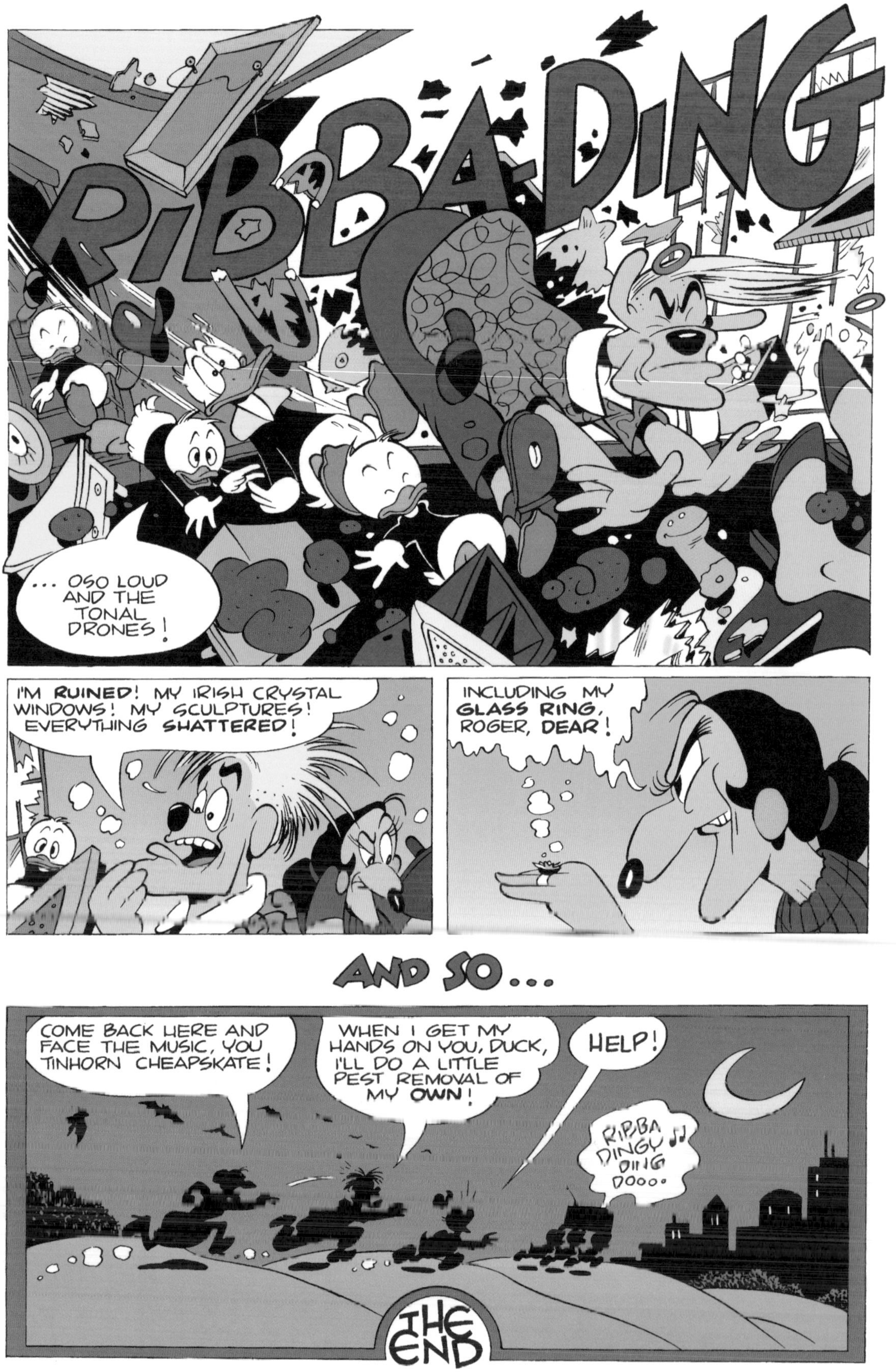
RIBBA-DING
... OSO LOUD AND THE TONAL DRONES!
I'M RUINED! MY IRISH CRYSTAL WINDOWS! MY SCULPTURES! EVERYTHING SHATTERED!
INCLUDING MY GLASS RING, ROGER, DEAR!
AND SO...
COME BACK HERE AND FACE THE MUSIC, YOU TINHORN CHEAPSKATE!
WHEN I GET MY HANDS ON YOU, DUCK, I'LL DO A LITTLE PEST REMOVAL OF MY OWN!
HELP!
RIBBA DINGY DING DOOO.
THE END

William Van Horn

by JOHN CLARK *and* DAVID GERSTEIN

BORN FEBRUARY 15, 1939, William Van Horn began his lifelong love affair with comics and cartoons when he was about five years old. "I drew mostly war scenes and pictures of Mickey Mouse," Van Horn says. "Later I tried my hand at Dick Tracy and the Lone Ranger."

Around 1954, Van Horn decided that he would one day work in animation and, upon his graduation from the California College of Arts and Crafts in 1961, secured a position with Imagination, Inc., a small animation studio in San Francisco. After working a number of years as a writer, animator, background artist, and U.S. Army illustrator—he was drafted and on duty from 1962 to 1964—Van Horn began writing and illustrating children's books. "The first... was *Harry Hoyle's Giant Jumping Bean* [1978]," he recalls. "It sold on its first submission and, believe me, that was absolutely the last time it was ever so easy."

In 1966, Van Horn married Frances Elaine Dixon and in 1980 they relocated from the bay area to Vancouver, British Columbia. "Elaine is a Canadian citizen, so she was able to get the rest of us in. The children and myself are landed immigrants." Those children included son Noel—later a Disney comics creator himself—and daughter Tish.

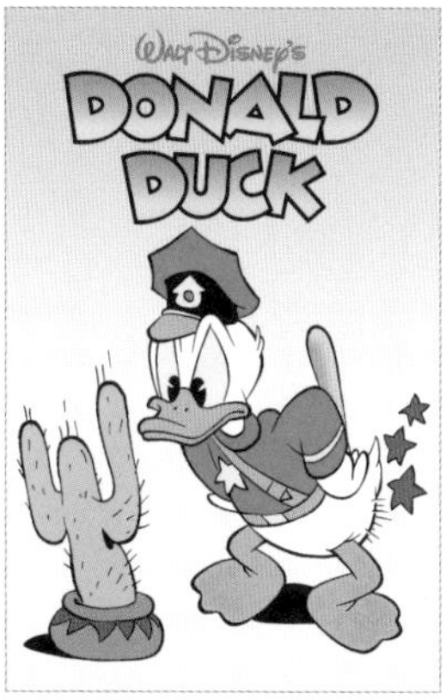
Walt Disney's
DONALD DUCK

A 1990 cover drawing only used, at the time, as an editorial page illustration. It later became a true front cover for *Walt Disney's Comics and Stories* 678 (2007).

William Van Horn's own first comics effort, the self-created dinosaur character *Nervous Rex*, immediately highlighted the senses of whimsy and cynicism that would characterize his best work. But an effort to join the Disney ranks still awaited. When Gladstone took over publishing Disney comics from Western Publishing in 1986, Bill saw an opportunity to return to some of the pleasures of his youth, and sent samples to Gladstone's Editor-in-Chief, Byron Erickson. But the task proved an arduous one for Van Horn. Although Erickson was initially impressed with Van Horn's work, he felt it to be too "off spec" to justify buying anything for publication. Undaunted, Van Horn continued his efforts until his stories began being accepted.

Erickson's initial needs centered around short filler stories, which Van Horn was happy to provide, beginning with "A Prickly Relation" (*Uncle Scrooge* 226) and "A Sound Deal" (*Mickey and Donald* 2) in May of 1988. Van Horn made the jump in 1990 when Disney began publishing domestic comic books in-house, an arrangement that continued until 1993. Finally Van Horn began working for the Danish-based creative house Egmont, producing Duck stories for the Northern European market.

Van Horn's initial Gladstone work included short Uncle Scrooge and Donald Duck stories and longer *DuckTales* sagas, often starring Launchpad McQuack. For Disney's in-house comics, this changed to a run of Donald twelve-page stories, a pattern that continued for Egmont. Mixing Barksian personality with out-of-control silliness, Van Horn created a Duckburg full of mocking irony and looney frustrations for Donald and Scrooge. Often teaming up with Van Horn was writer John Lustig, a sharp-witted satirist beloved today for his romance-comic spoof *Last Kiss*.

In time, Van Horn confounded the Ducks with new supporting characters of his own. Baron Itzy Bitzy, the legendary whistling flea who debuts in this book's "Lost On a Dog," was a Van Horn invention. Later came Scrooge's layabout half-brother Rumpus McFowl and cat-faced con man Woimly Filcher.

Up through 2017, William Van Horn continued to write and draw stories for Egmont, some of which—as of this writing—are still just now debuting in Europe. As for North America, while Van Horn's early *DuckTales* work has been anthologized elsewhere, we are excited to offer—in this volume—the first-ever complete collection of Van Horn's early Donald Duck and Uncle Scrooge stories and covers, many of them out of print for decades.

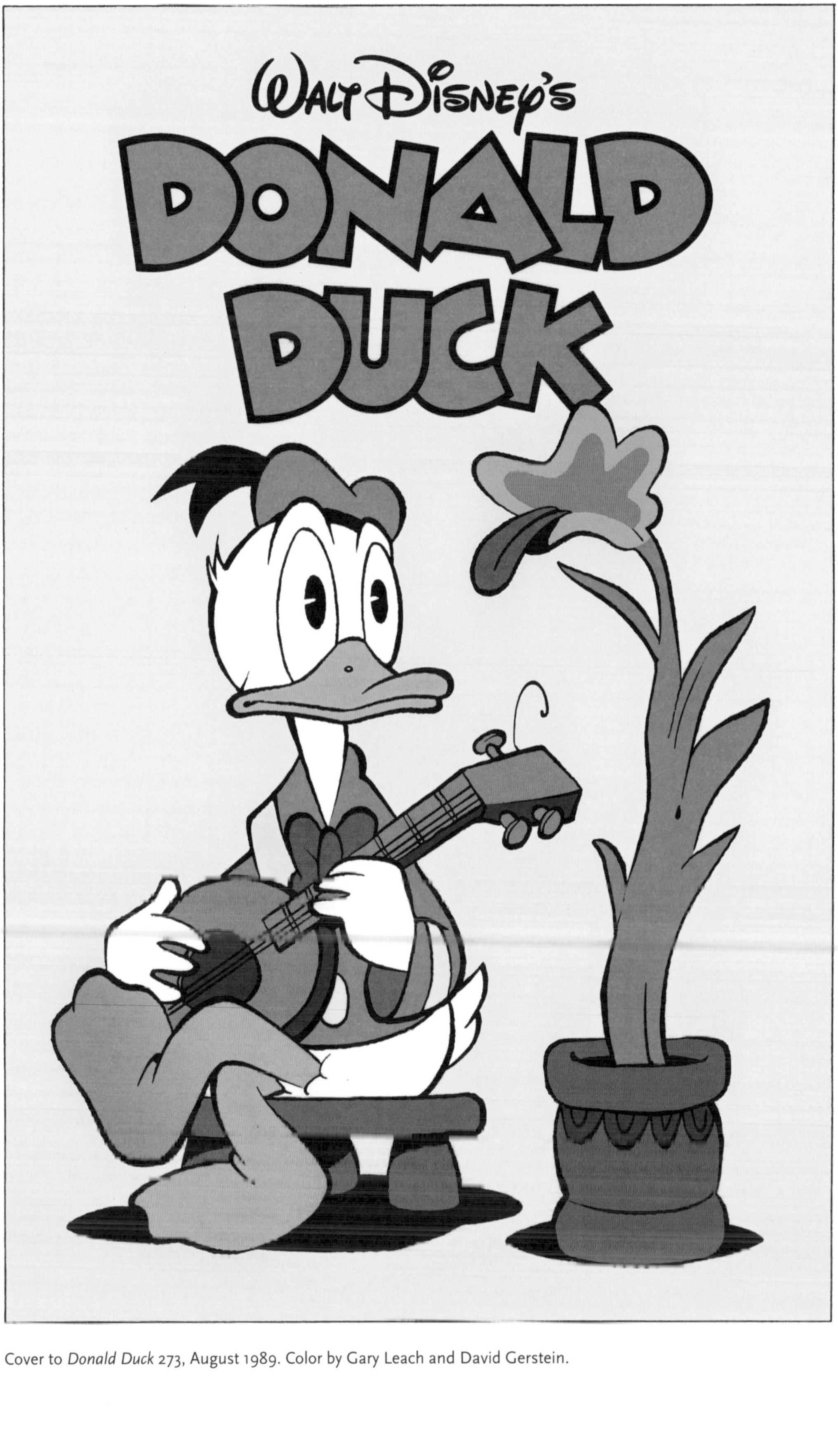
WALT DISNEY'S
DONALD DUCK

Cover to *Donald Duck* 273, August 1989. Color by Gary Leach and David Gerstein.

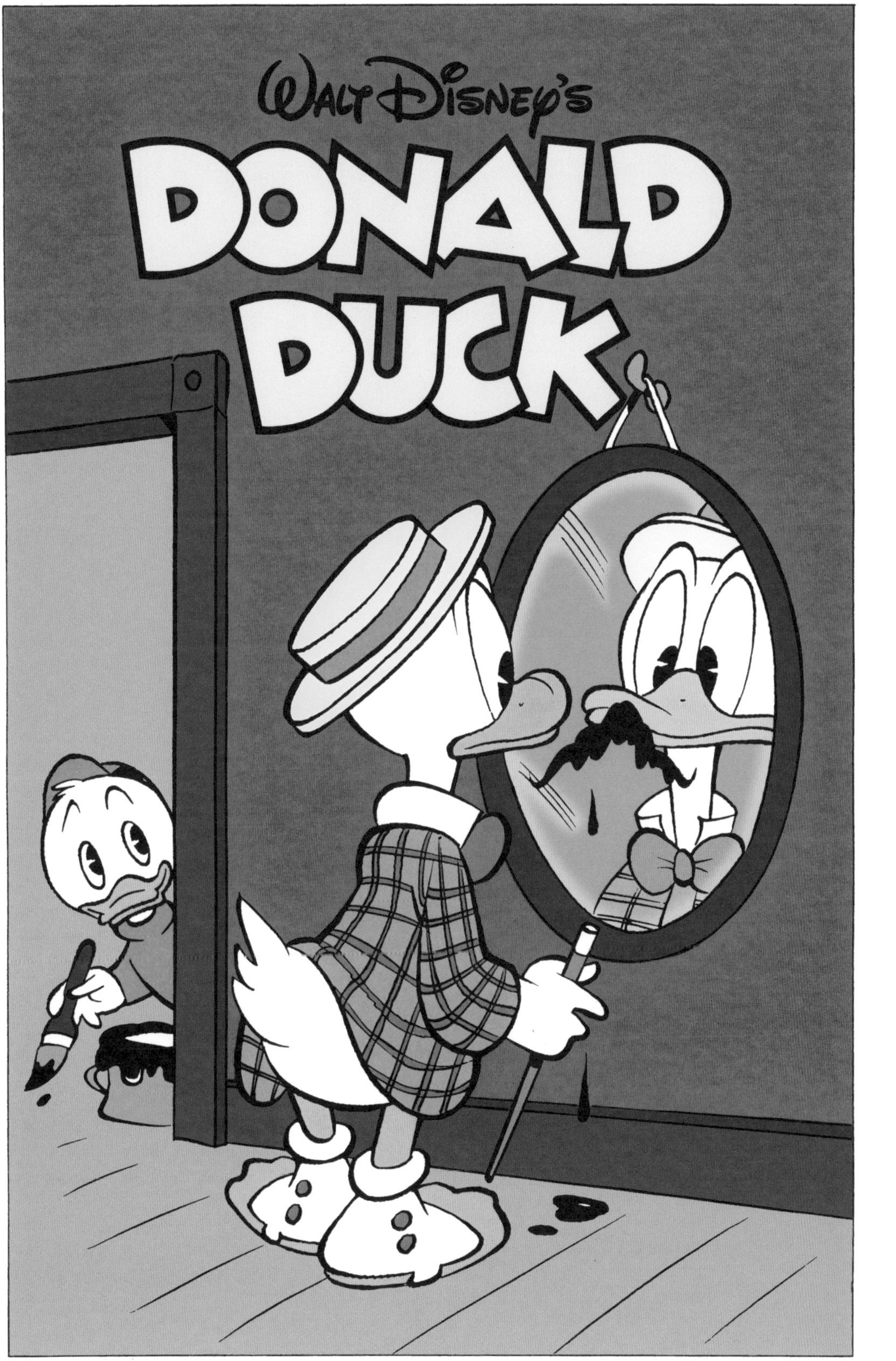
Walt Disney's
DONALD DUCK

Cover to *Donald Duck* 274, September 1989. Color by Gary Leach and David Gerstein.

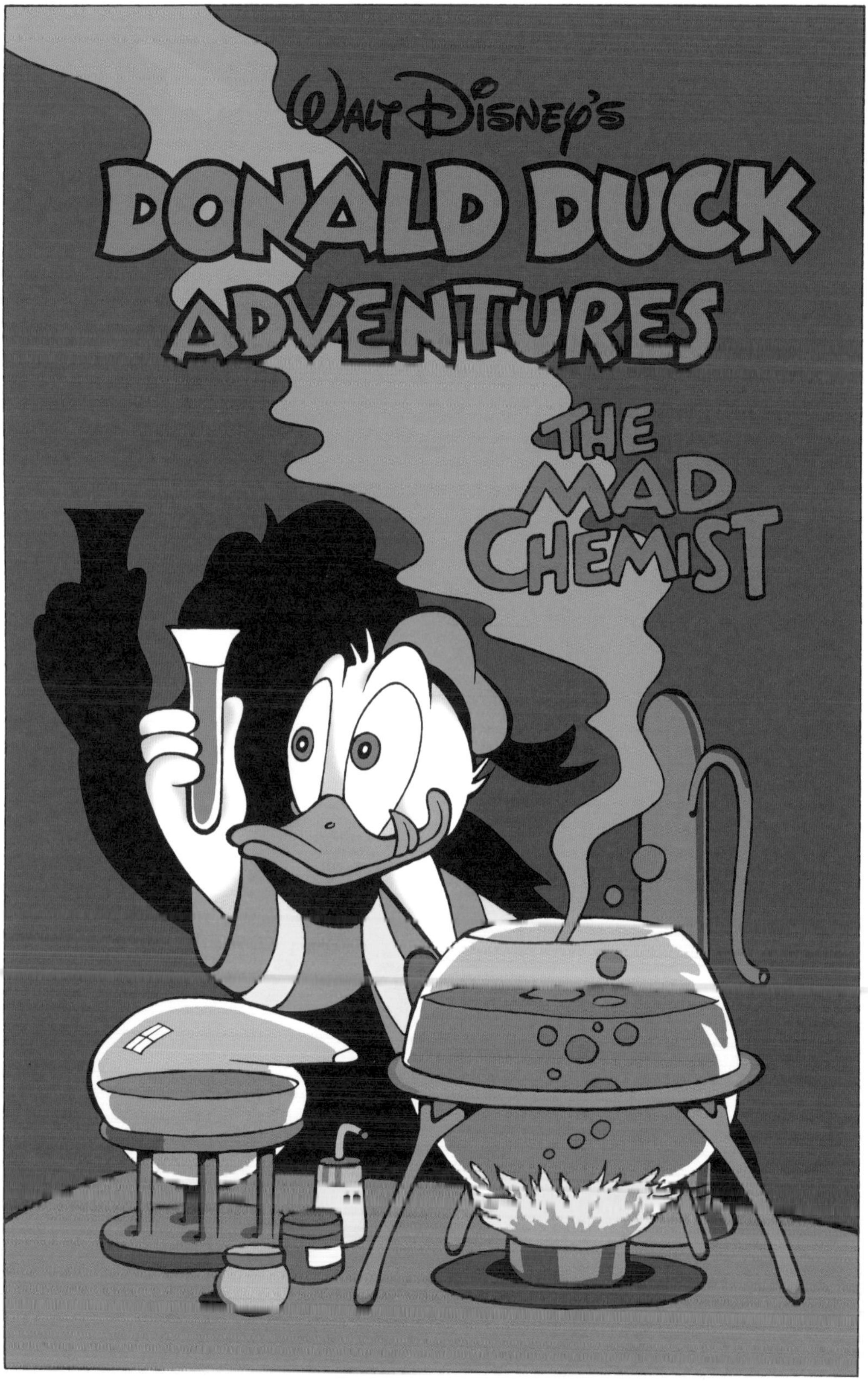
WALT DISNEY'S
DONALD DUCK
ADVENTURES
THE MAD CHEMIST

Cover to *Donald Duck Adventures* [series I] 15, September 1989; illustrating a classic story by Carl Barks. Color by Gary Leach and Erik Rosengarten.

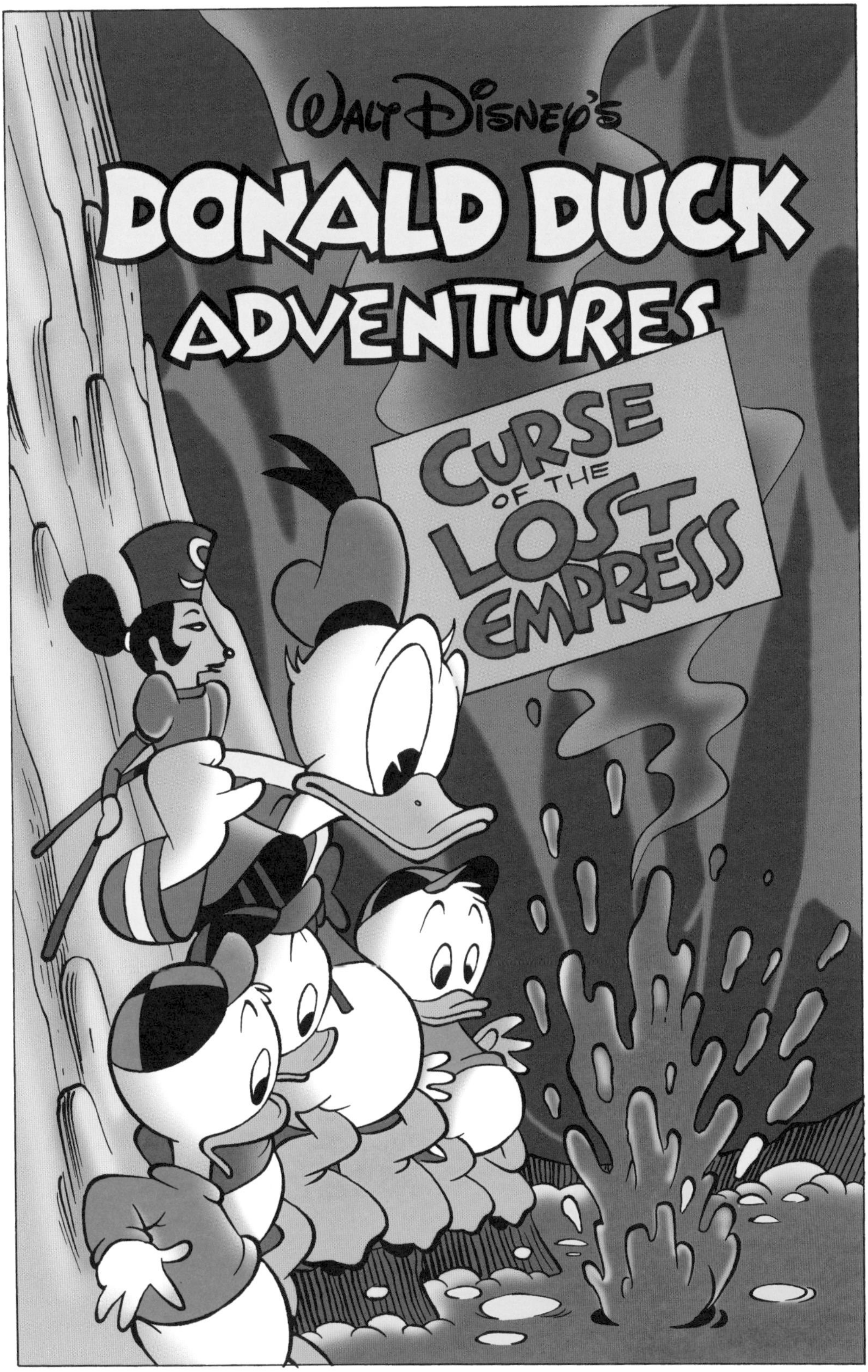
WALT DISNEY'S
DONALD DUCK
ADVENTURES
CURSE OF THE LOST EMPRESS

Cover to *Donald Duck Adventures* [series I] 17, November 1989; illustrating a new story by Ben Verhagen.
Color by Gary Leach and Digikore Studios.

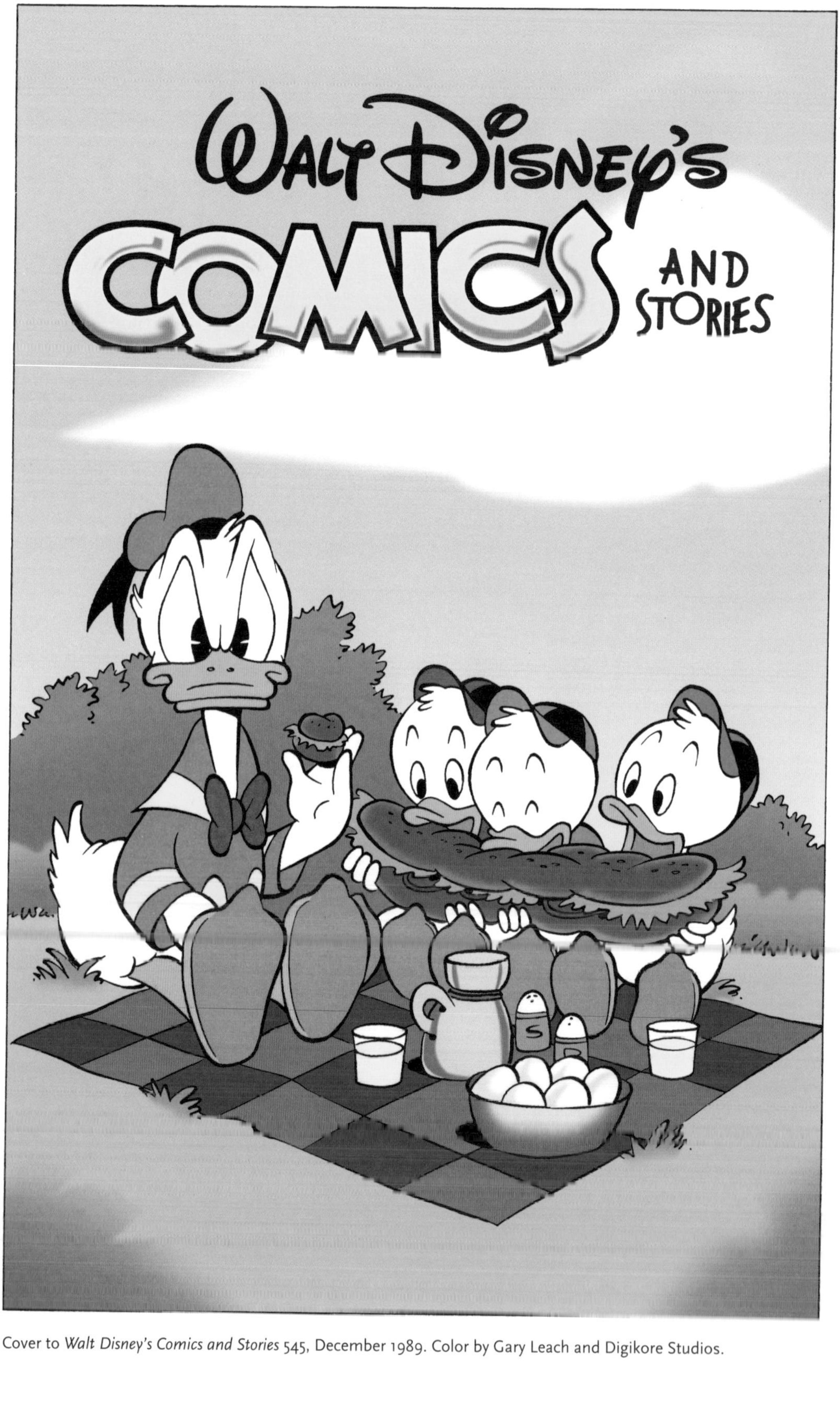
WALT DISNEY'S
COMICS
AND STORIES
S
Cover to *Walt Disney's Comics and Stories* 545, December 1989. Color by Gary Leach and Digikore Studios.

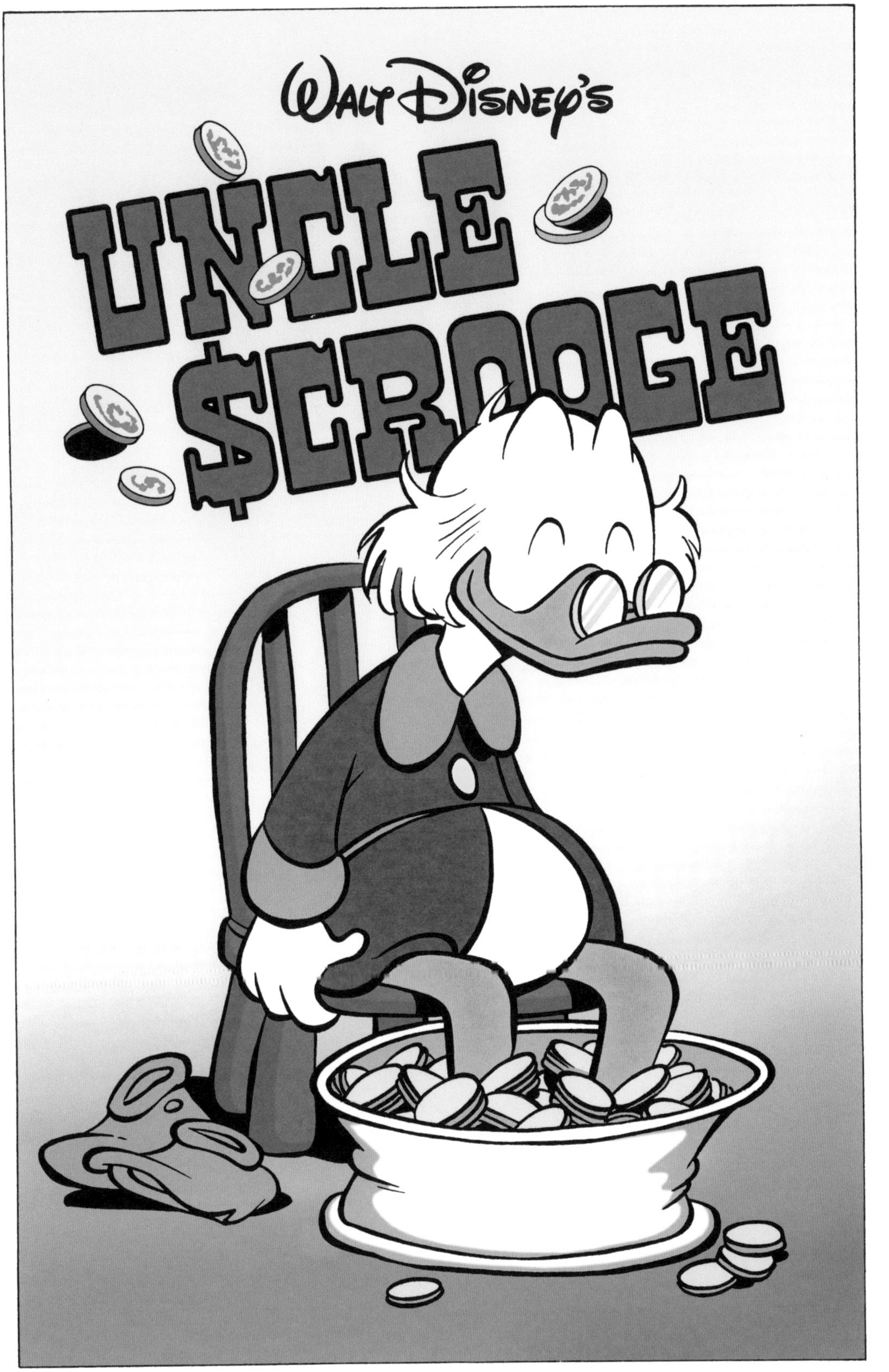
Walt Disney's
UNCLE $CROOGE

Cover to *Uncle Scrooge* 240, December 1989. Color by Gary Leach and Erik Rosengarten.

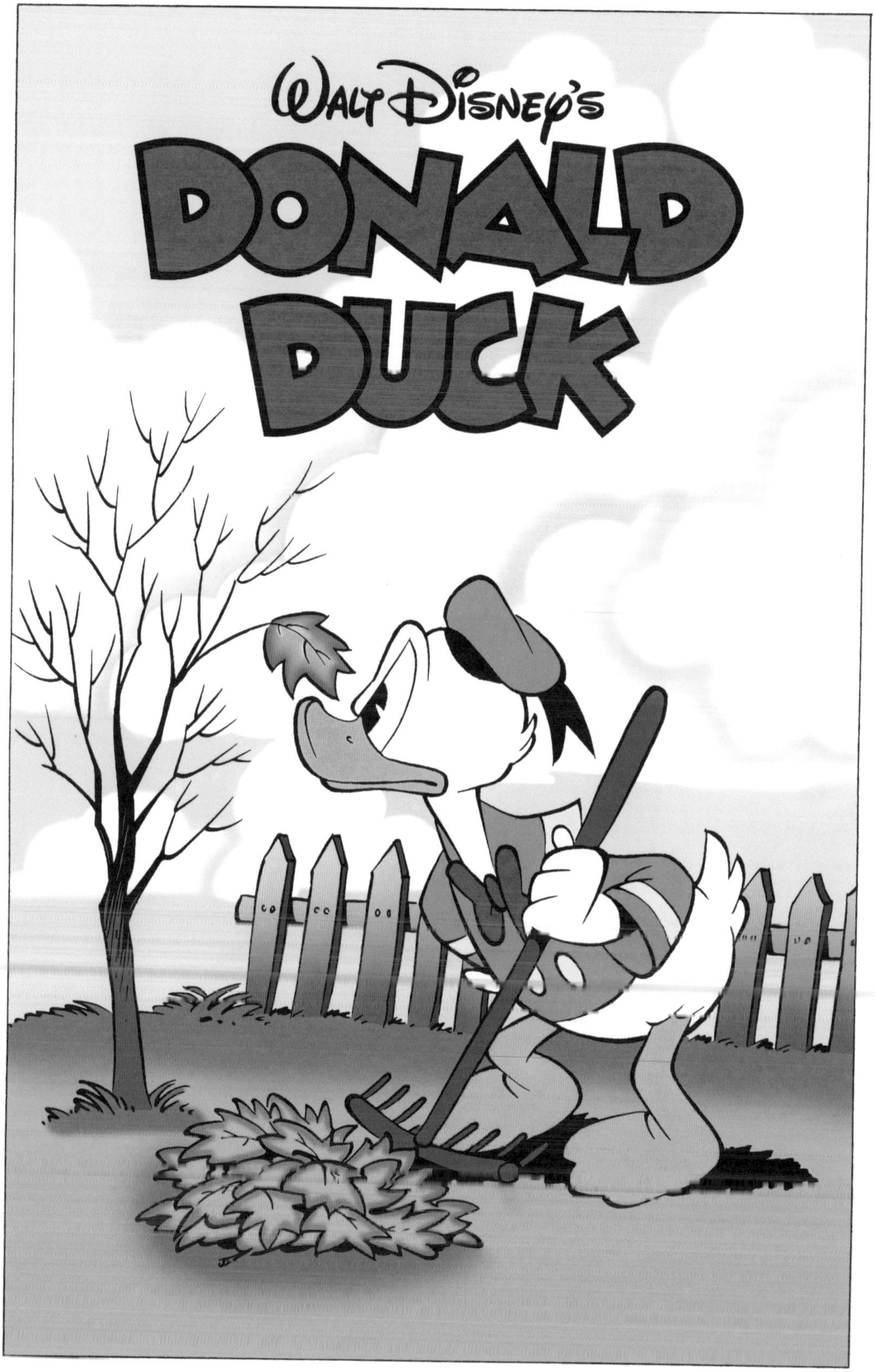
Walt Disney's
DONALD DUCK

Cover to *Donald Duck* 277, January 1990. Color by Gary Leach and Digikore Studios.

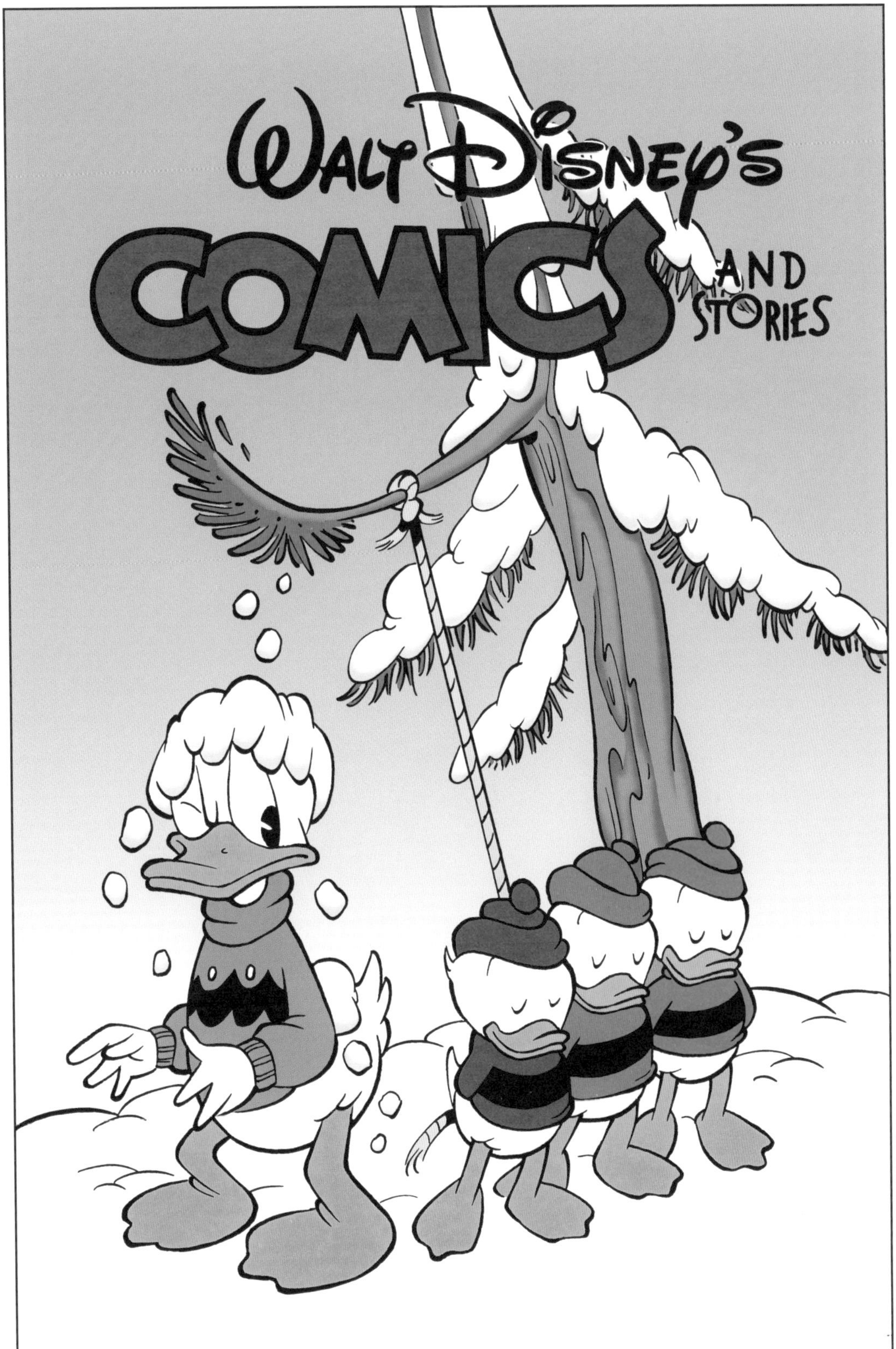
WALT DISNEY'S
COMICS AND STORIES

Cover to *Walt Disney's Comics and Stories* 547, April 1990. Color by Gary Leach.

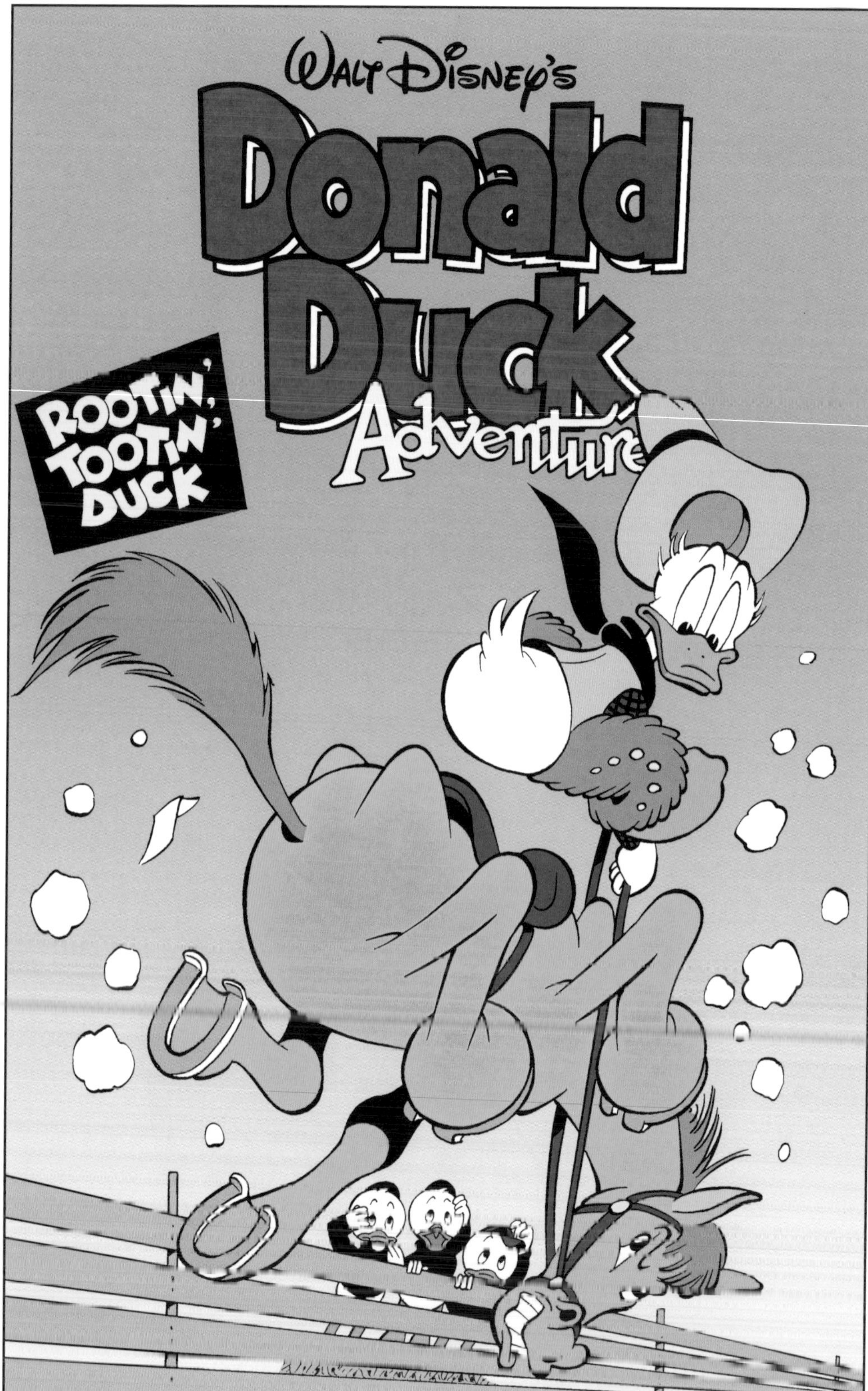

WALT DISNEY'S
Donald Duck
Adventure
ROOTIN', TOOTIN' DUCK

Cover to *Donald Duck Adventures* [series II] 2, July 1990. Color by Gail Bailey and David Gerstein.

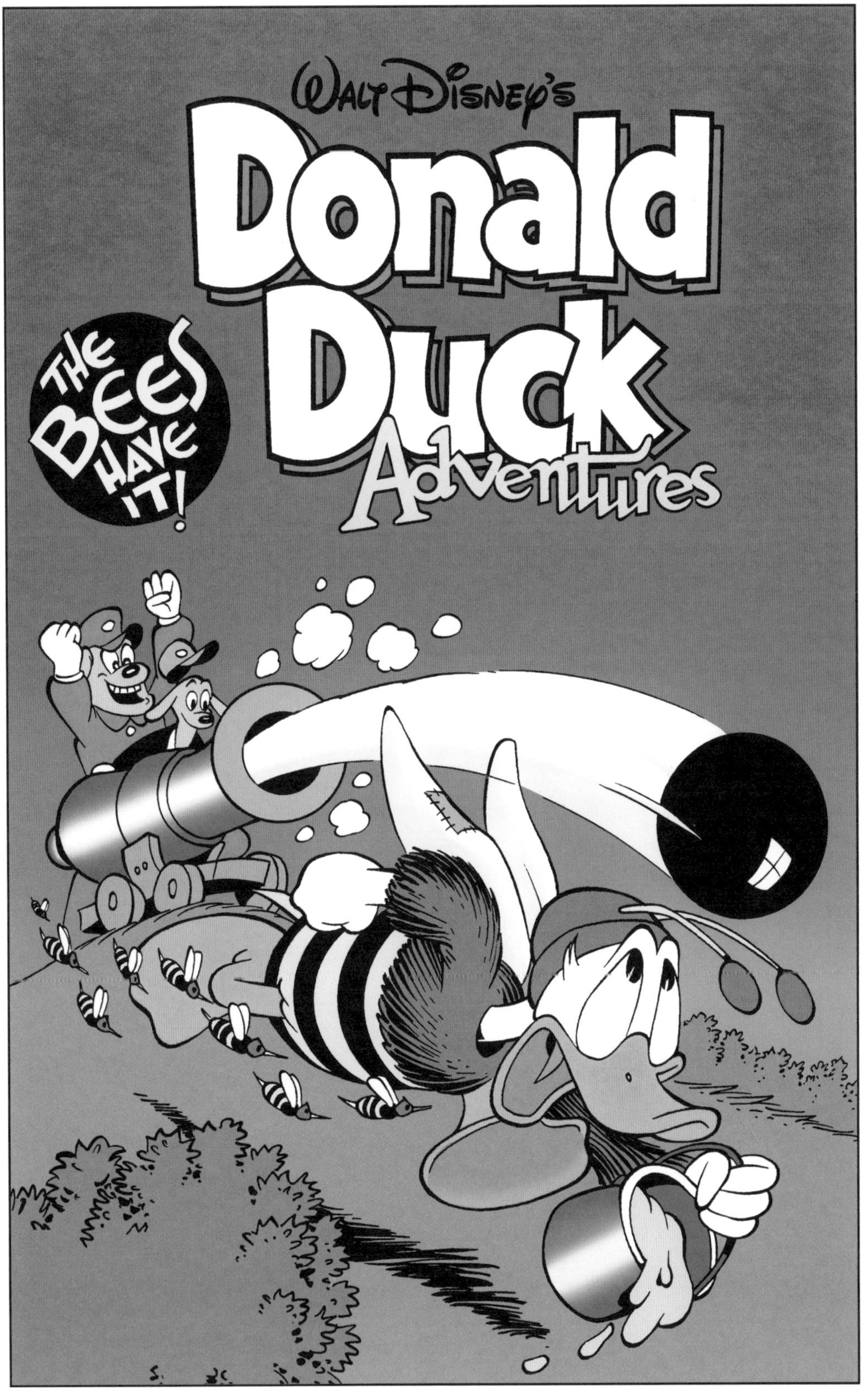
WALT DISNEY'S
Donald Duck
Adventures
THE BEES HAVE IT!

Cover to *Donald Duck Adventures* [series II] 4, September 1990. Color by Gail Bailey and Erik Rosengarten.

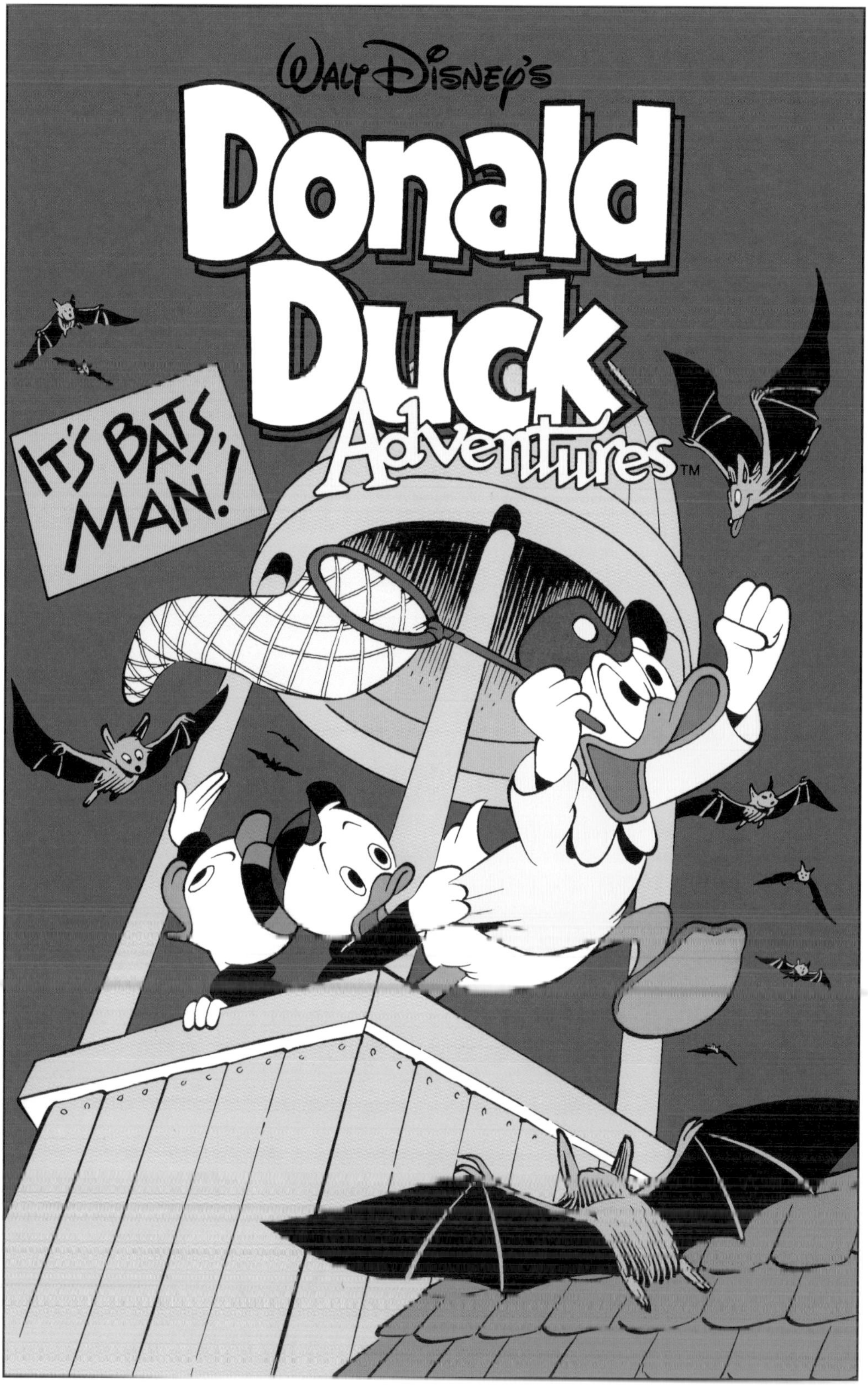
WALT DISNEY'S
Donald Duck
Adventures
TM
IT'S BATS, MAN!

Cover to *Donald Duck Adventures* [series II] 6, November 1990. Restoration and color by Paul Baresh.